EIGHT EDITION

Building Classroom Discipline

C. M. Charles
Emeritus, San Diego State University

Collaboration by
Gail W. Senter
California State University San Marcos

PEARSON

Boston   New York   San Francisco
Mexico City   Montreal   Toronto   London   Madrid   Munich   Paris
Hong Kong   Singapore   Tokyo   Cape Town   Sydney

Senior Editor: Arnis E. Burvikovs
Editorial Assistant: Audrey Beth Stein
Marketing Manager: Tara Whorf
Editorial-Production Service: Omegatype Typography, Inc.
Composition and Prepress Buyer: Linda Cox
Manufacturing Buyer: Andrew Turso
Cover Administrator: Linda Knowles
Interior Design: Denise Hoffman
Electronic Composition: Omegatype Typography, Inc.

For related titles and support materials, visit our online catalog at www.ablongman.com

Between the time Website information is gathered and published, some sites may have closed. Also, the transcription of URLs can result in typographical errors. The publisher would appreciate notification where these errors occur so that they may be corrected in subsequent editions.

Library of Congress Cataloging-in-Publication Data

Charles, C. M.
　　Building classroom discipline / C. M. Charles ; collaboration by Gail W. Senter.—8th ed.
　　　　p. cm.
　　Includes bibliographical references and index.
　　ISBN 0-205-41257-2 (alk. paper)
　　　1. School discipline.　2. Classroom management.　I. Senter, Gail W.　II. Title.

LB3012.C46 2005
371.5—dc22

2003070677

Printed in the United States of America

10   9   8   7   6   5   4   3   2   1   09   08   07   06   05   04

CONTENTS

3 Lee and Marlene Canter's *Assertive Discipline*   37

4 Fred Jones's *Positive Classroom Discipline*   55

5 William Glasser's *Noncoercive Discipline*   73

6 Marvin Marshall's *Discipline through Raising Responsibility*   93

7 Jane Nelsen, Lynn Lott, and H. Stephen Glenn's *Positive Discipline in the Classroom*   111

8 Richard Curwin and Allen Mendler's *Discipline with Dignity*   128

9   Barbara Coloroso's *Inner Discipline*   **147**

10   Budd Churchward's *Honor Level System of Discipline*   **164**

11 Spencer Kagan, Patricia Kyle, and Sally Scott's *Win-Win Discipline*   181

12 Linda Albert's *Cooperative Discipline*   199

13 C. M. Charles's *Synergetic Discipline*   218

14 Alfie Kohn's *Beyond Discipline*   239

15 Working Effectively with All Students   256

A pleasant classroom environment in which students behave responsibly is essential for high-quality teaching and learning. Teachers, in their efforts to maintain such an environment, routinely exert influence on students to help them show initiative and interact positively with others. This influence is commonly called "discipline," which is comprised of a number of different strategies and techniques. In the past, discipline was often demanding and occasionally harsh. Although it helped students behave civilly and stay on task, it produced undesirable side effects such as student fearfulness, loss of motivation, and dislike for school. That kind of discipline is no longer desired in school or elsewhere. It is now replaced with discipline that promotes student self-direction and a positive attitude toward school, teachers, and others. Techniques for maintaining such discipline are presented in this book.

Regarding This Book

Beginning with the first edition of *Building Classroom Discipline* almost 25 years ago, the overriding purpose of this book has been to help teachers develop personal systems of discipline tailored to their individual philosophies and personalities as well as to the needs, traits, and social realities of their schools and communities. None of the excellent commercial models of discipline described in this book are likely to provide a perfect match for any given teacher's needs. Yet, all teachers will find portions of the various models that suit them well. They can select judiciously from the hundreds of ideas in the models and organize them into a system of behavior management that best fits their situation and preferences. Suggestions for facilitating that process are presented here.

Over the past two decades, many advances have been made in discipline. Whereas discipline prior to that time hinged on reward and punishment, newer techniques now encourage students to behave acceptably because they feel it is the right thing to do and see it as advantageous to themselves and their classmates. *Building Classroom Discipline,* Eighth Edition, describes a variety of such approaches set forth by leading authorities. These approaches show teachers how to work with students helpfully and respectfully, ensuring learning while preserving student dignity and positive teacher–student relationships.

Building Classroom Discipline, Eighth Edition, is designed for use in preservice courses in discipline and classroom management, learning and instruction, methods of teaching, and educational psychology. It is equally appropriate for teachers already in service who are seeking more effective and enjoyable ways of working with students. Instructors in school district training programs and teacher institutes will also find the book useful.

The book is comprehensive enough to serve as a single or primary text, yet compact enough for use with other texts. It describes 18 models of discipline developed by some of the most astute educational thinkers of the past half century. Six of these models, summarized in Chapter 2, are presented as historical models. They were all groundbreaking approaches in their day and have contributed powerfully to the best of today's approaches. An additional 12 models, all widely used at present, are presented in greater detail. These 12 models are referred to as "application models." They depict today's most popular views on the nature and purpose of discipline, as well as how effective discipline should be organized and used.

How Application Models Are Presented

Application models are presented in individual chapters organized for maximum clarity, understanding, and applicability. The chapters review the work of individual authorities or teams of authorities and consist of the following:

1. A preview of the authority's discipline scheme, including focus, logic, contributions, and principal suggestions
2. A brief biographical sketch of the authority
3. The authority's contributions to discipline
4. The authority's central focus
5. The authority's principal teachings
6. Analysis of the authority's discipline model
7. Strengths of the model
8. Initiating the model in the classroom
9. Review of terminology particular to the model
10. The Selected Seven—seven selected points that summarize each model
11. Application exercises including questions, activities, concept cases, and a "You Are the Teacher" scenario that calls for application to resolve a real-life situation
12. References

Review and Feedback from Authorities

Before publication of the models presented herein, authorities whose approaches are presented as application models have reviewed the chapter devoted to their work and have interacted with the author so that the descriptions of concepts, approaches, and terminology are all depicted accurately. These authorities and others are continually modifying their ideas and developing new approaches. The ongoing cooperative liaison between discipline authorities and the author of this book ensures that the information you read is accurate and up-to-date.

Material Related to the Models of Discipline

In addition to the application models of discipline, other chapters are included in this book for the following purposes:

1. To establish the general context of concerns about discipline.
2. To identify competencies teachers require in discipline and teaching in general.
3. To establish a sense of professionalism in teaching and what it entails and requires.
4. To provide a framework to be used as readers move through the book to construct a quality personal system of discipline.
5. To identify trends in discipline and establish relationships between historical models and application models.
6. To provide helpful information on working with diverse groups of students and their parents and guardians.
7. To help users of the book formalize personal approaches to discipline that are appropriate to the needs and social realities of their students as well as to their own personalities, philosophies, and preferences.

■ *Chapter 1* reviews the widespread concern about student behavior and school discipline, pointing out problem areas and suggesting remedies for those problems. The nature of misbehavior is discussed, its effects on students and teacher are described, and schools' attempts to deal with behavioral problems are reviewed. The chapter describes the INTASC competencies that are desired in teachers and used for teacher licensing in many states, the Praxis Series from Educational Testing Service for assessing teacher competencies, and Charlotte Danielson's observations concerning competencies required for effective classroom teaching. Finally, the chapter reviews the nature of teacher professionalism and provides a framework for developing one's personal system of discipline.

■ *Chapter 2* presents condensed analyses of historical models of discipline that allow readers to comprehend earlier attempts at dealing with inappropriate classroom behavior, recognize the origins of important concepts and approaches, and identify the trends that have led to today's application models.

■ *Chapter 15* reviews the behavioral characteristics one can expect to see in students who are economically disadvantaged; are members of diverse racial, ethnic, and linguistic groups; and/or face special challenges associated with specific learning and behavioral difficulties.

■ *Chapter 16* provides assistance in helping readers clarify their personal views on the philosophy, theory, and practice of discipline, and from that point readers proceed to finalize a personal system of discipline attuned to student characteristics and needs, as well as their own personality and preferences.

■ *Reviews of terms and concepts* are presented at the ends of chapters.

■ *Selected Seven* key points are presented to summarize each chapter.

■ *Application activities and exercises* are presented at the ends of chapters. They include Questions and Activities, Concept Cases, and classroom scenarios involving misbehavior at different grade levels and subject areas. Called You Are the Teacher, these scenarios are for practice in applying the chapter's discipline techniques in resolving true-to-life classroom situations and concerns.

■ *A Glossary of Terms* is presented at the end of the book, as is a comprehensive *Bibliography.*

New to This Edition

Since publication of the previous edition of *Building Classroom Discipline,* new and promising approaches have appeared that enable educators to work with students in ways that are ever more humane and productive. At the same time, certain older models of discipline have ceased to be used in their entirety, although portions of them have been incorporated into the newer approaches. *Building Classroom Discipline,* Eighth Edition, presents two new application models, while Thomas Gordon's *Discipline as Self-Control* has been moved to Chapter 2, Great Pioneers in Classroom Discipline. Dr. Gordon died in 2002. The following are new to this edition.

Chapter 6, Marvin Marshall's *Discipline through Raising Responsibility.* This new program, quickly gaining popularity worldwide, helps students willingly assume greater responsibility for personal behavior. Dr. Marshall has been a teacher and school administrator at various levels. He now writes, lectures, and conducts seminars on topics related to his Raise Responsibility System.

Chapter 10, Budd Churchward's *Honor Level System.* This new program helps students conduct themselves in accordance with the highest levels of honorable behavior. It is managed by computer and is used in a number of school systems across the United States. Mr. Churchward was for many years a classroom teacher and now presents lectures, seminars, and training sessions related to his Honor Level System.

Chapter 15, Working Effectively with All Students. This chapter presents information to help teachers work more effectively with students identified as belonging to one or more of the following groups: economically disadvantaged; recently arrived immigrants; African American; American Indian/Alaska Native; Asian American; Hispanic American; behaviorally at risk of failure; having Attention Deficit Hyperactivity Disorder (ADHD); those who abuse drugs and alcohol; and those prone to violence, bullying, and hate crimes.

Chapter 16, Formalizing Your Personal System of Discipline, has been reorganized to help readers more easily construct a personal system of discipline that meets their needs and those of their students. The structural scheme for accomplishing this end, called Five Principles for Building a Personal System of Discipline, is introduced in Chapter 1 and followed through to the end of the text.

As noted, new information is also included in Chapter 1, focusing on teacher professionalism, teacher competencies as described in INTASC and Praxis, and a framework for helping readers develop their own personal systems of discipline.

Acknowledgments

The author gratefully acknowledges the valuable contributions made to this and previous editions by the following people:

Teachers and Administrators

Roy Allen	Constance Bauer	Linda Blacklock
Tom Bolz	Michael Brus	Gail Charles

Ruth Charles	Diana Cordero	Keith Correll
Barbara Gallegos	Nancy Girvin	Kris Halverson
Leslie Hays	Charlotte Hibsch	Elaine Maltz
Colleen Meagher	Nancy Natale	Linda Pohlenz
David Sisk	Deborah Sund	Mike Straus
Virginia Villalpando		

Critical Reviewers

Linda Albert, Cooperative Discipline
Dale Allee, Southwest Missouri State University
James D. Burney, University of North Alabama
Lee Canter and Marlene Canter, Assertive Discipline
Budd Churchward, Honor Level System of Discipline
Barbara Coloroso, Kids Are Worth It!
Richard Curwin, Discipline with Dignity
Philip DiMattia, Boston College
Karen M. Dutt, Indiana State University
Carolyn Eichenberger, St. Louis University
James D. Ellsworth, Northern Arizona University
Sara S. Garcia, Santa Clara University
Robert E. Gates, Bloomsburg University
William Glasser, Choice Theory in the Classroom
Thomas Gordon (deceased), Effectiveness Training International
Marci Green, University of South Florida at Ft. Myers
C. Bobbi Hansen, University of San Diego
Fredric Jones and JoLynne Jones, Positive Classroom Discipline
David I. Joyner, Old Dominion University
Deborah Keasler, Southwestern Oklahoma State University
Spencer Kagan, Win-Win Discipline
Alfie Kohn, Beyond Discipline: From Compliance to Community
Thomas J. Lasley, The University of Dayton
Lawrence Lyman, Emporia State University
Bernice Magnus-Brown, University of Maine
Marvin Marshall, Raise Responsibility System
Vick McGinley, West Chester University
Janey L. Montgomery, University of Northern Iowa
Janice L. Nath, University of Houston
Jane Nelsen, Positive Discipline in the Classroom
Merrill M. Oaks, Washington State University
Jack Vaughan Powell, University of Georgia
Elizabeth Primer, Cleveland State University
Mary C. Shake, University of Kentucky
Alma A. Shearin, University of Central Arkansas
Terry R. Shepherd, Southern Illinois University at Carbondale
JoAnne Smatlan, Seattle Pacific University

Kay Stickle, Ball State University
Marguerite Terrill, Central Michigan University
Sylvia Tinling, University of California, Riverside
Bill Weldon, Arizona State University
Kathleen Whittier, State University of New York at Plattsburgh

Editors at Allyn and Bacon

Arnis E. Burvikovs, Education Editor
Audrey Beth Stein, Editorial Assistant

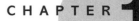

CHAPTER 1

Classroom Discipline
The Problem and the Solution

This chapter reviews the unsettling status of student misbehavior, often referred to as "poor discipline," and presents a plan for helping teachers resolve the problem. That plan involves taking steps to prevent misbehavior, teaching more effectively, and dealing with misbehavior in a constructive manner. It is strongly suggested that you undertake to organize a system of discipline that fits your needs and those of your students. Information and a guide are presented for beginning this task.

Comparing Classrooms 314 and 315

The scene is an inner-city school. Classroom 314 is quiet as students listen attentively to the teacher's questions about a recent lesson. Suddenly, eager hands begin to wave and bodies twist out of their seats amidst shouts of Aooh me! I know! Aooh-oh! Quiet returns when one student is chosen to answer. As soon as she has responded, others begin to yell out refutations or additions and compete again for teacher recognition. As they participate wholeheartedly in class, several students are simultaneously but secretly passing notes and candy and signaling to each other in sign and face language. When the questions end and seat work begins, some students offer to help others who are unsure of how to proceed.

But across the hall in room 315, chaos reigns. The room is noisy with the shouting, laughter, and movement of many children. Though most students are seated, many are walking or running aimlessly around the classroom. Some stop at others' desks, provoke them briefly, and move on. Several students who are lining up textbooks as "race courses" for toy cars laugh when the teacher demands their attention. As the teacher struggles to ask a question over the noise, few if any students volunteer to answer. When one student does respond correctly, others yell out, "You think you're so smart." (Schwartz, 1981, p. 99)

By most teachers' standards, the discipline in Room 314 is acceptable, whereas that in Room 315 is not. But what is the difference? In both rooms students are making noise and behaving in ways not usually condoned. Yet the teacher in Room 314 is probably satisfied with the lesson, whereas the teacher in Room 315 is not. Why? The answer lies in the teacher's sense that the classroom situation is productive. The students in 314 are showing initiative but are still responsive to the teacher. Their personal interactions are positive and reasonably respectful. The teacher feels progress is being made and is happy to see students displaying reasonable manners while actively involved in the lesson.

In contrast, the students in 315 are barely in touch with the lesson. They are accomplishing little that is worthwhile. They are doing more or less what they want, disregarding what the teacher says. Their behavior is haphazard and their interactions frequently disrespectful of the teacher and each other. The teacher is rightfully concerned about the behavior in this class, for it is keeping students from learning and is encouraging habits that are self-defeating for students. An impartial judge would consider the lesson a failure.

If you were the teacher in Room 315, what would you hope to see? Think about this a moment. How would you want students to respond to your lessons? To you? How would you want them to relate to each other? What would, or could, you do to make things as you'd like them to be? Could you work out a detailed plan concerning how you'd work with the class so it would be productive and rewarding? Suppose you did make such a plan and found that students disregarded what you asked them to do. Then what? Questions such as these are difficult to answer and in truth are more difficult to answer in a real classroom than when discussing hypothetical situations. If the answers were easy, we'd have no teachers feeling unfulfilled or ready to leave teaching because they could no longer tolerate dealing with disrespectful, unmotivated students.

The Problem of Student Misbehavior

Student misbehavior is one of the most troubling phenomena in education today. In many classes it interferes with teaching, stifles learning, produces great stress, and leads to poor class morale. It upsets both teachers and students and ruins many classes. It causes more teachers to fail than does any other factor. That needn't be the case, however. As you will see, misbehavior can easily be brought to manageable proportions by employing three strategies simultaneously. The first is to *prevent* the occurrence of as much misbehavior as possible. This is done by identifying factors that lead to misbehavior and then eliminating or reducing those factors. The second is to *introduce classroom conditions* that lead to student enjoyment, sense of purpose, self-direction, and sense of responsibility. The third is to deal with misbehavior that does occur in a *positive manner* rather than a negative one. This involves encouraging students, relating with them personally, teaching them to behave acceptably, and helping them understand how to conduct themselves responsibly while seeing the personal value of doing so.

These three strategies are routinely employed by a great many very successful teachers, working in all types of schools with all types of students. They find teaching joyful and rewarding. They are proud to see their students interacting positively and behaving considerately. They feel close to many of them and enjoy trusting relationships. Of course, at times they experience problems and stress, as will always happen in teaching. But they have learned that behavior problems are kept to a minimum when teacher and students work together in a spirit of goodwill. Unfortunately, many teachers do not yet know how to employ these newer discipline strategies. As a result, their teaching days are burdened with turmoil that wears them down. It has a debilitating effect on students, too, and many teachers and students dread their daily experiences together.

Let's now dispose of the fear of student misbehavior. In this book you will learn how to work happily and productively with your students, helping them become solid, productive citizens able to control themselves and get along with each other. The results will bring you great satisfaction and, perhaps, the greatest prize in teaching—the esteem of your students.

The Meanings of Behavior and Misbehavior

Misbehavior is best understood as a condition of overall behavior. **Behavior** refers to everything people do, good or bad, right or wrong, helpful or useless, productive or wasteful. **Desirable school behavior** is that in which students show self-control, responsibility, and consideration and respect for others. It usually involves cooperation and helpfulness. You can see that this definition of good classroom behavior is different from the traditional definition, which often connotes obeying, acquiescing, keeping quiet, following directions, and doing as expected.

Misbehavior is behavior that is *inappropriate* for the setting or situation in which it occurs. If you look back to what students were doing in Room 315, you will see that some of their actions merely showed careless disregard for expectations whereas others seemed to be intentional transgressions. Throughout the history of education, misbehavior has been a catchall term for behavior teachers didn't like. That is a rather useless definition. In its place, let's agree on the following: Classroom misbehavior is any behavior that, through *intent or thoughtlessness,*

1. interferes with teaching or learning
2. threatens or intimidates others
3. oversteps society's standards of moral, ethical, or legal behavior

Types of Misbehavior You Will Encounter

Teachers typically encounter 13 types of student misbehavior. Take note of them here, and as you progress through this book, you will learn how to deal positively with all of them.

1. *Inattention*—daydreaming, doodling, looking out the window, thinking about things irrelevant to the lesson.
2. *Apathy*—a general disinclination to participate, sulking, not caring, not wanting to try or do well.
3. *Needless talk*—students chatting during instructional time about things unrelated to the lesson.

4. *Moving about the room*—getting up and moving about without permission, congregating in parts of the room.
5. *Annoying others*—provoking, teasing, picking at, calling names.
6. *Disruption*—shouting out during instruction, talking and laughing inappropriately, causing "accidents."
7. *Lying*—falsifying to avoid accepting responsibility or admitting wrongdoing, or to get others in trouble.
8. *Stealing*—taking things that belong to others.
9. *Cheating*—making false representations or wrongly taking advantage of others for personal benefit.
10. *Sexual harassment*—making others uncomfortable through touching, sex-related language, or sexual innuendo.
11. *Aggression and fighting*—showing hostility toward others, threatening them, shoving, pinching, wrestling, hitting.
12. *Malicious mischief*—doing damage intentionally to school property or the belongings of others.
13. *Defiance of authority*—talking back to the teacher, refusing in a hostile manner to do as the teacher requests.

It is natural to assume that students are to blame when they exhibit these misbehaviors. At this point, let's suspend judgment about blame. As we move ahead, we will see that many different factors can "cause" students to misbehave. Instead of blaming someone, we will give attention to factors that often lead to misbehavior and learn how to deal with them.

The Roles of Discipline and Behavior Management

Overall, the tactics teachers use to manage student behavior are referred to as discipline or behavior management. These terms are used interchangeably. **Discipline** is the more familiar and has two meanings in relation to behavior. The first refers to a condition of misbehavior, for example, "The discipline in that room is pretty bad." The second refers to what teachers do to try to get students to behave acceptably, for example, "Mr. Smythe's discipline system is one of the best I've seen." Both meanings are used in this book, with the context indicating which is intended.

Because the term *discipline* has traditionally suggested teacher control, coercion, and forceful tactics, educators today often use the term **behavior management** for preventing, suppressing, and redirecting misbehavior. Please understand that when the word *discipline* is used as a verb in this book, it does not refer to harsh, abusive tactics but rather to positive actions that lead to improved student behavior and good relations between teacher and students.

Educators once considered teaching and discipline to be separate endeavors. They believed teaching was concerned with imparting knowledge, whereas discipline was concerned with making students behave themselves in an acceptable manner. As recently as

30 years ago, teachers expected students to misbehave and were ready to impose harsh measures when they did. Today we have a different conception of discipline. We now realize it is an integral part of teaching, not an effort that stands apart. We know, furthermore, that instruction affects behavior, and behavior affects instruction. That is why discipline is now considered a strand of teaching, along with instruction, communication, relations with parents, and classroom structure and management.

Toward Resolving the Discipline Problem

The solution to the discipline problem is for teachers to develop approaches to teaching that meet the needs of their students while remaining consistent with teacher personality and the social realities of the community. Let's begin our journey into improving discipline by reviewing some basic principles of working effectively with students. These principles will help you develop a mind-set for understanding better what is to come. After reviewing these principles, we will begin considering how you can build a personal system that meets your students' needs and your own needs as well.

Basic Principles of Working with Students

Here are basic principles of working with students in a manner that establishes a positive, productive, enjoyable classroom in which students learn and have a satisfying educational experience overall.

Maintain focus on your major task in teaching. Your major task is to help your students become more capable and successful, both in school and in later years. Inform them of this task and indicate how you will try to help them. Then back up your words with actions. Help students develop self-direction and responsibility. Help them become progressively better at making good decisions, treating others well, and accepting responsibility for their actions. They do not learn these things by reading about them or listening to you lecture about them. They learn them through experience, in which they will make frequent mistakes. The only process known for accomplishing these ends involves repeated experience in trying to make good choices, accepting that mistakes will be made, reflecting on those mistakes and learning from them, and in this manner gradually becoming more capable.

Know what causes misbehavior and how to deal with those causes. Understand the known causes of student misbehavior, where they reside, and how they are manifested. Take steps to soften or remove those causes.

Understand your students' needs and how to meet them. Know what motivates students. Know what they like and find attractive, as well as what they dislike and try to avoid. Know their typical behaviors, as affected by age, economic level, ethnicity, and other factors. Know how the students usually react to teachers and the school situation. Align your program to meet student needs. Emphasize topics important to them. Keep them involved. Use activities they enjoy. Keep learning lively and upbeat. Allow groups to work cooperatively on projects. Eliminate drudgery, boredom, frustration, and overload.

Give up trying to coerce students.   Effective teaching and behavior management depend on enticement rather than coercion. Please give up once and for all any notion that you can, with good results, make students do anything they don't want to do. When you use force, students resist. When you make demands, students subvert them. When you speak derogatorily, they lose respect for you. When you treat them inconsiderately, they lose trust in you and reciprocate. When you lecture them, they tune you out. It is true that when you have very highly motivated learners (or very fearful ones) you can deal with them demandingly and abrasively and get some of the results you want. But most students in school today are not highly motivated to please you, some are not afraid of you, and a few are quite willing to defy you in front of others.

Treat all students as your social equals.   Although you must maintain a mature, adult viewpoint, talk with students as your social equals. Confer dignity on all students. Communicate clearly and effectively. Never embarrass students, put them down, or make fun of them. Never speak to them sarcastically. Don't struggle against them. Don't make demands or threats. Don't argue with them. Don't spend a lot of time telling them what to do or going on about what they should have done.

Teach and relate to students in a charismatic way.   Keep yourself interesting and your outlook positive. Share some of your talents, experiences, and interests. Show personal attention to all your students. Take time to exchange pleasant words with as many as you can every day.

Involve students meaningfully in making decisions.   These include decisions about the class, the instructional activities, behavioral expectations, and how interventions should occur in the event of misbehavior. Take students seriously. Communicate with them respectfully. Encourage them to look for ways to treat each other well and help each other be successful. Encourage them to assume individual responsibility.

Establish a positive set of tactics for responding to misbehavior.   It is essential that students be involved in determining this process and the decisions that result. The tactics should stop the misbehavior, keep students positively on track, and preserve good relations.

Involve parents and guardians to a reasonable degree. Keep them informed about your class and what it is doing for their children. Make it clear you want and need their support. Show that you value their children and will do all you can to help them succeed in school.

Organizing a Personal System of Discipline

You can put all of these factors together into an organized approach that is suited to the realities of the students with whom you work, as well as to your personality and preferences. This becomes your personal system of teaching and discipline, which this book is organized to help you develop. This personal system will give you an effective approach to working with all students, no matter what their age or background. It will be effective because you will base it on human needs, make it supportive and encouraging, and ensure student acceptance and cooperation. For it to acquire those qualities, you must make sure it is never harsh, abrasive, demanding, or coercive. This **personal system of behavior management** will draw students into a sense of togetherness in the classroom, with a high likelihood of the following:

■ *An effective environment for learning.* The prime purpose of education is to help the young acquire attitudes, values, skills, and information that improve the quality of their lives and society as a whole. Such learning occurs best in environments that are reasonably well ordered, free from threat, relatively free from disruptions, and encouraging of exploration and interaction.

■ *A heightened student sense of purpose.* Humans want to find meaning in life and experience a sense of purpose. Each of us, knowingly or unknowingly, tries to identify what is important to us, how our lives are made better by those things, how we can best pursue them, and how we can avoid damaging others or the environment in their pursuit. Effective behavior management helps students develop a clearer sense of purpose concerning what they wish to experience, what they want to learn, and how they want their lives to progress.

■ *Increased learning.* As misbehavior declines, students have more time and incentive to focus on instructional activities and put forth their best effort. Because behavior management has to do with maintaining interest and productivity, students become more likely to engage willingly with the material being learned and profit more easily from the experience.

■ *A joyful, satisfying experience in school.* Most students don't really enjoy school because they don't find the classes adequately interesting, attractive, or rewarding. Many claim the only thing they like about school is the opportunity to be with friends. This picture changes significantly when you make your classes enjoyable and satisfying.

■ *Good personal relations.* Our personal sense of accomplishment and satisfaction is dependent in large measure on how we are treated by others. And, of course, the treatment we receive from others depends in large part on how we treat them. Most of us want to be respected, accepted as worthwhile, and treated with consideration. We want to enjoy friendships and work with others harmoniously. We are more likely to experience those benefits when we accord the same things to others. When we have disagreements, we want to resolve them equitably, while maintaining positive feelings. We cannot expect to do so if we don't treat others respectfully. Effective behavior management emphasizes the golden rule. At times you will be required to teach students how to speak effectively with others, cooperate, and show respect and consideration.

■ *Student self-control.* Personal self-control enables students to learn better. It helps them maintain a sense of purpose and direction and avoid incidents that take them on tangents or lead to damaging confrontations. One of the major purposes of behavior management is to help students develop inner discipline, the ability to control and direct themselves in various situations.

■ *Student responsibility.* Our society emphasizes individual freedom of choice concerning expression, activity, and relationships. However, in a democratic society all freedoms are linked to responsibility, meaning that the rights of others must be taken into account and not transgressed. Responsibility entails showing consideration, behaving ethically, and accepting the legitimate consequences of one's behavior, whether positive or negative. Effective behavior management heightens student initiative and choice but is always anchored in responsibility.

Your Entry Point for Developing a Personal System of Discipline

There are many outstanding programs of discipline available to you, as you will see in later chapters of this book. Excellent though those programs are, it is unlikely that any one of them will adequately address all your needs. Students differ from place to place and class to class. They usually behave in keeping with the realities of their social situations. In addition to that, you have your own distinct personality, philosophy, and preferred ways of teaching. You will find it easy and reassuring to design a discipline system that is consistent with all these needs and preferences.

You are now at an appropriate point to begin that undertaking. To begin, please do the following: (1) Respond to the 20 questions that follow concerning students and their behavior. The purpose of this activity is to open and orient your thinking still further. Discuss these questions with colleagues, if possible. (2) Consider the advice that comes from INTASC, the Praxis Series, and Charlotte Danielson, which you will encounter presently. (3) Explore the **five principles for a personal system of discipline** provided after the questions and suggestions. They will guide you progressively toward a system of discipline that meets your particular needs and those of your students. (4) Read and incorporate into your thinking the suggestions and caveats associated with professional, ethical, and legal aspects of teaching.

20 Questions about Discipline for Preliminary Reflection

Think about the following questions and answer them as best you can. Discuss them with colleagues if possible. Ultimately, you will be able to answer all these questions in a professional manner.

1. *How should students behave?* How, generally and specifically, do you want your students to conduct themselves in class? Clarify your reasons for wanting them to behave as you envision.
2. *What are appropriate behavior and misbehavior?* What is meant by the terms *appropriate behavior* and *misbehavior* as used in education? Give two notable examples of each. Do teachers ever misbehave when working with students? If so, in what ways?
3. *What is bad about misbehavior?* In what ways does misbehavior interfere with teaching and learning? How seriously does it affect effort, progress, and morale? Is there a positive side to misbehavior?
4. *Why do students misbehave when they know they shouldn't?* Why don't students always behave as teachers would like them to? Identify some factors that seem to lead to misbehavior. Do teachers have any control over those factors?
5. *What do we need to know about student needs?* What do we know about the nature and needs of students that can help us work with them more effectively? What about students with special needs related to disabilities, economic realities, or racial, ethnic, cultural, or linguistic diversity?

6. *What do we mean by "positive" discipline?* What is meant by positive discipline and behavior management? Is there a corresponding "negative" type of discipline? If so, how do the two differ, and what is each good for?

7. *What can teachers do to help students behave properly?* How would you explain the teacher's role in helping today's students behave more appropriately? List five things teachers can do toward this end.

8. *Does teaching method affect behavior?* In what ways can method(s) of teaching affect student behavior? Is it possible to teach in such a way that students actually want to conduct themselves appropriately?

9. *Does the physical environment affect behavior?* In what ways can the physical learning environment affect student behavior? What can you do to enhance the quality of the physical environment in which you teach?

10. *Does the psychosocial environment affect behavior?* In what ways can the psychosocial learning environment (comprised of emotions, feelings, and attitudes) affect student behavior? What can you and your students do to enhance the quality of the psychosocial environment?

11. *What role does communication play in discipline?* How, specifically, can you speak with and otherwise communicate with students in order to influence them in a positive manner?

12. *How can you help students work together productively?* What, specifically, can you do to help all members of your class work together effectively, enjoy success, and display positive personal interaction?

13. *What role can parents or guardians play in discipline?* What do you see as advantages of establishing and maintaining good relationships with students' parents or guardians? How can those people be helpful to you and your students?

14. *How can teachers establish good relations with parents?* What can you do to enhance your relationship with students' parents? How do you enlist their support? How do you communicate with them?

15. *In what ways do trust, ethics, and teacher charisma affect student behavior?* To what do these terms refer? Who is responsible for seeing that they become part of the class environment and procedures?

16. *What should you do when students misbehave?* When students misbehave, how can you intervene positively to stop the misbehavior, keep students on track, and maintain positive feelings and relationships? What are specific things you feel comfortable saying and doing?

17. *How can you best deal with problems in your classroom?* What is the difference between a problem and misbehavior? When general problems arise in your classes that involve students and their behavior, how can you best deal with them?

18. *How can you best deal with conflict?* What is meant by conflict? How does it differ from misbehavior and problems? When conflicts occur among students or between you and students, how can you best deal with them?

19. *How do you make your class energetic and lively when you want it that way?* What steps can you take to energize your class so students enjoy learning in a helpful, active, cooperative manner?

20. *Why is a structured approach to discipline desirable?* Why is it important for you to rely on a well-organized strategy for maintaining positive behavior in your classroom? Why is it important that you organize the strategy to suit your specific needs?

Guidance from INTASC, Praxis, and Charlotte Danielson

At this point, let's take a moment to review some of the major suggestions that are presently being used to guide your development as a professional educator. These suggestions come from (1) the Interstate New Teacher Assessment and Support Consortium (INTASC), (2) the Praxis Series of tests produced by Educational Testing Service, and (3) Charlotte Danielson who worked on developing the Praxis III tests of teacher competence in the classroom.

INTASC Recommendations

In 1987 the *Interstate New Teacher Assessment and Support Consortium (INTASC)* was established to assist in rethinking teacher education, especially as concerns preparation and licensing. The consortium articulated 10 desired outcomes of teacher education, which follow in abridged form. These 10 principles, as they are now called, are widely emphasized in teacher education and often used to evaluate beginning and experienced teachers. The principles indicate competencies required for effective teaching and discipline. For a more detailed presentation of INTASC, consult the following website: www.ccsso.org/content/pdfs/corestrd.pdf.

Principle 1. The teacher understands the central concepts, tools of inquiry, and structures of the discipline(s) he or she teaches and can create learning experiences that make these aspects of subject matter meaningful for students. Examples of evidence of such understanding can be seen when the teacher:

- Uses multiple representations and explanations of disciplinary concepts that capture key ideas and link them to students' prior understandings.
- Represents and uses differing viewpoints, theories, "ways of knowing," and methods of inquiry in his or her teaching of subject matter concepts.
- Engages students in generating knowledge and testing hypotheses according to the methods of inquiry and standards of evidence used in the discipline.
- Develops and uses curricula that encourage students to see, question, and interpret ideas from diverse perspectives.

Principle 2. The teacher understands how children learn and develop and can provide learning opportunities that support their intellectual, social, and personal development. Examples of evidence for such understanding can be seen when the teacher:

- Assesses individual and group performance in order to design instruction that meets learners' current needs and leads to the next level of development.

- Stimulates student reflection on prior knowledge and linking new ideas to already familiar ideas, making connections to students' experiences, providing opportunities for active engagement, manipulation, and testing of ideas and materials, and encouraging students to assume responsibility for shaping their learning tasks.
- Accesses students' thinking and experiences as a basis for instructional activities by, for example, encouraging discussion, listening and responding to group interaction, and eliciting samples of student thinking orally and in writing.

Principle 3. *The teacher understands how students differ in their approaches to learning and creates instructional opportunities that are adapted to diverse learners.* Evidence for this understanding is seen when the teacher:

- Identifies and designs instruction appropriate to students' stages of development, learning styles, strengths, and needs.
- Uses teaching approaches that are sensitive to the multiple experiences of learners and that address different learning and performance modes.
- Makes appropriate provisions (in terms of time and circumstances for work, tasks assigned, and communication and response modes) for individual students who have particular learning differences or needs.
- Seeks to understand students' families, cultures, and communities, and uses this information as a basis for connecting instruction to students' experiences (e.g., drawing explicit connections between subject matter and community matters, making assignments that can be related to students' experiences and cultures).
- Creates a learning community in which individual differences are respected.

Principle 4. *The teacher understands and uses a variety of instructional strategies to encourage students' development of critical thinking, problem solving, and performance skills.* Examples of evidence for this understanding are evident when the teacher:

- Carefully evaluates how to achieve learning goals, choosing alternative teaching strategies and materials to achieve different instructional purposes and to meet student needs (e.g., developmental stages, prior knowledge, learning styles, and interests).
- Uses multiple teaching and learning strategies to engage students in active learning opportunities that promote the development of critical thinking, problem solving, and performance capabilities and that help students assume responsibility for identifying and using learning resources.
- Constantly monitors and adjusts strategies in response to learner feedback.
- Develops a variety of clear, accurate presentations and representations of concepts, using alternative explanations to assist students' understanding and presenting diverse perspectives to encourage critical thinking.

Principle 5. *The teacher uses an understanding of individual and group motivation and behavior to create a learning environment that encourages positive social interaction, active engagement in learning, and self-motivation.* Evidence supporting this understanding occurs as the teacher:

- Creates a smoothly functioning learning community in which students assume responsibility for themselves and one another, participate in decision making, work collaboratively and independently, and engage in purposeful learning activities.
- Engages students in individual and cooperative learning activities that help them develop the motivation to achieve by, for example, relating lessons to students' personal interests, allowing students to have choices in their learning, and leading students to ask questions and pursue problems that are meaningful to them.
- Organizes, allocates, and manages the resources of time, space, activities, and attention to provide active and equitable engagement of students in productive tasks.
- Helps the group concerning interactions, academic discussions, and individual and group responsibility that create a positive classroom climate of openness, mutual respect, support, and inquiry.

Principle 6. *The teacher uses knowledge of effective verbal, nonverbal, and media communication techniques to foster active inquiry, collaboration, and supportive interaction in the classroom.* Examples of evidence that support these communication qualities are seen when the teacher:

- Models effective communication strategies in conveying ideas and information and in asking questions (e.g., monitoring the effects of messages, restating ideas and drawing connections, using visual, aural, and kinesthetic cues, and being sensitive to nonverbal cues given and received).
- Supports and expands learner expression in speaking, writing, and other media.
- Asks questions and stimulates discussion in different ways for particular purposes, for example, probing for learner understanding, helping students articulate their ideas and thinking processes, promoting risk taking and problem solving, facilitating factual recall, encouraging convergent and divergent thinking, stimulating curiosity, and helping students to question.
- Communicates in ways that demonstrate a sensitivity to cultural and gender differences (e.g., appropriate use of eye contact, interpretation of body language and verbal statements, and acknowledgment of and responsiveness to different modes of communication and participation).

Principle 7. *The teacher plans instruction based on knowledge of subject matter, students, the community, and curriculum goals.* Evidence of this capability is seen when the teacher:

- Plans for learning opportunities that recognize and address variation in learning styles and performance modes.
- Creates short-range and long-term plans that are linked to student needs and performance, and adapts the plans to ensure and capitalize on student progress and motivation.

Principle 8. *The teacher understands and uses formal and informal assessment strategies to evaluate and ensure the continuous intellectual, social, and physical development of the learner.* Evidence of this understanding is seen when the teacher:

- Uses a variety of formal and informal assessment techniques (e.g., observation, portfolios of student work, teacher-made tests, performance tasks, projects, student self-assessments, peer assessment, and standardized tests).
- Solicits and uses information about students' experiences, learning behavior, needs, and progress from parents, other colleagues, and the students themselves.
- Uses assessment strategies to involve learners in self-assessment activities, to help them become aware of their strengths and needs, and to encourage them to set personal goals for learning.
- Evaluates the effect of class activities on both individuals and the class as a whole, collecting information through observation of classroom interactions, questioning, and analysis of student work.
- Monitors his or her own teaching strategies and behavior in relation to student success, modifying plans and instructional approaches accordingly.
- Maintains useful records of student work and performance and can communicate student progress knowledgeably and responsibly, based on appropriate indicators, to students, parents, and other colleagues.

Principle 9. *The teacher is a reflective practitioner who continually evaluates the effects of his or her choices and actions on others (students, parents, and other professionals in the learning community) and who actively seeks out opportunities to grow professionally.* Evidence for reflective practice is seen when the teacher:

- Uses classroom observation, information about students, and research as sources for evaluating the outcomes of teaching and learning and as a basis for experimenting with, reflecting on, and revising practice.
- Seeks out professional literature, colleagues, and other resources to support his or her own development as a learner and a teacher.

Principle 10. *The teacher fosters relationships with school colleagues, parents, and agencies in the larger community to support students' learning and well-being.* Evidence that supports the existence of such relationships is seen when the teacher:

- Participates in collegial activities designed to make the entire school a productive learning environment.
- Makes links with the learners' other environments on behalf of students, by consulting with parents, counselors, teachers of other classes and activities within the schools, and professionals in other community agencies.
- Identifies and uses community resources to foster student learning.
- Establishes respectful and productive relationships with parents and guardians from diverse home and community situations and seeks to develop cooperative partnerships in support of student learning and well-being.
- Talks with and listens to students, is sensitive and responsive to clues of distress, investigates situations, and seeks outside help as needed and appropriate to remedy problems.

The Praxis Series of Tests

In 1987, Educational Testing Service (ETS) undertook to establish tests that could be used by schools to assess the quality level of their teachers and for teacher licensing agencies to use in granting certification to new teachers. The resultant tests are called the Praxis Series. (Praxis is a word that refers to reflection on and application of accepted ways of doing things—in other words, what one does in practice.) Many states now use these tests in teacher licensing. There are three phases of Praxis tests. Praxis I is for assessing basic skills teachers require in reading, writing, and mathematics. Praxis II is for assessing competencies emphasized in programs of teacher education. Praxis III is for assessing the competence levels of teachers in the classroom. Several states and individual writers have worked to align the INTASC principles and the Praxis criteria. To see one such example from the Utah State Department of Education, consult the following website: www.ed.utah.edu/TandL/NCATE/correlationINTASC-PRAXIS.pdf.

Danielson and Professional Teaching Competencies

Charlotte Danielson (1996) worked in the development of Praxis III. In the course of that work, it became evident to her that teachers have, or make, little opportunity to discuss teaching with each other. Yet, teachers trained to serve as assessors in Praxis III reported that the interactions with fellow professionals provided great new insights into teaching. Danielson, therefore, devised a framework for teaching that teachers can use as a basis of discussion to enrich their professional lives. The framework lists four components of professional teaching: planning and preparation; the classroom environment; communicating clearly and accurately; and reflecting on teaching. Danielson further devised forms that depict clearly the relationships between the INTASC principles and teacher performance.

Five Principles for Building a Personal System of Discipline

In keeping with the foregoing stipulations in the INTASC, Praxis, and Danielson contributions, five principles are set forth here that will help you prepare yourself to work with students in ways that bring satisfaction to all. You will be encouraged to reflect and take notes on these five principles as you read the remainder of this book. When you have completed the book, you will have at hand an organized collection of notes from which you can formalize your personal system of discipline.

Principle 1. *Present and conduct yourself in a professional manner.* Make sure you know and put into practice the following:

- Standards of professionalism
- Ethical considerations
- Legal considerations

Principle 2. *Clarify how you want your students to behave, now and in the future.* You may identify attitudes and behaviors such as:

- Show positive attitude
- Behave considerately toward others
- Take initiative
- Show self-direction
- Make a strong effort to learn
- Assume personal responsibility for behavior

Principle 3. *Establish and maintain classroom conditions that help students become the kinds of people you hope they will be.* You may wish to give attention to:

- Good environment for learning
- Compatibility with students' nature, needs, interests, and preferences
- Sense of community
- Positive attention
- Good communication
- Consideration for others
- Attention to special needs
- Trust
- Interesting activities
- Student knowledge of expectations
- Continual helpfulness
- Preservation of dignity
- Minimizing causes of misbehavior
- Teacher charisma
- Student involvement in planning the program

Principle 4. *Do all you can to help students conduct themselves responsibly.* Consider the following:

- Identify and reduce the known causes of misbehavior.
- Build a sense of community in your classroom that emphasizes collaboration, joint decision making, responsibility, and consideration for others.
- Communicate clearly and effectively with students. Keep them fully informed.
- Speak with students in ways that build dignity and invite cooperation.
- Work in a collaborative way with students and allow them to help make class decisions.
- Reach a set of agreements about how the class is to function and how you and the students will conduct yourselves.
- Build group spirit and otherwise energize the class.
- Bring parents into meaningful partnership with your class and program.
- Use activities that increase student self-direction and responsibility.
- Resolve class problems effectively and fairly while maintaining good personal relationships.

Principle 5. *Intervene helpfully when misbehavior occurs.*

■ Understand the nature of helpful interventions and devise approaches that are suited to you and your students.
■ Develop a repertoire of helpful things to say and do when students misbehave.
■ Identify tactics and words you want to make sure to avoid.
■ Establish a clear procedure for dealing with misbehavior. Involve students in developing the procedure. Follow that procedure consistently.
■ Help students accept responsibility for their behavior and commit to better behavior in the future.

Getting Started on Principle 1: Presenting and Conducting Yourself in a Professional Manner

At this point, we explore important professional, ethical, and legal considerations related to working with students. This information applies to the first of the five principles for developing your personal system of discipline.

Author's note: The author is not qualified to provide legal advice. The legal aspects of this chapter are believed to be correct, but the interpretations presented here cannot be considered the final word. Please, therefore, obtain from your school district a description of legal responsibilities of its teachers and consider that information authoritative.

Standards of Professionalism

The National Education Association (1975) has set forth professional and ethical provisions for educators. All teachers are expected to abide by them. This code stipulates, among other things, that the educator:

■ Shall not misrepresent his or her professional qualifications in any way.
■ Shall not knowingly make false or malicious statements about a colleague.
■ Shall not accept any gratuity, gift, or favor that might impair or appear to influence professional decisions or action.
■ Shall not suppress or distort subject matter relevant to the student's progress.
■ Shall not intentionally expose students to embarrassment or disparagement.
■ Shall not disclose information about students obtained in the course of professional service unless disclosure serves a compelling professional purpose or is required by law.

In addition to the NEA stipulations, professionalism requires you to do the following:

- Dress professionally, as an adult in a professional situation.
- Use appropriate language for the educational setting with correct speech patterns and complete avoidance of obscenities.
- Treat others with respect and courtesy.

Legalities Pertaining to Student Safety and Well-Being

Schools have traditionally operated under the doctrine of *in loco parentis,* which means "in place of parents." This doctrine has to do with student care and safety and it means that you should watch over students as if you were their parent (actually, even more closely than that). It gives you and other school officials authority over students in school matters involving academics and discipline and permits you to take actions that a reasonable parent would take under similar circumstances.

Due Diligence

Teachers and other school personnel have a duty to oversee—to exercise reasonable care to protect students from harm (see Goorian and Brown, 2002). Many teachers are not aware they are required to keep a diligent eye on all students under their supervision. They may feel that their mere presence satisfies their duty. In general, diligence means taking reasonable care or giving reasonable attention to a matter. In school settings this principle is applied in relation to established policies and is judged in terms of what a reasonable and prudent professional would do in a similar circumstance.

Negligence and Breach of Duty

If a student is injured mentally or physically while at school, and the teacher on duty did not exercise due diligence, the teacher and school may be sued for negligence (Drye, 2000). The following guidelines will help you make sure you are in a defensible position should questions arise about negligence and breach of duty:

- Perform your assigned duties as directed, even those that seem boring and unnecessary.
- Oversee your students. Be vigilant in monitoring their behavior. Do not leave students unattended in your classroom, shop, or instructional area.
- Provide thorough instructions and teach safety procedures before undertaking activities that involve risk to students.
- Be vigilant for signs that students might harm themselves. Pay attention to what they do, say, and write. Observe them for changes in behavior. Speak to the counselor about your concerns.
- You are required by law to report if you suspect one of your students is being abused. Follow your school guidelines to familiarize yourself with signs of abuse. If you are suspicious, report your concerns to the school counselor or administrator, who will follow up.

Concerns Related to Physical Contact with Students

Don't allow yourself to be alone in the classroom with a student, unless you are in plain sight of others. If you are male, refrain from touching students, other than on the hands or arms or with pats to the head or shoulder. If students frustrate or anger you, never grab any part of their body, as it is difficult to justify or defend physical contact motivated by anger. Also make sure you never throw pencils, pens, erasers, books, desks, or chairs, no matter how strongly you are provoked.

Ethics of Instruction

Ethics refers to right and wrong, proper and improper. There are certain ethics of the profession by which all teachers are expected to abide. They affect your approach to teaching and your overall strategy for working with students. They also impinge on a large number of factors associated with interacting with students, presenting lessons, and managing behavior. It is strongly recommended that you emphasize the following seven qualities in your overall teaching style.

1. *Give your genuine best effort to the profession.* Your obligation is to do the best you can to help each and every student profit from the educational experience and experience satisfaction in doing so. This applies to all students under your direction, without favoritism. It also applies to how you work and relate with parents and colleagues.

2. *Do your best to teach effectively.* Teach in a manner deemed most conducive to success for all learners. This implies careful selection of subject matter, focus on worthwhile learning, provision of interesting activities, relating with students effectively, and insisting on considerate, humane treatment by and for everyone in the class.

3. *Always do what you can to help students.* Helpfulness is an indispensable ingredient of effective teaching. You will see it emphasized and reemphasized in the most popular models of behavior management. As Haim Ginott (1971) said, always ask yourself what you can do, at a given moment, that would be most helpful to your students.

4. *Treat students civilly, respectfully, and fairly.* Treat all students as your social equals. Give each some personal attention every day. Learn their names quickly and remember important things about them. Give them credit for work well done and for exemplary behavior. Smile and interact with them in a friendly manner but don't single out any as your favorites. Spread your attention around evenly. Be friendly but don't try to become pals with students.

5. *Emphasize same-side cooperation with students.* Involve students in planning and decision making. Try to establish the understanding that you and they must work together in order to attain class goals and have a satisfying time doing so. Show you are considerate of their desires and feelings. Always treat them as you would like to be treated in similar circumstances. Do not attack their dignity or disparage them in any way.

6. *Communicate effectively.* Make sure students know what is expected of them. Take time to listen to their concerns. Consider using class meetings to discuss important matters with the class. When you listen to students, try to see their perspective. When you speak to them, be helpful and encouraging, but take care that you don't give too much advice or begin preaching or moralizing. Don't grill students about their behavior or otherwise put them on the defensive. Instead, politely ask them to help you understand why they have done or said a certain thing. When they explain, listen to them attentively. When you reply with a suggestion, indicate it is something for them to consider or simply your opinion.

7. *Maintain a charismatic demeanor.* Charisma is a quality of attractiveness that draws attention and makes others want to be in your presence and interact with you. You acquire charisma by making yourself personally interesting to students. Be upbeat and pleasant, with a touch of wit (don't try to overdo it). Share some of your interests, experiences, and talents. Let students know a bit about your family life and what you like to do outside of school. Use humor but without being silly. Never weave sarcasm into what you say. Show personal interest, be helpful, and treat students considerately.

KEY TERMS AND CONCEPTS PRESENTED IN THIS CHAPTER

The following terms and concepts are important in understanding the discipline problem and the solutions proposed in this book. Check yourself to make sure you understand them:

behavior
desirable school behavior
misbehavior
types of misbehavior (13)
discipline

behavior management
personal system of behavior
  management
five principles for a personal system
  of discipline

prevention of misbehavior
legal concerns
ethics
INTASC
Praxis

QUESTIONS AND ACTIVITIES

1. In pairs or small groups, discuss the 20 questions presented in the entry point section. See if you can arrive at group consensus concerning answers to the questions.

2. Refer to the five principles for building a personal system of discipline. In a notebook or journal, copy the outline headings, leaving a few blank pages following each of the five principles. Then review this chapter and enter in your notebook information you feel applies to each of the principles. By repeating this activity at the end of every chapter, you will accumulate a wealth of ideas and techniques to use in organizing your own personal system of discipline.

REFERENCES

Danielson, C. 1996. *Enhancing professional practice: A framework for teaching.* Alexandria, VA: ASCD.

Drye, J. 2000. *Tort liability 101: When are teachers liable?* Atlanta, GA: Educator Resources. www.Educator-Resources.com.

Ginott, H. 1971. *Teacher and child.* New York: Macmillan.

Goorian, B., and Brown, K. 2002. Trends and issues: School law. ERIC Clearinghouse on Educational Management. http://eric.uoregon.edu/trends_issues/law/index.html.

Interstate New Teacher Assessment and Support Consortium. 2003. Model standards for beginning teacher licensing, assessment and development: A resource for state dialogue. www.ccsso.org/content/pdfs/corestrd.pdf. pp. 14–33.

National Education Association. 1975. Code of Ethics of the Education Profession. www.nea.org/aboutnea/code.html.

Schwartz, F. 1981. Supporting or subverting learning: Peer group patterns in four tracked schools. *Anthropology and Education Quarterly, 12*(2), 99–120.

CHAPTER 2

Great Pioneers in Classroom Discipline

CHAPTER PREVIEW

This chapter describes contributions made between 1951 and 1989 by six influential pioneers in classroom discipline. Although their models are rarely used today as complete systems of behavior management, their ideas strongly influence present-day practice. Prior to 1951, teachers used an authoritative approach to discipline, which was considered to be something essentially separate from teaching. In 1951, this picture began to change and has continued to do so. Discipline is now seen as an integral part of teaching, due in large part to the influence of the authorities featured in this chapter.

The Evolution of Classroom Discipline

Prior to the middle of the twentieth century, classroom discipline was forceful and demanding, often harsh and punitive. Please understand that teachers were persons of good intent doing the best they could to help students learn. Their control tactics were reflective of the times. Everyone expected teachers to make students toe the mark. When students got out of line, they were to be reprimanded and often punished. Teachers possessed authoritative power and used it, seldom taking into account that their tactics produced fear and caused students to dislike school.

Why did teachers use methods that caused student resentment rather than encouraging cooperation? The answer lies in tradition, ignorance, and desire for success. Although they tried not to show it, teachers were also afraid of losing control, of being terrorized by their students, of being failures as teachers. They didn't yet know that humane procedures, properly used, could deflect student resistance and replace it with cooperation.

The years following World War II brought many social changes toward equality and democracy. Correspondingly, society's view of classroom discipline slowly changed. That change became evident in the early 1950s, although it took a while to catch on, slowed by an absence of formalized discipline procedures that were gentle, yet effective.

What we now call modern discipline consists of techniques that entice, persuade, and assist students, rather than using intimidation and punishment to force student compliance. It received a major push in 1951 when Fritz Redl and William Wattenberg set forth the first organized, systematic discipline plan based on humane tactics. Their work opened educators' minds to new possibilities and set a pattern for changes to come.

In this chapter we examine the contributions of Fritz Redl and William Wattenberg and other great pioneers in modern discipline. We begin with Redl and Wattenberg's conclusions concerning group behavior and proceed to the pivotal discoveries by B. F. Skinner on behavior shaping, Jacob Kounin on lesson management, Haim Ginott on communication in discipline, Rudolf Dreikurs on discipline through democratic teaching, and Thomas Gordon on improving discipline through helping students develop greater self-control.

Fritz Redl and William Wattenberg: Discipline through Influencing Group Behavior

Fritz Redl

Fritz Redl and William Wattenberg (1951) presented the first theory-based approach to discipline. It was designed specifically to help teachers understand and deal considerately with group misbehavior and the effects it had on individual students. Their work inaugurated the modern era in classroom discipline. Both Redl and Wattenberg were specialists in human behavior.

Redl and Wattenberg's Principal Teachings

- *People in groups behave differently than they do individually.*

  Students in classrooms do things they would not do if by themselves and will not do certain things they would do if by themselves. When teachers understand how individual behavior is affected by the group, they can better help students be successful in school.

William Wattenberg

- *Group dynamics, defined as forces generated by and within groups, produce the group currents that strongly affect behavior.*

  Redl and Wattenberg claimed that if teachers are to deal effectively with *group behavior,* they must understand group dynamics, how those dynamics develop, and how they affect students in the classroom. Group dynamics—psychological forces that grow within groups of people—are manifested in effects such as group spirit, imitative behavior, desire to excel, scapegoating of certain students, hiding places for nonachievers, group norms and expectations, and the adoption of certain roles by members of the group.

- *Students adopt identifiable **roles** in the classroom.*

  Within any group, students take on roles such as leaders, followers, clowns (the show-offs), instigators (who provoke misbehavior), and scapegoats (those on whom blame is placed even when not deserved). Teachers should be watchful for the emergence of these roles, bring them to the class's attention, be prepared to encourage or discourage them as appropriate, and know how to limit their detrimental effects.

● *Teachers are also cast into many different roles that affect student behavior.*

Students see teachers as role models, sources of knowledge, referees, judges, and surrogate parents. Teachers must be aware that students hold these expectations of them. They can discuss these matters with students for clarification.

● *Teachers should involve students in setting class standards and deciding how transgressions should be handled.*

They should keep student attitude in mind at all times, show a desire to be helpful, remain as objective as possible, show tolerance, and maintain a sense of humor.

● *Teachers should use* **influence techniques,** *rather than punishment, to control behavior.*

Positive influence techniques include **supporting self-control,** offering **situational assistance,** and **appraising reality,** where teachers help students become aware of underlying causes of proper and improper behavior.

● *Punishment is a last resort in dealing with misbehavior.*

If used at all, punishment should never be physically hurtful but should consist only of preplanned consequences that are unpleasant to students, such as sitting by themselves, making up work that has not been done, or not being allowed to participate in certain class activities. Never should it involve angry outbursts from the teacher or attempts to teach students a lesson.

Review of Redl and Wattenberg's Contributions

Redl and Wattenberg made five notable contributions to modern discipline. First, they described how groups behave differently from individuals, thus helping teachers understand classroom behaviors that are otherwise perplexing. Second, they provided the first well-organized, systematic approach to improving student behavior in the classroom, replacing aversive techniques with humane approaches that promoted long-term positive relationships. Third, they showed how to diagnose the causes of student misbehavior, believing that by attending to causes teachers could eliminate most misbehavior. Fourth, they established the value of involving students in making decisions about discipline, which is now advocated by all authorities. And, fifth, they pointed out the detrimental effects of punishment and showed why it should not be used in class discipline. These five contributions established a pattern that newer discipline trends have followed.

But despite its remarkable advances and contributions to later developments in classroom discipline, Redl and Wattenberg's approach was never put widely into practice. Teachers couldn't seem to get a handle on the concept and implications of group dynamics, nor did they understand how to deal with the roles that they and students assumed in the group. They found they could not put the recommended procedures into effect quickly enough, given the harried context of the classroom, and felt they had insufficient expertise to carry them out properly. Thus, although Redl and Wattenberg's work broke new ground in discipline and although teachers found it interesting, persuasive, and in many ways helpful, the approach was too cumbersome to implement efficiently.

B. F. Skinner:
Discipline through Shaping Desired Behavior

Even before Redl and Wattenberg published their suggestions for working with the group, Harvard behavioral psychologist Burrhus Frederic Skinner (1904–1990) was discovering how our voluntary actions are influenced by what happens to us immediately after we perform a given act. Skinner earned his doctorate in psychology at Harvard in 1931 and, from that time almost until his death in 1990, he published articles and books based on his findings and beliefs about human behavior. Skinner (1953, 1954, 1971) never concerned himself directly with classroom discipline. His followers devised and popularized **behavior modification,** which is still used extensively in different realms of human learning. Behavior modification came strongly into vogue in the early 1960s, especially for controlling the behavior of young children, and its principles are used everywhere in teaching.

B. F. Skinner

Skinner's Principal Teachings

- *Much if not most of our voluntary behavior is shaped as we receive reinforcement immediately after we perform an act.*

  (For our purposes here, reinforcement can be thought of as reward, though *reward* is a term Skinner avoided.) We do something, and if rewarded for it, we become more likely to repeat the act.

- *If stimuli are to have a reinforcing effect on behavior, they must be received soon after the behavior occurs.*

  Reinforcing stimuli common in the classroom include knowledge of results, peer approval, awards and free time, and smiles, nods, and praise from the teacher.

- *Behavior modification refers to the overall procedure of* **shaping student behavior** *intentionally through reinforcement.*

  Skinner did not invent or use the term *behavior modification.*

- **Constant reinforcement,** *given every time a student behaves as desired, helps new learning become established.*

  The teacher might praise Jonathan every time he raises his hand or privately compliment Mary every time she turns in required homework.

- **Intermittent reinforcement,** *given occasionally, is sufficient to maintain desired behavior once it has become established.*

  After students have learned to come into the room and get immediately to work, the teacher will only occasionally need to express appreciation.

- *Behaviors that are not reinforced eventually disappear or become* **extinguished.**

  If Roberto raises his hand in class but is never called on, he will eventually stop raising his hand.

● *Successive approximation is a behavior-shaping progression in which behavior comes closer and closer to a preset goal.*

This process is evident when skills are being built. Here students are rewarded regularly for improvement.

● *Punishment often has negative effects in behavior modification and, hence, is not used in the classroom.*

Skinner was uncertain as to whether punishment could extinguish inappropriate behavior.

Review of Skinner's Contributions

Although Skinner did not concern himself with classroom discipline per se, his discoveries concerning the shaping of desired behavior through reinforcement led directly to behavior modification, which is still used to speed and shape academic and social learning. Years ago many primary-grade teachers used behavior modification as their entire discipline system, rewarding students who behaved properly and ignoring those who misbehaved. Very few teachers now use behavior modification as their discipline system, yet Skinner's principles of reinforcement are regularly applied at all levels of teaching.

In the 1960s teachers very much liked behavior modification. They found it unusually effective in promoting desired behavior, especially at the primary grade level, and many built it into every aspect of their daily teaching. After a few years, however, behavior modification was being used not so much for discipline as for encouraging and reinforcing learning. Even teachers who enjoyed its effectiveness began to worry that it might be simply bribing students to behave properly. Beyond primary grades, teachers had found behavior modification unsuitable as a total discipline package for several reasons. A major concern was that although it was effective in teaching students desirable behavior, it was inefficient in teaching them what *not* to do. Teachers grew tired of hoping that by ignoring misbehaving students they could get them to behave properly; they saw that misbehavior often brought enough rewards from peers to keep it going. Also, students can be taught or shown almost instantly how to behave desirably. They don't have to learn it through lengthy nonverbal and nonimitative processes as do pigeons and rats.

Jacob Kounin:
Improving Discipline through Lesson Management

Jacob Kounin

In 1971 a new work appeared that opened yet another window on classroom discipline. Previously, teaching and discipline had been seen as separate aspects of education. Although everyone knew they affected each other, teaching was thought of as helping students learn, whereas discipline was what teachers did to keep students working, paying attention, and behaving themselves.

This changed somewhat following the publication of Jacob Kounin's book *Discipline and Group Management in Classrooms.* Kounin was an educational psychologist at Wayne State University. He became known for his detailed investigations into the effects of classroom management and lesson management on student behavior.

Kounin's Principal Teachings

- *Teachers need to know what is going on in all parts of the classroom at all times.*
  Kounin verified that teachers good in discipline displayed this trait, which he called **withitness.**

- *Good lesson momentum helps keep students on track.*
  Kounin used the term **momentum** to refer to teachers starting lessons with dispatch, keeping lessons moving ahead, making transitions among activities efficiently, and bringing lessons to a satisfactory close.

- *Smoothness in lesson presentation helps keep students involved.*
  The term **smoothness** refers to steady progression of lessons without abrupt changes or disturbing incidents.

- *Effective teachers have systems for gaining student attention and clarifying expectations.*
  Kounin called this tactic **group alerting.**

- *Effective teachers keep students attentive and actively involved.*
  Such student **accountability** is maintained by regularly calling on students to respond, demonstrate, or explain.

- *Teachers good in behavior management are able to attend to two or more events simultaneously.*
  This skill, which Kounin called **overlapping,** is exemplified in teachers' answering questions for students doing independent work while at the same time instructing a small group of students.

- *Effective teachers see to it that students are not overexposed to a particular topic.*
  Overexposure produces **satiation,** meaning students have had their fill of the topic as indicated through disengagement, boredom, and misbehavior.

- *Effective teachers make instructional activities enjoyable and challenging.*
  Kounin described how fun and challenge delay satiation.

Review of Kounin's Contributions

Kounin identified a number of teacher strategies that helped students remain engaged in lessons with resultant reduction in misbehavior. The interconnection he identified between ways of teaching and control of behavior led to a new line of thought concerning how teaching influences misbehavior. He suggested that the best way to maintain good discipline is to keep students actively engaged in class activities.

Kounin explained that he had expected to find a relationship between what teachers did when students misbehaved and the subsequent misbehavior of those students. But no such findings emerged from his research, prompting Kounin to write:

> That unexpected fact required unlearning on my part, in the sense of having to replace the original question by other questions. Questions about disciplinary techniques were eliminated and replaced by questions about classroom management in general, [and] *preventing* misbehavior was given higher investigative priority than *handling* misbehavior. (1971, p. 143, italics added)

He went on to describe what teachers should understand about operating their classrooms:

> . . . the business of running a classroom is a complicated technology having to do with developing a nonsatiating learning program; programming for progress, challenge, and variety in learning activities; initiating and maintaining movement in classroom tasks with smoothness and momentum; coping with more than one event simultaneously; observing and emitting feedback for many different events; directing actions at appropriate targets; maintaining a focus upon a group; and doubtless other techniques not measured in these researches. (1971, pp. 144–145)

Kounin made outstanding contributions concerning how lesson management can forestall misbehavior, and he provided a valuable service in drawing attention to the close connection between teaching and discipline. However, teachers never found his approach satisfactory as a total system of discipline. They agree that proper teaching can cut down markedly on the incidence of class misbehavior. But misbehavior occurs even in the best of circumstances, and Kounin provided no help in what teachers should do when misbehavior disrupts lessons. Kounin stated that he couldn't identify teacher tactics that, when used in response to misbehavior, did anything to improve the behavior. Improve it or not, teachers feel they must be able to put a stop to disruptive or defiant behavior simply in order to continue with their lessons. Unfortunately, they found little in Kounin's work that helped in that regard.

Haim Ginott: Discipline through Congruent Communication

In the same year that Kounin published his work on lesson management, there appeared another small book that had even greater influence. That was Haim Ginott's *Teacher and Child* (1971) in which Ginott illuminated the critical role of communication in discipline, especially concerning how teachers talk to and with their students. In many ways, Ginott did more than anyone else to set the tone that prevails in today's systems of discipline.

Haim Ginott

Ginott (1922–1973) was a classroom teacher early in his career. Later, he earned his doctorate at Columbia University and went on to hold professorships in psychology at Adelphi University and at New York University Graduate School. He also served as a UNESCO consultant in Israel, was resident psychologist on the *Today* show, and wrote a weekly syndicated column entitled *Between Us* that dealt with interpersonal communication.

Ginott's Principal Teachings

- *Learning always takes place in the present tense,* meaning teachers must not prejudge students or hold grudges.

- *Learning is always a personal matter to the student.*
  Large classes often make teachers forget that each student-learner is an individual who must be treated as such.

- *Teachers should always endeavor to use* **congruent communication,** which is communication that is harmonious with students' feelings about situations and themselves.

- *The cardinal principle of congruent communication is that it addresses situations.*
  It never addresses students' character or personality.

- **Teachers at their best,** *using congruent communication, do not preach, moralize, impose guilt, or demand promises.*
  Instead, they **confer dignity** on their students by treating them as social equals capable of making good decisions.

- **Teachers at their worst** *label students, belittle them, and denigrate their character:*
  They usually do these things inadvertently.

- *Effective teachers* **invite cooperation** *from their students by describing the situation and indicating what needs to be done.*
  They do not dictate to students or boss them around, acts that provoke resistance.

- *Teachers have a* **hidden asset** *on which they should always call, namely, "How can I be most helpful to my students right now?"*
  Most classroom difficulties are avoided when teachers employ that asset.

- *Teachers should feel free to express their anger and other feelings, but when doing so should use* **I-messages** *rather than* **you-messages.**
  Using an I-message, the teacher might say, "I am very upset." Using a you-message, the teacher might say, "You are being very rude."

- *It is wise to use* **laconic language** *when responding to or redirecting student misbehavior.*
  Laconic means short, concise, and brief, which describes the sort of responses Ginott advocates.

- **Evaluative praise** *is worse than none at all and should never be used.*
  An example of evaluative praise is saying, "Good boy for raising your hand."

- *Teachers should use **appreciative praise** when responding to effort or improvement.*
This is praise in which the teacher shows appreciation for what the student has done, without evaluating the student's character (e.g., "I can almost smell those pine trees in your drawing").

- *Always respect students' privacy.*
Teachers should never pry when students do not wish to discuss personal matters but should show they are available should students want to talk.

- *When correcting students, teachers should provide directions concerning the behavior desired.*
Instead of reprimanding students, teachers should help them behave properly.

- *Teachers should not use **why questions** when discussing behavior.*
Why questions only make students feel guilty. An example of a why question is, "Why did you speak to Susan that way?"

- *Sarcasm is almost always dangerous and should not be used when discussing situations with students.*

- *Punishment should not be used in the classroom.*
Punishment only produces hostility, rancor, and vengefulness, while never making students really desire to improve.

- *Teachers should strive continually for **self-discipline** in their work with students.*
Teachers must be careful not to display the very behaviors they are trying to eradicate in students, such as raising their voice to end noise, acting rude toward students who are impolite, and berating students who have used bad language.

- *Classroom discipline is attained gradually, as a series of little victories* in which the teacher, through self-discipline and helpfulness, promotes humaneness and self-control within students.

Review of Ginott's Contributions

Ginott insisted that the only true discipline is self-discipline, which all teachers should try to promote in students. He made a number of especially helpful contributions concerning how teachers can communicate with students to foster positive relations while reducing and correcting misbehavior. He showed the importance of the teacher being self-controlled and, beyond that, the value of congruent communication, which is teacher communication that is harmonious with student feelings and self-perception.

Ginott urged teachers to use **sane messages** when addressing misbehavior, messages that focus calmly on what needs to be corrected without attacking the student's character or personality. He helped clarify his contentions by describing teachers at their best and at their worst, pointing out the positive effects that accrue from treating students considerately and helpfully and the negative effects that result when teachers lose self-control, berate students, or speak to them sarcastically. He cautioned educators that his suggestions would not produce instantaneous results. Guidance through communication had to be used repeatedly over time for its power to take effect. Although misbehavior can be squelched, **genuine discipline** (by which Ginott meant self-discipline) never occurs instantaneously, but rather in a series of small steps that result in genuine changes in student attitude.

Ginott's (1971) overall view on teaching and working with students is summarized in the following excerpt from *Teacher and Child:*

> As a teacher I have come to the frightening conclusion that I am the decisive element in the classroom. It is my personal approach that creates the climate. It is my daily mood that makes the weather. As a teacher I possess tremendous power to make a child's life miserable or joyous. I can be a tool of torture or an instrument of inspiration. I can humiliate or humor, hurt or heal. In all situations it is my response that decides whether a crisis will be escalated or de-escalated, and a child humanized or dehumanized. (p. 13)

It would be difficult to find a teacher who does not agree with Ginott's views on the value of communication and his suggestions concerning how it should be done. Indeed, his ideas are reiterated in virtually all of today's popular systems of discipline. Yet, teachers who have tried to use Ginott's suggestions as their total system of discipline have found something lacking. Teachers want their discipline system to be humane, but they also want it to put an immediate stop to behavior that is offensive or disruptive. Ginott does not provide adequate suggestions in that regard. His suggestions are more helpful in maintaining good relationships with students than in dealing with students who are disruptive in the classroom.

Rudolf Dreikurs:
Discipline through Democratic Teaching

On the heels of the influential books by Jacob Kounin and Haim Ginott there appeared yet another great contribution to discipline, one by psychiatrist Rudolf Dreikurs that emphasized seeking out and dealing with underlying causes of misbehavior. Dreikurs formulated strategies for helping students acquire self-discipline based on understanding of its social value. Dreikurs taught that self-discipline could best be achieved within the context of a democratic classroom.

Rudolf Dreikurs

Dreikurs (1897–1972) was born in Vienna, Austria. After receiving his medical degree from the University of Austria, he entered into a long association with the renowned Austrian psychiatrist Alfred Adler, with whom he worked in family and child counseling. Dreikurs immigrated to the United States in 1937 and eventually became director of the Alfred Adler Institute in Chicago. He also served as professor of psychiatry at the Chicago

Medical School. In keeping with his interest in child and family counseling, he turned attention to misbehavior and discipline in school classrooms.

Dreikurs's Principal Teachings

● *Discipline at its best is seen in student **self-control** based on **social interest.***

Self-controlled students are able to show initiative, make reasonable decisions, and assume responsibility in ways that benefit themselves and others, thus improving the school experience for all concerned.

● *Good discipline occurs best in a **democratic classroom.***

A democratic classroom is one in which teacher and students work together to make decisions about how the class will function.

● *Good discipline cannot occur in autocratic or permissive classrooms.*

In **autocratic classrooms,** the teacher makes all decisions and imposes them on students, leaving no opportunity for student initiative and responsibility. In **permissive classrooms,** the teacher fails to require that students comply with rules, conduct themselves humanely, or endure consequences for their misbehavior.

● *Almost all students have a primary compelling desire to feel they are a valued member of the class, that they belong. This sense of belonging is the **genuine goal** of most school behavior.*

Students sense **belonging** when the teacher and others give them attention and respect, involve them in activities, and do not mistreat them.

● *When students are unable to gain a sense of belonging in the class, they often turn to the **mistaken goals** of attention, power, revenge, and inadequacy.*

When seeking attention, students talk out, show off, interrupt others, and demand teacher attention. When seeking power, they drag their heels, make comments under their breath, and sometimes try to show that the teacher can't make them do anything. When seeking revenge, they try to get back at the teacher and other students by lying, subverting class activities, and maliciously disrupting the class. When seeking to display inadequacy, they withdraw from class activities and make no effort to learn.

● *Teachers should learn how to **identify mistaken goals** and deal with them.*

When teachers see evidence that students are pursuing mistaken goals, they should point out the fact by identifying the mistaken goal and discussing the faulty logic involved. They should do this in a friendly, nonthreatening manner. Dreikurs suggests calmly asking, "Do you need me to pay more attention to you?" or "Could it be that you want to show that I can't make you do the assignment?"

● *Rules for governing class behavior should be formulated jointly by teacher and students. Associated with those rules should be **logical consequences** for compliance or violation.*

Good behavior (following the rules) brings pleasant consequences such as enjoyment of learning and associating positively with others. Misbehavior brings unpleasant consequences such as having to complete work at home or being excluded from normal class activities.

● *Punishment should never be used in the classroom.*

Punishment is just a way for teachers to get back at students and show who's boss. It usually humiliates the student and has additional undesirable effects. It should, therefore, be replaced with logical consequences agreed to by the class.

Review of Dreikurs's Contributions

Dreikurs contributed several valuable concepts and strategies, many of which are evident in today's most popular systems of discipline. He called self-discipline **true discipline,** and was the first to base his discipline scheme on the premise of social interest, that is, of students' seeing that their personal well-being is closely associated with what is good for the group. He was among the first to clarify how democratic teachers and democratic classrooms promote sound discipline. He was the first to pinpoint a prime goal (that of belonging) as an underlying motivator of student behavior and to identify the mistaken goals of attention, power, revenge, and inadequacy that students turn to when unable to achieve the primary goal of belonging. He urged teachers to involve students jointly in formulating rules of class behavior and link those rules with logical consequences that occur as students comply with, or break, the class rules.

Dreikurs also provided a number of more specific suggestions concerning how teachers should interact with students. He said teachers should never use punishment and should avoid using praise, which he felt made students dependent on teacher reactions. Instead of praise, Dreikurs would have teachers use **encouragement.** Praise, by its nature, is directed at the character of the student. Encouragement, by its nature, is directed at what the student does or can do. Instead of saying, "You can certainly play the piano well," an enlightened teacher would say, "I notice a great deal of improvement," or "I can see you enjoy playing very much." Dreikurs gave encouragement a very strong role in how teachers should speak with students. He made the following suggestions (Dreikurs and Cassel, 1995, pp. 51–54):

- Always speak in positive terms; never be negative.
- Encourage students to strive for improvement, not perfection.
- Emphasize student strengths while minimizing weaknesses.
- Help students learn from mistakes, which are valuable in learning.
- Encourage independence and the assumption of responsibility.
- Show faith in students; offer them help in overcoming obstacles.
- Encourage students to help each other.
- Show pride in students' work; display it and share it with others.
- Be optimistic and enthusiastic—a positive outlook is contagious.
- Use encouraging remarks such as, "You have improved," "Can I help you?" "What did you learn from that mistake?"

Because Dreikurs contributed so much to discipline, it might seem strange that teachers did not adopt his approach wholeheartedly. Teachers do like his ideas but have found his system a bit daunting because it is too unwieldy to be implemented easily. They had trouble seeing the interconnections among democracy, prime motive, mistaken goals, social interest, and logical consequences. But most of all, they found it lacking in the ingredient they most wanted, namely, what to do to put an immediate stop to student disruptions, aggression, and defiance.

Thomas Gordon: Discipline as Self-Control

Clinical psychologist Thomas Gordon (1918–2002) founded Gordon Training International, one of the largest human relations training organizations in the world. He pioneered the teaching of communication skills and conflict resolution to parents, teachers, youth, and managers of organizations. Almost 2 million people have undergone his training programs worldwide. Gordon is the author of eight books, including *Parent Effectiveness Training: A Tested New Way to Raise Responsible Children* (1970), *T.E.T.: Teacher Effectiveness Training* (1974, 1987), and *Discipline That Works: Promoting Self-Discipline in Children* (1989). His books and training programs offer parents and teachers strategies for helping children become more self-reliant, self-controlled, responsible, and cooperative. In 1999 Gordon received the American Psychological Foundation's Gold Medal Award for Enduring Contributions to Psychology in the Public Interest. Gordon Training International can be contacted through the following website: www.gordontraining.com.

Thomas Gordon

Gordon's Principal Teachings

- *Teachers should try to influence students rather than control them.*
  The more teachers try to control, the less they are able to exert positive influence.

- *Students' coping mechanisms are strategies that students use when confronted with coercive power.*
  The three coping mechanisms are *fighting* (combating the person with whom they have the conflict), *taking flight* (trying to escape the situation), and *submitting* (giving in to the other person). None of these strategies is conducive to good education.

- *Noncontrolling methods of behavior change are available for influencing students to behave properly.*
  It is counterproductive for teachers to use authoritative power or rewards and punishments to control students.

- *I-messages are statements in which people tell how they personally think or feel about another's behavior and its consequences. They should be used when attempting to influence others.*
  The following is an example of an I-message: "I am having trouble concentrating because there is so much noise in the room."

- *You-messages are statements of blame leveled at someone's behavior. They should NOT be used when attempting to influence others.*
  This is an example of a you-message: "You girls are making too much noise."

● *Shifting gears is a tactic that involves changing from a confrontational to a listening posture.*
This strategy is helpful when students resist the teacher's I-messages or defend themselves.

● *Win-lose conflict resolution can end disputes temporarily but is usually ineffective.*
This type of conflict resolution produces a winner and a loser and usually has a detrimental effect on the loser. For example, Samuel and Justin scuffle and Samuel is made to apologize to Justin, which supposedly resolves the conflict. However, Samuel feels wronged and humiliated and, therefore, declines to cooperate with Justin or the teacher.

● *No-lose conflict resolution is a way of ending disputes by enabling both sides to emerge as "winners."*
For example, when Samuel and Joaquin get in a scuffle, the teacher takes them aside and says sincerely, "I wonder what we might do so that you boys won't feel like fighting any more." Then discussion produces a solution with no winner or loser, and neither boy feels unjustly treated.

● ***Communication roadblocks*** *are comments by well-meaning teachers that shut down student willingness to communicate.*
Two examples of roadblocks are moralizing and telling the student what he or she ought to do.

● ***Participative classroom management*** *makes students more inclined to abide by rules they have helped formulate.*
Students share in problem solving and decision making concerning the classroom, desirable behavior, and class rules.

● *Problem solving is a process that should be taught and practiced in all classrooms.*
Students help clarify problems, put forth possible solutions, select solutions that are acceptable to all, implement the solutions, and evaluate them.

Review of Gordon's Contributions

Gordon believed that classroom discipline is best accomplished by helping students acquire an inner sense of self-control. He rejected as counterproductive the traditional intervention techniques of power-based authority, reward and punishment, and win-lose conflict resolution. Although reward and punishment had been a cornerstone of the behavior management process, Gordon (1989) had this to say about them:

> Using rewards to try to control children's behavior is so common that its effectiveness is rarely questioned . . . the fact that rewards are used so often and unsuccessfully by so many teachers and parents proves they don't work very well. . . . (pp. 37–38)

Gordon urged teachers to replace reward and punishment with **noncontrolling methods** including:

- **Modifying the environment** to reduce student misbehavior.
- Sending I-messages that do not set off the coping mechanisms students use in response to power.

- Practicing the no-lose method of conflict resolution.
- Acknowledging feelings and perceptions, actively listening to students, and avoiding roadblocks to communication, such as giving orders, warning, preaching, advising, lecturing, criticizing, name-calling, analyzing, praising, reassuring, questioning, and withdrawing.
- Participative problem solving and decision making, in which students and teachers work together to make class decisions.

The **no-lose method of conflict** resolution was one of Gordon's greatest contributions. It is usually referred to now as win-win conflict resolution. Gordon urged teachers to defuse conflict situations and bring about solutions acceptable to everyone. In **win-lose conflict resolution,** egos are on the line, and ultimately one person emerges as "winner" and the other as "loser." The loser may comply with the verdict but develop feelings of resentment and disinclination to cooperate. In the no-lose (win-win) approach, both sides find a mutually acceptable solution to their disagreement. No power is applied; hence, egos are preserved and personal relations remain undamaged.

Another of Gordon's prime emphases, although advocated by authorities who preceded him, was **collaborative class management** in which students and teacher jointly plan and make decisions about certain aspects of the classroom, curriculum, and procedures. This concept is now emphasized in virtually all application models of discipline. It includes setting rules collaboratively, making joint decisions about room arrangement and preferred activities, and using a style of management that motivates students, encourages them to take risks, and helps them conduct themselves responsibly.

Although Gordon made a number of valuable additions to our knowledge about maintaining positive discipline in the classroom, his approach *en toto* never attracted a wide following. The reason for this possibly lies in Gordon's detailed attention to concepts of who owns the problem, behavior windows, tactics for opening communication, and avoiding communication roadblocks. The attendant discussions seemed tedious to teachers and not immediately germane to their concerns.

KEY TERMS AND CONCEPTS PRESENTED IN THIS CHAPTER

The following terms and concepts are pivotal in the contentions of pioneers in modern discipline and appear frequently in systems of discipline now in use.

From Redl and Wattenberg's Group Dynamics: appraising reality, diagnostic thinking, group behavior, group dynamics, influence techniques, situational assistance, student roles, teacher roles, supporting self-control.

From Skinner's Behavior Shaping: behavior modification, constant reinforcement, extinction, intermittent reinforcement, positive reinforcement, punishment, reinforce, reinforcement, reinforcer, shaping student behavior, successive approximations.

From Kounin's Lesson and Group Management: accountability, group alerting, momentum, overlapping, satiation, smoothness, withitness.

From Ginott's Discipline through Communication: appreciative praise, conferring dignity, congruent communication, evaluative praise, genuine discipline, invite cooperation, laconic language, sane messages, teacher self-discipline, teachers at their worst, teachers at their best, teachers' hidden asset, why questions, I-messages, you-messages.

From Dreikurs's Discipline through Democratic Teaching: attention, autocratic classroom, belonging, democratic classroom, encouragement, genuine goal of behavior, inadequacy, logical consequences, mistaken goals, permissive classroom, power, punishment, revenge, self-control, social interest, true discipline.

From Gordon's Discipline as Self-Control: collaborative class management, communication roadblocks, active listening, I-messages, you-messages, noncontrolling methods, participative management, helping skills, modifying the environment, no-lose conflict resolution.

QUESTIONS AND ACTIVITIES

1. Enter into your journal items of information that are pertinent to the five guiding principles for building a personal system of discipline.

2. It was noted that none of the discipline systems described in this chapter found widespread use *as a total system*. What do you understand to be the reason for this, given the number of excellent suggestions they contain?

3. Of the approaches reviewed in this chapter, which seemed most useful to you? Which seemed least useful? Why?

4. Despite the presence today of many effective systems of discipline, one can still see teachers who try to maintain discipline by outshouting their students, speaking sarcastically, and treating students disrespectfully. Why do you believe they persist with these tactics? How effective do you think these tactics are with today's students?

REFERENCES

Dreikurs, R., and Cassel, P. 1995. *Discipline without tears.* New York: Penguin-NAL. Originally published in 1972.

Ginott, H. 1971. *Teacher and child.* New York: Macmillan.

Gordon, T. 1970. *Parent Effectiveness Training: A tested new way to raise responsible children.* New York: New American Library.

Gordon, T. 1974, 1987. *T.E.T.: Teacher Effectiveness Training.* New York: David McKay.

Gordon, T. 1989. *Discipline that works: Promoting self-discipline in children.* New York: Random House.

Kounin, J. 1971. *Discipline and group management in classrooms.* New York: Holt, Rinehart & Winston. Reissued in 1977.

Redl, F., and Wattenberg, W. 1951. *Mental hygiene in teaching.* Rev. ed. New York: Harcourt, Brace & World. Revised and reissued in 1959.

Skinner, B. F. 1953. *Science and human behavior.* New York: Macmillan.

Skinner, B. F. 1954. The science of learning and the art of teaching. *Harvard Educational Review, 24,* 86–97.

Skinner, B. F. 1971. *Beyond freedom and dignity.* New York: Knopf.

CHAPTER 3

Lee and Marlene Canter's *Assertive Discipline*

OVERVIEW OF THE CANTERS' MODEL

Focus

- Maintaining a calm, productive classroom environment.
- Meeting students' needs for learning and ensuring that their rights are attended to.
- Helping the teacher remain calmly and nonstressfully in charge of the classroom.

Logic

- Teachers have the right to teach in a professional manner without disruption.
- Students have the right to learn in a safe, calm environment with full support.
- These rights are best met by in-charge teachers who do not violate students' best interests.
- Trust, respect, and perseverance enable teachers to earn student cooperation.

Contributions

- A classroom control strategy that places teachers humanely in charge in the classroom.
- A system that allows teachers to apply positive support and corrective actions calmly and fairly.
- Techniques for teaching students how to behave and for dealing with difficult students.

Canters' Suggestions

- Maintain a leadership role in the class but not in a hostile or authoritarian manner.
- Teach students how to behave acceptably in the classroom.
- Understand students' personal needs and show your willingness to help.
- Continually strive to build trust between yourself and your students.

About Lee and Marlene Canter

Lee Canter is founder of Canter & Associates, an organization that provides training in classroom discipline and publishes related materials for educators and parents. Marlene Canter collaborates in the work. For many years the Canters have been refining their system of discipline, which they call *Assertive Discipline*, to help teachers interact with students in a calm, helpful, and consistent manner. The overall goal of their program is to help teachers establish classrooms where students may learn and teachers may teach effectively. Through workshops, graduate courses, and a variety of published materials, the Canters have brought *Assertive Discipline* to over one and a half million teachers and administrators worldwide. In addition to offering books, tapes, and training programs in discipline, the Canters produce materials and offer graduate-level courses on topics such as motivation, instructional strategies, homework, dealing with severe behavior problems, and activities for positive reinforcement. For lists of their publications and more information on *Assertive Discipline*, contact the Canter & Associates website at www.canter.net.

Lee Canter

Marlene Canter

The Canters' Contributions to Discipline

The Canters have made several major contributions to classroom discipline. They popularized the concept of rights in the classroom—the rights of students to have teachers help them learn in a calm, safe environment and the rights of teachers to teach without disruption. They explained that students need and want limits that assist their proper conduct and that it is the teacher's responsibility to set and enforce those limits. The Canters were the first to insist that teachers have a right to backing from administrators and cooperation from parents in helping students behave acceptably and were also the first to provide teachers with a workable procedure for correcting misbehavior efficiently through a system of easily administered corrective actions. Over the years, the Canters have continually modified their popular approach to ensure that it remains effective as social realities change. Earlier they focused mainly on teachers being strong leaders in the classroom, whereas now they place more emphasis on building trusting, helpful relationships with students, providing **positive recognition** and support, and taking a proactive approach to dealing with problems of behavior.

The Canters' Central Focus

The Canters' model focuses on establishing a classroom climate in which needs are met, behavior is managed humanely, and learning occurs as intended. This climate is accomplished by attending closely to student needs, formalizing effective class rules of behavior, teaching students how to behave properly, regularly giving students positive attention, talking helpfully with students who misbehave, and establishing a sense of mutual trust and respect. The Canters explain how to take a proactive approach to working effectively with students.

The Canters' Principal Teachings

- *Today's students have clear rights and needs that must be met if they are to be taught effectively.*
  These **student rights and needs** include a caring teacher who persistently works to foster the best interests of students.

- *Teachers have rights and needs in the classroom as well.*
  Teachers' rights include teaching in a classroom that is free from disruption with support from parents and administrators as they work to help students.

- *The most effective teachers are those who remain in control of the class while always remembering that their main duty is to help students learn and behave responsibly.*
  Teachers must continually model through their own behavior the kind of trust and respect for students that they want students to show toward others.

- *A good discipline plan, based on trust and respect, is necessary for helping students limit their counterproductive behavior.*
  Such a discipline plan contains rules and corrective actions, and the plan must be fully understood and supported by students and parents.

- *Teachers should practice **positive repetitions**.*
  Positive repetitions involve repeating directions as positive statements to students who are complying with class rules, for example, "Fred remembered to raise his hand. Good job," or "The equipment is all back neatly in place. Good going."

- *Students should enjoy **positive support** when they behave acceptably.*
  Positive support is provided through kind words or facial expressions that teachers offer when students comply with class expectations. The Canters consider positive acknowledgment to be very powerful.

- *Today's teachers must not only model proper class behavior but often must directly teach it as well.*
  It is not enough for teachers simply to set limits and apply corrective actions. They must help students understand and practice behavior that leads to success in school.

- *Teachers can successfully teach the majority of students typically thought of as difficult to manage.*
  They can accomplish this by reaching out to those students, learning about their needs, interacting with them personally, and showing a constant willingness to help.

- *Teachers are most effective when they use a proactive, rather than a reactive, approach to discipline.*
  Reactive means you wait until students misbehave and then try to decide what to do to get them back on course. **Proactive** means you anticipate misbehavior and plan in advance how you will deal with it in a positive manner.

Analysis of the Canters' *Assertive Discipline*

In 1976, the Canters set forth the basic premises and practices of *Assertive Discipline,* which almost overnight brought relief to teachers everywhere who were beleaguered by classroom misbehavior. They have progressively modified their approach over time. Their main assertions follow.

Needs and Rights in the Classroom

Canter and Canter (2001) explain that students have a need for and the right to a warm, supportive classroom environment in which to learn, where teachers do all they can to help students be successful. Teachers have needs and rights in the classroom as well, which include the need and right to teach in a professional manner without disruptions and with support from administrators.

Types of Teachers and Their Effects on Students

The Canters describe three types of teachers, differentiated on the basis of how they relate to students. They call the three types hostile teachers, nonassertive teachers, and assertive teachers.

Hostile teachers appear to view students as adversaries. They seem to feel if they are to maintain order and teach properly, they must keep the upper hand. They attempt to do so by laying down the law, accepting no nonsense, and using commands and stern facial expressions. They sometimes give needlessly strong admonishments such as: "Sit down, shut up, and listen!" Such messages suggest a dislike for students and cause students to feel they are being treated unjustly.

Nonassertive teachers take an overly passive approach to students. They fail to help the class formulate reasonable expectations or are inconsistent in dealing with students, allowing certain behaviors one day while strongly disapproving them the next. They often make statements such as, "For heaven's sake, please try to behave like ladies and gentlemen," or "How many times do I have to tell you no talking?" They come across as wishy-washy, and after a time students stop taking them seriously. Yet, when those teachers become overly frustrated, they sometimes come down very hard on students. This inconsistency leaves students confused about expectations and enforcement.

Assertive teachers clearly, confidently, and consistently model and express class expectations. They work hard to build trust with the class. When necessary, they teach students how to behave so they can better learn and relate to others, and they implement a discipline plan that encourages student cooperation. Such teachers help students understand which behaviors promote success and which lead to failure. Assertive teachers are not harsh taskmasters. They recognize students' needs for consistent limits on behavior but at the same time are ever mindful of students' needs for warmth and encouragement. Because they know that students may require direct instruction in how to behave acceptably in the classroom, they might be heard to say, "Our rule is no talking without raising your hand. Please raise your hand and wait for me to call on you."

Each of the response styles produces certain effects on teachers and students. The **hostile response style** takes away most of the pleasure that teachers and students might otherwise enjoy in class. Its harshness curtails the development of trusting relationships and can produce negative student attitudes toward teachers and school. The **nonassertive response style** leads to student feelings of insecurity and frustration. Nonassertive teachers cannot get their needs met in the classroom, which produces high levels of stress for them. These teachers frequently become hostile toward chronically misbehaving students. Students in turn feel manipulated and many feel little respect for their teachers. The **assertive response style** provides several benefits that the other styles do not. Assertive teachers create a classroom atmosphere that allows both teacher and students to meet their needs. They invite student collaboration and help students practice acceptable behavior. Students learn they can count on their teacher to provide clear expectations, consistency, and an atmosphere of warmth and support. All this engenders a feeling of comfort for everyone and allows teaching and learning to flourish.

Striking a Balance between Structure and Caring

The Canters point out that if you want students to choose appropriate behavior and cooperate with you, they need to know that you are concerned about them personally—about their personal lives and their success in school. The Canters encourage teachers to say, "It is the way I perceive the student and the way I act toward him or her that will put me in the position to make some major changes and help the student succeed in school" (2001, p. 20). At the same time, students need structure and clearly defined limits on behavior. Teachers should strive to develop a classroom climate that is safe, peaceful, calm, and predictable, suffused with personal concern for students. Sustaining such a climate will enable teachers to help students conduct themselves responsibly despite problems they may bring with them to school.

Moving toward Trust as an Element of Discipline

The Canters (Canter, 1996) stress that good discipline does not depend on many rules linked with harsh corrective actions. Rather, good discipline grows out of mutual trust and respect. The Canters provide abundant advice to help teachers develop this sort of discipline in their classrooms. In order to develop trust and respect in the classroom, teachers must always model the trust and respect they wish to see in their students. They must listen carefully to students, speak to them respectfully, and treat everyone fairly. Furthermore, they should get to know their students as individuals and acknowledge them as such. Toward this end the Canters suggest that teachers greet students by name with a smile, acknowledge birthdays and other important events in students' lives, learn about students' interests and preferences, and chat with them individually in and out of the classroom. They also suggest establishing strong ties with parents or guardians. This can be done through purposeful communication via positive notes and occasional phone calls.

Teaching Students How They Are Expected to Behave in the Classroom

Students do not automatically know how to behave in all settings and situations. Therefore, teachers must make sure to teach acceptable behavior through modeling, explanation, and practice. The Canters say that the most important classroom rule is "Follow directions." Recognizing that different teachers have their own ways of doing things, the Canters suggest you remind students they need to follow your expectations, not another teacher's expectations. The Canters advise teachers to identify the academic activities, routine procedures, and special procedures for which directions are needed and then determine the specific directions that students need. The following are two examples, one for an academic activity and one for a routine procedure (Canter and Canter, 1992, pp. 126–127):

Teacher conducting a directed lesson teaches students how to follow these directions:

1. Please clear your desks of everything but paper and pencil.
2. Eyes on me. No talking while I'm talking.
3. Raise hand and wait to be called on before speaking.

For routine procedure for entering the room, the teacher teaches students how to:

1. Walk into the room.
2. Go directly to their seat and sit down.
3. Cease talking when the bell rings.

The best time for teaching directions is immediately prior to the first (or next) time the activity is to take place. For young children, give demonstrations and have children act them out. Frequent reteaching and reinforcement are necessary.

For older students, explain the reasons behind the directions and the benefits they provide. The Canters (1992, pp. 131–138) suggest the following procedure:

1. Explain the rationale for the direction.
2. Involve the students by asking questions.
3. Explain the specific directions.
4. Check for student understanding (by asking questions or having students role-play).

Once taught, the specific directions should be reinforced regularly through **positive repetition.** Rather than correcting a student who is not following directions, the teacher repeats the desired behavior. For example, a primary-grade teacher notes one or more who are following directions and says, "Joshua has remembered to raise his hand. So has Elsa." A secondary teacher addresses the class rather than individuals: "Practically everyone began work quickly. I appreciate that very much." Directions should be reviewed each time the activity is repeated for the first two weeks. For the next month the directions should be reviewed each Monday as a refresher, and for the remainder of the year they should be reviewed after vacations and before special events such as holidays and field trips.

Establishing Discipline That Provides Structure and Identifies Behavior Limits

The Canters advocate a written discipline plan that clarifies rules, positive recognition, and corrective actions. **Rules** state exactly how students are to behave. They should indicate observable behaviors such as "Keep your hands to yourself" rather than vague ideas such as "Show respect to other students." Rules should be limited in number (three to five) and refer only to behavior, not to academic issues. They remain always in effect. **Directions**, in contrast, only last for a given activity.

Positive recognition refers to giving sincere personal attention to students who behave in keeping with class expectations. Positive recognition should be used frequently, as it tends to increase self-esteem, encourage good behavior, and build a positive classroom climate. Common ways of providing recognition include giving encouragement, expressing appreciation, and communicating with positive notes and phone calls to parents.

Corrective actions are applied when students interfere with other students' right to learn. **Positive support** is given when students behave appropriately. Corrective actions are never harmful physically or psychologically, although they will usually be slightly unpleasant for students. The Canters stress that it is not severity that makes corrective actions effective, but rather the teacher's consistency in applying them. Students have full knowledge of probable corrective actions in advance. When corrective actions must be invoked, students are reminded that, by their behavior, they have chosen the consequence. Teachers usually don't like to invoke corrective actions, but the Canters remind us that we fail our students when we allow them to disrupt or misbehave without showing we care enough to limit their unacceptable behavior.

Using the Discipline Hierarchy

With advance preparation, misbehavior can be dealt with calmly and quickly. The Canters advise making what they call a **discipline hierarchy** that lists corrective actions and the order in which they will be imposed within the day. (Each day or secondary class period begins afresh.) Each consequence in the hierarchy is a bit more unpleasant than its predecessor. The Canters (1992, p. 85) illustrate the discipline hierarchy with the following examples:

> *First time a student disrupts.* Consequence: "Bobby, our rule is no shouting out. That's a warning."
>
> *Second or third time the same student disrupts.* Consequence: "Bobby, our rule is no shouting out. You have chosen 5 minutes time out at the back table."
>
> *Fourth time the same student disrupts.* Consequence: "Bobby, you know our rules about shouting out. You have chosen to have your parents called." The teacher

informs Bobby's parents. This is done by telephone and is especially effective if Bobby is required to place the call and explain what has happened.

Fifth time the same student disrupts. Consequence: "Bobby, our rule is no shouting out. You have chosen to go to the office to talk with the principal about your behavior."

Severe clause. Sometimes behavior is so severe that it is best to invoke the *severe clause*—being sent to the principal—on the first offense. Consequence: "Bobby, fighting is not allowed in this class. You have chosen to go to the principal immediately. We will talk about this later."

To employ the discipline hierarchy effectively, teachers must keep track of offenses that students commit. This can be done by recording on a clipboard students' names and the number of violations. Other options include recording this information in the plan book or, in primary grades, using a system of colored cards that students "turn" or change after each violation. The Canters advise that names of offending students *not* be written on the board.

Teaching the Discipline Plan

The Canters stress that in order to make a discipline plan work effectively, teachers must **teach the discipline plan to** their students. It is not enough just to read it aloud or display it on a poster. The Canters provide a number of sample lessons showing how the plan can be taught at different grade levels. The plans follow this sequence:

1. Explain why rules are needed.
2. Teach the specific rules.
3. Check for understanding.
4. Explain how you will reward students who follow rules.
5. Explain why there are corrective actions for breaking the rules.
6. Teach the corrective actions and how they are applied.
7. Check again for understanding.

Providing Positive Support

The Canters (2001) say that the best way to build responsible behavior is regularly to provide positive support and recognition to students who are on task. Both should be integrated naturally into lessons being taught. The Canters go on to say that **verbal recognition** is the most effective technique for encouraging responsible behavior, and they provide guidelines for its use:

■ Effective verbal recognition is personal. The student's name is mentioned along with the desired behavior: "Jack, thank you for working quietly back there."

- Effective verbal recognition is genuine. It must be related to the situation and behavior, and the teacher's demeanor should show that it is sincere.
- Effective verbal recognition is descriptive and specific. It lets students know when and why they are behaving appropriately: "Good, Susan. You went right to work on your essay."
- Effective verbal recognition is age appropriate. Young children like to be praised publicly. Older students like praise but usually prefer to receive it privately. The Canters make several recommendations concerning how to go about providing positive verbal recognition and support, such as scanning the room to note students who are working appropriately, circulating around the classroom to give one-on-one attention, and for young children writing names on the board of those who are behaving responsibly. They suggest setting a goal with the class for getting at least 20 names on the board each day.

Redirecting Nondisruptive Off-Task Behavior

Often students break class rules in a nondisruptive way. They may look out the window instead of working, read a book instead of doing their assignment, or doodle instead of completing their work. Rather than applying corrective actions for these benign misbehaviors, teachers should redirect students back to the assigned task. The Canters describe four techniques teachers can use in these circumstances:

- Use "the look": Make eye contact and use an expression that shows awareness and disapproval.
- Use **physical proximity:** Move beside the student. Usually there is no need to do more.
- Mention the offending student's name. The teacher says, "I want all of you, including Tanya and Miguel, to come up with the answer to this problem."
- Use **proximity verbal recognition:** Jason is not working, but Suni and Maria, seated nearby, are working. The teacher says, "Suni and Maria are doing a good job of completing their work."

These redirecting techniques are usually quite effective. If they do not produce the desired results, the teacher should assume that the offending student needs more help for self-control and should turn to the discipline hierarchy and issue a warning.

Invoking Corrective Actions

When the discipline program is first implemented, students are clearly informed of positive recognition and negative corrective actions associated with class rules, and they may have role-played situations involving both. They realize that negative corrective actions naturally follow misbehavior. The Canters make these suggestions for invoking negative corrective actions:

- Provide corrective actions calmly in a matter-of-fact manner: "Nathan, speaking like that to others is against our rules. You have chosen to stay after class."
- Be consistent: Provide a consequence every time students choose to disrupt.
- After a student receives a consequence, find the first opportunity to recognize that student's positive behavior: "Nathan, I appreciate how you are working. You are making a good choice."
- Provide an escape mechanism for students who are upset and want to talk about what happened: Allow the student to describe feelings or the situation in a journal or log.
- When a younger student continues to disrupt—move in: Nathan again speaks hurtfully to another student. The teacher moves close to Nathan and quietly and firmly tells him his behavior is inappropriate. She reminds him of the corrective actions he has already received and of the next consequence in the hierarchy.
- When an older student continues to disrupt—move out: Marta once again talks during work time. The teacher asks Marta to step outside the classroom, where she reminds Marta of the inappropriate behavior and possible corrective actions. All the while, the teacher stays calm, shows respect for Marta's feelings, and refrains from arguing.

Working with Difficult Students

The Canters have found that the techniques described to this point help almost all students behave in a responsible manner, but they recognize that a few students require additional consideration. Those are the difficult-to-handle students the Canters (1993) describe as:

> . . . students who are continually disruptive, persistently defiant, demanding of attention or unmotivated. They are the students who defy your authority and cause you stress, frustration and anger. Many of these students have severe emotional or behavioral problems. They may have been physically or psychologically abused, or born substance-addicted to alcohol, cocaine, or other drugs. Many of them come from home environments where parents have very little influence or control over their behavior.

> Difficult students are *not* the students in your class who act up occasionally. They're not the ones who once in a while may cause you to lose your temper. Difficult students are those who engage in disruptive, off-task behavior with great intensity and frequency. (p. 6)

Teachers do not like having to contend with these students, but they are most in need of attention and adult guidance. The Canters acknowledge that "You can't 'cure' or change these students, but you can create an environment that will help (them) achieve" (1993, p. 11). This is accomplished in three phases, which the Canters call (1) reaching out to difficult students, (2) meeting the special needs of difficult students, and (3) communicating with difficult students.

Reaching Out to Difficult Students

Teachers must take the initiative in working with difficult students. Instead of continually reacting to misbehavior, they have to reach out to those students and try to gain their trust. The Canters remind us that most students arrive in the classroom feeling they can trust the teacher and they, therefore, accept teacher guidance. But difficult students are different. For a number of reasons, they do not see teachers as positive, caring role models. They do not trust teachers, do not like school, and do not see any point in behaving properly in school. They find satisfaction in ignoring teacher requests and behaving impudently. A teacher's first priority in working with such students is, therefore, to build a sense of trust.

The process is not an easy one. Teachers can begin by trying to put themselves in the student's place, trying to see teachers and school from the student's point of view. Then they can change the ways they *respond* to the difficult student. They need to decide beforehand how they will react when the student behaves defiantly or confrontationally. This involves **proactive teacher behavior,** which the Canters contrast with **reactive teacher behavior.** When responding reactively to a difficult student, teachers usually lose their tempers, fail to impose their will on the student, and end up sending the student to the principal's office. This accomplishes nothing positive. The teacher feels bad, stress is increased, and a sense of frustration and failure remains. The student does not become more willing to comply with teacher requests but rather more resistant and less trusting, and the class is left feeling uneasy.

By preparing proactive responses, teachers can avoid much of the uneasiness and begin building a sense of trust. The Canters (1993, pp. 32–34) advise teachers as follows:

- Anticipate what the difficult student will do and say. Think through how you will respond.
- Remember that you have a choice in your responses. You can choose *not* to respond angrily or defensively. You can choose *not* to let your feelings get hurt.
- Do not give up on difficult students. They need to see that you care about them.

Building Trust with Difficult Students

Teachers can show that they care about students as individuals by treating every student as they would want their own child to be treated. Furthermore, they can reach out to students in ways such as the following:

- Take a student interest inventory. Find out about brothers and sisters, friends, preferred activities, hobbies, favorite books and TV shows, future hopes, and what students like their teachers to do.
- Greet students individually at the door. Say something special to each, personally.
- Spend some individual time with students. Give one-on-one attention when possible.
- Make a phone call to the student after school and express appreciation, empathy, or regret, as appropriate.
- When a student is ill, send a get-well card or use the phone to convey best wishes.

Meeting Difficult Students' Needs

Some of difficult students' strongly felt needs are not being met at school. Teachers must find ways to meet those needs if they are to be successful with these students. The Canters explain that difficult students typically have three kinds of special needs: (1) a need for extra attention, (2) a need for firmer limits, and (3) a need for motivation. The way to succeed with difficult students who are disruptive or noncompliant is to attend to these three special needs.

How does a teacher identify which of these three needs is predominating at a given time? By doing the following, the Canters say: (1) Look at the student's behavior, (2) look at your own response to the student's behavior, and (3) look at the student's reaction to your response. Suppose fourth-grader Juan continually makes silly noises, gets out of his seat, makes irrelevant comments, shouts out, and grins at others. His behavior annoys you greatly, and after days of it you feel he is driving you crazy. Every time you reprimand Juan he gets quiet for a little while, then begins disrupting again. Juan is annoying you (a sign of persistent attention-seeking behavior) and is satisfied temporarily when you give him attention. It is clear that Juan has a need for extra attention.

Suppose ninth-grader Alicia talks back to you, argues with others, and refuses to do what you ask of her. She doesn't want you or anyone else telling her what to do. Alicia's behavior makes you angry, and after a time you feel threatened. You want to put her in her place. When you reprimand and redirect her, she refuses to comply with your reasonable requests. Alicia shows a need for firmer limits.

Suppose eleventh-grader Arthur is always reluctant to begin an assignment, never completes one, continually makes excuses, and projects an "I-can't" attitude. Arthur's behavior over time frustrates you. You try everything you know to get him going. He doesn't fight back, but nothing you do seems to work. In the Canters' scheme, Arthur has a need for extra motivation.

Meeting the Student's Predominant Need   Once a difficult student's predominant need is identified, the teacher can address it in a beneficial manner, in accordance with the following suggestions (Canter and Canter, 1993, pp. 68–73):

If the student needs *attention,* provide the maximum amount of attention in the shortest amount of time. Plan some proactive steps, such as greeting the student at the door, taking him or her aside for occasional brief chats, giving personal attention during directions and work time, and providing positive recognition for effort and attentiveness. Through the process, help the student see how to obtain recognition through appropriate, rather than inappropriate, behavior.

If the student needs *firmer limits,* enforce class rules in a nonconfrontational way. Do not give these students occasion to show how tough and defiant they can be. Quietly and privately remind them of rules and show appreciation when they comply.

If the student needs *greater motivation,* show faith in his or her ability. Make sure the assignment is within the student's capability. Break the task down into small parts if possible. Compliment the student on any effort or progress he or she makes.

Providing Positive Support   Positive interactions with difficult students are one of the keys to success, but most teachers find this task difficult, since they are so often provoked by the students' misbehavior. For these situations, the Canters (1993, pp. 100–116) provide a number of suggestions, including:

- In the plan book, enter reminders of whom you wish to acknowledge, what for, and when.
- Post reminders at strategic points in the classroom, such as beside the clock.
- Put a sticker on your watch face, so that every time you look at your watch you will be reminded to provide positive recognition to someone in need of it.
- Walk around the room and look for positive behavior, then supply recognition.

As noted earlier, the Canters believe positive support is best provided in the form of *verbal recognition*. It can also be given effectively in notes and phone calls home, special privileges, behavior awards, and tangible rewards.

Redirecting Nondisruptive Misbehavior

Difficult students often misbehave in ways that do not disrupt the class, such as daydreaming, doodling, looking out the window, and withdrawing. Teachers usually react to this kind of misbehavior by either ignoring it or giving an immediate consequence. The Canters suggest, however, that nondisruptive misbehavior offers a good opportunity to build positive relationships with the student. The strategy proceeds this way (Canter and Canter, 1993, pp. 120–124): The teacher says quietly to the student, "Your behavior is inappropriate, but I care about you and I'm going to give you the chance to choose a more appropriate behavior." This gives the student an opportunity to meet the teacher's expectations. Further help will probably be needed, which the teacher provides by establishing eye contact, moving into physical proximity, or softly calling the student's name. If this is not sufficient, the student can be reminded of the rules and seated near the teacher. Teachers must remember to give encouragement as the student shows signs of complying with the rules.

Interacting with Difficult Students

The Canters make a number of suggestions for interacting with difficult-to-manage students, related to how to handle oneself, how to defuse confrontations, and how to use one-to-one problem solving. They begin by cautioning against "reactive responses" that usually make relationships worse, not better. They remind us that when a student becomes increasingly upset or defiant, we should stay calm and deescalate the situation. When meeting in a problem-solving conference with a student, we can communicate both firmness and caring. And by using effective communication skills we can build trust with a student even in difficult circumstances (1993, p. 190).

Defusing Confrontations The Canters point out that when you set limits and hold difficult students accountable, there will be confrontations. Teachers intensely dislike confrontations with students, which put teachers on the defensive and stir up heated emotions. How do you deal with them? The Canters (1993, pp. 162–175) make suggestions that include the following:

- Tell yourself to stay calm. Do not speak for a moment or two. Take a slow, deep breath and count to three, four, or five. This will help you relax.
- Depersonalize the situation. Realize that the student is not attacking you personally, but rather the situation. Think of it as a scene in a movie. The calmer you remain, the harder it is for the student to stay upset.
- Differentiate between covert and overt confrontations. In covert confrontations, the student mumbles or sneers but does not attack you verbally. In this case, step away from the student, but later speak to him or her privately. Overt confrontations are treated differently. Here, the student reacts defiantly to the teacher's requests, drawing other students' attention. In this case, remain calm and refuse to engage the student hostilely. Instead, acknowledge the student's emotion and restate what the student needs to do. If the student remains hostile, take him or her aside, acknowledge the student's feelings, and again request cooperation.
- If the student is especially hostile, you should back off. Drop the matter temporarily so the class may continue. Later, talk with the student privately.

Difficult though it may be, teachers should not view confrontations as setbacks, but rather as new opportunities to show commitment to the student. A calm, caring attitude will do much toward building trust between teacher and student.

One-to-One Problem Solving   Students who continue to misbehave seriously require still more in-depth, personal guidance from the teacher. This can be provided in what the Canters call one-to-one problem-solving conferences, useful when the student's misbehavior is chronic, when there is a sudden change in behavior, or when there is a serious problem (such as fighting) that cannot be overlooked. The Canters (1993, pp. 180–189) provide these guidelines for personal conferences:

- Meet privately with the student and keep the meeting brief.
- Show empathy and concern. The meeting is about the student's behavior, not about your classroom and not about you.
- Focus on helping the student gain insight into the misbehavior and into more appropriate behavior that will meet the student's needs. Try to find out why the problem behavior persists—is there a problem at home, with other students, with the difficulty of assignments? Listen and show respect for the student.
- Help the student determine how his or her behavior can be improved.
- Disarm the student's criticism of you. Ask for specific examples of what you are doing that bothers the student. Show empathy. Focus on the student's needs.
- State your expectations about how the student is to behave. Make it clear (in a calm, friendly manner) that you will not allow the student to continue disruptive behavior.

Strengths of the Canters' *Assertive Discipline*

The Canters have developed and refined a system of discipline for helping promote a pleasant, supportive classroom environment that frees teachers to teach and students to learn. Their approach has broken new ground in several ways—effectiveness, ease of implementation, meeting teachers' and students' needs, teaching students how to behave responsibly, and insistence on support from administrators and parents. A great many teachers are very enthusiastic about *Assertive Discipline* because it helps them deal with students positively and teach with little interruption. It also preserves instructional time and helps relieve the annoyance of verbal confrontations. In the past, *Assertive Discipline* was criticized for being unnecessarily harsh and too focused on suppressing unwanted behavior rather than on helping students learn to control their own behavior. The Canters have been sensitive to those concerns and have taken pains to make sure that teachers understand this central point: Students must be taught, in an atmosphere of respect, trust, and support, how to behave responsibly. Perhaps the most telling evidence of the strength of *Assertive Discipline* is its continued widespread popularity, which indicates it provides tactics that work well for students and teachers alike.

Initiating the Canters' *Assertive Discipline*

Assertive Discipline can be introduced in the class at any time, although the first few days of a new school year or semester are especially appropriate. Decide on behaviors you want from students, what you will do to build trust, what positive recognitions you will provide, and what corrective actions you will invoke. Meet with your class and discuss the kinds of behavior that will make the classroom pleasant, safe, and productive. Solicit students' ideas. Using their input, jointly formulate three to five rules to govern behavior. Sincerely ask all students if they can agree to abide by the rules. Discuss with students the positive recognitions you will provide and the hierarchy of corrective actions that you will invoke. Make sure students realize that the rules apply to every member of the class all the time. Take your plan to the principal for approval and administrative support. Send a copy of the discipline plan home for parents to read. Ask parents to sign and return a slip indicating their approval and support. With students, role-play rules, recognitions, and corrective actions and emphasize repeatedly that the plan helps everyone enjoy a safe, positive environment.

KEY TERMS AND CONCEPTS PRESENTED IN THIS CHAPTER

The following terms are emphasized in the Canters' *Assertive Discipline*. Check to make sure you understand them:

student rights and needs	positive recognition	positive support
teacher rights	proactive posture	verbal recognition
assertive response style	reactive posture	positive repetitions
assertive teachers	setting limits	physical proximity
hostile response style	corrective actions	rules
hostile teachers	severe clause	directions
nonassertive response style	teaching the discipline plan	discipline hierarchy
nonassertive teachers	teaching proper behavior	proximity verbal recognition

SELECTED SEVEN—SUMMARY SUGGESTIONS FROM LEE AND MARLENE CANTER

The Canters suggest that you emphasize the following, as well as their many other suggestions.

1 Make sure that your students' needs, and your own needs, get met in the classroom. That is necessary for happy, productive classes.

2 Maintain focus on your main duties in the classroom, which are to help students learn and to help them behave responsibly.

3 You must model appropriate behavior and may have to teach it to students as well.

4 Your discipline system should establish limits on behavior and provide the necessary structures to help students behave acceptably. You must teach your discipline plan to students so they understand and accept it.

5 You are far more effective when you use a proactive approach to teaching rather than a reactive one. This means thinking through and anticipating situations and how to deal with them rather than trying to react without prior consideration.

6 Good student behavior is best maintained by providing students continual positive support and the help they need.

7 The crucial factors in working with difficult students are (1) reaching out to these students, (2) gaining their trust, and (3) meeting their needs.

CONCEPT CASES

■ CASE 1 *Kristina Will Not Work*

Kristina, a student in Mr. Jake's class, is quite docile. She socializes little with other students and never disrupts lessons. However, despite Mr. Jake's best efforts, Kristina will not do her work. She rarely completes an assignment. She is simply there, putting forth no effort at all. *How would the Canters deal with Kristina?*

They would advise Mr. Jake to do the following: Quietly and clearly communicate class expectations to Kristina. Redirect her to on-task behavior. Have private talks with her to determine why she is not doing her work and what Mr. Jake might do to help. Provide personal recognition regularly and try to build a bond of care and trust with Kristina. Contact Kristina's parents about her behavior. See if they can provide insights that will help Mr. Jake work with Kristina. If necessary, make an individualized behavior plan for helping Kristina do her work. As she shows signs of progress, provide positive corrective actions.

■ CASE 2 *Sara Cannot Stop Talking*

Sara is a pleasant girl who participates in class activities and does most, though not all, of her assigned work. She cannot seem to refrain from talking to classmates, however. Her teacher, Mr. Gonzales, has to speak to her repeatedly during lessons, to the point that he often becomes

exasperated and loses his temper. *What suggestions would the Canters give Mr. Gonzales for dealing with Sara?*

■ CASE 3 *Joshua Clowns and Intimidates*

Larger and louder than his classmates, Joshua always wants to be the center of attention, which he accomplishes through a combination of clowning and intimidation. He makes wise remarks, talks back (smilingly) to the teacher, utters a variety of sound-effect noises such as automobile crashes and gunshots, and makes limitless sarcastic comments and put-downs of his classmates. Other students will not stand up to him, apparently fearing his size and verbal aggression. His teacher, Miss Pearl, has come to her wit's end. *Would Joshua's behavior be likely to improve if the Canters' techniques were used in Miss Pearl's classroom? Explain.*

■ CASE 4 *Tom Is Hostile and Defiant*

Tom has appeared to be in his usual foul mood ever since arriving in class. On his way to sharpen his pencil, he bumps into Frank, who complains. Tom tells him loudly to shut up. Miss Baines, the teacher, says, "Tom, go back to your seat." Tom wheels around, swears loudly, and says heatedly, "I'll go when I'm damned good and ready!" *How would the Canters have Miss Baines deal with Tom?*

QUESTIONS AND ACTIVITIES

1. Make notes in your journal from what you encountered in the Canter model that applies to the five principles of building a personal system of discipline.

2. Each of the following exemplifies an important point in the Canter model of discipline. Identify the point illustrated by each.

    a. Miss Hatcher, on seeing her class list for the coming year, exclaims, "Oh no! Billy Smythe in my class! Nobody can do a thing with him! There goes my sanity!"

    b. "If I catch you talking again during the class, you will have to stay an extra five minutes."

    c. "I wish you would try your best not to curse in this room."

    d. Students who receive a fourth check mark must go to the office and call their parents to explain what has happened.

    e. If the class is especially attentive and hardworking, students earn five minutes they can use for talking quietly at the end of the period.

3. For a grade level and/or subject you select, outline an *Assertive Discipline* plan that includes the following:
    • four rules
    • positive recognition and corrective actions associated with the rules
    • the people you will inform about your system, and how you will inform them

YOU ARE THE TEACHER

Fifth Grade

Your new fifth-grade class consists of students from a small, stable community. Because the transiency rate is low, many of your students have been together since first grade, and during those years they have developed certain patterns of interacting and assuming various roles such as clowns and instigators. Unfortunately, their behavior often interferes with teaching and learning. During the first week of school you notice that four or five students enjoy making smart-aleck remarks about most things you want them to do. When such remarks are made, the other students laugh and sometimes join in. Even when you attempt to hold class discussions about serious issues, many of the students make light of the topics and refuse to enter genuinely into an exploration of the issues. Instead of the productive discussion you have hoped for, you find that class behavior often degenerates into flippancy and horseplay.

A Typical Occurrence

You have begun a history lesson that contains a reference to Julius Caesar. You ask if anyone has ever heard of Julius Caesar. Ben shouts out, "Yeah, they named a salad after him!" The class laughs and calls out encouraging remarks such as "Good one, Ben!" You wait for some semblance of order and then say, "Let us go on." "Lettuce, continue!" cries Jeremy from the back of the room. The class bursts into laughter and chatter. You ask for their cooperation and no more students calling out or making remarks, but you know several are continuing to smirk and whisper, with a good deal of barely suppressed giggling. You try to ignore it, but because of the disruptions you are not able to complete the lesson on time or to get the results you hoped for.

Conceptualizing a Strategy

If you followed the suggestions of Lee and Marlene Canter, what would you conclude or do with regard to the following?

1. Preventing the problem from occurring in the first place.
2. Putting a clear end to the misbehavior now.
3. Involving other or all students in addressing the situation.
4. Maintaining student dignity and good personal relations.
5. Using follow-up procedures that would prevent the recurrence of the misbehavior.
6. Using the situation to help the students develop a sense of greater responsibility and self-control.

REFERENCES

Canter, L. 1996. First, the rapport—then, the rules. *Learning, 24*(5), 12, 14.

Canter, L., and Canter, M. 1976. *Assertive Discipline: A take-charge approach for today's educator.* Seal Beach, CA: Lee Canter & Associates. The second and third editions of the book, published in 1992 and 2001, are entitled *Assertive Discipline: Positive behavior management for today's classroom.*

Canter, L., and Canter, M. 1993. *Succeeding with difficult students: New strategies for reaching your most challenging students.* Santa Monica, CA: Lee Canter & Associates.

Fred Jones's *Positive Classroom Discipline*

OVERVIEW OF
JONES'S
MODEL

Focus

- Establishing classroom environment and routines that encourage good behavior.
- Teaching in a manner that promotes student attention and participation.
- Using incentive systems to foster responsibility, good behavior, and productivity.
- Providing help efficiently to students who need guidance during independent work.

Logic

- Teachers can relate to students in ways that promote consideration and responsibility.
- The best way to deal with behavior problems is by preventing their occurrence.
- Good body language is the most effective control strategy available to teachers.
- Interactive teaching (Say, See, Do) holds student attention and reduces misbehavior.

Contributions

- Clarified the value and techniques of effective body language.
- Explained how to use Say, See, Do Teaching as a means of limiting misbehavior.
- Showed how to use incentive systems and PAT to motivate responsible behavior.
- Explained how to provide help efficiently to students during independent work.

Jones's Suggestions

- Take steps to eliminate the vast time wasting that is evident in most classrooms.
- Use good classroom organization and efficient help to forestall misbehavior.
- Use effective body language and incentives to manage incipient misbehavior.
- Use Say, See, Do Teaching to increase student attention and involvement in lessons.
- Teach responsibility; don't do for students what they can do for themselves.

About Fred Jones

Fred Jones

Fredric H. Jones is the developer and disseminator of Tools for Teaching (formerly known as Positive Classroom Management). He is based in Santa Cruz, California. A clinical psychologist, Jones has worked for many years to develop training procedures for improving teacher effectiveness in motivating, managing, and instructing students. His procedures have grown from extensive field observations of effective teachers that he conducted while on the faculties of the UCLA Medical Center and the University of Rochester School of Medicine and Dentistry. An independent consultant since 1978, Jones now devotes full efforts to his training programs.

Jones's management system is described in his books, *Positive Classroom Discipline* (1987a), *Positive Classroom Instruction* (1987b), and *Fred Jones's Tools for Teachers* (2001). Jones also makes available a video course of study called *The Video Toolbox* (2002). The manual for the videos is authored by JoLynne Talbott Jones. These materials and others for Jones's programs are available from the Fredric H. Jones & Associates, Inc., website: www.fredjones.com (2003).

Jones's Contributions to Discipline

For over 30 years, Fred Jones has been studying highly successful teachers, those often referred to as "naturals," to pinpoint what they do to make teaching and discipline seem so effortless. He has concluded that their success derives from a set of core competencies they use in various situations. Those competencies help students learn how to manage themselves, which results in a significant reduction in teacher workload and stress.

Jones was the first to place major emphasis on the importance of **nonverbal communication** such as teachers' body language, facial expressions, gestures, eye contact, and physical proximity. He was also the first to furnish a solution for what he calls **helpless handraising** by students who get stuck during seat work. He emphasizes the value of good classroom organization and management and stresses the importance of teaching students to behave responsibly. He advocates an instructional approach he calls **Say, See, Do Teaching,** which calls for frequent student response during lessons, thus ensuring attention and active participation.

Jones's Central Focus

The main focus of Jones's efforts is on helping students support their own self-control so that they behave properly and maintain a positive attitude. Toward that end he emphasizes good classroom management, effective use of body language, teaching in a way that calls for much student interaction, providing incentives that motivate desired behavior, helping students assume personal responsibility, and providing efficient help to students during independent work time.

Jones's Principal Teachings

- *Approximately 95 percent of all student misbehavior consists of talking to neighbors and being out of one's seat, as well as generally goofing off, such as daydreaming and making noise.*
  But it is this behavior that most often disrupts teaching and learning.

- *On the average, teachers in typical classrooms lose approximately 50 percent of their teaching time because students are off task or otherwise disrupting learning.*
  This amounts to *massive time wasting.*

- *Most teaching time that is otherwise lost can be recouped when teachers establish clear classroom structures, use effective body language, use Say, See, Do Teaching, use incentive systems, and provide efficient help to students.*
  These are the hallmarks of good behavior management.

- *Efficient arrangement of the classroom improves the likelihood of successful teaching and learning.*
  This includes seating arrangements that permit teachers to **work the crowd** as they supervise student work and provide help.

- *Proper use of body language is one of the most effective discipline skills available to teachers.*
  Body language includes eye contact, physical proximity, body carriage, facial expressions, and gestures.

- *Teachers set limits on student behavior not so much through rules as through subtle interpersonal skills.*
  These are the skills that convey that teachers mean business.

- *Say, See, Do Teaching is an instructional method that calls for frequent student response to teacher input.*
  It keeps students actively alert and involved in the lesson.

- *Students will work hard and behave well when given incentives to do so.*
  These incentives are teachers' promises that students will receive, in return for proper behavior, rewards in the form of favorite activities that can be earned by all members of the group for the enjoyment of all members of the group.

- *To be effective, an incentive must be attractive to the entire group and be available equally to all.*
  Incentives that are available only to certain members of the class will affect only the behavior of those few individuals and leave the class as a whole little changed.

- *Students must learn to do their work without the teacher hovering over them.*
  Jones refers to students who rely on teacher presence as helpless handraisers. He devised a method of providing help very efficiently to students who call for teacher assistance during independent work. Jones says to "be positive, be brief, and be gone."

- *The goal of discipline is for students to assume responsibility for their actions.*
  All aspects of learning are improved when students do so.

Analysis of Jones's *Positive Classroom Discipline*

Misbehavior and Loss of Teaching-Learning Time

Since the early 1970s, Jones and his associates have spent thousands of hours observing and recording what transpires in hundreds of elementary and secondary classrooms. Jones's main interest has been in identifying the methods of classroom management used by highly successful teachers, especially the methods for keeping students working on task, providing individual help when needed, and dealing with misbehavior.

Jones's observations led him to several important conclusions. Principal among them was that discipline problems are usually quite different from the way they are depicted in the media and perceived by the public. Even though many of the classrooms studied were located in inner-city schools and alternative schools for students with behavior problems, Jones found very little hostile student defiance—the behavior that teachers fear and that many people believe predominates in schools. Instead, he found what he called **massive time wasting,** in which students talked when they shouldn't, goofed off, daydreamed, and moved about the room without permission. Jones found that in well-managed classrooms, one of those disruptions occurred about every two minutes. In loud, unruly classes the disruptions averaged about 2.5 per minute. In attempting to deal with those misbehaviors, teachers lost an average of almost 50 percent of the time available for teaching and learning (Jones, 1987a).

Jones also discovered a critical time during lessons in which misbehavior was most likely to occur. He found that most lessons go along fairly well until students are asked to work on their own. That is when, Jones (1987b) says, "The chickens come home to roost." Until that point, students seem to pay attention and give the impression they are learning perfectly. But when directed to continue work on their own, hands go up, talking begins, students rummage around or stare out the window, and some get out of their seats. The teacher often doesn't know what to do except nag and admonish. This, Jones says, is "another day in the life of a typical classroom" (1987b, p. 14) where the teacher ends up reteaching the lesson to a group of helpless hand-raisers during time that should be devoted to supervising independent work.

Teachers everywhere relate to that scenario as one that leaves them feeling frustrated and defeated. When discussing the phenomenon, many express bitterness over never having received training in how to deal effectively with such misbehavior. New teachers say they expected that they would quickly learn to maintain order in their classrooms but were only partially successful and found themselves resorting to punitive measures.

Jones concluded that teachers were correct about not receiving training in behavior management and, furthermore, that many, if not most, were unable to develop needed skills while working on the job. Jones decided to observe and document the methods used by teachers who were notably successful with discipline. Those observations provided the basis of Jones's system of discipline.

Skill Clusters in Jones's Model

Jones says that the purpose of discipline is to help students engage in learning, with the discipline as positive and unobtrusive as possible. His analysis of the numerous classroom observations uncovered five clusters of teacher skills that keep students productively at work, thus preventing misbehavior or allowing teachers to deal with it efficiently. Those skill clusters have to do with (1) classroom structure to discourage misbehavior, (2) setting limits through body language, (3) Say, See, Do Teaching to maximize student attention and involvement, (4) responsibility training through incentive systems, and (5) providing efficient help to individual students. Let us explore these skill clusters further.

Skill Cluster 1: Classroom Structure to Discourage Misbehavior

Jones emphasizes that the best way to manage behavior problems is to prevent their occurrence. In turn, the best way to prevent their occurrence is by providing a **classroom structure** that gives specific attention to room arrangement, class rules, classroom chores, and routines to begin class.

Room Arrangement   An effective way to prevent students' goofing off is to minimize the physical distance between teacher and students. This allows teachers to **work the crowd.** Through movement, proximity, personal interaction, and occasional pauses, looks, or slow turns, teachers keep most students most of the time actively attentive and involved with no inclination to misbehave.

Teachers with minimum discipline problems constantly move among students during seat work, group discussions, and cooperative learning. This calls for room arrangements with generous walkways that allow teachers to move easily among the students. Jones suggests the *interior loop* as ideal, where desks or tables are set with two wide aisles from front to back and enough distance between side-to-side rows for teachers to walk comfortably among the students.

Classroom Rules   Classroom rules should be both general and specific. **General rules,** fairly few in number, define the teacher's broad guidelines, standards, and expectations for work and behavior. They can be reviewed and posted. **Specific rules** describe procedures and routines, detailing specifically what students are to do and how they are to do it. These rules must be taught and rehearsed until they are learned like any academic skill. Jones advocates spending the first two weeks making sure students understand the specific rules.

Classroom Chores   Jones believes in assigning as many classroom chores to students as possible. This gives them a sense of buy-in to the class program and helps develop a sense of responsibility.

Opening Routines   Class sessions in most schools begin in a fragmented way with announcements, taking attendance, handling tardies, and the like. This fragmentation is typically accompanied by students wasting time and misbehaving. Jones says that, on average, about five to eight minutes are wasted in most classrooms immediately after the bell rings. It is much preferable that teachers begin lessons promptly. Jones suggests beginning the class with **bell work,** which does not require active instruction from the teacher. Bell work engages and focuses students on the day's lesson, and they can begin on their own upon entering the room. Examples of bell work are review questions, warm-up problems, brain teasers, silent reading, and journal writing.

Skill Cluster 2: Limit Setting through Body Language

Jones maintains that good discipline depends in large measure on teachers making effective use of **body language.** Jones says teachers are most effective in **setting limits** when they use their bodies correctly but say nothing and take no other action. He reminds teachers that they cannot discipline with their mouths. He says if that were possible, nagging would have fixed every kid a million years ago. When you open your mouth, he says, you run the risk of slitting your own throat. The specific body language that Jones emphasizes is discussed in the following paragraphs.

Proper Breathing Teachers do well to remain calm in all situations. Calm conveys strength. It is attained in part through proper breathing. The way teachers breathe when under pressure signals how they feel and what they are likely to do next. Skilled teachers breathe slowly and deliberately before responding to situations. Jones notes that some teachers take two deep breaths before turning to a misbehaving student. He believes doing so enables them to maintain self-control.

Eye Contact Miss Remy is demonstrating and explaining the process of multiplying fractions. She sees that Jacob has stopped paying attention. She pauses in her explanation. The sudden quiet causes Jacob to look at Miss Remy and find that she is looking directly at his eyes. He straightens up and waits attentively. Few physical acts are more effective than **eye contact** for conveying the impression of being in control. Jones says that turning and pointing the eyes and the feet toward talking students shows teacher commitment to discipline.

Physical Proximity Miss Remy has completed her demonstration of the multiplication of fractions. She has directed students to complete some exercises on their own. After a time she sees from the back of the room that Jacob has stopped working and has begun talking to Jerry. She moves toward him. Jacob unexpectedly finds Miss Remy's shadow at his side. He immediately gets back to work, without Miss Remy having to say anything. Jones observed that teachers who use **physical proximity** rarely need to say anything to the offending students to get them to behave.

Body Carriage Jones also finds that posture and **body carriage** are quite effective in communicating authority. Students read body language and are able to tell whether the teacher is feeling in charge, tired, disinterested, or intimidated. Good posture and confident carriage suggest strong leadership, whereas a drooping posture and lethargic movements suggest resignation or fearfulness. Effective teachers, even when tired or troubled, tend to hold themselves erect and move assertively.

Facial Expressions Like their body carriage, teachers' **facial expressions** communicate much to students. Facial expressions can show enthusiasm, seriousness, enjoyment, and appreciation, all of which tend to encourage good behavior; or they can reveal boredom, annoyance, and resignation, which may encourage misbehavior. Perhaps more than anything else, facial expressions such as winks and smiles demonstrate a sense of humor, the trait that students most enjoy in teachers.

Skill Cluster 3: Using Say, See, Do Teaching

Jones says that many teachers beyond primary grades spend major portions of their class periods presenting information to students while the students remain relatively passive. Finally, toward the end of the lesson, students are asked to do something with the information they have received. Jones (2001) graphically depicts this old fashioned approach as follows:

>   (Teacher) input, input, input, input, input—(Student) output

This instructional approach contains some built-in factors that contribute to student misbehavior, including:

- The large amount of teacher input produces cognitive overload in students, which makes them disengage from the lesson.
- The students sit passively for too long. The urge to do something builds up.
- The teacher does not adequately work the crowd, that is, interact with individual students, particularly in the back of the classroom.

Teachers who are more effective, Jones contends, put students to work from the beginning. They present information and then quickly have students do something with it. This approach is "doing" oriented, with activities occurring often at short intervals, and is depicted as follows:

>   Teacher input—student output—teacher input—student output—teacher input—
>   student output

Jones calls this approach **Say, See, Do Teaching.** The teacher says (or does), the students see, and the students do something with the input. This approach, along with the use of **Visual Instruction Plans (VIPs),** greatly reduces the amount of student fooling around because the students are kept busy while the teacher circulates and interacts with students at work. The VIP is a series of picture prompts that represents the process of the activity or thinking and clearly guides students through the process of the task and performance.

Skill Cluster 4: Responsibility Training through Incentive Systems

Jones observes that teachers have three different management styles: Some teach well and reward well; some nag, threaten, and punish; and some lower their standards and accept whatever they can get from students. These management styles are closely related to success in the classroom. Mr. Sharpe tells his class that if all of them complete their work in

45 minutes or less, they can have the last 10 minutes of class time to talk quietly with a friend. Mr. Naeve tells his class he will allow them to begin the period by discussing their work with a friend, provided they promise to work very hard afterward. Which teacher is likely to get the best work from his students? This question has to do with incentives and how they affect responsibility.

An **incentive** is something outside of the individual that prompts the individual to act. It is something that is promised as a consequence for desired behavior but is held in abeyance to occur or be provided later. It might be popcorn, a preferred activity, an unspecified surprise, or the like. It is an effective incentive if students behave as desired in order to obtain it later. Jones gives a prominent place in his classroom management program to incentives as a means of motivating students. He found that some of the most effective teachers use incentives systematically, although most teachers use them ineffectively or not at all.

What, then, are characteristics of effective incentives, and how should they be used? Responsibility training gains most of its strength, Jones says, from the "bonus" portion of the incentive. Bonuses encourage students to save time they would normally waste in order to get it back in the form of preferred activity time. It gives members of the class a shared vested interest in cooperating to save time rather than wasting it in small snippets throughout the period or day. Jones suggests that in order to make best use of incentives, teachers should carefully consider (1) Grandma's rule, (2) student responsibility, (3) genuine incentives, (4) preferred activities, (5) educational value, (6) group concern, (7) ease of implementation, (8) omission training, and (9) backup systems. Let us see what is involved in each.

Grandma's Rule   **Grandma's rule** states: "First eat your vegetables, and then you can have your dessert." Applied to the classroom, this rule requires that students first do what they are supposed to do, and then for a while after that they can do what they want to do. Just as children (and most adults) want their dessert first, promising to eat their vegetables afterward, students ask to have their incentive first, pledging on their honor to work feverishly afterward. As we all know, even the best intentions are hard to remember once the reason for doing so is gone. Thus, teachers who wish to use effective incentive systems must, despite student urging, delay the rewards until last and make the reward contingent on the students doing required work acceptably. In other words, if they don't eat their broccoli, they don't get their ice cream.

Student Responsibility   Jones believes that incentives, used correctly, can help everyone take responsibility for their actions. For example, one way students can show responsibility is through cooperating with others. However, cooperation is voluntary; it is difficult to force anyone to cooperate. Students who enjoy goofing off and daydreaming, when asked to cooperate, can ask themselves, "Why should I? What's in it for me?" Jones suggests that when students show responsibility by doing what teachers ask them to do, it is because teachers have used encouragement and incentives, rather than trying to force responsibility through nagging, threatening, or punishing.

Genuine Incentives There is a wide difference between what many teachers hope will be incentives (e.g., "Let's all work in such a way that we will later be proud of what we do") and what students consider **genuine incentives** (e.g., "If you complete your work on time, you can have five minutes of preferred activity time"). Jones cautions against allowing students to earn "free time" to do whatever they wish. He says students won't work for long to earn free time, but they will for *activity* time they enjoy. This shows that what teachers believe to be an incentive may, in actuality, not work for most students in the class. Further examples: A teacher may say, "The first person to complete a perfect paper will receive two bonus points." This may motivate a few of the most able students, but all the others know they have little chance to win so there is no reason to try. Or the teacher may say, "If you really work hard, you can be the best class I have ever had." This sounds good to the teacher but means little to the students and is not sufficient to keep them diligently at work.

Jones believes that activities students enjoy are the best overall incentives. Students respond well to the anticipation of activities such as art, viewing a film, or having time to pursue personal interests or talk with friends. Such group activities are genuine incentives in that, first, almost all students desire them sufficiently to make extra effort to obtain them and, second, they are available to all students, not just a few. Tangible objects, awards, and certificates should not be used as incentives. They tend to be costly or difficult to dispense or, worse, have little educational value.

Preferred Activity Time Preferred activity time (**PAT**) is time allotted for activities such as learning games and enrichment activities that can serve as incentives. *Preferred activity* means that the activity is one students enjoy, such as using vocabulary words to play hangman, an art project, or reading a book for pleasure—activities they prefer to most others. Jones advises that when selecting and introducing PAT, teachers must make sure that students want the activity, that they earn the activity by showing responsibility, and that the teacher can live with the PAT.

PAT may be earned in a number of different ways. Mr. Jorgensen gives his fourth graders three minutes to put away their language arts materials and prepare for math. Any time left over from the three minutes goes to later PAT. In Mrs. Nguyen's English class, if everyone is seated and ready when the bell rings, the class earns two additional minutes of PAT. However, if the class or some of its members continue to be noisy, the class loses the amount of PAT that they have wasted. Some PAT may be used the day it is earned, whereas other PAT may be accumulated for a future activity, such as a field trip. In some instances, PAT may be earned as individual bonuses. When Mickey continues to be unprepared and, consequently, loses PAT for the class, Mr. Duncan decides to work with him individually. Mickey's irresponsibility no longer penalizes the entire class, but as he improves, he might earn PAT for the entire class, which improves his status with peers.

Educational Value To the extent feasible, every class period should be devoted to activities that have **educational value.** Work that keeps students occupied but teaches them nothing can seldom be justified. This principle applies to incentive systems. Although few educators would be loath never to allow a moment of innocent frivolity, the opposite extreme of daily or weekly parties as incentives is difficult to condone. What then should one use as PAT?

There are many activities with educational value that students enjoy greatly, both individually and in groups. Students are not left to do just anything, nor do they proceed without guidance. The freedom lies in being able to choose from a variety of approved activities. Activities can be chosen by vote, and all students engage in the same activity during the time allotted. Elementary school students often select physical education, art, music, drama, construction activities, or being read to by the teacher. Secondary students often choose to watch a video, hold class discussions on special topics, watch performances by class members, or work together on projects such as producing a class magazine. JoLynne Talbott Jones posts on the Jones website (www.fredjones.com) suggestions from teachers for a large number of educationally sound activities that students of various grade levels enjoy greatly and that, therefore, serve as good preferred activities.

Group Concern Jones emphasizes the importance of making sure every student has a stake in earning the incentive for the entire class. This **group concern** motivates all students to keep on task, behave well, and complete assigned work. Here is how it is done.

The teacher agrees to set aside a period of time in which students might be allowed to engage in a preferred activity. In keeping with Grandma's rule, this PAT period must come after a significant amount of work time has been devoted to the normal curriculum. The PAT can be at the end of the school day for self-contained classes—perhaps 15 to 20 minutes. For departmentalized classes, the time can be set aside at the end of the week—perhaps 30 minutes on Friday. The students can decide on the activity for their dessert time, and to earn it they have only to work and behave as expected.

The teacher manages the system by keeping track of the time that students earn. Of course, it is possible that a single student, by misbehaving, can prevent the class from earning full PAT. Teachers often think it unfair to penalize the entire class for the sins of a few. In practice this is rarely a problem, because the class quickly understands that this is a group, not an individual, effort. The group is rewarded together and punished together regardless of who might transgress. A strength of this approach is that it brings peer pressure to bear against misbehavior. Ordinarily a misbehaving student obtains reinforcement from the group in the form of attention, laughter, or admiration. With proper PAT, the opposite is true. The class is likely to discourage individual misbehavior because it takes away something the class members want. Nevertheless, some students do occasionally misbehave to the detriment of other responsible students. When this occurs, the teacher may decide to work with the offending student individually.

Ease of Implementation Incentive systems will not work unless they are easy to implement. Jones (2001) suggests:

1. Establish and explain the system.
2. Allow the class to vote from time to time on the approved activities they wish to enjoy during incentive time.

3. Keep track of the bonus time students have earned for PAT.
4. Be prepared when necessary to conduct the class in low-preference activities for the amount of time that students might have lost from the time allotted to their preferred activity.

Omission Training   Generally speaking, incentives and PAT bonuses are earned by the entire class. Teachers cannot possibly monitor incentives for all students individually. The exception lies in the occasional student whose misbehavior repeatedly ruins PAT for the rest of the class. For those few students Jones describes **omission training,** a plan that allows a student to earn PAT for the entire class by omitting a certain misbehavior.

Kevin is one such student. In Ms. VanEtten's class he simply does not seem to care about PAT and, consequently, is late, loud, and unprepared, thus ruining PAT for the others. Ms. VanEtten privately explains to Kevin that he doesn't have to participate in PAT, particularly since he doesn't care about it, but she does want him to be successful with his own work and behavior. She explains that she will use a timer, and when Kevin behaves in accordance with class rules, he will earn time for himself, and also PAT for the class. When he misbehaves, he loses time for himself but not for the class.

Backup Systems   As a last option for students like Kevin, Jones suggests **backup systems,** which are hierarchical arrangements of sanctions intended to put a stop to unacceptable student behavior. Jones identifies three levels of backup:

1. Small backup responses, said privately or semiprivately to the student: "I expect you to stop talking so we can get on with our work." With such low-keyed messages the student knows the teacher means business. Whispering privately is a constructive way of protecting students' dignity.
2. Medium backup responses, delivered publicly in the classroom: "Emily, sit in the thinking chair for three minutes and consider how you are acting that causes me to send you there." Or "Brian, you are late again. You'll have detention with me tomorrow after school." Other medium backup responses include warnings, reprimands, loss of privilege, and parent conferences. Because these are public, they are risky. Students may try to get even with teachers if they feel humiliated in front of their peers.
3. Large backup responses require at least two professionals, usually the teacher and an administrator, and deal with chronically repeated disruptions or other intolerable behavior. Large backup responses include trips to the office, in- or out-of-school suspension, special class, and special school.

Skill Cluster 5: Providing Efficient Help to Individual Students

One of the most interesting, important, and useful findings in Jones's research has to do with the way teachers help students who are stuck during seat work. Suppose a grammar lesson is in progress. The teacher introduces the topic, explains the concept on the board, asks a couple of questions to determine whether the students are understanding, and then assigns exercises for students to complete at their desks. Very soon Arnell raises his hand signaling that he needs help. If only three or four students raise hands during work time, the teacher has no problem. But if 20 students fill the air with waving arms, most sit for several minutes doing nothing while waiting for the teacher. This waiting time is pure waste and an invitation to misbehave.

Jones asked teachers how much time they thought they spent on the average when providing help to individuals who signaled. The teachers felt that they spent from one to two minutes with each student, but when Jones's researchers timed the episodes, they found that teachers actually spent around four minutes with each student. This consumed much time and made it impossible for the teacher to attend to more than a few students during the work period. Even if the amount of time were only one minute per contact, several minutes would pass while some students sat and did nothing.

Jones noted an additional phenomenon that compounded the problem. He called it **helpless handraising,** wherein some students routinely raised their hands for teacher help even when they did not need it. To have the teacher unfailingly come to their side and give personal attention proved rewarding for those students, and the constant reinforcement furthered their dependency.

Jones concluded that independent seat work is typically beset with four problems: (1) insufficient time for teachers to answer all requests for help; (2) wasted student time; (3) high potential for misbehavior; and (4) perpetuation of dependency. Jones determined that all four problems can be solved through teaching teachers how to give **efficient help,** which is accomplished as follows:

First, organize the classroom seating so that students are within easy reach of the teacher. The interior loop seating arrangement previously described is suggested because it gives the teacher free, easy movement in the room. Unless able to get quickly from one student to another, the teacher uses too much time and energy.

Second, use Visual Instruction Plans and graphic reminders, such as models or charts, that provide clear examples and instructions. These reminders might show steps in algorithms, proper form for business letters, or written directions for the lesson. The reminders are posted and can be consulted by students before they call for teacher help.

Third, reduce to a minimum the time used for giving students individual help. To see how this can be accomplished, consider that teachers normally give help very inefficiently through a questioning tutorial that proceeds something like this:

"What's the problem?"

"All right, what did we say was the first thing to do?" *[Waits; repeats question.]*

"No, that was the second. You are forgetting the first step. What was it? Think again." *[Waits until student finally makes a guess.]*

"No, let me help you with another example. Suppose . . . "

In this manner the teacher often reteaches the concept or process to each student who requests help. Four minutes can be unexpectedly spent in each interaction. Jones trains teachers to give help in a very different way, and he insists that each help episode be done in 20 seconds or less, with an optimal goal of about 10 seconds. To reach this level of efficiency, the teacher should do the following when arriving beside the student:

1. (Optional for initial contact). Quickly find anything that the student has done correctly and mention it favorably: "Your work is very neat" or "Good job up to here."
2. Give a straightforward prompt that will get the student going: "Follow step two on the chart" or "Regroup here." Jones says to teach students to ask themselves "What do I do next?" instead of tutoring them through the whole task.
3. Leave immediately. Jones puts it like this: "Be positive, be brief, and be gone."

Help provided in this way solves the time and attention problems that teachers face during instructional work time. Every student who needs help can receive proper attention. Students waste little time waiting for the teacher. Misbehavior is much less likely. Helpless handraising is diminished, especially if the teacher gives attention to students who work without calling for assistance. Rapid circulation by the teacher also permits better monitoring of work being done by students who do not raise their hands. When errors are noted in those students' work, the teacher should provide help just as for students who have raised their hands.

Study Group Activity Guide

Jones makes available a free Study Group Activity Guide for educators that can be downloaded from his Internet site. *The Video Toolbox* aligns with the Study Guide and book and is designed for small groups of teachers or student teachers who meet regularly to discuss and put into practice the skills Jones advocates. He stresses the value of working with colleagues in this manner. The Study Group Activity Guide and *The Video Toolbox* structure learning activities that can be used indefinitely as teachers perfect their management skills. He recommends that the study groups consist of three to eight teachers who meet on a weekly basis. The structure for meetings includes focus questions, study group questions, and performance checklists. The 12 meeting topics have to do with:

1. Working the Crowd and Room Arrangement
2. Praise, Prompt, and Leave
3. Visual Instructional Plans
4. Say, See, Do Teaching
5. Rules, Routines, and Standards
6. Understanding Brat Behavior
7. Calm Is Strength
8. The Body Language of Meaning Business
9. Eliminating Backtalk
10. Responsibility Training
11. Omission Training and Preferred Activity Time
12. Dealing with Typical Classroom Crises

Strengths of Jones's *Positive Classroom Discipline*

The Jones model provides effective tactics for preventing misbehavior and supporting proper behavior and does so in a balanced way. Jones has been successful in identifying and compiling discipline techniques used by teachers who are so effective they are often called "naturals." That is why teachers' heads nod in agreement with his suggestions. Jones has found that the strategies he advocates are all teachable, though many teachers do not learn them well on their own, given the pressures of day-to-day teaching. Through specific training episodes, most teachers can acquire the techniques that are normally used only by their most effective colleagues.

The tactics Jones describes must be understood and then practiced repeatedly. Fortunately, teachers can assess their classroom behavior in light of Jones's suggestions and isolate certain control tactics they would like to incorporate into their teaching. They can practice what Jones suggests and apply their new skills in the classroom. That is one of the most appealing qualities of Jones's suggestions: The entire *Positive Classroom Discipline* program does not have to be put into place as a full-blown system but can instead be practiced, perfected, and added incrementally.

Initiating Jones's *Positive Classroom Discipline*

Jones (1987a, p. 321) suggests that his model of discipline be initiated as a five-tiered system of closely related management methodologies: (1) classroom structure, (2) limit setting, (3) Say, See, Do Teaching, (4) incentives, and (5) backup systems. All five tiers are carefully planned out in advance and introduced simultaneously. It is important to understand that *Positive Classroom Discipline* is a system in which the parts interrelate. For example, if classroom structure is inadequate, some of the unmanaged behavior is likely to surface as misbehavior that disrupts teaching and learning. If this happens often, the cost in time and effort skyrockets. Say, See, Do Teaching keeps students attentive and actively involved with smaller amounts of input, thus preventing problems that occur when input becomes more than students can handle. If potential discipline problems are not circumvented at this point, they end up requiring responsibility training, which again consumes much instructional time.

To introduce *Positive Classroom Discipline* to students, you can begin with a discussion of limit setting, which leads to the formulation of agreements (rules) about what students may and may not do in the classroom. Explain to the students that when they violate rules, their behavior will be corrected with body language that reminds the students or, at most, makes the misbehaving student slightly uncomfortable. Examples such as eye contact, stares, and physical proximity are given and demonstrated.

To make limit setting work effectively, mild discomfort is counterbalanced with incentives and social rewards, such as acknowledgment and approval, in return for students' observing rules and agreements. Desirable incentives are discussed, and procedures for managing incentives are described. Students are reminded that the incentives they select are to have instructional value.

You will also need to discuss with students the **backup systems** you will use when students misbehave seriously and refuse to comply with your requests. Such sanctions receive relatively little attention in Jones's system, which attempts to move teachers away from reliance on admonition and threat. Yet, Jones acknowledges that at times the teacher may be unable to get misbehaving students to comply with the rules. At those times, teachers may tell the student, "If you are not going to do your work, sit there quietly and don't bother others." And for yet more serious situations of defiance or aggression, teachers must have a plan by which they isolate the student or call for help as needed.

KEY TERMS AND CONCEPTS PRESENTED IN THIS CHAPTER

The following terms are central to Jones's *Positive Classroom Discipline.* Check yourself to make sure you can explain their meanings:

massive time wasting	preferred activity time (PAT)	setting limits
Say, See, Do Teaching	educational value	general rules
Visual Instruction Plan (VIP)	group concern	specific rules
body language	Grandma's rule	classroom structure
efficient help	omission training	eye contact
interior loop	physical proximity	body carriage
helpless handraising	bell work	facial expressions
incentives	nonverbal communication	work the crowd
genuine incentives	backup systems	

SELECTED SEVEN—SUMMARY SUGGESTIONS FROM FRED JONES

Fred Jones suggests that you emphasize the following, as well as his many other suggestions:

1. Do what you can to save instructional time that is so frequently wasted because of student misbehavior and other factors. A number of simple management techniques will conserve this time.

2. Structure your classroom and program to encourage attention, active involvement, and responsibility. Use an effective seating arrangement, establish clear routines, and assign individual chores to students.

3. Use body language and personal skills more than verbal messages to limit misbehavior and help students stay on track.

4. Emphasize Say, See, Do Teaching as a means of increasing student alertness, involvement, and learning.

5. Use class incentives as a means of increasing student involvement and responsibility.

6. Learn how to give individual help to students in 20 seconds or less. Doing so eliminates student dependence on your presence and enables you to provide help as needed to all students quickly.

7. Actively "work the crowd," which means interacting frequently with individual students during instruction.

CONCEPT CASES

CASE 1 *Kristina Will Not Work*

Kristina, a student in Mr. Jake's class, is quite docile. She socializes little with other students and never disrupts the class. However, Mr. Jake cannot get Kristina to do any work. She rarely completes an assignment. She is simply there, putting forth almost no effort at all. *How would Jones deal with Kristina?*

Jones would probably suggest that Mr. Jake take the following steps to improve Kristina's behavior:

1. Make frequent eye contact with her. Even when she looks down, Mr. Jake should make sure to look directly at her. She will be aware of it, and it may be enough to encourage her to begin work.
2. Move close to Kristina. Stand beside her while presenting the lesson.
3. Give Kristina frequent help during seat work. Check on her progress several times during the lesson. Give specific suggestions and then move quickly on.
4. Increase the amount of Say, See, Do Teaching with Kristina so she has less information to deal with and is called on to respond frequently.
5. Set up a personal incentive system with Kristina, such as doing a certain amount of work to earn an activity she especially enjoys.
6. Set up a system in which Kristina can earn rewards for the entire class. This brings her peer attention and support.

CASE 2 *Sara Cannot Stop Talking*

Sara is a pleasant girl who participates in class activities and does most, though not all, of her assigned work. She cannot seem to refrain from talking to classmates, however. Her teacher, Mr. Gonzales, has to speak to her repeatedly during lessons, to the point that he often becomes exasperated and loses his temper. *What suggestions would Jones give Mr. Gonzales for dealing with Sara?*

CASE 3 *Joshua Clowns and Intimidates*

Larger and louder than his classmates, Joshua always wants to be the center of attention, which he accomplishes through a combination of clowning and intimidation. He makes wise remarks, talks back (smilingly) to the teacher, utters a variety of sound-effect noises such as automobile crashes and gunshots, and makes limitless sarcastic comments and put-downs of his classmates. Other students will not stand up to him, apparently fearing his size and verbal aggression. His teacher, Miss Pearl, has come to her wit's end. *What specifically do you find in Jones's suggestions that would help Miss Pearl deal with Joshua?*

CASE 4 *Tom Is Hostile and Defiant*

Tom has appeared to be in his usual foul mood ever since arriving in class. On his way to sharpen his pencil, he bumps into Frank, who complains. Tom tells him loudly to shut up. Miss Baines, the teacher, says, "Tom, go back to your seat." Tom wheels around, swears loudly, and says heatedly, "I'll go when I'm damned good and ready!" *How effective do you believe Jones's suggestions would be in dealing with Tom?*

QUESTIONS AND ACTIVITIES

1. Makes notes in your journal concerning elements from Jones's model that contribute to the five principles of building a personal system of discipline.
2. For each of the following scenarios, first identify the problem that underlies the undesired behavior and then describe how Jones would have the teacher deal with it.
   a. Mr. Anton tries to help all of his students during independent work time but finds himself unable to get around to all who have their hands raised.

b. Ms. Sevier wants to show trust for her class. She accepts their promise to work hard if she will allow them first to listen to a few favorite recordings. After listening, the students talk so much that they fail to get their work done.

c. Mr. Gregory wears himself out every day dealing with three class clowns who disrupt his lessons.

The other students always laugh at the clowns' antics.

d. Mrs. Swanson, who takes pride in her lectures, is becoming frustrated because students begin to gaze out the window and whisper before she has completed what she wants to tell them.

 ## YOU ARE THE TEACHER

Student Teacher

You are a student teacher in an inner-city magnet school that emphasizes academics. Half of your students are African American. The other half, of various ethnic groups, have been bused in to take advantage of the instructional program and rich resources. All are academically talented and none has what would be called a bad attitude toward school. Mrs. Warde, the regular teacher of the class, does not seem to rely on any particular scheme of discipline, at least not any which is obvious to you. She simply tells the students what to do and they comply. For the first few lessons you have taught, Mrs. Warde has remained in the room, serving as your aide. The students worked well, and you felt pleased and successful.

When Mrs. Warde Leaves the Room

Mrs. Warde tells you that she will leave the room during the math lesson so that you can begin getting the feel of directing the class on your own. Mrs. Warde warns her that the class might test you with a bit of naughtiness, though nothing serious is likely to occur. Just be in charge, Mrs. Warde counsels. The math lesson begins well, without incident. The lesson has to do with beginning algebra concepts, which you approach through a discovery mode. You tell the class, "I want you to work independently on this. Think your way through the following equations and decide if they are true for all numbers."

$$a + 0 = a$$
$$a + b = b + a$$
$$a\,(b + c) = ab + c$$
$$a + 1 = 1$$
$$a \times 0 = a$$

The students begin work, but within two minutes hands are shooting up. You go to help Alicia, who is stuck on the third equation. "What's the matter?" you whisper.

"I don't understand what this means."

"It was like what I showed you on the board. The same."

"Those were numbers. I don't understand it with these letters."

"They are the same as the numbers. They take the place of the numbers. I showed you how they were interchangeable, remember? Go ahead, let me see. Tell me what you are doing, step-by-step."

You do not realize it, but you spend almost five minutes with Alicia. Meanwhile, a few of the students have finished and are waiting, but most are holding tired arms limply in the air. You rush to the next student and repeat your questioning tutorial. Meanwhile, Matt and Alonzo have dropped their hands and are looking at each other's papers. They begin to talk, then laugh. Others follow, and soon all work has stopped and the classroom has become quite noisy. You repeatedly say, "Shhh, shhh!" but with little effect. At last you go to the front of the room, demand attention, and tell the class how disappointed you are in their rude behavior.

Conceptualizing a Strategy

If you followed the suggestions of Fred Jones, what would you conclude or do with regard to the following?

1. Preventing the problem from occurring in the first place.
2. Putting a clear end to the misbehavior.

3. Involving other or all students in addressing the situation.
4. Maintaining student dignity and good personal relations.

5. Using follow-up procedures that would prevent the recurrence of the misbehavior.
6. Using the situation to help the students develop a sense of greater responsibility and self-control.

REFERENCES

Jones, F. 1987a. *Positive classroom discipline.* New York: McGraw-Hill.

Jones, F. 1987b. *Positive classroom instruction.* New York: McGraw-Hill.

Jones, F. 1996a. Did not! Did, too! *Learning, 24*(6), 24–26.

Jones, F. 2001. *Fred Jones's tools for teachers.* Santa Cruz, CA: Fredric H. Jones & Associates.

Jones, F. 2003. Tools for teaching. www.fredjones.com.

Jones, J. 2002. *The Video Toolbox.* Santa Cruz, CA: Fredric H. Jones & Associates.

CHAPTER 5

William Glasser's
Noncoercive Discipline

**OVERVIEW OF
GLASSER'S
MODEL**

Focus

- Improving student satisfaction with school, which promotes motivation and learning.
- Helping teachers change from being boss teachers to lead teachers.
- Emphasizing quality in curriculum, teaching, and learning.
- Applying principles of Choice Theory for quality teaching, learning, and behavior.

Logic

- Most misbehavior occurs when students are bored or frustrated by class expectations.
- Students whose basic needs are being met do not often misbehave in school.
- Curriculum is most effective when focused on what students consider to be important.
- The best teaching is done in a leading manner rather than a bossing manner.

Contributions

- The concept and practice of regularly held classroom meetings.
- Focus on meeting students' basic needs as essential in teaching and discipline.
- Concepts and practices of quality in curriculum, teaching, and learning.
- Concepts of Choice Theory applied to teaching, learning, and behavior.

Glasser's Suggestions

- Do your best to meet student needs for security, belonging, freedom, power, and fun.
- Make quality paramount in all aspects of teaching, learning, and curriculum.
- Work with students through "lead teaching" rather than "boss teaching."
- Use noncoercive techniques to help students make responsible choices.

About William Glasser

William Glasser, a psychiatrist and educational consultant, has for many years written and spoken extensively on issues related to education and discipline. Born in 1926 in Cleveland, Ohio, he first studied chemical engineering but later turned to psychology and then to psychiatry. He achieved national acclaim in psychiatry for his theory called *reality therapy* (*Reality Therapy: A New Approach to Psychiatry*, 1965), which shifted the focus in treating behavior problems from past events to present reality. Glasser later extended reality therapy to the school arena. His work with juvenile offenders

William Glasser

convinced him that teachers could help students make better choices concerning how they behaved in school. He explained how to do this in his book *Schools without Failure* (1969), judged to be one of the twentieth century's most influential books in education. In 1986, Glasser published *Control Theory in the Classroom*, which gave a new and different emphasis to his contentions concerning discipline, encapsulated in his pronouncement that if students are to continue working and behaving properly, they must "believe that if they do some work, they will be able to satisfy their needs enough so that it makes sense to keep working" (p. 15). Since the publication of that book, Glasser has emphasized the school's role in meeting basic needs as the primary means of encouraging participation and desirable behavior. In 1996, he changed the name of his approach from Control Theory to "Choice Theory," reemphasizing that all behavior is based on personal choice. This theme is furthered in his books *The Quality School: Managing Students without Coercion* (1998a), *Choice Theory in the Classroom* (1998c), *The Quality School Teacher* (1998b), and *Every Student Can Succeed* (2001). Glasser can be contacted through the William Glasser Institute, 22024 Lassen Street, Suite 118, Chatsworth, CA 91311. Phone: 800-899-0688; 818-700-8000. Fax: 818-700-0555. Website: www.wglasser.com. Email: wginst@wglasser.com.

Glasser's Contributions to Discipline

Glasser has greatly influenced thought and practice in school discipline. He was the first to insist that students are in control of their behavior, that no unseen factors are forcing them to do this or that, and that they actually choose to behave as they do. He claimed that misbehavior simply resulted from bad choices, whereas good behavior resulted from good choices. He insisted that teachers have the power and the obligation to help students make better behavioral choices, and he provided numerous suggestions for interacting with students in ways that help them succeed. He set forth the concept of **class-room meetings,** now widely used, in which teacher and students jointly discuss class matters and resolve problems. These contributions were all made in Glasser's earlier work.

Since 1985, Glasser has made many new contributions to thought and practice in discipline. His central contentions at present are:

- Virtually all human behavior is internally motivated and chosen by the individual.
- All of our behavior is our best attempt to satisfy one or more of five basic needs built into our genetic structure.
- All human behavior is purposeful.
- We make the best behavior choices we can, given the information we have.
- We are responsible for our own behavior.
- Effective discipline is based on meeting students' needs for survival, belonging, freedom, fun, and power.
- All students can do competent work and some quality work in school.

In developing these themes, Glasser contributed the concepts of Choice Theory, quality curriculum, quality learning, and quality teaching, maintaining that all play important roles in good discipline.

Glasser's Central Focus

Glasser believes that improvement in education and discipline can only be accomplished by changing the way classrooms function. He says it is clear that trying to force students to learn or behave properly will not succeed. His work, therefore, focuses on providing a curriculum that is naturally attractive to students and on working with students in ways that encourage their making responsible choices that lead to personal success.

In particular, Glasser emphasizes quality in curriculum, teaching, and learning. He says that if schools are to survive, they must be redesigned to emphasize quality throughout. They must give up trying to coerce or force students to learn or behave in a particular manner. Force does not work, but students willingly pursue matters they find interesting and that meet their needs for security, belonging, power, fun, and freedom. Glasser feels these are **basic needs,** built into the genetic codes. By genuinely trying to meet those needs, educators can entice students to engage in meaningful learning while conducting themselves appropriately. No pressure need be applied.

Glasser's Principal Teachings

- *Virtually all human behavior is internally motivated and chosen by the individual.*
  True motives lie within the individual. Behavior is chosen, in keeping with those motives.

- *All human behavior is purposeful.*
  Our behavior is never aimless or accidental. It reflects our attempts to meet certain specific needs.

- *We are responsible for our own behavior.*
  Because our behavior is purposeful and chosen, we cannot blame our transgressions on circumstances, fate, or others. Any credit or blame goes to us.

● *All of our behavior is our best attempt to control ourselves to meet five basic needs: survival, belonging, power, fun, and freedom.*

The school experience should be refined to enable students to meet these five needs more easily.

● *Students feel pleasure when their basic needs are met and frustration when they are not.*

Students are usually contented and well behaved when their needs are being met but discontented and inclined to misbehave when their needs are not being met.

● *At least half of today's students will not commit themselves to learning if they find their school experience boring, frustrating, or otherwise dissatisfying.*

There is no way teachers can make students commit to learning, though they can usually force behavioral compliance temporarily.

● *Few students in today's schools do their best work.*

The overwhelming majority is apathetic about schoolwork. Many students do no schoolwork at all.

● *Today's schools must create quality conditions in which fewer students and teachers are frustrated.*

Students must feel they belong, enjoy a certain amount of power, have some fun in learning, and experience a sense of freedom in the process.

● *What schools require is a new commitment to quality education.*

Quality education occurs when the curriculum is attractive and students are encouraged, supported, and helped to learn.

● *The school curriculum should be limited to learnings that are useful or otherwise relevant to students' lives.*

Usefulness and relevance are hallmarks of quality curriculum, which is delivered through activities that attract student interest, involve students actively, provide enjoyment, and lead to meaningful accomplishments.

● *Students should be allowed to acquire in-depth information about topics they consider useful or relevant in their lives.*

This increases the likelihood of quality learning.

● *Quality learning is evident when students become able to demonstrate or explain how, why, and where their learnings are valuable.*

The opportunity for making such explanations should be incorporated in the daily classroom activities.

● *Instead of scolding, coercing, or punishing, teachers should try to befriend their students, provide encouragement and stimulation, and show unending willingness to help.*

Their ability to do these things is a mark of quality teaching.

● *Teachers who dictate procedures, order students to work, and berate them when they do not are increasingly ineffective with today's students.*

Teachers who function in this manner are called "boss teachers."

● *Teachers who provide a stimulating learning environment, encourage students, and help them as much as possible are most effective with today's learners.*

Teachers who function in this way are called "lead teachers."

● *Motivation is the key ingredient in learning. Students are motivated by what they find pleasurable at any given time.*

It is up to teachers to make the curriculum and instruction pleasurable for students. When that is done, most learning difficulties and behavior problems disappear.

Analysis of Glasser's *Noncoercive Discipline*

Glasser points out the futility of attempting to force students to behave against their will. For example, when a student is not paying attention because the lesson is boring, it is a losing battle to try to force the student's attention. On the other hand, when lessons are interesting, students pay attention naturally and don't have to be continually cajoled. This fact has caused Glasser to focus on what he calls **quality education,** which entices students to engage willingly in the curriculum. **Choice Theory,** which helps teachers and students understand human nature and use it to advantage, plays a key role in quality education.

Earlier, Glasser concluded that the majority of students today are content to do low-quality schoolwork or even none at all. It was his conclusion that "no more than half of our secondary school students are willing to make an effort to learn, and therefore cannot be taught" (1986, p. 3), and that " . . . no more than 15 percent of high school students do quality work" (1990, p. 5). His solution to the problem is to offer instruction in a different manner—one in which a substantial majority of students willingly do high-quality schoolwork. Nothing less, he says, will suffice.

For many years now, Glasser has been refining procedures for achieving the quality education he envisions. What must be done, he says, is to provide instruction, support, and other conditions in the classroom that meet students' basic needs. This requires only modest changes in curricula, materials, and physical facilities but a significant change in the way teachers work with students. Glasser recognizes how difficult teaching can be. He expresses sympathy for beleaguered secondary teachers who yearn to work with dedicated, high-achieving students but are continually frustrated by students who make little effort to learn. Those teachers report that their main discipline problems are not defiance or disruption but, rather, students' overwhelming apathy, resignation, and unwillingness to participate in class activities or assignments. Students, for their part, tell Glasser that the problem with schoolwork is not that it is too difficult but that it is too boring. For Glasser, this is another way of saying that schoolwork does not meet students' psychological needs. He has a remedy for this problem, which he puts forth in three fundamental propositions:

1. The school curriculum must be organized to meet students' basic needs for survival, belonging, power, fun, and freedom.

2. **Quality schoolwork** and **self-evaluation** (of quality) by students must replace the fragmented and boring requirements on which students are typically tested and evaluated. This requires that teachers abandon traditional teaching practices and move toward **quality teaching** as described in **competency-based classrooms.**

3. **Choice Theory,** which contributes to success and responsibility, must be given central attention in teaching, learning, and behavior management.

Meeting Students' Needs

Glasser is adamant that education that does not give priority to students' five basic needs is bound to fail. Meeting the needs is not difficult. Glasser says students' need related to **survival** is met when the school environment is kept safe and free from personal threat. They sense **belonging** when they are involved in class matters, receive attention from the teacher and others, and are brought into discussions of matters that concern the class. Students sense **power** when the teacher asks them to participate in decisions about topics to be studied and procedures for working in the class. A sense of power also comes from being assigned responsibility for class duties, such as helping take attendance, caring for class animals, helping distribute and take care of materials, being in charge of audiovisual equipment, and so forth. Students experience **fun** when they are able to work and talk with others, engage in interesting activities, and share their accomplishments. And they sense **freedom** when the teacher allows them to make responsible choices concerning what they will study, how they will do so, and how they will demonstrate their accomplishments. Glasser frequently mentions the value of cooperative learning groups and **learning teams** in helping students meet their basic needs (Glasser, 1998c).

Quality Curriculum

Glasser finds much fault with the present school curriculum, the way it is presented, and how student learning is evaluated. He claims that present-day education consists too much of memorizing facts irrelevant to students' lives, and that its quality is judged by how many fragments of information students can retain long enough to be measured on tests. He says school should be converted into a place where students learn useful information and learn it well. To make that possible, a **quality curriculum** is necessary. The old curriculum should be revised so that it consists only of learnings that students find enjoyable and useful. The rest should be discarded as "nonsense" (Glasser, 1992).

When teachers introduce new segments of learning, they should hold discussions with students and, if the students are old enough, ask them to identify what they would like to explore in depth. Adequate time should then be allowed so the identified topics can be learned well. Quality learning requires depth of understanding together with a good grasp of its usefulness. Learning a smaller number of topics very well is always preferable to covering many topics superficially. As part of evaluating in-depth learning, students should expect to explain why the material they have learned is valuable and how and where it can be used. They should regularly be asked to assess the quality of their efforts as well.

Quality Teaching

Quality teaching is rather easy to accomplish, but it requires a change in approach. Even teachers who are committed intellectually to quality teaching may find the change difficult, as it is not easy to change one's teaching style. Glasser (1993, p. 22 ff) says it can be done by working toward the following:

1. *Provide a warm, supportive classroom climate.* This is done by helping students know and like you. Use natural occasions over time to tell students who you are, what you stand for, what you will ask them to do, what you will not ask them to do, what you will do for them, and what you will not do for them. Show that you are always willing to help.

2. *Use lead teaching rather than boss teaching.* This means using methods that encourage students and draw them out rather than trying to force information into them. (You will see how this is done in the section called "More on Lead Teaching," which follows presently.)

3. *Ask students only to do work that is useful.* **Useful work** involves developing skills that are useful in students' lives rather than merely acquiring information. At times teachers may have to point out the value of the new skills, but that value must become quickly apparent to students or they will not make a sustained effort to learn. Students should not be required to memorize information except that which is essential to the skill being learned. However, information should be taught and learned provided it meets one or more of the following criteria (1993, p. 48):

- The information is directly related to an important skill.
- The information is something that students express a desire to learn.
- The information is something the teacher believes to be especially useful.
- The information is required for college entrance exams.

4. *Always ask students to do the best they can.* The process of doing quality work occurs slowly and must be nurtured. Glasser (1998b) suggests that a focus on quality can be initiated as follows:

- Discuss quality work enough so that students understand what you mean.
- Begin with an assignment that is clearly important enough to do well.
- Ask students to do their best work on the assignment. Do not grade their work because grades suggest to students that the work is finished.

5. *Ask students to evaluate work they have done and improve it.* Quality usually comes from modifications through continued effort. Glasser suggests that when students feel they have completed a piece of work on a topic they consider important, the teacher should help them make **value judgments** about it, as follows:

- Ask students to explain why they feel their work has high quality.
- Ask students how they think they might improve their work further. As students see the value of improving their work, higher quality will result naturally.
- Progressively help students learn to use **SIR,** a process of self-evaluation, improvement, and repetition, until quality is achieved.

6. *Help students recognize that doing quality work makes them feel good.* This effect will occur naturally as students learn to do quality work. Glasser (1993) says,

> There is no better human feeling than that which comes from the satisfaction of doing something useful that you believe is the very best you can do and finding that others agree. As students begin to sense this feeling, they will want more of it. (p. 25)

7. *Help students see that quality work is never destructive to oneself, others, or the environment.* Teachers should help students realize that it is not possible to achieve the good feeling of quality work if their efforts harm people, property, the environment, or other creatures.

More on Lead Teaching

Glasser has much to say about the style of teaching required for quality education. In essence, he says that teachers must move away from "boss teaching" and begin replacing it with "lead teaching." Teachers typically function as bosses, Glasser contends, because they do not realize they cannot provide motivation—that instead they must call on motivation already residing within students.

Boss teachers, as Glasser describes them, do the following:

- Set the tasks and standards for student learning.
- Talk rather than demonstrate and rarely ask for student input.
- Grade the work without involving students in the evaluation.
- Use coercion to ensure students comply with expectations.

To illustrate how a boss teacher functions, consider the example of Mr. Márquez, who introduces his unit of study on South American geography in the following way:

> Class, today we are going to begin our study of the geography of South America. You will be expected to do the following things:
>
> 1. Learn the names of the South American countries.
> 2. Locate those countries on a blank map.
> 3. Describe the types of terrain typical of each country.
> 4. Name two products associated with each country.
> 5. Describe the population of each country in terms of ethnic origin and economic well-being.
> 6. Name and locate the most important river in each country.
>
> We will learn this information from our textbooks and encyclopedias. You will have two tests, one at. . . .

Mr. Márquez's boss approach limits productivity and quality of work. It is unlikely that his students will pursue the work eagerly. Most will do only enough, and only well enough, to get by.

Lead teachers work differently. They realize that genuine motivation to learn resides within students, in the form of needs and interests, and must be activated. Toward that end, lead teachers spend most of their time organizing interesting activities and providing assistance to students. They teach in a way similar to the following:

- Discuss the curriculum with the class in such a way that many topics of interest are identified.
- Encourage students to identify topics they would like to explore in depth.
- Discuss with students the nature of the schoolwork that might ensue, emphasizing quality and asking for input on criteria of quality.
- Explore with students resources that might be needed for quality work and the amount of time such work might require.
- Demonstrate ways in which the work can be done, using models that reflect quality.
- Emphasize the importance of students' continually inspecting and evaluating their own work in terms of quality.
- Make evident to students that everything possible will be done to provide them with good tools and a good workplace that is noncoercive and nonadversarial.

To illustrate how lead teaching might proceed, consider the example of Mr. Garcia's introduction to a unit of study on the geography of South America:

Class, have any of you ever lived in South America? You did, Samuel? Which country? Peru? Fantastic! What an interesting country! I used to live in Brazil. I traveled in the Amazon quite a bit and spent some time with jungle Indians. Supposedly they were headhunters at one time. But not now. At least so they say. Tomorrow I'll show you a bow and arrow I brought from that tribe. Samuel, did you ever eat monkey when you were in Peru? I think Peru and Brazil are very alike in some ways but very different in others. What was Peru like compared to here? Did you get up into the Andes? They have fabulous ruins all over Peru, I hear, and those fantastic Chariots of the Gods lines and drawings on the landscape. Do you have any photographs or slides you could bring for us to see? What a resource you could be for us! You could teach us a lot!

Class, Samuel lived in Peru and traveled in the Andes. If we could get him to teach us about that country, what do you think you would most like to learn? (The class discusses this option and identifies topics.)

We have the opportunity in our class to learn a great deal about South America, its mountains and grasslands, its dense rain forests and huge rivers, and its interesting people and strange animals. Did you know there are groups of English, Welsh, Italians, and Germans living in many parts of South America, especially in Argentina? Did you know there are still thought to be tribes of Indians in the jungles that have no contact with the outside world? Did you know that almost half of all the river water in the world is in the Amazon Basin, and that in some places the Amazon River is so wide that from the middle you can't see either shore?

Speaking of the Amazon jungle, I swam in a lake there that contained piranhas, and look, I still have my legs and arms. Surprised about that? If you wanted to learn more about living in the Amazon jungle, what would you be interested in knowing? (Discussion ensues.)

How about people of the high Andes? Those Incas, for example, and their ancestors who in some unknown way cut and placed enormous boulders into gigantic, perfectly fitting fortress walls? Samuel has seen them. The Incas were very civilized and powerful, with an empire that stretched for three thousand miles. Yet they were conquered by a few Spaniards on horseback. How in the world could that have happened? If you could learn more about those amazing people, what would you like to know? (Discussion continues in this manner. Students identify topics about which they would be willing to make an effort to learn.) Now let me see what you think of this idea: I have written down the topics you said you were interested in, and I can help you with resources and materials. I have lots of my own, including slides, South American music, and many artifacts I have collected. I know two other people who lived in Argentina and Colombia that we could invite to talk with us. We can concentrate on what you have said you would like to learn. But if we decide to do so, I want to see if we can make this deal: We explore what interests you; I help you all I can; and you, for your part, agree to do the best work you are capable of. We would need to discuss that to get some ideas of what you might do that would show the quality of your learning. In addition, I hope I can persuade each of you regularly to evaluate yourselves as to how well you believe you are doing. Understand, this would not be me evaluating you, it would be you evaluating yourself—not for a grade but for you to decide what you are doing very well and what you think you might be able to do better. What do you think of that idea? Want to give it a try?

Choice Theory in the Classroom

Motivation is an extremely important contributor to academic and behavioral success. Students who like what they are doing and want to learn more about it almost always do well and conduct themselves appropriately. Glasser notes that educators have traditionally assumed that "external control" (what we do to students or for them) is teachers' most reliable means of motivating school learning. He points out that this assumption is seriously flawed because all students will do what is most satisfying to them at any given time, if they can. If they choose to work hard and comply with expectations, it is because they get satisfaction from doing so. If students do not experience that natural satisfaction, they will seldom work hard for long. The payoff for doing so is too remote to serve as a reliable motivator.

It has become clear that threat and punishment do not motivate students to do well in school. They can be replaced with principles of Choice Theory that help produce the results teachers desire. Choice Theory helps everyone become more realistic about human behavior, and it can be used to establish learning environments that lead to success and quality. The following are some of the main tenets of Choice Theory:

- We can control no one's behavior except our own.
- We cannot successfully make a person do anything. All we can do is open possibilities and provide information.
- All behavior is best understood as Total Behavior, comprised of four components: acting, thinking, feeling, and physiology (how we function).
- All Total Behavior is chosen, but we only have direct control over the acting and thinking components. In other words, we can choose how to act and how to think. Feeling and physiology are controlled indirectly through how we choose to act and think.
- What we do is not automatically determined by external causes. It is determined primarily by what goes on inside us.
- One way to improve behavior is through clarifying what a quality existence would be like and planning the choices that would help achieve that existence. In the classroom, this process occurs best when teachers establish warm, trusting relationships with students.

Applications of Choice Theory to the classroom are reflected in the work of Kathy Curtiss and Steven English (2003), who have been providing services to schools across the country for many years (see www.kathycurtissco.com/what_we_do.htm). Curtiss and English advocate using classroom meetings, integrating character development into curriculum content, and developing instructional strategies that lead to student ownership of learning. They also work on strengthening student reflection and self-evaluation with the aim of increasing students' responsibility for making the most of their educational opportunity. They recommend the use of portfolios and assessment rubrics (procedures) based on standards, as well as developing stronger partnerships between teachers and students. They point out that these provisions accomplish little unless the classroom is imbued with trust and respect and students learn to resolve their problems without hurting each other. Instructional strategies that make this possible include cooperative learning, conflict resolution, classroom meetings, and character education.

The Relation of Quality Teaching to Discipline

Teachers who function as leaders of quality classrooms assiduously avoid adversarial relationships with their students because they destroy incentives for student learning as well as pleasure in teaching. When teachers stay out of the adversity trap, they not only have an opportunity to foster quality learning but also reduce discipline problems to a minimum.

Glasser acknowledges that no approach can eliminate all behavior problems. He urges teachers to work with students to establish standards of conduct in the classroom. Toward that end, he makes the following suggestions: Begin with a discussion of the importance of quality work (to be given priority in the class) and explain that you will do everything possible to help students learn and enjoy themselves without using force. That discussion should lead naturally to asking students about class behavior they believe will help them get their work done and truly help them learn. Glasser says that if teachers can get students to see the importance of courtesy, no other rules may be necessary.

Teachers should also solicit student advice on what should happen when behavior agreements are broken. Glasser says students usually suggest punishment, though they know punishment is not effective. If asked further, they will agree that behavior problems are best solved by looking for ways to remedy whatever is causing the rule to be broken. Glasser urges teachers to ask, "What could I do to help?" and to hold classroom meetings to explore alternatives to inappropriate behavior. Once agreements and consequences are established, they should be put in writing and all students should sign the document, attesting that they understand the agreements and that, if they break them, they will try—with the teacher's help—to correct the underlying problem. Agreements established and dealt with in this way, says Glasser, show that the teacher's main concern lies in quality, not power, and that the teacher recognizes that power struggles are the main enemy of quality education.

When Rules Are Broken

Glasser reminds us that when class agreements or rules are broken teacher interventions are required. These interventions should be nonpunitive acts that stop the misbehavior and get the student's mind back on class work. Suppose that Jonathan has come into the room obviously upset. As the lesson begins, he turns heatedly and throws something at Michael. Glasser would suggest that the teacher do the following:

Teacher: It looks like you have a problem, Jonathan. How can I help you solve it? [Jonathan frowns, still obviously upset.]

Teacher: If you will calm down, I will discuss it with you in a little while. I think we can work something out.

Glasser says you should make it clear that you are unable to help Jonathan unless he calms down. You say this without emotion in your voice, recognizing that anger on your part will only put Jonathan on the defensive. If Jonathan doesn't calm down, there is no good way to deal with the problem. Glasser (1990) says to allow him 20 seconds, and if he isn't calm by then, admit that there is no way to solve the problem at that time. Give Jonathan time out from the lesson but don't threaten or warn him. Say something like the following: "Jonathan, I want to help you work this out. I am not interested in punishing you. Whatever the problem is, let's solve it. But for now you must go sit at the table. When you are calm, come back to your seat." Later, at an opportune time, discuss the situation with Jonathan approximately as follows:

Teacher: What were you doing when the problem started? Was it against the rules? Can we work things out so it won't happen again? What could you and I do to keep it from happening?

If the problem involves hostilities between Jonathan and Michael, the discussion should involve both boys and proceed along these lines:

> *Teacher:*   What were you doing, Jonathan? What were you doing, Michael? How can the three of us work things out so this won't happen anymore?

It is important to note that no blame is assigned to either Jonathan or Michael. No time is spent trying to find out whose fault it was. You remind the boys that all you are looking for is a solution so that the problem won't occur again. Glasser says if you treat Jonathan and Michael with respect and courtesy, if you show you don't want to punish them or throw your weight around, and if you talk to them as a problem solver, both their classroom behavior and the quality of their work will likely improve.

Moving toward Quality Classrooms

As of October 2001, there were 10 schools in the United States officially designated by William Glasser as Glasser Quality Schools (GQS). Glasser (2001) describes them as schools in which:

- Relationships are based on trust and respect, and all discipline problems (meaning intentional misbehavior) have disappeared.
- Total learning competence is stressed. Student work does not receive credit until it has reached the B level of quality on the traditional ABCDF grading system.
- Students and staff are taught to use Choice Theory in their lives and in their work at school.
- Students score significantly above average on proficiency tests and college entrance exams, typically at the 80th percentile or better.
- Staff, students, parents, and administrators view the school as a joyful place.

A fundamental operating principle of Glasser Quality Schools is that teachers and administrators endeavor to help students be happy at school. Glasser claims that if you are having trouble with a student, you can be absolutely sure that student is unhappy in your class and very likely unhappy in school. Almost all problems that occur between teachers and students are caused by unsatisfactory relationships. Glasser, therefore, stresses the fundamental importance of maintaining good relationships between teachers and students. Such relationships are established when teachers completely stop using what he calls "the seven deadly habits" and replace them with what he calls "the seven connecting habits."

The Seven Deadly Habits

The seven deadly habits that prevent the establishment of caring relationships between teachers and students are *criticizing, blaming, complaining, nagging, threatening, punishing, and rewarding students to control them.* (These same deadly habits function equally in relationships outside of school.) If teachers are to establish good relationships with students and gain their willing cooperation, they must decide they will never again use any of these deadly habits.

The Seven Connecting Habits

In place of the seven deadly habits that damage relationships, teachers should use behaviors that increase a sense of connection between them and their students. The seven connecting habits are *caring, listening, supporting, contributing, encouraging, trusting, and befriending*. Glasser believes—and his quality schools support his contentions—that all students who come to school can do competent work. In order for this to happen, teachers must strongly "connect" with their students. This connection is accomplished when teachers use the seven connecting habits and *give up* trying to use external controls to make students behave as they want them to. External control is exemplified in the seven deadly habits. It effectively prevents the close relationships needed between teachers and students. Glasser illustrates his contentions by describing how we relate to friends (and he does indeed urge teachers to befriend their students). He says we do not speak harshly to our friends, or criticize or blame them. Rather, we use connecting habits when relating with them.

Gaining the Benefits of Quality Classrooms

Here is a brief outline of Glasser's suggestions for working with your class in order to obtain the benefits of quality classrooms.

1. *Ways of relating.* Determine that, beginning today, you will assiduously avoid the seven deadly habits when working with your students and replace them with connecting habits.
2. *The basic message.* The message you want to get across to students is the following: "We are in this class together. I want to help you to be competent or go beyond. My job is to teach you and help you learn, not to find out what you don't know and punish you for not knowing it. If you have a question, ask me. If you need more time, I'll give it to you. If you have an idea how to do what we are trying to do better, tell me. I'll listen" (Glasser, 2001, p. 113).
3. *Befriending students.* Instead of telling students what they must do and not do, endeavor to befriend all of them. To set the stage, say something like, "I think an important part of my job is to do all I can to make sure you have a good time learning. You have to come to school and no one's going to pay you for doing schoolwork. So the least I can do is make this class fun for both you and me. I think we can learn a lot and still have a very good time" (Glasser, 2001, p. 54). Then assiduously use the seven connecting habits.
4. *Rules for the class.* Rely on one fundamental rule of behavior—the golden rule. Discuss the golden rule with students. A few other rules may occasionally be necessary, but the golden rule is fundamental to all others.
5. *Dealing with misbehavior.* Replace traditional discipline (external control) with talking and listening to students as soon as you sense impending trouble. Listen carefully. Inject humor into the situation if you can but only if, when doing so, you do not make light of students' concerns.

6. *Selecting knowledge.* Expect your students to learn only information and skills that will be useful to them in school and in life. They must be able to use what they learn. There is no memorizing information simply for the sake of "knowing" it. Explain to students that you will not ask them to learn anything that is not useful to them, and when there is doubt, you will explain clearly how the new learning will benefit them.

7. *Competency.* Tell students you have a new way of teaching in which everyone can do competent work and everyone will make good grades (meaning a grade of B or better.) Explain that you will ask students to work at any given assignment until they have brought it to a competent level. Nobody will fail or receive a low grade. They can use any resources available to help them, including textbooks, parents, and other students. The primary objective is to do competent work.

8. *Quality.* Often encourage students to work for still higher quality. This means they work at assignments until they have brought them to the A level.

9. *Teach, then test.* Use tests as much as you want. Teach students using your best techniques, then give them a test. Explain that the tests are for learning only. Since memorization is not emphasized, use short essay or multiple choice tests. Promise students no one will fail or receive a bad grade. When they have completed the test, have them go back over it and correct any incorrect or incomplete answers. Ask them to explain why the correction is better. Give them the time and help needed to get everything right.

10. *Understanding and using.* Ask students always to focus on understanding and using the information and skills being taught. Ask them to share and discuss the learnings with parents and guardians.

11. *For older students.* For students in middle school and high school, explain that you will teach and test for educational competence. This will involve thinking about the new knowledge being acquired and then using that thinking in speaking, listening, reading, writing, and problem solving. The point of this effort is always to improve knowledge.

12. *After competence is achieved.* Students who complete their work competently can then have the option of helping other students or moving ahead to doing something of yet higher quality.

To experience the full flavor and sense of Glasser's ideas, read his small book entitled *Every Student Can Succeed* (2001). Glasser suggests that this will be his culminating book in education.

Strengths of Glasser's *Noncoercive Discipline*

Glasser points out that schools traditionally expect students to do boring work while sitting and waiting, which goes strongly against students' nature and severely limits achievement for many. He says that expecting students to do boring work in school "is like asking someone who is sitting on a hot stove to sit still and stop complaining" (1986, p. 53) and that "teachers should not depend on any discipline program that demands that they do something to or for students to get them to stop behaving badly in unsatisfying classes. Only a discipline program that is also concerned with classroom satisfaction will work" (1986, p. 56).

Glasser has also given us much to think about regarding quality in teaching and learning. He has shown how teachers can function more effectively as leaders who provide continual support and encouragement but do not coerce, intimidate, or punish. They know that if they meet students' needs adequately, students will stay in school and do better-quality work. In schools and classes that operate on the basis of quality, discipline problems will be few and relatively easily resolved.

Glasser's approach does not have to be set into place as a total and complete system of teaching and discipline. His suggestions for teachers acting as problem solvers without arguing or punishing should be seriously considered by all teachers. His procedures for increasing quality in teaching and learning can be put gradually into practice, thus allowing teachers to evaluate for themselves the effect on classroom climate and morale. Glasser's suggestions, although they may require some changes in teaching techniques, help bring about what all teachers desire, which is for their students to learn well and enjoy school while becoming more self-directing and responsible.

Initiating Glasser's *Noncoercive Discipline*

Suppose you like Glasser's ideas on schooling and discipline and want to try them in your classroom. How do you go about putting them into practice? You would begin by holding discussions with your class to get students' thoughts on how school could be made more interesting and enjoyable. You could do something like the following:

- Involve students in discussions about the curriculum, topics they would like to explore, ways in which they would like to work, procedures for reporting or demonstrating accomplishment, personal conduct that would make the class function better, and how disruptions might be handled positively and effectively. The process is mainly for student input, but you might offer some of your opinions as well.
- Make plain to students that you will try to organize a few activities as they have suggested and that you will do all you can to help them learn and succeed.

Meanwhile, you would also take the following steps:

- Learn how to function as a lead teacher rather than a boss teacher.
- Use the seven connecting habits while avoiding the seven deadly habits.
- Hold regular class meetings to discuss curriculum, procedures, behavior, and other educational topics. These meetings should always be conducted with an eye to improving learning conditions for students, never as a venue for finding fault, blaming, or criticizing.
- When students misbehave, discuss their behavior and why it was inappropriate for the class. Ask them what they feel they could do to avoid misbehaving in the future. If the misbehavior is serious or chronic, talk with the involved students privately at an appropriate time.

KEY TERMS AND CONCEPTS PRESENTED IN THIS CHAPTER

The following terms are central to Glasser's suggestions regarding education, teaching, learning, and discipline. Check yourself for understanding.

Choice Theory	freedom	lead teachers
responsibility	quality education	class rules
useful work	quality curriculum	classroom meetings
value judgments	quality learning	self-evaluation
basic needs	quality schoolwork	learning teams
survival	quality teaching	seven deadly habits
belonging	competency-based classrooms	seven connecting habits
power	SIR	
fun	boss teachers	

SELECTED SEVEN—SUMMARY SUGGESTIONS FROM WILLIAM GLASSER

William Glasser suggests that you emphasize the following, as well as his many other suggestions:

1 Remember that your students' behavior is internally motivated and purposeful, directed toward meeting certain needs. Therefore, adjust your curriculum and instructional activities to allow students to meet those needs.

2 A majority of your students will not commit themselves to learning they find boring, frustrating, or otherwise dissatisfying. Do away with that type of learning and replace it with instruction students enjoy.

3 Encourage your students to pursue in-depth information about socially approved topics they consider useful or relevant in their lives.

4 Encourage students to demonstrate or explain how, why, and where their preferred learnings are valuable in their lives.

5 Instead of coercing, scolding, and punishing your students to get them to learn and behave properly, befriend them, provide encouragement and stimulation, and show unending willingness to help.

6 Ask students what kinds of class behaviors will help them acquire quality learning. Ask them to reach agreements about such behavior in the class. Ask them what should happen when anyone breaks a behavior agreement. Ensure that the steps are positive, not negative.

7 When working with students, avoid the seven deadly habits of criticizing, blaming, complaining, nagging, threatening, punishing, and rewarding students to control them. Instead, rely on the seven connecting habits of caring, listening, supporting, contributing, encouraging, trusting, and befriending.

CONCEPT CASES

■ CASE 1 *Kristina Will Not Work*

Kristina, a student in Mr. Jake's class, is quite docile. She socializes little with other students and never disrupts class. However, despite Mr. Jake's best efforts, Kristina never does her work. She rarely completes an assignment. She is simply there, putting forth no effort. *How would Glasser deal with Kristina?*

Glasser would first suggest that Mr. Jake think carefully about the classroom and the program to try to determine whether they contain obstacles that prevent Kristina from meeting her needs for survival, belonging, power, fun, and freedom. He would then have Mr. Jake discuss the matter with Kristina, not blaming her but noting the problem of nonproductivity and asking what the problem is and what he might be able to do to help. In that discussion, Mr. Jake might ask Kristina questions such as the following:

1. You have a problem with this work, don't you? Only you can decide whether to do it. Is there anything I can do to help you?
2. Is there anything I could do to make the work more interesting for you?
3. Is there anything in this class that you especially enjoy doing? Do you think that, for a while you might like to do only those things?
4. Is there anything we have discussed in class that you would like to learn very, very well? How could I help you do that?
5. What could I do differently that would help you want to learn?

Glasser would not want Mr. Jake to use a disapproving tone of voice with Kristina, but every day he should make a point of talking with her in a friendly and courteous way about nonschool matters such as trips, pets, and movies. He would do this casually, showing he is interested in her and willing to be her friend. Glasser would remind Mr. Jake that there is no magic formula for success with all students. Mr. Jake can only encourage and support Kristina. Scolding and coercion are likely to make matters worse, but as Mr. Jake befriends Kristina she is likely to begin to do more work and better-quality work.

■ CASE 2   *Sara Cannot Stop Talking*

Sara is a pleasant girl who participates in class activities and does most, though not all, of her assigned work. She cannot seem to refrain from talking to classmates, however. Her teacher, Mr. Gonzales, has to speak to her repeatedly during lessons, to the point that he often becomes exasperated and loses his temper. *What suggestions would Glasser give Mr. Gonzales for dealing with Sara?*

■ CASE 3   *Joshua Clowns and Intimidates*

Larger and louder than his classmates, Joshua always wants to be the center of attention, which he accomplishes through a combination of clowning and intimidation. He makes wise remarks, talks back (smilingly) to the teacher, utters a variety of sound-effect noises such as automobile crashes and gunshots, and makes limitless sarcastic comments and put-downs of his classmates. Other students will not stand up to him, apparently fearing his size and verbal aggression. His teacher, Miss Pearl, has come to her wit's end. *How do you think Glasser would have Miss Pearl deal with Joshua?*

■ CASE 4   *Tom Is Hostile and Defiant*

Tom has appeared to be in his usual foul mood ever since arriving in class. On his way to sharpen his pencil, he bumps into Frank, who complains. Tom tells him loudly to shut up. Miss Baines, the teacher, says, "Tom, go back to your seat." Tom wheels around, swears loudly, and says heatedly, "I'll go when I'm damned good and ready!" *How would Glasser have Miss Baines deal with Tom?*

QUESTIONS AND ACTIVITIES

1. Make notes in your journal concerning information from Glasser that relates to the five principles for developing a personal system of discipline.
2. Select a grade level and/or subject you enjoy teaching. Outline what you would consider and do, along the lines of Glasser's suggestions, concerning the following:
   a. Organizing the classroom, class, curriculum, and activities to better meet your students' needs for belonging, fun, power, and freedom
   b. Your continual efforts to help students improve the quality of their work

3. Do a comparative analysis of Glasser's system with that of either Canter or Jones, as concerns:
   a. Effectiveness in suppressing inappropriate behavior
   b. Effectiveness in improving long-term behavior
   c. Ease of implementation
   d. Effect on student self-concept
   e. Effect on bonds of trust between teacher and student
   f. The degree to which each model accurately depicts realities of student attitude and behavior.

YOU ARE THE TEACHER

Middle School World History

Your third-period world history class is comprised of students whose achievement levels vary from high to well below average. You pace their work accordingly, ask them to work cooperatively, and make sure everyone understands what they are supposed to do. For the most part you enjoy the class, finding the students interesting and refreshing. Your lessons follow a consistent pattern. First, you ask the students to read in groups from the textbook. Then you call on students at random to answer selected questions about the material. If a student who is called on is unable to answer a question, the group he or she represents loses a point. If able to answer correctly, the group gains a point. For partially correct answers, the group neither receives nor loses a point. For the second part of the period, the class groups do something productive or creative connected with the material they have read, such as making posters, writing a story, doing a skit, or the like. As appropriate, these efforts are shared with members of the class.

Typical Occurrences

You call on Hillary to answer a question. Although she has been participating, she shakes her head. This has happened several times before. Not wanting to hurt Hillary's feelings, you simply say, "That costs the group a point," and you call on someone else. Unfortunately, Hillary's group gets upset at her. The other students make comments under their breath. Later, Clarisse does the same thing that Hillary has done. When you speak with her about it, she replies, "You didn't make Hillary do it." You answer, "Look, we are talking about you, not Hillary." However, you let the matter lie there and say no more. Just then Deonne comes into the class late, appearing very angry. He slams his pack down on his desk and sits without opening his textbook. Although you

want to talk with Deonne, you don't know how to approach him at that time. Will is in an opposite mood. Throughout the oral reading portion of the class, he continually giggles at every mispronounced word and at every reply students give to your questions. Will sits at the front of the class and turns around to laugh, seeing if he can get anyone else to laugh with him. He makes some oooh and aaaah sounds when Hillary and Clarisse decline to respond. Although most students either ignore him or give him disgusted looks, he keeps laughing. You finally ask him what is so funny. He replies, "Nothing in particular," and looks back at the class and laughs. At the end of the period, there is time for sharing three posters students have made. Will makes comments and giggles about each of them. Clarisse, who has not participated, says, "Will, how about shutting up!" As the students leave the room, you take Deonne aside. "Is something wrong, Deonne?" you ask. "No," Deonne replies. His jaws are clenched as he strides past you.

Conceptualizing a Strategy

If you followed the suggestions of William Glasser, what would you conclude or do with regard to the following?

1. Preventing the problems from occurring in the first place.
2. Putting an immediate end to the undesirable behavior.
3. Involving other or all students in addressing the situation.
4. Maintaining student dignity and good personal relations.
5. Using follow-up procedures that would prevent the recurrence of the misbehavior.
6. Using the situation to help the students develop a sense of greater responsibility and self-control.

REFERENCES

Curtiss, K. 2003. Welcome. www.kathycurtissco.com.

Glasser, W. 1965. *Reality therapy: A new approach to psychiatry.* New York: Harper & Row.

Glasser, W. 1969. *Schools without failure.* New York: Harper & Row.

Glasser, W. 1977. 10 steps to good discipline. *Today's Education, 66,* 60–63.

Glasser, W. 1978. Disorders in our schools: Causes and remedies. *Phi Delta Kappan, 59,* 331–333.

Glasser, W. 1986. *Control theory in the classroom.* New York: HarperCollins.

Glasser, W. 1990. *The quality school: Managing students without coercion.* New York: Harper & Row.

Glasser, W. 1992. The quality school curriculum. *Phi Delta Kappan, 73*(9), 690–694.

Glasser, W. 1998a. *The quality school: Managing students without coercion.* New York: HarperCollins.

Glasser, W. 1998b. *The quality school teacher.* New York: HarperCollins. Glasser's progressive ideas on how teachers should work with students when quality is their primary goal.

Glasser, W. 1998c. *Choice theory in the classroom.* New York: HarperCollins.

Glasser, W. 2001. *Every student can succeed.* Chatsworth, CA: William Glasser Incorporated.

CHAPTER 6

Marvin Marshall's *Discipline through Raising Responsibility*

Focus

- Maintaining good discipline by increasing the level of student responsibility.
- Using noncoercive tactics to influence students to behave appropriately.
- Using questions to promote reflective self-analysis and choice in behavior.
- Avoiding external motivation and relying instead on internal motivation.

Logic

- Coercive methods are not effective in controlling classroom behavior.
- Most students are inclined to behave responsibly but must be helped to do so.
- As students begin to accept responsibility, their classroom behavior improves.
- Responsibility is important not only in discipline but also in all areas of endeavor.

Contributions

- A discipline system based on internal motivation and student responsibility.
- A hierarchy of social behavior that promotes responsibility.
- A discipline system that is easy to use and largely stress free.
- A support system of Internet newsletters and advice for teachers.

Suggestions

- Carefully teach students the four levels of social development.
- Use reflective questioning to encourage students to reflect on personal behavior.
- Help students learn how to make responsible choices.
- Use no rewards for appropriate behavior, no punishments, and no coercion.
- When disruptions continue, elicit rather than impose consequences so students take ownership of the solution.

About Marvin Marshall

Marvin Marshall

Marvin Marshall (Ed.D. in Guidance and Instruction, University of Southern California) has been a teacher, counselor, and administrator at all levels of public education. Born in 1933, he is an author, professional speaker, and staff developer who makes presentations at conferences, universities, businesses, and schools around the world. His writings have been published in several prestigious journals, he is a featured columnist for <teachers.net>, and he writes a monthly electronic newsletter related to raising responsibility, improving relationships, and increasing effectiveness. He set forth his conclusions and suggestions about classroom discipline in a 1998 article entitled "Fostering Social Responsibility," in his book entitled *Discipline without Stress, Punishments, or Rewards: How Teachers and Parents Promote Responsibility & Learning* (2001), and in his monthly newsletter entitled *Raising Responsibility*, which is available free of charge via email from www.MarvinMarshall.com.

Marshall's Contributions to Discipline

Marshall's model of discipline is designed to raise individual **responsibility** so students do what is right and proper, regardless of personal temptations or outside influences. Marshall believes almost all students are inclined to behave responsibly but need help to do so. He maintains this help is best provided by teaching students about levels of social development, having them reflect on their personal behavior, encouraging them to make responsible decisions, and helping them know how to circumvent the often destructive influences of peer pressure. He has found that when student responsibility increases, classroom misbehavior decreases. Marshall's Raise Responsibility System is rapidly gaining popularity. Teachers find it appealing because it rings true and is easy to understand and apply.

Marshall's Central Focus

Marshall focuses on helping students conduct themselves in a socially and personally responsible manner. His approach leads to desirable classroom behavior for students at all levels. He also shows how parents can use it to raise responsibility in their children and suggests that all of us can benefit from adopting and using the principles in our daily lives.

Marshall's Principal Teachings

● *Almost all students are inclined to behave responsibly.*
They sometimes don't know how to do so, however, and therefore require teacher help.

● *As students show more personal responsibility, classroom behavior improves.*
This improvement occurs automatically.

● *In order to achieve this improvement, external manipulators of student behavior must be abandoned.*
This means teachers must stop using rewards for appropriate behavior, using punishments for inappropriate behavior, telling students what to do, warning them, and criticizing them.

● ***Noncoercive influence*** *tactics must replace coercion.*
Students cannot be forced to learn or behave responsibly, but they can be influenced to do so through noncoercive approaches. A major noncoercive tactic involves posing questions that prompt students to reflect on their behavior. The primary question teachers ask students is, *"At what level is that behavior?"* Students answer with the appropriate level. The misbehavior usually ceases at this point.

● *A **hierarchy of social behavior** is used to facilitate the reflective process.*
The hierarchy consists of four levels: *Level A, Anarchy; Level B, Bothering/Bossing/Bullying; Level C, Cooperating/Conforming;* and *Level D, Taking the Initiative to Be Responsible.* Students must understand the hierarchy and what the levels mean before reflective questioning can be used effectively. The Raise Responsibility System is designed to help students function at Level D, which relies on internal motivation.

● *When students function at Level D, they make enlightened decisions about personal behavior.*
Their decisions result in their conducting themselves responsibly, regardless of circumstances, personal urges, and influence from others.

● *When students reflect on their inappropriate behavior, they immediately see how they could behave better.*
They begin to *want* to behave properly because they recognize the benefits of doing so for themselves and for the class.

● *In relatively rare cases in which students continue to misbehave after identifying the level of behavior, teachers ask follow-up questions.*
These follow-up questions enable students to make decisions that lead to responsible behavior. In rare cases in which students continue to misbehave after identifying the level of behavior, a consequence is elicited from the student (i.e., the student is asked to suggest a consequence as well as a plan for redirecting the inappropriate behavior.)

● *Undesirable behavior is considered separately from students as persons.*
Students feel no need to be defensive about their behavior because reference is made to levels of behavior rather than to the student or the behavior itself.

● *A number of specific teaching strategies can be used to improve the likelihood that students will conduct themselves responsibly.*
Those strategies can be used easily as a normal part of teaching. Nothing complicated or elaborate is required.

Analysis of Marshall's
Discipline through Raising Responsibility

The Nature of the Raise Responsibility System

The **Raise Responsibility** System is a program for helping students become self-disciplined and responsible. Marshall describes the program as proactive (versus reactive), noncoercive (versus coercive), empowering (versus overpowering), responsible (versus dependent), and positive (versus negative). It makes students and teachers aware of their ability to respond to any stimulus, situation, or urge (versus lack of control), and it is reflective (versus impulsive). It emphasizes the principles of positivity, choice, and reflection about choices that have been made. Teachers use it in the classroom by teaching students the levels of social development, asking questions to make sure students understand the levels and how they relate to classroom behavior, and eliciting **guided choices** from students that bring misbehavior to an end and replace it with proper behavior. The program uses internal student motivation to promote responsibility, which in turn leads to students behaving appropriately because they want to do so.

Theory of How to Manage Others

Marshall refers to **Theory X** and **Theory Y**, proposed by Douglas McGregor in 1960, as contrasting views of how to manage workers. Theory X holds that people dislike work, try to avoid it, and must be directed, coerced, controlled, and threatened with punishment to do their work. Theory Y holds that people will work gladly if their tasks bring satisfaction and will exercise self-direction, self-control, and personal responsibility in doing so. Marshall extends these concepts to the classroom and, as you can see, bases his Raise Responsibility System on Theory Y.

Developing Responsible Behavior

Marshall contends that the best way to help students conduct themselves properly is to encourage them to accept personal responsibility for their behavior. In school, responsible behavior is considered to be behavior that leads to better learning and better personal relations. It benefits both the individual and the class. It is involves students taking ownership of the results of choices they make and is strengthened through exercising self-direction, making decisions, accepting the results, and endeavoring to improve. Over time, accepting responsibility becomes an integral part of one's personality. Marshall explains that discipline occurs best when students continually reflect on their personal behavior, clarify the level of that behavior, and try to behave in ways that benefit themselves and others.

Marshall maintains that most students are inclined to behave responsibly but require help to do so because they either don't know how or else peer pressure or lack of self-control overrides their better judgment. Educators, he says, want students to behave responsibly but have been using the wrong approaches to help them do so. He advises teachers to put aside all inclinations to coerce students. Coercion doesn't work. It must be replaced with noncoercive influences that give students ownership of their behavior. Marshall's Raise Responsibility approach is designed to accomplish that. He lists its benefits as follows:

- Reduces discipline problems, referrals, class removals, and suspensions
- Handles classroom disruptions simply and easily
- Uses authority without resorting to punishment
- Raises individual and social responsibility
- Reduces the influence of peer pressure
- Integrates character education
- Promotes learning
- Reduces stress

Marshall says that whenever students give an excuse for unacceptable behavior that is within their control, an appropriate comment is, "Responsibility finds a way; irresponsibility finds an excuse." Encourage students to ask themselves questions such as, "If I wanted to be responsible in school right now, what would I be doing?" In most cases, the answer will be apparent to them.

Calling on Internal Rather Than External Motivation

Marshall urges teachers to rely on **internal motivation** and forget about trying to motivate students externally, as most do today. (He intentionally uses the terms *internal* and *external* rather than *intrinsic* and *extrinsic* to indicate clearly the source of motivation at any given time, pointing out that much internal motivation is learned, not genetically determined.) Internal motivation includes what students like, enjoy, find fascinating, are curious about, and so forth. **External motivation** includes what teachers do to try to make students behave in certain ways, such as giving rewards, praising, making demands, making threats, and criticizing. Using internal rather than external motivation is pivotal in Marshall's Raise Responsibility System.

Marshall has a great deal to say about rewards, punishment, and admonitions. He acknowledges they can sometimes make students comply but insists they do not motivate responsible behavior. In fact, he says, they reduce responsibility rather than increase it. Students think of **rewards** as bribes. They may want the rewards, but the desire for them does nothing to develop a sense of responsibility toward oneself and others. Socially there is nothing of value in rewarding students for behaving as they know they ought to.

Punishment is equally ineffective in developing responsibility. Marshall lists the following downsides of punishment: It satisfies the *punisher* but has little lasting effect on the person being *punished*. It leads to avoidance, fear, fleeing, and fighting. It produces animosity, not responsibility. It puts student and teacher in adversarial roles and stifles motivation to learn and effective personal relations, the very things we are hoping to achieve. It prompts students to make excuses, cover their tracks, and become evasive. It does not induce them to change. Change requires taking ownership of situations and behavior. Imposed punishment manifests ownership for the teacher, not for the student.

Telling students what to do does not accomplish much either. Students interpret telling as criticism, which annoys them and promotes defensiveness, not responsibility. Moreover, it makes them resistant because it implies they are incapable of thinking or have not been performing well enough. Marshall proves the short-range ineffectiveness of telling (in contrast to sharing) by asking teachers to complete this sentence and consider its results: "If I have told you once, I have told you. . . ."

The same is true for other forms of coercion that attempt to overpower students and make them behave in certain ways. Students resist this pressure. In contrast, noncoercive tactics encourage students to behave appropriately because they see the value of doing so. Noncoercion moves the locus of control away from the teacher and places it on the students. This encourages students to set up expectations for themselves, reflect on their behavior, accept responsibility for it, and see the personal value of behaving appropriately.

The Futility of Trying to Change Students

Marshall strongly insists that teachers cannot change students. Although they can control students temporarily, they cannot control their thinking or the way they *want* to behave. Students change themselves based on the influence they receive. Influence based on force is counterproductive, but when teachers promote responsibility instead of making demands, classroom behavior becomes more self-directed and considerate, resulting in a better educational experience for everyone and reduced stress for both teacher and students. Marshall presents specific tactics, easily understood and applied, to help teachers accomplish that end.

The Hierarchy of Social Behavior

In the Raise Responsibility System, a hierarchy of four levels of social behavior is explained to students and emphasized continually. When a change in student behavior is needed, students are asked to identify which of the four levels is consistent with their behavior. This simple act promotes self-reflection that leads to responsible behavior.

Levels in the Hierarchy

Level A, Anarchy. When functioning at this lowest level, students pay no heed to expectations or standards. They have no sense of order or purpose and they seldom accomplish anything worthwhile.

Level B, Bossing/Bullying/Bothering. When functioning at this level, students are bothering others with no consideration of the effects. They obey the teacher (or other students) only when teacher or classmates demonstrate more strength of authority.

Level C, Cooperation/Conformity. When functioning at this level, students conform to expectations set by the teacher or others. They are cooperative with the teacher and fellow students and are easily influenced by peer pressure. Here they are relying on external motivation, coming from others rather than from their personal beliefs concerning what is proper.

Level D, Taking Initiative to Be Responsible. When functioning at this level, students take the initiative and do what is right and proper—that is, they behave responsibly without having to be told because they rely on internal motivation and, therefore, do what is proper. Self-discipline is a natural outcome of accepting responsibility.

Note: Marshall says that only Levels D and C are acceptable in the classroom. Level D is preferable by far, but level C is acceptable. Level A and Level B are unacceptable levels of behavior.

Value of the Hierarchy

Marshall lists numerous benefits associated with using the hierarchy of social behavior. It directs attention to self-control and then to social responsibility. It causes students to aspire to Level D, which they know is best. It separates the act from the actor, the deed from the doer, irresponsible behavior from a good person. Without that separation, students are too defensive about their behavior to take positive action. The hierarchy helps students realize they are constantly making choices, both consciously and unconsciously. It helps them understand and deal with peer pressure. It fosters intrinsic motivation to behave responsibly. It promotes good character without giving specific attention to values, ethics, or morals. It serves as a vehicle for communication that uses the same conceptual vocabulary for youth and adults. It encourages students to help maintain an environment conducive to learning rather than always relying on the teacher to do so. It raises awareness of individual responsibility. It empowers students by helping them analyze and correct their own behavior. It serves as an inspiration to improve and encourages mature decision making. It labels behavior, not individuals, and fosters understanding about internal and external incentives. And it promotes self-management. Democracy calls for responsibility and doing the right thing, even when no one else is watching.

Teaching the Hierarchy to Students

Marshall suggests explaining to students that a democratic way of life requires that citizens make decisions for themselves, rather than having decisions made for them and imposed by a king or dictator. Democracy requires that people be able to do the right thing because they believe it is best. Students should be helped to understand that such is the essence of responsible behavior.

In teaching the levels of social behavior, Marshall (2001, pp. 70–80) describes hands-on activities that help students learn and remember the four levels. This involves visualizing each level and then drawing a picture of it, describing it in writing, describing it orally to others, and listening to others' interpretations. He explains that by using these various modalities, the four levels become fixed in students' minds. He urges teachers to emphasize that the difference between Levels C and D, both of which are acceptable, is usually in the motivation involved. Level C is behaving acceptably because of peer pressure or teacher directions, rewards, or punishments. Level D is being responsible without being asked, told, rewarded, or punished. On this level, students *take the initiative* to do the right thing because it is best for the class, the school, and themselves.

How to Intervene When Misbehavior Occurs

You have seen that the hierarchy of behavior provides a reference for students to identify their level of behavior and then, one hopes, to change to a more responsible level. Let's suppose a student misbehaves and the teacher needs to intervene. How should the intervention be done? Marshall does not present his advice in exactly the same form as you see here. This description assumes that the hierarchy has been taught well and students understand it. It then indicates what the teacher would do first, second, third, and so forth.

Step 1. Use an unobtrusive tactic. Suppose Syong is annoying Neri. Before saying anything to Syong, you would influence her to stop by using an unobtrusive technique, such as facial expression, eye contact, hand signal, moving near to Syong, changing voice tone, thanking students for working, saying "excuse me," or asking students for help.

Step 2. Check for understanding. If the unobtrusive tactic doesn't stop Syong's misbehavior, determine if she understands its level in the hierarchy. Use a neutral, unemotional tone of voice and phrase the question as, "Syong, which level of behavior is that?" No mention is made of the nature of the behavior or that Syong was doing it but only of its level. In the exchange that follows, Syong is somewhat uncooperative: (T—teacher; S—Syong):

> *T:* Syong, on what level is that behavior?
>
> *S:* She was doing it, too.
>
> *T:* That was not the question. Let's try it again. On what level is that behavior?
>
> *S:* I don't know.
>
> *T:* What level is it when someone *bothers* others?
>
> *S:* B.
>
> *T:* Thank you.

You see that the teacher's questions separate Syong from the behavior. Without the separation, a teacher may ask, "What are you doing?" This can lead to a confrontational situation if Syong reponds, "Nothing." However, asking *"On what level is that behavior?"* prompts not only acknowledgment but also self-evaluation. You are not "attacking" Syong; you are **separating** her as a good person from the bad behavior, something educators often talk about but find difficult to do. Because of the separation, Syong doesn't feel she must defend herself. Your ability to pose such questions improves through practice. Keep in mind that effective questions are those that prompt the student to self-evaluate.

Step 3. Use guided choice. At this point, Syong has probably stopped misbehaving and has selected a more responsible way of conducting herself. In the unlikely event that she continues to bother Neri even after acknowledging that her behavior is at an unacceptable level, you ask her to make a guided choice, which is designed to do four things: (1) stop the disruption, (2) isolate the student from the class activity, (3) provide the student a responsibility-producing activity to encourage self-reflection, and (4) allow the teacher to return promptly to the lesson. Marshall suggests several options for use at various grade levels (see Marshall, 2001, pp. 102–104). Students are given the choice of doing the activity by themselves or with another student, in the room or in the office, and so forth. Examples of activities used in guided choices that encourage self-evaluation are:

- Primary grades—have student draw what he or she did; describe the event to a tape recorder; describe the incident to another student; create a story that is similar to the event.
- Other grades—complete an "essay form" (Marshall, 2001, p. 274) that asks the student to write about
  What did I do? (acknowledgment)
  What can I do to prevent its happening again? (choice)
  What will I do? (commitment)

If, after identifying the level of behavior, Syong continues to bother Neri or someone else, Marshall suggests you move to *authority without punishment,* which is epitomized in guided choices. You give Syong a choice, using only one question, such as: "Would you rather complete the activity by yourself or would you like someone else to help you?"

Similar questions might be:

Would you prefer to complete the activity in your seat or in the rear of the room?
Would you rather complete the activity in the room or in the office?

Your selection of a question is determined by what you know about the student, the dynamics of the class, and the situation itself. Guided choice options should be adjusted in accordance with grade level, individual student, and choices already used. In checking for understanding and providing guided choices, the teacher is asking the student, not telling. This reduces confrontation and minimizes stress. This empowerment through guided options helps preserve student dignity.

Marshall says teachers typically use the checking for understanding phase with 15 to 20 percent of their students. Its self-evaluative quality prevents most repeat offenses. He says that teachers need to use guided choices with only 2 to 5 percent of their students.

It is very unlikely that Syong, once she has done one of these activities, will continue to bother others, but teachers always want to know what to do in case she continues to misbehave. Marshall suggests the following, although he does not refer to them as steps:

Step 4. Make a self-diagnostic referral.   Syong is given a form that she must complete in writing, following the instructions it contains. Again, she is allowed choices in how and where she will complete the activity. The self-diagnostic referral contains items such as the following:

- Describe the problem that led to doing this referral.
- Identify the level of behavior.

- Explain why this level of behavior is not acceptable.
- On what level should you act in order to be socially responsible?
- If you had acted on an acceptable level, what would have happened?
- List three solutions that would help you act more responsibly.

Marshall advises keeping the completed referrals on file for the entire year, as they might need to be used for follow-up.

Step 5. Give an additional self-diagnostic referral.   If Syong continues to bother other students, assign an additional referral to complete in the same manner as the first. Then mail a copy of the first and second referrals to Syong's parents or guardian, together with a brief note explaining the problem.

Step 6. Give a final self-diagnostic referral.   If Syong continues to bother other students, assign her a final self-diagnostic referral. Mail a copy along with copies of the first two referrals and both notes to parents. The final note indicates to parents that you have exhausted all positive means of fostering social responsibility and will refer future disruptions to the administrator. Marshall points out that in all these cases, it is the student who identifies the problem and proposes positive solutions. All the teacher does is write brief notes to parents and mail them copies of the student's self-diagnostic referral. Thus, the student has done most of the thinking and planning, which is necessary if behavior is to become more responsible.

Note: It is essential that before you use this approach, you explain it in writing to your building administrator. This informs the administrator so (1) he or she is not caught off guard and (2) your approach receives official sanction from the administrator.

Tactics That Assist Internal Motivation in Students

Marshall describes various tactics teachers can use to increase students' internal motivation. They include the following (the numbering has no significance other than to permit easy referral should you discuss the points with colleagues):

1. *Think and speak positively.*   We learn and perform better when we feel good, but we often make ourselves and our students feel bad because we project negativism. We should strive to have a *positive outlook* and speak and conduct ourselves in an upbeat manner. As we help students do the same, we reduce stress, improve relationships, and exert stronger influence. Therefore, to the extent feasible, maintain a sunny disposition. Our outlook is in large part what we make of it. If we react positively to people and situations, we enjoy ourselves and are more likely to please our students.

2. *Emphasize the power of choice.*   We all have the power to choose our responses and attitudes to situations, events, impulses, and urges. An optimistic (versus pessimistic) perception of our choices gives us an additional sense of control. The power of choice-response thinking gives students control and responsibility rather than consigning them as victims of life events. Regardless of age, everyone likes to feel they have control over their life. When we are encouraged to make choices, we sense that control. Consider

offering your students a choice of activities, including homework assignments. By providing two, three, or even four alternative activities and letting students choose among them, you increase their opportunity to select something that appeals to them.

3. *Think and ask reflective questions.* Thinking reflectively reinforces both positivity and choice. Reflection, when applied to oneself, can lead to self-evaluation and correction, which are the ingredients for growth and change. Ask questions of students and encourage them to ask themselves questions. The questioning process jump-starts the thinking process. When students ask themselves "Why?" and "How?" both alertness and interest increase.

4. *Control the conversation, but not the behavior, by asking questions.* One way of exerting positive influence is to control the conversations we have with students. "Control" doesn't sound good to advocates of humane discipline, but in this case it refers to conversation, not the student. What it means is that we shape the topic and what is said rather than responding to whatever students might say. When someone asks you a question and you enter into a discussion about it, that person is *controlling the conversation.* If you want to control the conversation, you must pull out of the responsive mode and regain control by answering with a question of your own. For example, a student asks you, "Why do we have to do this assignment?" Instead of arguing with the student, you can say, "Do you feel there is another way we can learn this information more easily?" The key point to remember is that the person who asks the question controls the conversation.

This is but one of many ways to exert influence without trying to control behavior. Marshall says if you look around at your family and friends, you will see that the happiest people are the ones who don't try to control anyone but themselves. You will further see that the people who are the most miserable are those who are always trying to control others. Although you cannot control student behavior for long, you can influence students so they want to conduct themselves more appropriately. That is the best way to maintain good discipline in the classroom. You will rarely, if ever, solve a discipline problem by trying to make the student see that you are right and he or she is wrong. On the other hand, you are likely to get good results by asking, "What can I do to improve the situation?"

5. *Create curiosity.* Marshall says curiosity may be the greatest of all motivators for learning. Much of the learning we do on our own occurs because of it. Marshall suggests presenting a problem or a challenge to students and allowing them to grapple with it. This naturally engenders curiosity.

6. *Create desire.* Spend some time at the beginning of each lesson to talk about what the lesson offers. Students always want to know what's in it for them. Mention specific new knowledge, skills, adventures, or insights. Point out how they make life easier, better, or more enjoyable. Also show how they can help students make better decisions, solve problems, get along better with others, or live life more effectively.

7. *Emphasize a sense of personal responsibility.* As you have seen, Marshall places major emphasis on encouraging students to develop personal responsibility. Toward that end, you might find it helpful to give students an opportunity at the beginning of the class to indicate the expectations they have, the outcomes they desire, and what they are willing to

do in order to achieve those results. Discuss your responsibilities in this regard, as well. For younger students, a preview of the activity usually suffices.

8. *Use acknowledgment and recognition.* Acknowledgment and recognition help students feel affirmed and validated. Such simple comments as "I see you did your homework" foster reflection and feelings of competence, as do comments such as, "Evelyn raises an interesting question, one that applies to what we've been exploring."

9. *Encourage students.* One of the most effective techniques is to let students know you believe they can accomplish the task. A word of encouragement following a mistake is worth more than a great deal of praise after a success. Emphasize that learning is a process and that no one can learn something and be perfect at the same time. Doing something in a particular way and not being successful is a valuable way of learning. It should be seen as a mistake, not as a failure.

10. *Use collaboration.* Allow students to work together cooperatively. Generally speaking, cooperation is a much better teaching tactic than is competition, which can be fun for short periods. But competing with others is not good for youngsters who never reach the winner's circle. Those students soon drop out of the activity. Instead of competition, consider using learning buddies. Even a very shy student will share with one other person. Pose a question for a pair of learning buddies that calls on them to think and discuss. This ensures that every student will participate.

11. *Get yourself excited.* You can't expect others to get excited about what you are teaching if you are not excited about it yourself. Show enthusiasm for the lesson. When lecturing, use just a little more enthusiasm than when you are conversing, facilitating, or reviewing.

12. *Foster interpersonal relationships.* Connecting with your students on a one-to-one basis is extremely valuable, but helping them connect with each other one-to-one can be even more valuable. Sometimes allow students an opportunity to socialize for short periods before learning activities start. Relationships are extremely important to young people.

13. *Use variety.* Variety spices up topics that students might otherwise find tedious. A myriad of visual, auditory, and manipulative techniques can be employed in teaching. Examples are charts, cartoons, models, selected parts of films, videos, DVDs, PowerPoint creations, overhead transparencies, listening to music, recording music, rapping, creating verse, creating rhythms, physical movements, enacting the roles of characters in stories or events, large group discussions, case studies, and working with small groups or buddies.

14. *Stress responsibility rather than rules.* If you want to teach toward obedience, establish and use *rules.* If you want to emphasize self-directed appropriate behavior, emphasize and help students develop *responsibility.* Simply using the term *responsibilities* rather than *rules* facilitates the process.

15. *See situations as challenges, not problems.* If we help students take a positive approach and view situations as *challenges* rather than problems, we help them deal better with what life brings. This also helps students feel they have some control rather than being victims of circumstance. We can emphasize that students can use adversity as a catalyst to becoming better, stronger, wiser, and more aware of the realities of life.

16. *Use listening to influence others.* It is surprising how strongly we can influence students simply by listening to them. In fact, the more we are open to students, the greater our influence is. One tactic for listening is to pretend we are the other person who is talking. Doing this requires us to set aside some of our views and redirect some of our impulsive reactions. Also, we must ask *reflective questions* rather than give advice. We can learn these skills, but they take practice.

17. *Be careful about challenging students' ideas.* Very few people like to have their ideas and beliefs challenged. We interpret our positions as being criticized or at least not being acknowledged. Under those circumstances, students may defend themselves or begin to fear you. Instead of challenging, ask questions such as, "Interesting. How did you come to that conclusion?" or "An alternative point of view is (such and such). Have you ever considered that view?"

18. *Avoid telling students what to do.* No one likes to be told what to do. Depending on the other person's mental frame at the time, when we tell him or her to do something, regardless of how admirable our intentions might be, the message is usually perceived as criticism or as an attempt to control. Rather than telling, phrase your idea as a question, stated as if you were curious about the possibilities. For example, if you disapprove of what a student wants to do, ask, "What would be the long-term effect of doing that?" or "That's an interesting point. How did you come to that conclusion?" Three more questions you will find useful are:

Is there any other way this could be handled?
What would a responsible action look like?
What do you think a highly responsible person would do in this situation?

19. *Raise your likeability level.* Most teachers want students to like them and believe they can make that happen by trying to be friends with students. There is much to be said for a friendly demeanor, but personal friendship is not what students need most from teachers. Encouragement and empowerment are what students need. If you provide those things while preserving student dignity, your students will like you very much indeed.

20. *Improve your teaching.* Great teachers know that learning is based on motivation and students are best motivated when they can build on existing interests and strengths. That doesn't mean we should ignore the negative or disregard what needs improvement. But students achieve success through their assets, not their shortcomings. This is especially true for students at risk who have negative perceptions of school.

21. *Nurture students' brains.* Marshall refers to Marian Diamond, an internationally known neuroscientist who has studied mammalian brains for decades. She and Janet Hopson (1998) are the authors of *Magic Trees of the Mind: How to Nurture Your Child's Intelligence, Creativity, and Healthy Emotions from Birth through Adolescence.* Their work encourages teachers to think of enriching students' brains to increase academic success. They make the following recommendations:

■ Set the stage for enriching the cortex by first providing a steady source of positive emotional support.

- Encourage students to eat a nutritious diet with enough proteins, vitamins, minerals, and calories.
- Stimulate all the senses, though not necessarily all at the same time.
- Maintain an atmosphere free of undue pressure and stress but suffused with a degree of pleasurable intensity.
- Present a series of novel challenges that are neither too easy nor too difficult for the students.
- Allow social interaction in a significant percentage of the activities. Peers are intrigued with and enjoy each other.
- Promote the development of a broad range of mental, physical, aesthetic, social, and emotional skills and interests.
- Allow students to select many of their instructional activities. Each brain is unique. Allow that uniqueness to develop.
- Offer opportunities for students to assess the results of their learning and modify it as they think best.
- Provide an enjoyable atmosphere that promotes exploration and fun in learning. Encourage active participation rather than passive observation. The brain needs time to relate new information to existing associations. Students need time to reflect and think about what is happening.

22. *Emphasize the four classical virtues.* The *four classical virtues* are prudence, temperance, justice, and fortitude. Prudence is making proper choices without doing anything too rash. Temperance is remaining moderate in all things, including human passions and emotions. Justice refers to ensuring fair outcomes based on honesty. Fortitude is showing courage in pursuit of the right path, despite the risks, with strength of conviction. Marshall believes we can do no better for our students than to pass on the wisdom of former generations. He says doing so will put our children in a strong position to care for themselves.

23. *Tutor a few students every day.* Tutoring students one-on-one is the easiest, quickest, and most effective way of establishing personal relationships with students. It provides an excellent venue for encouraging students personally.

24. *Hold frequent classroom meetings.* They provide excellent opportunities to work together with students to consider and resolve challenges that confront the class.

25. *Resolve conflict in a constructivist manner.* When people are involved in conflict, ask each of them what they are willing to do to resolve the situation. Get across the notion that we can't make other people change. We can, however, influence them to change through what we do and through changes we make in ourselves.

Strengths of Marshall's Raise Responsibility System

Marshall's Raise Responsibility System has major strengths beyond those found in many other systems of discipline. It makes sense and rings true to teachers. It focuses on developing responsibility, an enduring quality that remains useful throughout life. It removes the stress that students and teachers normally experience in discipline. It is easy to teach, apply, and live by. It is long-lasting because it leads to changes in personality. Educators find these strengths especially compelling, hence, the surge of interest in Marshall's model.

Initiating Marshall's Raise Responsibility System

The Raise Responsibility System is put into effect and maintained by doing the following:

- Outline the program and indicate for yourself how you will use it. Show your plan to your administrator for approval. Prepare the outline and its rationale to send to parents when you are ready to implement it.
- Plan how you will set and maintain a positive classroom climate. This chapter has presented several suggestions for doing so. You will find many others elsewhere in this book.
- Introduce the program to your students. Explain the rationale and how the program works. Teach students the hierarchy of social behavior, what it means, and how it will be used. Teach this through hands-on activities and scenarios in which students can participate.
- Check to make sure students understand the program, the hierarchy, reflective questions, and how all components will be used.
- Ask students to take a copy of the plan home for their parents to read. In the copy ask for parental support. Ask parents to sign their approval and return the copy to you. Post your plan on your classroom Internet site so parents and students can refer to it.
- When students misbehave, follow the sequence of influence techniques described earlier in the chapter.
- Make no use of punishment for misbehavior or reward for appropriate behavior, but instead ask students to comment on their feelings as they experience responsibility and self-control.

KEY TERMS AND CONCEPTS PRESENTED IN THIS CHAPTER

The following terms are important in Marshall's Raise Responsibility System:

responsibility	reflective questions	controlling the conversation
Raise Responsibility	noncoercive influence	responsibility versus rules
guided choices	external (extrinsic) motivation	Theory X
hierarchy of social behavior	internal (intrinsic) motivation	Theory Y
Level A	rewards	self-diagnostic referral
Level B	punishment	four classical virtues
Level C	separating student from behavior	
Level D	positive outlook	

SELECTED SEVEN—SUMMARY SUGGESTIONS FROM MARVIN MARSHALL

Marvin Marshall suggests that you emphasize the following, as well as his many other suggestions:

1 One of the most important life skills you can teach students is that of behaving responsibly. Such behavior can be learned and in the process most class misbehavior disappears.

2 Responsible behavior in the classroom is behavior that leads to more satisfactory learning and personal relations for all class members. Ask students about this behavior, if they want it in the class, and if they are willing to do their part in achieving it. When they agree, ask for their commitment.

3 Teach students about a hierarchy of behavior consisting of the following levels: Level A, Anarchy; Level B, Bothering/Bossing/Bullying; Level C, Cooperating/Conforming; and Level D, Taking the Initiative to Be Responsible. Students must understand the hierarchy fully before reflective questions can be used effectively. The goal for all students is to function at Level D, which calls into play internal motivation to behave responsibly.

4 Ask students to reflect on their behavior and identify the level of the behavior in question. When they do so, they almost always want to function at Level D.

5 Weave tactics for increasing responsibility into your normal teaching routines.

6 When working with students, avoid management Theory X, which holds that people dislike work, try to avoid it, and must be directed, coerced, controlled, and threatened with punishment to do their work. In its place, use management Theory Y, which holds that people will work gladly if their tasks bring satisfaction and will exercise self-direction, self-control, and personal responsibility in doing so.

7 Remember that you cannot force students to change their behavior. However, they will change for the better if you provide influence for self-direction and responsible behavior.

CONCEPT CASES

■ CASE 1 *Kristina Will Not Work*

Kristina, a student in Mr. Jake's class, is quite docile. She socializes little with other students and never disrupts lessons. However, despite Mr. Jake's best efforts, Kristina will not do her work. She rarely completes an assignment. She is simply there, putting forth no effort at all. *How would Marshall deal with Kristina?*

He would take the following approach: He will not attempt to force Kristina to learn, knowing that he could not force her even if he wanted to. To learn or not to learn is Kristina's choice. He has seen that she is capable of learning and reassures her of this fact. If she chooses to put forth the effort to learn, she will feel more competent, enjoy herself more, and be happier. But this is her choice. Accordingly, Marshall would (1) ask Kristina to identify the level of her behavior, (2) ask her how a responsible person would behave in the circumstance, (3) positively reiterate his belief that Kristina is capable, (4) provide Kristina with a few guided choices, (5) ask her to self-reflect on her subsequent behavior and future decisions.

■ CASE 2 *Sara Cannot Stop Talking*

Sara is a pleasant girl who participates in class activities and does most, though not all, of her assigned work. She cannot seem to refrain from talking to classmates, however. Her teacher, Mr. Gonzales, has to speak to her repeatedly during lessons to the point that he often becomes exasperated and loses his temper. *What suggestions would Marshall give Mr. Gonzales for dealing with Sara?*

■ CASE 3 *Joshua Clowns and Intimidates*

Larger and louder than his classmates, Joshua always wants to be the center of attention, which he accomplishes through a combination of clowning and intimidation. He makes wise remarks, talks back (smilingly) to the teacher, utters a variety of sound-effect noises such as automobile crashes and gunshots, and makes limitless sarcastic comments and put-downs of his classmates. Other students will not stand up to him, apparently fearing his size and verbal aggression. His teacher, Miss Pearl, has come to her wit's end. *Would Joshua's behavior be likely to improve if Marshall's techniques of noncoercion and reflection were used in Miss Pearl's classroom? Explain.*

■ CASE 4 *Tom Is Hostile and Defiant*

Tom has appeared to be in his usual foul mood ever since arriving in class. On his way to sharpen his pencil, he bumps into Frank, who complains. Tom tells him loudly to shut up. Miss Baines, the teacher, says, "Tom, go back to your seat." Tom wheels around, swears loudly, and says heatedly, "I'll go when I'm damned good and ready!" *How would Marshall have Miss Baines deal with Tom?*

QUESTIONS AND ACTIVITIES

1. In your journal on the five principles of a personal system of behavior management, add notes from Marshall's model as appropriate.

2. Describe your overall impression of Marshall's Raise Responsibility System. What do you see as its strengths and shortcomings? How easily do you feel it could be used in the classroom? How well do you think it can stop aggressive behavior?

3. With a fellow student, practice asking the reflective questions and giving the guided choices Marshall suggests for identifying level of behavior and behaving at Level C or Level D.

4. With a fellow student, discuss the key terms used in Marshall's model. Check for meaning and application.

YOU ARE THE TEACHER

High School American Literature

You teach an eleventh-grade one-semester course in American literature. The course is required for graduation. Among your 33 students are eight seniors who failed the course previously and are retaking it. The students at your school are from middle-class affluent families, and many of them are highly motivated academically. But there is also a significant number who have little interest in school aside from the opportunity to socialize. Your teaching routine proceeds as follows: First, you begin the period with a three-question quiz of assigned reading. The quiz focuses on facts such as names, places, and description of plot. Second, when the quiz papers are collected, you conduct a question-and-answer session about the assigned reading. You call on individual students, many of whom answer, "I don't know." Third, you have the class begin reading a new chapter in the work under study. They take turns reading orally until the end of the period. The remainder of the assignment not read orally is to be completed as homework.

A Typical Occurrence

The students enter your classroom lethargically and begin taking the quiz from questions you have written on the board. You notice that many of their answers are simply guesses. You see that Brian, who has already failed the class and must pass it now in order to graduate, doesn't know the answers to any of the questions. You say, "I can tell that many of you didn't read your assignment. What's going on?" When oral reading begins, you notice that Brian does not have his copy of *Huckleberry Finn*, the work being studied. This is nothing new. You lend Brian a spare copy. Brian follows along in the reading for a while, then begins doodling on a sheet of paper. You call on him to read. He cannot find the place. You say, "Brian, this is simply unacceptable. You have failed the class once; fail it again now and you know you don't graduate."

Brian does not look up but says, "Want to make a bet on that?"

"What?"

"I guarantee you I'll graduate."

"Not without summer school, you won't!"

"That's okay by me. That will be better. This class is too boring, and the assignments are too long. I've got other things to do besides read this stupid story. Who cares about this anyway? Why can't we read something that has to do with real life?"

You are offended and reply, "You couldn't be more wrong! Other students enjoy this work, and it is one of the greatest books in American literature! There is nothing wrong with the book! What's wrong, Brian, is your attitude!"

Brian's eyes are hot, but he says nothing further. His book remains closed. You struggle through the final 10 minutes of class. Brian is first out of the room when the bell rings.

Conceptualizing a Strategy

If you followed the suggestions of Marvin Marshall, what would you conclude or do with regard to the following?

1. Preventing the problem from occurring in the first place.
2. Putting an immediate end to the misbehavior.
3. Involving other or all students in addressing the situation.
4. Maintaining student dignity and good personal relations.
5. Using follow-up procedures that would prevent the recurrence of the misbehavior.
6. Using the situation to help students develop a sense of greater responsibility and self-control.

REFERENCES

Diamond, M., and Hopson, J. 1998. *Magic trees of the mind: How to nurture your child's intelligence, creativity, and healthy emotions from birth through adolescence.* New York: Dutton.

Marshall, M. 1998. *Fostering social responsibility.* Bloomington, IN: Phi Delta Kappa Educational Foundation.

Marshall, M. 2001. *Discipline without stress, punishments, or rewards: How teachers and parents promote responsibility & learning.* Los Alamitos, CA: Piper Press.

Marshall, M. (Monthly since August 2001). *Promoting Responsibility: The Monthly Newsletter.* www.MarvinMarshall.com.

McGregor, D. 1960. *The human side of enterprise.* New York: McGraw-Hill.

CHAPTER 7

Jane Nelsen, Lynn Lott, and H. Stephen Glenn's *Positive Discipline in the Classroom*

OVERVIEW OF NELSEN, LOTT, AND GLENN'S MODEL

Focus

- Seeing misbehavior (mistakes) as opportunities for learning social and life skills.
- Mutual respect: humane, dignified regard for self and others.
- A learning environment that encourages rather than discourages and humiliates.
- Involvement in looking for solutions to misbehavior rather than punishment.

Logic

- Students can learn to behave with dignity, self-control, and concern for others.
- These traits develop in classrooms that are accepting, encouraging, and supportive.
- The process that serves best is cooperative planning infused with humane concern.

Contributions

- A strategic approach to positive interaction rather than a packaged system.
- Help for teachers on how to stop directing students and begin working with them.
- Clear strategy for intervening respectfully and helpfully when students misbehave.
- Suggestions to help empower students and prepare them for later success.

Nelsen, Lott, and Glenn's Suggestions

- Help students see they are capable, significant, and able to control their own lives.
- Help students develop intrapersonal, interpersonal, strategic, and judgmental skills.
- Learn to be a caring teacher who works with, rather than against, your students.
- Replace barriers to relationships with builders of relationships.

About Jane Nelsen, Lynn Lott, and H. Stephen Glenn

Jane Nelson

Jane Nelsen, Lynn Lott, and H. Stephen Glenn are educators who promote their concepts on Positive Discipline through lectures, workshops, and private practice. Their goal is to help adults and children learn to respect themselves and others, behave responsibly, and contribute to the betterment of the groups of which they are members. Their book *Positive Discipline in the Classroom* (2000) helps teachers establish learning climates that foster responsibility, mutual respect, and cooperation. They believe that such climates do away with most of the discipline problems teachers otherwise encounter, since students learn the value, for themselves, of respect and helpfulness toward others.

Lynn Lott

Nelsen, Lott, and Glenn have authored or coauthored a number of books, of which the following are most significant for teachers: *Raising Self-Reliant Children in a Self-Indulgent World* (Glenn and Nelsen , 1989, 2000), *Positive Discipline* (Nelsen, 1989, 1996), *Positive Discipline for Teenagers* (Nelsen and Lott, 2000), and *Positive Discipline in the Classroom* (Nelsen, Lott, and Glenn, 2000). Jane Nelsen and H. Stephen Glenn can be contacted at Empowering People, P.O. Box 1926, Orem, UT 84059–1926, phone 1-800-456-7770, website: www.empoweringpeople.com. Lynn Lott can be reached at 707-526-3141, ext. 3 or email: Maxlynski@aol.com.

Nelsen, Lott, and Glenn's Contributions to Discipline

H. Stephen Glenn

Nelsen, Lott, and Glenn's main contribution is an approach to discipline that emphasizes students' ability to control themselves, cooperate, assume responsibility, and behave in a dignified manner. They believe that these desirable traits grow especially well in groups where Positive Discipline concepts are discussed and practiced in regular class meetings. They suggest that concerns of students or teacher be written into a notebook and be made agenda items for class meetings. In those meetings, everyone participates in attempting to resolve problems in a manner satisfactory to all concerned. Involvement in that process teaches students important life skills.

Nelsen, Lott, and Glenn's Central Focus

Nelsen, Lott, and Glenn help teachers develop classrooms where students are treated respectfully and taught the skills needed for working with others. These are classrooms where students (1) never experience humiliation when they fail but instead learn how to turn mistakes into successes, (2) learn how to cooperate with teachers and fellow students to find joint solutions to problems, and (3) are provided an environment that instills excitement for life and learning in place of fear, discouragement, and feelings of inadequacy. In the process, students develop a sense of connection, belonging, and significance.

Nelsen, Lott, and Glenn's Principal Teachings

● *Discipline problems gradually become insignificant in classrooms where there is a climate of acceptance, dignity, respect, and encouragement.*
Teacher and students must work together to maintain this climate.

● *Students need to perceive themselves as capable, significant, and in control of their own lives.*
These perceptions grow best in classes that hold regular class meetings that employ the principles of *Positive Discipline.*

● *It is crucial for students to develop skills of self-control, adaptability, cooperation, and judgment.*
Classroom meetings are good venues for developing these skills.

● *Teachers must show that they truly care about their students.*
This is necessary if the desired perceptions and skills are to develop properly.

● *Teachers demonstrate caring by showing personal interest, talking with students, offering encouragement, and providing opportunities to learn important life skills.*
These tactics are crucial for every teacher.

● *Teachers can greatly facilitate desirable student behavior by removing barriers to good relationships with students and replacing them with builders of good relationships.*
By simply avoiding certain barriers, teachers quickly bring about great improvement in student behavior.

● *Class meetings should emphasize participation by everyone, group resolution of problems, and win-win solutions.*
The meetings should also be a place where everyone, teacher and students alike, practices communication, respect, support, encouragement, and cooperation.

Analysis of Nelsen, Lott, and Glenn's *Positive Discipline in the Classroom*

Positive Discipline in the Classroom is intended to empower students at all levels to become more successful, not only in the classroom but also in all walks of life. The belief that underlies this approach is that behavior problems can be greatly diminished as students acquire the skills of accepting and respecting others, communicating effectively, and focusing on solutions to problems. These outcomes are most likely to occur within a class atmosphere of kindness and firmness, where dignity and mutual respect prevail. There the mistaken goals of behavior are clarified and diminished. Positive discipline management tools are used, including encouragement and positive feedback. Collaboration occurs with other faculty, and parent/teacher/student conferences are held to communicate progress and find better ways to encourage and support students.

The authors say that class meetings are uniquely suited to implementing *Positive Discipline in the Classroom*. Although the meetings are not a cure-all, they significantly promote social skills such as listening, taking turns, hearing different points of view, negotiating, communicating, helping one another, and taking responsibility for one's own behavior. Academic skills are strengthened in the process as well because students must practice language skills, attentiveness, critical thinking, decision making, and problem solving, all of which enhance academic performance.

Class meetings also alter students' perception of teachers by helping students see that teachers and other adults need nurturing and encouragement just as much as they do. When teachers involve themselves as partners with students in class meetings, a climate of mutual respect is encouraged. Teachers and students listen to one another, take each other seriously, and work together to solve problems for the benefit of all. Antagonisms so often seen in most classrooms tend to fade away.

The Significant Seven

Nelsen, Lott, and Glenn have identified three perceptions and four skills that contribute to the special benefits of *Positive Discipline in the Classroom*. They call these perceptions and skills the significant seven, which they describe as follows:

The Three Empowering Perceptions

Class meetings help students develop **three self-perceptions** that lead to success in life:

1. Perception of *personal capabilities.* (I have ability; I can do this.)
2. Perception of *significance in primary relationships.* (I am needed; I belong.)
3. Perception of *personal power* to influence one's life. (I have control over how I respond to what happens to me.)

The Four Essential Skills

Class meetings help students develop **four essential skills** that contribute significantly to success in life:

1. *Intrapersonal skill.* (I understand my emotions and can control myself.)
2. *Interpersonal skill.* (I can communicate, cooperate, and work with others.)
3. *Strategic skill.* (I am flexible, adaptable, and responsible.)
4. *Judgmental skill.* (I can use my wisdom to evaluate situations.)

Intrapersonal Skills Young people seem more willing to listen to one another than to adults. They gain understanding of their personal emotions and behavior by hearing feedback from classmates. In a nonthreatening climate, young people are willing to be accountable for their actions. They learn to distinguish between their feelings and their actions; that is, what they feel (anger) is separate from what they do (hit someone), and although feelings are always acceptable, some actions are not.

Interpersonal Skills Class meetings encourage students to develop **interpersonal skills** by means of dialogue, sharing, listening, empathizing, cooperating, negotiating, and resolving conflicts. Teachers, instead of stepping in and resolving problems for students, can suggest putting the problem on the class meeting agenda so everyone can work to solve it together.

Strategic Skills Students develop **strategic skills,** the ability to adapt to problems, by responding to the limits and consequences imposed by everyday life. Through the problem-solving process, they learn alternative ways to express or deal with their thoughts or feelings.

Judgmental Skills Young people develop **judgmental skills,** the ability to evaluate situations and make good choices, when they have opportunity and encouragement to practice doing so. This process is fostered in classes that acknowledge effort rather than success or failure. There students find themselves in a setting that allows them to make mistakes safely, learn, and try again.

Nelsen, Lott, and Glenn suggest that teachers involve students in classroom meetings as often as feasible. There students can make mistakes in a safe atmosphere, take responsibility for the mistakes, and learn from them without being judged negatively for what they say. This helps them give up a **victim mentality** in which they blame others ("The teacher has it in for me") and accept an **accountability mentality** in which they accept personal responsibility ("I received an F because I didn't do the work"). They also learn that even when they can't control what happens, they *can* control their own responses and their resultant actions.

The Importance of Caring

The approach to discipline advocated by Nelsen, Lott, and Glenn requires that teachers truly care about students' welfare and that such caring be made evident. Teachers show they care when they go out of their way to learn about students as individuals, encourage them to see mistakes as opportunities to learn and grow, and have faith in their ability to make meaningful contributions. Students know teachers care when they feel teachers are listening to them and taking their thoughts and feelings seriously.

Relationship Barriers and Builders

Certain teacher behaviors act as barriers to developing caring relationships with students, whereas other behaviors help build such relationships. Nelsen, Lott, and Glenn identify five pairs of contrasting behaviors, which they call barriers and builders. **Barriers** are behaviors that prevent good relationships because they are disrespectful and discouraging to students, whereas **builders** are behaviors that build good relationships because they are respectful and encouraging. Here are some examples of barriers versus builders (the barrier is shown first, followed by the builder).

1. *Assuming versus Checking.* All too often teachers *assume,* without checking with students, that they know what students think and feel, what they can and cannot do, and how they should or shouldn't respond. Teachers then deal with students on the basis of those assumptions. When they do so, however, they often prevent students' unique capabilities from becoming evident. It is greatly preferable that teachers verify what students actually think and feel, which is done by *checking* with them instead of assuming.

2. *Rescuing/Explaining versus Exploring.* Teachers wish to be helpful to students. They usually think they are helpful when they explain things, rescue students from difficulties, or do some of their work for them. Students progress better, however, when allowed to perceive situations for themselves and proceed on the basis of personal perceptions. Elementary teachers explain and rescue, for example, when they say, "It's cold outside, so don't forget your jackets." They help explore when they say, "Take a look outside. What do you need to remember in order to take care of yourself?"

3. *Directing versus Inviting/Encouraging.* Teachers do not realize they are being disrespectful to students when they say, "Pick that up"; "Put that away"; "Straighten up your desk before the bell rings." But such commands have many negative effects: They build dependency, eliminate initiative and cooperation, and suggest to students it is all right to do as little as possible on their own. Directives of this type stand in contrast to *inviting and encouraging* students to become self-directed. Instead of commanding, the teacher might say, "The bell will ring soon. I would appreciate anything you might do to help get the room straightened up for the next class."

4. *Expecting versus Celebrating.* It is important that teachers hold high expectations of students and believe in their potential. However, when students are judged for falling short of expectations, they become easily discouraged, as when teachers say, "I really thought you could do that," or "I thought you were more responsible than that." Students respond far better when teachers look for improvements and then call attention to them. Attention to their improvement is quite motivating to students.

5. *"Adult-isms" versus Respecting.* Nelsen, Lott, and Glenn use the term *adult-ism* for teacher statements that suggest what students *ought to do,* such as: "How come you never . . . ?" "Why can't you ever . . . . ?" "I can't believe you would do such a thing!" These adult-isms produce guilt rather than support and encouragement. Instead of handing an unacceptable paper back and saying, "You knew what I wanted on this project!" a teacher could say, "What is your understanding of the requirements for this project?" Nelsen, Lott, and Glenn (1993) flatly state:

> We guarantee 100% improvement in student–teacher relationships when teachers simply learn to recognize barrier behaviors and stop demonstrating them. Where else can you get such a generous return for ceasing a behavior? And when the builders are added, the payoff is even greater. (p. 18)

In addition to emphasizing builders while avoiding barriers, teachers can do a number of things to show that they care about their students, such as:

- Using a supportive tone of voice.
- Listening to students and taking them seriously.
- Acting as though they enjoy their jobs.
- Appreciating the uniqueness of individual students.
- Showing a positive attitude (e.g., eagerly trying to help students).
- Showing a sense of humor.
- Showing interest in and respect for students' outside interests.
- Involving students in making decisions about the class and curriculum.
- Looking for improvement, not perfection, in student work and behavior.

Eight Building Blocks to Effective Class Meetings

As you have seen, class meetings are the primary venue for identifying and implementing the caring, supportive, and cooperative climate desired in *Positive Discipline in the Classroom*. Nelsen, Lott, and Glenn maintain that training in **eight building blocks** for effective class meetings is the surest route to the kind of classroom climate desired by students and teachers. Each of the building blocks focuses on a particular skill. It takes about two hours to introduce the eight building blocks to students. After that, about four additional class meetings will be needed to give adequate attention to what they entail.

Preliminary Considerations

Before beginning to explore the eight building blocks, introduce the concept of class meetings and get students to buy into the idea. This can be done by explaining you would like to begin holding class meetings where students can express concerns and use their power and skills to help make decisions. Elementary students are usually eager to try class meetings, but middle school and high school students may need some persuading. Using language appropriate for your grade level, begin by initiating a discussion about power, how problems are usually handled in school, and how that method results in teachers telling students what to do. The students then comply or rebel, without being brought into the decision-making process.

Next, ask students questions such as the following: Who has an example they would like to share about what happens when someone tries to control you? What do you feel? What do you do? What do you learn? Students will usually say that they feel angry or scared or manipulated. What they learn is to rebel, comply, or withdraw. Ask them also how they try to control or manipulate others, including teachers.

Continue by asking students if they would like to be more involved in the decisions that affect their lives. Would they be willing to do the work required to come up with solutions they like? Point out that some students actually *prefer* having adults boss them around so that they can rebel, or so they don't have to take responsibility themselves. It takes time and personal responsibility from everyone to use class meetings effectively. Make it clear that you don't intend to waste time teaching and learning a respectful method if they prefer continuing with the usual way in which the teacher is in control and students' only options are to comply, rebel, and/or spend time in detention. This kind of discussion is especially helpful and effective in classrooms where students have been taught with authoritarian methods.

Finally, once students indicate support for classroom meetings, decide together when the meetings will be held. Preferences vary from weekly half-hour meetings to three shorter meetings per week. A meeting every day is advisable for the first week, as students learn the eight building blocks.

Building Block 1: Form a Circle

The first step in implementing class meetings is to establish an atmosphere that allows everyone an equal right to speak and be heard and where **win-win solutions** can take place. A circular seating arrangement serves best. Ask students for suggestions about how to form the circle, listen to them, and write their ideas on the board. Make decisions based on their suggestions.

Building Block 2: Practice Giving Compliments and Showing Appreciation

It is important to begin class meetings on a positive note, which can be accomplished by having students and teacher say complimentary things to each other. Many students at first have difficulty giving and receiving compliments. Practice helps. Ask them to recall when someone said something that made them feel good about themselves. Let them share their examples with the group. Then ask them to think about something they would like to thank others for, such as thanking a classmate for lending a pencil or eating lunch together. See if they can put their feelings into words.

Receiving compliments is often as difficult as giving them. The best response to a compliment is a simple "Thank you." The notion of giving and receiving compliments seems embarrassing to some older students. When that is the case, use the term *show appreciation* instead of *compliment*.

Building Block 3: Create an Agenda

All class meetings should begin with a specific agenda. When students and teachers experience concerns, they can jot them down in a special notebook. This can be done at a designated time and place, such as when students leave the room. The class meetings will address only the concerns that appear in the notebook.

Building Block 4: Develop Communication Skills

Nelsen, Lott, and Glenn suggest a number of activities for developing communication skills, such as taking turns speaking (begin by going around the circle and letting each person speak), listening attentively to what others say, learning to use I-statements (saying "I think," "I feel," and so forth), seeking solutions to problems rather than placing blame on others, showing respect for others by never humiliating or speaking judgmentally about them, learning how to seek and find win-win solutions to problems, and framing conclusions in the form of "we decided," showing it was a group effort and conclusion.

Building Block 5: Learn about Separate Realities

In this building block, teachers focus on helping students understand that not everyone is the same or thinks the same way. Nelsen, Lott, and Glenn describe an activity that poses problem situations involving turtles, lions, eagles, and chameleons. Students discuss how each would probably feel, react, and deal with the problem. This can lead to helping students see that different people perceive situations, feel, and react in different ways.

Building Block 6: Recognize the Five Reasons People Do What They Do

Ask students if they have ever wondered why people do what they do. Ask for their ideas, acknowledge them, and then ask if they have ever heard of the primary goal of belonging and the four mistaken goals of misbehavior. Proceed by using examples to illustrate the goal of belonging and the mistaken goals of undue attention, power, revenge, and giving up.

> Author's Note: Nelsen, Lott, and Glenn use Rudolf Dreikurs's explanation of why students behave as they do. As you have seen, there are alternative explanations concerning student motivation and causes of misbehavior (see William Glasser; C. M. Charles). Nelsen, Lott, and Glenn's recommendations pertain regardless of the causes of behavior that are identified.

Building Block 7: Practice Role-Playing and Brainstorming

By the third class meeting, students are usually ready to begin considering problems and seeking solutions to them. Here are some suggestions for exploring problems in a tactful manner: (1) Discuss the key elements of the problem situation. (2) Have students act out roles involved in the problem. (3) Brainstorm a number of possible solutions to the difficulty or problem and allow students to select a solution they believe will work best.

Building Block 8: Focus on Nonpunitive Solutions

Ask students the following and write their answers on the board: "What do you feel like when someone bosses you? What do you want to do? What do you want to do when someone calls you names or puts you down? When others do these things to you, does it help you behave better?" Then ask them how their behavior is affected when someone is kind to them, helps them, or provides stimulation and encouragement. Have them compare their answers, which you have written on the board. Use the comparison to draw attention to the value of encouragement versus punishment.

Tell the students that you intend never to punish or belittle them in any way and that when they do something wrong you will try to help them behave more appropriately. Explain that what you will do to help will always be *related* to what they have done wrong, *respectful* of them as persons, and *reasonable*. These are what Nelsen, Lott, and Glenn call the **three R's of good solutions.** They explain the concept this way: If students don't do their homework, sending them to the office is not related to missed homework. A *related* solution might be to have them make up the homework or not get points for that assignment. *Respectful* means addressing the solution with dignity and consideration: "Would you like to make up the homework assignment at home or right after school?" *Reasonable* means you don't add punishment such as, "Now you'll have to do twice as much."

Standard Format for Class Meetings

Consistent with the building blocks, Nelsen, Lott, and Glenn suggest that teachers use the following format for class meetings. The teacher normally initiates the meeting and makes sure everyone abides by the rules and has an equal right to speak:

1. *Express compliments and appreciation.* Each session begins in this way as a means of setting a positive tone.
2. *Follow up on earlier solutions applied to problems.* Any suggested solution is to be tried only for a week, so it is important to determine if the solution has been working. If it hasn't, the class may wish to put the issue back on the agenda for future problem solving.
3. *Go through agenda items.* When an agenda item is read, ask the person (student or teacher) with the issue if he or she still wants help with it. If so, ask that person what a satisfactory solution could be. If he or she can't think of any, go around the circle giving every student an opportunity to offer a suggestion. Ask the student to select the most helpful solution from the suggestions offered.
4. *Make future plans for class activities.* End the class meeting by discussing a fun activity for the entire class at a future date. For example, the class might decide to set aside some time on Friday to discuss an upcoming event, view a videotape, or complete homework assignments with a friend.

What a Positive Discipline Class Meeting Looks Like

The following description was provided personally by Jane Nelsen (December 2002).

1. Students sit in a circle, and the teacher sits in the circle at the same level. (In other words, if the students are on the floor, so is the teacher. If the students are sitting in chairs, so is the teacher—as opposed to standing and teaching.)
2. As soon as possible, students lead the meeting.
3. The student in charge will start the compliments by passing an item (such as a talking stick or koosh ball) around the circle so every student has an opportunity to give a compliment, pass, or ask for a compliment.
4. The receiver of a compliment will say, "Thank you."
5. The teacher or student in charge will handle the agenda and read off the next item to be discussed.
6. After the agenda item is read, the student who placed the item on the agenda can choose among (a) sharing feelings while others listen, (b) discussing without fixing, or (c) asking for problem-solving help.
7. If the student asks for discussing without fixing or for problem-solving help, the item will be passed around the circle again for students to discuss without fixing or to brainstorm for solutions. (Short comments are also allowed.)
8. The teacher refrains from commenting on the students' suggestions (except to make sure the student is giving a suggestion. It may be necessary to say, "How could you turn that into a suggestion?"). When the item reaches the teacher, he or she can make a comment or suggestion—but only then.

9. Each suggestion is written in a notebook or on chart paper.
10. In most cases, the item will go around the circle twice to give children an opportunity to make a suggestion they didn't think of before listening to others. (This doesn't take as long as some fear.)
11. A vote will be taken only if the problem involves the whole class. Otherwise, the student who put the problem on the agenda can choose the suggestion he or she thinks will be most helpful.

Six Reasons Class Meetings Fail

The following information was provided personally by Jane Nelsen (December 2002).

1. Not forming a circle.
2. Not having the meetings regularly (three to five times per week for elementary; less often for secondary).
3. Teacher censoring what students say.
4. Not allowing students to learn nonpunitive problem-solving skills.
5. Talking down to students patronizingly instead of showing faith in their abilities.
6. Not going around the circle and allowing every student a chance to speak or pass.

Respectful Interventions and Management

Nelsen, Lott, and Glenn continually emphasize mutual respect among all members of the class. They make suggestions such as:

1. *Give students choices but make the choices appropriate and limit their number.* **Appropriate choices** are those that further the educational program. Instead of saying, "What do you want to do first this morning?" say "We can begin with our directed work or our group discussion—which do you prefer?" An **acceptable choice** is one that you, the teacher, deem worthwhile. Do not provide unacceptable choice options to students.

2. *Ask students to use a problem-solving process to settle disputes.* A **four-step problem-solving process** should be introduced for this purpose and its steps posted in the room:

Step 1. Ignore the situation. This encourages students either to avoid involvement or else leave the area of conflict for a cooling-off period.

Step 2. *Talk it over respectfully with the other students.* This is an opportunity for students to tell each other how they feel, to listen to and respect their own feelings, to figure out what they did to contribute to the problem, and to tell the other person what they are willing to do d*ifferently.*

Step 3. *Find a win-win solution.* This might involve brainstorming for solutions or simply apologizing.

Step 4. (If no solution is agreed to) *Put it on the class meeting agenda.* This shows students it is all right to ask for help.

When students come to you with a problem, refer them to the four problem-solving steps chart, and ask if they have tried any of the steps. If they haven't tried any, ask which one they would like to try. This keeps you out of the role of perpetual problem solver.

3. *When you cannot wait for a class meeting, follow through immediately.* At times, kind and firm action is called for. In 10 words or less, identify the issue and redirect the student's behavior: "I need your help to keep the noise down."

4. *When conflict occurs, ask students about it rather than telling them what to do.* Teachers tend to tell students what happened, why it happened, how they should feel about it, and what they should do. Instead of telling, teachers should ask students their perception of why it happened, how they feel about it, and how they could use that information next time. This encourages students to use judgment and be accountable for their actions. Nelsen, Lott, and Glenn say whenever you feel like telling students, stop yourself and *ask*. This is usually enough to get students to think about their behavior and decide what ought to be done.

5. *Use questions that redirect behavior.* Certain questions cause students to think about what they are doing and decide on better behavior. For example, the teacher might say, "How many of you think it is too noisy in here for people to concentrate? How many do not?"

6. *Be willing to say no with dignity and respect.* It is all right to say no. Many teachers don't think they have the right to say no without giving a lengthy explanation, but often a kind and succinct "no" is all that is required.

7. *Act more but talk less.* Most teachers would be amazed if they could hear the number of useless words they speak. It is better to let one's behavior do the talking. Use hand signals, body posture, and facial expressions.

8. *Put everyone in the same boat.* It is almost impossible to identify the culprit and judge behavior correctly in every situation that arises. When some students are talking and others are not, say, "It is too noisy in here." If someone says, "It wasn't me; I wasn't doing anything wrong," simply say, "I'm not interested in finding fault or pointing fingers but in getting the problem resolved."

Solutions Rather Than Consequences

Nelsen, Lott, and Glenn caution that it is easy to misuse logical consequences. They point out that well-meaning teachers often perpetuate the use of punishment even though they call it "logical consequences." Nelsen, Lott, and Glenn urge teachers always to think in terms of solutions rather than consequences. The following illustrates their point.

During a class meeting, students in a fifth-grade class were asked to brainstorm logical consequences for two students who didn't hear the recess bell and were late for class. Following is their list of consequences:

- Make them write their names on the board.
- Make them stay after school that many minutes.
- Take away that many minutes from tomorrow's recess.
- No recess tomorrow.
- The teacher could yell at them.

The students were then asked to forget about consequences and brainstorm for solutions that would help the students be on time. The following is their list of solutions:

- Someone could tap them on the shoulder when the bell rings.
- Everyone could yell together, "Bell!"
- They could play closer to the bell.
- They could watch others to see when they are going in.
- Adjust the bell so it is louder.
- They could choose a buddy to remind them that it is time to come in.

Notice the difference between these two lists. The first looks and sounds like punishment. It focuses on the past and making kids "pay" for their mistake. The second list looks and sounds like solutions that would help students do better in the future. It focuses on seeing problems as opportunities for learning. The first list is likely to hurt; the second is likely to help.

Among Nelsen, Lott, and Glenn's other suggestions for moving beyond consequences are:

Involve students in the solutions. When students participate in finding solutions to behavioral problems, they strengthen communication and problem-solving skills. They are also more likely to abide by agreements they have helped plan. Because they are made to feel part of the classroom community, they have less reason to misbehave and are more willing to work on solutions to problems.

Focus on the future instead of the past. When teachers apply logical consequences, they often are likely to be focusing on the past on the behavior the student has already committed. Rather than that, teachers should ask students to look to the future, thinking of solutions that will improve conditions in days to come.

Make connections between opportunity, responsibility, and consequence. Nelsen, Lott, and Glenn do not say that students should never experience logical consequences. Students need to learn that every new opportunity they encounter brings with it a related responsibility. If students are unwilling to take on the responsibility, they should not be allowed the opportunity. Nelsen, Lott, and Glenn illustrate this point as follows: Elementary students have the opportunity to use the playground during recess. Their related responsibility is to treat the equipment and other people with respect. If they treat things or people disrespectfully, the logical consequence is losing the opportunity of using the playground. A way to instill a sense of responsibility in students who have been given a consequence is to say, "You decide how much time you think you need to cool off and calm down. Let me know when you are ready to use the playground respectfully." Nelsen, Lott, and Glenn remind us that consequences are effective only if they are enforced respectfully and students are given another opportunity as soon as they are ready for the responsibility.

Be sure you don't piggyback. To piggyback is to add something to a consequence that isn't necessary and may actually be hurtful, such as, "Maybe this will teach you!" or, "You can just sit there and think about what you did!" Teachers who use piggybacking make punishment out of what would otherwise be a solution or even a respectful consequence.

Plan solutions carefully in advance.   A good way to prevent punishment's creeping into solutions is to plan out the solution in advance with student collaboration. During a class meeting, ask students to think about what sort of solutions would actually help them learn. Make the questions specific, such as, "What kind of solution do you think would help any of us to remember to use the school equipment respectfully?" "What do you think a helpful solution would be when we return books late to the library?"

Putting It All Together

When new procedures are implemented, it often takes some time before they begin to function smoothly. Nelsen, Lott, and Glenn say that if students do not respond to class meetings and other parts of Positive Discipline with the enthusiasm hoped for, don't be discouraged. You wouldn't stop teaching math or reading if students didn't grasp the concepts in a week or a month. Trust in the procedure; it will eventually come together. The goal is for long-term quality, not short-term convenience. Have faith that students and teachers can cooperate happily with each other. When putting class meetings into practice, be willing to give up *control over* students in favor of gaining *cooperation with* students. Forgo lecturing in favor of asking questions about students' thoughts and opinions. When students are encouraged to express themselves and are given choices, they become better able to cooperate, collaborate, and solve their problems.

Strengths of *Positive Discipline in the Classroom*

Nelsen, Lott, and Glenn provide a discipline program designed to help students accept responsibility and take positive control of their behavior. They say that punishment, rewards, and praise have no positive effect in developing self-directed people. They believe that each problem presents an opportunity for learning and that students learn important life skills when they help each other find positive solutions to problems. To accomplish the goals they identify, they advocate regular and frequent use of class meetings, which they believe afford the best opportunity for group discussions, identification of problems, and pursuit of solutions. They give many suggestions for making the meetings work effectively within the daily class program.

Although Nelsen, Lott, and Glenn provide lists of suggestions and cautions, the approach to discipline they advocate is not highly structured. Teachers who use it can adapt it to their needs and realities. This will be seen as a strength by teachers who like the ideas but want to make them part of their personal style of teaching. The Nelsen, Lott, and Glenn system will require some time for organizing and for student acclimatization. Therefore, its benefits may not be realized immediately, but over time they will be effective and lasting.

Initiating *Positive Discipline in the Classroom*

The Nelsen, Lott, and Glenn model of discipline depends on successful implementation of class meetings as an integral part of the instructional program. These meetings make it possible to involve students in discussions about curriculum and behavior and obtain their input in making decisions. They also furnish a venue for practicing many of the skills of communication, problem solving, and conflict resolution that Nelsen, Lott, and Glenn advocate. Therefore, a teacher wishing to implement *Positive Discipline in the Classroom* should set up class meetings and use the agenda suggested for them. They are best introduced at the beginning of the year or term. It will take time to get this approach functioning fully, but once under way it will help students develop skills that serve in life inside and outside the classroom. Any lost academic time will be regained once students begin behaving helpfully so that instruction is not disrupted.

KEY TERMS AND CONCEPTS PRESENTED IN THIS CHAPTER

The following terms are central to understanding the Nelsen, Lott, and Glenn model of discipline. Check yourself to make sure you understand them:

three self-perceptions: personal capabilities, significance in primary relationships, personal power
four essential skills: interpersonal skills, intrapersonal skills, judgmental skills, strategic skills

three R's of good solutions: related, respectful, reasonable
victim mentality
personal accountability
barriers to relationships
builders of relationships

eight building blocks for classroom meetings
win-win solutions
four-step problem-solving process

SELECTED SEVEN—SUMMARY SUGGESTIONS FROM NELSEN, LOTT, AND GLENN

Jane Nelsen, Lynn Lott, and H. Stephen Glenn suggest that you emphasize the following, as well as their many other suggestions:

1 Help students develop the skills of accepting and respecting others, communicating effectively, and focusing on solutions to problems. These skills not only lead to good behavior in the classroom but also empower students in all walks of life.

2 You must show you truly care about your students by learning about them as individuals, encouraging them to see mistakes as opportunities to learn and grow, and having faith in their ability to make meaningful contributions.

3 Work with your students in a kindly manner within a classroom climate of acceptance, dignity, respect, and encouragement. By doing so, you can gradually reduce discipline problems to an insignificant level.

4 Hold regular classroom meetings, in accordance with the eight building blocks of effective classroom

meetings. Give up some of your power in these meetings and allow students to make decisions that work for the class.

5 When working with students, remove the normal barriers to relationships and replace them with builders of relationships.

6 Help your students perceive themselves as capable, significant, and in control of their own lives. At the same time provide conditions that enable them to develop skills of self-control, adaptability, cooperation, and judgment.

7 When discussing class problems, always focus on solutions rather than consequences.

CONCEPT CASES

■ CASE 1 *Kristina Will Not Work*

Kristina, a student in Mr. Jake's class, is quite docile. She socializes little with other students and never disrupts lessons. However, despite Mr. Jake's best efforts, Kristina will not do her work. She rarely completes an assignment. She is simply there, putting forth no effort at all. *How would Nelsen, Lott, and Glenn deal with Kristina?*

One of the many possibilities they would advise Mr. Jake to do is the following: Ask Kristina if she would like to put the problem on the class meeting agenda to get ideas from the class that might be helpful. If she says yes, during a regular class meeting invite students to brainstorm ideas that might be helpful. Write down every suggestion. When finished, ask a volunteer to read the suggestions. Allow Kristina to choose the solution that would be most helpful to her, such as working with a buddy. Ask Kristina to try the solution for a week and report back in a class meeting how it is working. If she begins to do her work, give her a compliment in the class meeting. If she does not, ask her at the end of the week if she would like to put the problem on the agenda again to receive more suggestions from the class. It is rare that students do not follow through on suggestions they choose.

■ CASE 2 *Sara Cannot Stop Talking*

Sara is a pleasant girl who participates in class activities and does most, though not all, of her assigned work. She cannot seem to refrain from talking to classmates, however. Her teacher, Mr. Gonzales, has to speak to her re-

peatedly during lessons to the point that he often becomes exasperated and loses his temper. *What suggestions would Nelsen, Lott, and Glenn give Mr. Gonzales for dealing with Sara?*

■ CASE 3 *Joshua Clowns and Intimidates*

Larger and louder than his classmates, Joshua always wants to be the center of attention, which he accomplishes through a combination of clowning and intimidation. He makes wise remarks, talks back (smilingly) to the teacher, utters a variety of sound-effect noises such as automobile crashes and gunshots, and makes limitless sarcastic comments and put-downs of his classmates. Other students will not stand up to him, apparently fearing his size and verbal aggression. His teacher, Miss Pearl, has come to her wit's end. *Would Joshua's behavior be likely to improve if Nelsen, Lott, and Glenn's techniques were used in Miss Pearl's classroom? Explain.*

■ CASE 4 *Tom Is Hostile and Defiant*

Tom has appeared to be in his usual foul mood ever since arriving in class. On his way to sharpen his pencil, he bumps into Frank, who complains. Tom tells him loudly to shut up. Miss Baines, the teacher, says, "Tom, go back to your seat." Tom wheels around, swears loudly, and says heatedly, "I'll go when I'm damned good and ready!" *How would Nelsen, Lott, and Glenn have Miss Baines deal with Tom?*

QUESTIONS AND ACTIVITIES

1. In your journal, make entries from the Nelsen, Lott, and Glenn model that relate to the five principles of building a personal system of discipline.

2. Each of the following exemplifies an important point in the Nelsen, Lott, and Glenn model of discipline. Identify the point illustrated by each.
   - Miss Sterling, when Jacob interrupts her for the fifth time, says angrily, "Jacob, you go sit at the back table by yourself and stay there until you figure out how to act like a gentleman!"
   - "If I catch you talking again during the class, you will have to stay an extra five minutes."

   - "I am concerned about the lack of neatness in the work being turned in. I'd like to know your thoughts about neatness and what we might want to do, if anything, to improve."
   - "You are simply not working up to the standards I have for this class. You will need to put in more effort, or else I will have to increase the homework assignments."

3. For a grade level and/or subject you select, outline in one page what you would do if you wished to implement Nelsen, Lott, and Glenn's ideas in your classroom.

YOU ARE THE TEACHER

Middle School Library

You are a media specialist in charge of the middle school library. You see your job as serving as resource person to students who are seeking information and you are always eager to give help to those who request it. About half the students in your school are Caucasian. The remainder are African American, Hispanic American, and Asian American. Each period of the day differs as to the number and type of students who come under your direction. Small groups are usually sent to the library to do cooperative research. Some unexpected students always appear who have been excused from physical education for medical reasons but hate to be sent to the library, or else they bear special passes from their teachers for a variety of purposes.

Typical Occurrences

You have succeeded in getting students settled and working when Tara appears at your side, needing a book to read as makeup work for missing class. You ask Tara what kinds of books interest her. She resignedly shrugs her shoulders. You take her to a shelf of newly published books. "I read this one last night," you tell her. "I think you might like it. It's a good story and fast reading." Tara only glances at it. "That looks stupid," she says. "Don't you have any good books?" She glances down the shelf. "These are all stupid!" Another student, Jaime, is tugging at your elbow, with a note from his history teacher, who wants the source of a particular quotation. You ask Tara to look at the books for a moment while you take Jaime to the reference books. As you pass by a table of students supposedly doing research, you see that the group is watching Walter and Teo have a friendly pencil fight, hitting pencils together until one of them breaks. You ad-

dress your comments to Walter, who appears to be the more willing participant. Walter answers hotly, "Teo started it! It wasn't me!" "Well," you say, "if you boys can't behave yourself, just go back to your class." The other students smile and Walter feels he is being treated unjustly. He sits down and pouts. Meanwhile, Tara has gone to the large globe and is twirling it. You start to speak to her but realize that Jaime is still waiting at your side with the request for his teacher. Somehow, before the period ends, Tara leaves with a book she doesn't want and Jaime takes a citation back to his teacher. The research groups have been too noisy. You know they have done little work and wonder if you should speak to their teacher about their manners and courtesy. After the period is over, you notice that profane remarks have been written on the table where Walter was sitting.

Conceptualizing a Strategy

If you followed the suggestions of Jane Nelsen, Lynn Lott, and H. Stephen Glenn, what would you conclude or do with regard to the following?

1. Preventing the problem(s) from occurring in the first place.
2. Putting a clear end to the misbehavior now.
3. Involving other or all students in addressing the situation.
4. Maintaining student dignity and good personal relations.
5. Using follow-up procedures that would prevent the recurrence of the misbehavior.
6. Using the situation to help the students develop a sense of greater responsibility and self-control.

REFERENCES

Glenn, H., and Nelsen, J. 2000. *Raising self-reliant children in a self-indulgent world: Seven building blocks for developing capable young people.* Roseville, CA: Prima.

Glenn, H., Nelsen, J., Duffy, R., Escobar, L., Ortolano, K., and Owen-Sohocki, D. 2001. *Positive discipline: A teacher's A–Z guide.* Rocklin, CA: Prima.

Nelsen, J. 1987. *Positive discipline.* New York: Ballantine. Revised edition 1996.

Nelsen, J., and Lott, L. 2000. *Positive discipline for teenagers: Empowering your teens and yourself through kind and firm parenting.* Roseville, CA: Prima.

Nelsen, J., Lott, L., and Glenn, H. 1993. *Positive discipline in the classroom.* Rocklin, CA: Prima. Revised editions 1997, 2000.

Richard Curwin and Allen Mendler's *Discipline with Dignity*

OVERVIEW OF CURWIN AND MENDLER'S MODEL

Focus

- Establishing classroom discipline based on dignity and hope.
- Reclaiming students destined to fail in school because of their misbehavior.
- Finding long-term solutions to problems of misbehavior, including violence.
- Working productively with difficult-to-manage students.

Logic

- Through dignified discipline, we can save students who would otherwise fail in school.
- Many students misbehave when their sense of personal dignity is threatened.
- It is essential to restore a sense of hope in students who chronically misbehave.
- Violence and aggression, which teachers fear, can be dealt with effectively.

Contributions

- The concept of student dignity as the cornerstone of effective classroom discipline.
- The fact that most chronically misbehaving students have no sense of hope.
- A systematic approach to discipline based on preserving dignity and restoring hope.
- Concrete suggestions for dealing with violence, hostility, and aggression.

Curwin and Mendler's Suggestions

- Recognize that helping students behave acceptably is an integral part of teaching.
- In all circumstances, interact with students in a manner that preserves their dignity.
- Do all you can to reinstill hope of success in students who chronically misbehave.
- Never use any discipline technique that interferes with motivation to learn.

About Richard Curwin and Allen Mendler

Richard Curwin

Richard Curwin, born in 1944, began his teaching career in a seventh-grade class of boys whose behavior was seriously out of control. This experience led him to a career specialization in school discipline, first as a classroom teacher and later as a university professor and private consultant and writer. He earned a doctorate in education from the University of Massachusetts in 1972. Allen Mendler, born in 1949, earned a doctorate in psychology at Union Institute in 1981. His career has been devoted to serving as school psychologist and psychoeducational consultant. He has worked extensively with students and teachers at all levels.

Allen Mendler

Curwin and Mendler attracted national attention with their 1983 book, *Taking Charge in the Classroom.* They revised and republished that work in 1988 with the title *Discipline with Dignity,* which more accurately reflects the central concept of their approach. In 1992 Curwin published *Rediscovering Hope: Our Greatest Teaching Strategy,* a book devoted to helping teachers improve the behavior of difficult-to-control students who are otherwise likely to fail in school. In 1997 Curwin and Mendler published *As Tough as Necessary: Countering Violence, Aggression, and Hostility in Our Schools,* in which they provide suggestions for working with hostile, aggressive students. They followed in 1999 with *Discipline with Dignity for Challenging Youth,* designed to help teachers work productively with students with especially difficult behavioral problems. Curwin and Mendler regularly conduct training seminars in a wide variety of locations and make available a number of products including audio and video materials, which are listed on their website at www.disciplineassociates.com. They can be contacted through their website.

Curwin and Mendler's Contributions to Discipline

Curwin and Mendler have made two major contributions to school discipline: (1) strategies for improving classroom behavior through maximizing student dignity and hope and (2) strategies for interacting effectively with students who are hostile, aggressive, or violent. Their ideas have been especially useful to teachers who work with chronically misbehaving students. Those students—formerly about 5 percent of the student population but now a growing number—are the ones who disrupt instruction, interfere with learning, and make life miserable for teachers. Described by Curwin and Mendler as "without hope," such students deal out misery to teachers and will almost certainly fail in school unless they receive special consideration and care. Curwin and Mendler explain what without-hope students need if they are to have a chance for success in school, and they provide strategies to help teachers reclaim those students.

Curwin and Mendler's Central Focus

The central focus of Curwin and Mendler's work is on helping all students have a better opportunity for success in school through procedures that establish a sense of dignity and hope. They describe techniques that, in a dignified manner, encourage students to behave acceptably in school, and they provide a number of explicit suggestions for interacting productively with students, motivating them, ensuring success, and developing responsible behavior. In recent years they have given strong attention to working with students whose behavior is hostile and aggressive.

Curwin and Mendler's Principal Teachings

● *The number of students whose chronic classroom misbehavior puts them in imminent danger of failing in school is on the increase.*
These students are referred to as behaviorally at risk.

● *Most of these chronically misbehaving students have lost all hope of encountering anything worthwhile in school.*
A crucial responsibility of teachers is to help those students believe that school can be beneficial and that they can exert control over their own lives.

● *Students do all they can to prevent damage to their dignity, meaning their sense of self-worth.*
In attempting to protect themselves against such damage, students frequently transgress class rules and are justifiably considered to be behavior problems.

● *Five underlying principles of effective discipline should always be kept in mind.*
Those principles are that (1) discipline is a very important part of teaching, (2) short-term solutions are rarely effective, (3) students must always be treated with dignity, (4) discipline must not interfere with motivation to learn, and (5) responsibility is more important than obedience.

● *Responsibility, not obedience, is the goal of discipline.*
Responsibility, which involves making enlightened decisions, almost always produces better long-term behavior changes than does obedience to teacher demands.

● *Consequences, which are preplanned results that are invoked when class rules are broken, are necessary in discipline.*
Consequences are most effective when jointly planned by teacher and students.

● *Wise teachers deescalate potential confrontations by actively listening to the student, using I-messages, and keeping the discussion private.*
In most confrontations between teacher and student, both try to "win" the argument. The resulting struggle often escalates to a more serious level.

● *The behavior of difficult-to-manage students can be improved through providing interesting lessons on topics of personal relevance that permit active involvement and lead to competencies students consider important.*

Students who are very difficult to manage usually have little or no motivation to learn what is ordinarily taught in school, and they have little compassion or concern for others.

Analysis of Curwin and Mendler's *Discipline with Dignity*

Why Students Misbehave

All students misbehave at times. They talk without permission, call each other sarcastic names, and laugh when they shouldn't. Some do this out of boredom, some because they find certain misbehaviors (such as talking) irresistible, and some simply for expedience's sake. These kinds of misbehavior are relatively benign. They irritate teachers but do not place students in danger of failing. In contrast, other students break rules for more serious reasons, such as "gaining a measure of control over a system that has damaged their sense of dignity" (Curwin, 1992, p. 49). They exert their control by refusing to comply with teacher requests, arguing and talking back to the teacher, tapping pencils and dropping books, withdrawing from class activities, and increasing overt acts of hostility and aggression. These students have found they can't be good at learning but can be very good at being bad and, by doing so, can meet their needs for attention and power. Although such students are relatively few in number, they are not isolated. They are frequently at risk of failure in school, and they find others like themselves with whom to bond, which motivates further misbehavior.

Dignity

Dignity refers to respect for life and for oneself. It has long been at the center of Curwin and Mendler's approach to discipline. In their book *Discipline with Dignity* (2001), they point out that students with chronic behavior problems see themselves as losers and have stopped trying to gain acceptance in normal ways. In order to maintain a sense of dignity, those students tell themselves it is better to stop trying than to continue failing and that it is better to be recognized as a troublemaker than be seen as stupid.

The importance of personal dignity can hardly be overstated. Students try to protect their dignity at all costs, even with their lives when pushed hard enough. Teachers must take pains, therefore, to keep dignity intact and bolster it when possible. Curwin (1992) advises:

> We must . . . welcome high risk students as human beings. They come to school as whole people, not simply as brains waiting to be trained. Our assumptions about their social behavior need to include the understanding that their negative behaviors are based on

protection and escape. They do the best they can with the skills they have under the adverse conditions they face. . . . When they are malicious, they believe, rightly or wrongly, that they are justified in defending themselves from attacks on their dignity. (p. 27)

It is very difficult for most teachers to remain understanding and helpful when students behave atrociously. A steady diet of defiant hostility makes many teachers become cynical and give up trying to help students. Teachers who have to face such behavior on a daily basis often leave teaching because they don't feel its rewards are commensurate with the turmoil they must endure.

Students Who Are Behaviorally at Risk

Behaviorally at risk is a label given to students whose behavior prevents their learning and puts them in serious danger of failing in school. Like most labels, *at risk* is often misinterpreted and misapplied, and although helpful for communication, it provides no guidance for dealing with the problem. Curwin and Mendler, therefore, make plain that they use the term to refer solely to behavior, not to the nature of the student: "It is what students do under the conditions they are in, not who they are, that puts them at risk" (Curwin, 1992, p. xiii).

The students Curwin and Mendler refer to are those whom teachers consider to be out of control—students often referred to as lazy, turned off, angry, hostile, irresponsible, disruptive, or withdrawn. They are commonly said to have "attitude problems." They make little effort to learn, disregard teacher requests and directions, and provoke trouble in the classroom. Because they behave in these ways, they are unlikely to be successful in school. Curwin (1992) describes them as follows:

- They are failing.
- They have received, and do not respond to, most of the punishments and/or consequences offered by the school.
- They have low self-concepts in relation to school.
- They have little or no hope of finding success in school.
- They associate with and are reinforced by similar students.

The number of behaviorally at risk students is increasing steadily. Many can see no role for themselves in the mainstream. Increasingly, they experience depression and many contemplate suicide, which accounts for almost one quarter of all adolescent deaths (Curwin, 1992). Students without hope do not care how they behave in the classroom. It does not worry them if they fail, bother the teacher, or disrupt the class.

Behaviorally at risk students are difficult to control for several reasons. They usually, though not always, have a history of academic failure. Unable to maintain dignity through achievement, they protect themselves by withdrawing or acting as if they don't care. They have learned that it feels better to misbehave than to follow rules that provide no payoff. Curwin (1992) illustrates this point.

> Ask yourself, if you got a 56 on an important test, what would make you feel better about failing? Telling your friends, "I studied hard and was just too stupid to pass." Or, "It was a stupid test anyway, and besides I hate that dumb class and that boring teacher." (p. 49)

When students' dignity has been repeatedly damaged in school, it makes them feel good to lash back at others. As they continue to misbehave, they find themselves systematically removed from opportunities to act responsibly. When they break rules, they are made to sit by themselves in isolation. When they fight, they are told to apologize and shake hands. In such cases they are taken out of the very situations in which they might learn to behave responsibly. Curwin (1992) makes the point as follows:

> No one would tell a batter who was struggling at the plate that he could not participate in batting practice until he improved. No one would tell a poor reader that he could not look at any books until his reading improved. In the same way, no student can learn how to play in a playground by being removed from the playground, or how to learn time-management skills by being told when to schedule everything. Learning responsibility requires participation. (p. 50)

Students who are behaviorally at risk know and accept that they are considered to be discipline problems. They know that they can't do academic work as expected and that they are considered bothersome and irritating. Wherever they turn, they receive negative messages about themselves. They have become, in their own eyes, bad persons. How can teachers help students who see themselves as bad persons and whose only gratification in school comes from causing trouble?

Helping Students Regain Hope

Teachers can do little about the depressing conditions in society, but they can do much to help students regain a **sense of hope.** Hope is the belief that things will be better for us in the future. It inspires us and helps us live meaningfully. It provides courage and the incentive to overcome barriers. When hope is lost, there is no longer any reason to try. Students who are behaviorally at risk have, for the most part, lost hope that education will serve them. Curwin and Mendler contend that such students can be helped to regain hope and that as they do so their behavior will improve. This can be accomplished, they say, by making learning much more interesting and worthwhile. If students are to get involved in the learning process, they need something to hope for, something that will make their efforts seem worthwhile. Learning activities become successful when students see they build competence in matters students consider important (Curwin, 1992, p. 25).

Learning must not only be made attractive but, as mentioned, must bring success as well. At-risk students will not persevere unless successful, despite the initial attractiveness of the topic. To ensure success, teachers can explore ways to redesign the curriculum, encourage different ways of thinking, provide for various learning styles and sensory modalities, allow for creativity and artistic expression, and use grading systems that provide encouraging feedback without damaging the students' willingness to try.

Disciplining Difficult-to-Control Students

It should be recognized that traditional methods of discipline are ineffective with students who are behaviorally at risk. These students have grown immune to scolding, lecturing, sarcasm, detention, extra writing assignments, isolation, names on the chalkboard, or trips to the principal's office. It does no good to tell them what they did wrong; they already know. Nor does it help to grill them about their failure to do class work or follow rules. They already doubt their ability, and they know they don't want to follow rules. Sarcastic teacher remarks, because they attack students' dignity, only make matters worse. At-risk students need no further humiliation. Punishment destroys their motivation to cooperate. They see no reason to commit to better ways of behaving and, therefore, cannot achieve the results teachers hope for.

How, then, should teachers work with these students? Curwin and Mendler set forth principles and approaches they believe work significantly better than the discipline approaches normally used. They acknowledge that dealing with the chronic rule breaker is never easy and admit that the success rate is far from perfect, but they claim it is possible to produce positive changes in 25 to 50 percent of students considered to be out of control. Curwin (1992, pp. 51–54) would have teachers base their discipline efforts on the following principles:

1. *Dealing with student behavior is an important part of teaching.* Most teachers do not want to deal with behavior problems, but their attitude can change when they realize that being a professional means doing whatever they can to help each individual student. Teachers can look on misbehavior as an ideal opportunity for teaching responsibility. They should put as much effort into teaching good behavior as they put into teaching content.

2. *Always treat students with dignity.* Dignity is a basic need that is essential for healthy life; its importance cannot be overrated. To treat students with dignity is to respect them as individuals, to be concerned about their needs and understanding of their viewpoints. Effective discipline does not attack student dignity but instead offers hope. Curwin and Mendler advise teachers to ask themselves this question when reacting to student misbehavior: "How would this strategy affect my dignity if a teacher did it to me?"

3. *Good discipline must not interfere with student motivation.* Any discipline technique is self-defeating if it reduces motivation to learn. Students who become involved in lessons cause few discipline problems. Poorly behaved students usually lack motivation to learn what is being offered them. They need encouragement and a reason to learn. Curwin suggests that teachers, when about to deal with misbehavior, ask themselves this question: "What will this technique do to motivation?"

4. *Responsibility is more important than obedience.* Curwin differentiates between obedience and responsibility as follows: Obedience means "do as you are told." Responsibility means "make the best decision possible." Obedience is desirable in matters of health and safety, but when applied to most misbehavior it is a short-term solution against which students rebel. Responsibility grows, albeit slowly, as students have the opportunity to sort out facts and make decisions. Teachers should regularly provide such opportunities.

Consequences

Consequences refer to what teachers have students do when they break class rules. Curwin and Mendler differentiate among four types of consequences: logical, conventional, generic, and instructional. **Logical consequences** are those in which students must make right what they have done wrong. The consequence is logically related to the behavior. If students make a mess, they must clean it up. If they willfully damage material, they must replace it. If they speak hurtfully to others, they must practice speaking in ways that are not hurtful.

Conventional consequences are those that are commonly used in practice, such as time-out, removal from the room, and suspension from school. They are rarely logically related to the behavior. Curwin and Mendler suggest modifying conventional consequences so as to increase student commitment. For time out, they suggest that instead of banning the student for a specified length of time, teachers should say something such as "You have chosen time-out. You may return to the group when you are ready to learn."

Generic consequences are reminders, warnings, choosing, and planning that are invoked when misbehavior is noted. Often simple *reminders* are enough to stop misbehavior: "We need to get this work completed." *Warnings* are very firm reminders: "This is the second time I have asked you to get to work. If I have to ask you again, you will need time-out." *Choosing* allows students to select from three or four options a plan for improving their behavior. Planning, which Curwin (1992) calls "the most effective consequence that can be used for all rule violations" (p. 78), requires that students plan their own solution to a recurring behavior problem. Planning conveys that the teacher has faith in the student's competence. That faith often engenders a degree of commitment. The plan should name specific steps the student will follow and should be written, dated, and signed.

Instructional consequences teach students how to behave properly. Simply knowing what one ought to do does not ensure correct behavior. Some behaviors, such as raising one's hand or speaking courteously, are learned more easily when taught and practiced.

Curwin (1992, pp. 79–80) makes a number of suggestions concerning how teachers should use consequences, such as the following:

- Always implement a consequence when a rule is broken.
- Select the most appropriate consequence from the list of alternatives, taking into account the offense, situation, student involved, and the best means of helping that student.
- State the rule and consequence to the offending student. Nothing more need be said.
- Be private. Only the student(s) involved should hear.
- Do not embarrass the student.
- Do not think of the situation as win-lose. This is not a contest. Do not get involved in a power struggle.
- Control your anger. Be calm and speak quietly but accept no excuses from the student.
- Sometimes it is best to let the student choose the consequence.
- The professional (teacher) always looks for ways to help the client (student).

An **insubordination rule** should be established that removes the student from the classroom when the student refuses to accept an assigned consequence.

Preventing Escalation

When teachers respond to student misbehavior, students often dig in their heels and a contest of wills ensues, with neither side willing to back down. Curwin and Mendler remind teachers that their duty is not to win such contests but to do what they can to help the student. This requires keeping the channels open for rational discussion of problem behavior. That cannot be done if the teacher humiliates, angers, embarrasses, or demeans the student. This point is critical for high-risk students, who are predisposed to responding negatively. Curwin (1992) suggests that teachers do the following toward **preventing escalation** of incipient conflicts:

- Use active listening. Acknowledge and/or paraphrase what students say without agreeing, disagreeing, or expressing value judgments.
- Arrange to speak with the student later. Allow a time for cooling off. It is much easier to have positive discussions after anger has dissipated.
- Keep all communication as private as possible. Students do not want to lose face in front of their peers and so are unlikely to comply with public demands. Nor do teachers like to appear weak in front of the class. When communication is kept private, the chances for productive discussion are much better because egos are not so strongly on the line.
- If a student refuses to accept a consequence, invoke the insubordination rule. Don't use this provision until it is clear the student will not accept the consequence.

Motivating Difficult-to-Manage Students

Rules, consequences, and enforcement are necessary in all classrooms, but the key to better student behavior lies elsewhere—in motivation. Most students make an effort to learn and behave properly in school, whether because they find school interesting, like to please the teacher, or simply want to avoid failure. Such is not the case for students behaviorally at risk. It would be foolish to suggest that a magical set of techniques exists for helping such students. But teachers do know what motivates students in general. Students who are behaviorally at risk have the same general needs and interests as other students, but they have encountered so much failure that they have turned to resistance and misbehavior to bolster their egos. Curwin (1992, pp. 130–144) makes the following suggestions for increasing motivation among students who are behaviorally at risk:

- Select for your lessons as many topics as you can that have personal importance and relevance to the students.
- Set up authentic learning goals—goals that lead to genuine competence that students can display and be proud of.
- Help students interact with the topics in ways that are congruent with their interests and values.

- Involve students actively in lessons. Allow them to use their senses, move about, and talk. Make the lessons as much fun as possible. Lessons needn't be easy if they are important and enjoyable.
- Give students numerous opportunities to take risks and make decisions without fear of failure.
- Show your own genuine energy and interest in the topics being studied. Show that you enjoy working with students. Try to connect personally with them as individuals.
- Each day, do at least one activity that you love. Show pride in your knowledge and ability to convey it to your students. Don't be reluctant to ham it up.
- Make your class activities events that students look forward to. Make them wonder what might happen next.

Dealing with Aggression, Hostility, and Violence

Curwin and Mendler have concluded that students are becoming increasingly aggressive, hostile, and violent, and they are doing so at an earlier age. Teenagers are two and a half times more likely to experience **violence** than people over age 20. Curwin and Mendler say the increase in violence has occurred in part because society has been rewarding and punishing students in school, home, and community rather than teaching them values—such as that it is wrong to intimidate others, hurt them physically, or destroy their property. A large proportion of students who use violence lack a sense of compassion or remorse and, thus, do not respond to normal discipline techniques. This makes it especially difficult for teachers to work with them productively.

Curwin and Mendler have addressed this problem in their 1997 book *As Tough as Necessary: Countering Violence, Aggression, and Hostility in Our Schools.* They point out that by "as tough as necessary" they do not mean the zero-tolerance tactic now used in many schools. Instead, they mean using "a variety of ways to help aggressive, hostile, and violent children learn alternatives to hurting others" (p. ix). They contend that "behavior change among hardened, antisocial, and angry students cannot occur simply by offering more love, caring, and opportunities for decision making" (p. 16). They say that if schools are to deal with violence, they must adopt schoolwide approaches that (1) teach students how, when threatened or frustrated, to make nonviolent choices that serve them more effectively than do violent choices, (2) model for students nonhostile methods of expressing anger, frustration, and impatience, and (3) emphasize the teaching of values that relate to cooperation, safety, altruism, and remorse.

A Four-Phase Plan for Schools and Educators

Curwin and Mendler suggest a four-phase plan for schools and educators to help students move toward value-guided behavior. The four phases are (1) identifying the core values that the school wishes to emphasize, (2) creating rules and consequences based on the core values identified, (3) modeling the values during interactions with students and staff, and (4) eliminating interventions that violate the core values. The following are some suggestions they offer within each of the four phases.

Identify the Core Values of the School

Curwin and Mendler suggest that each school have faculty, staff, students, and parents work together to specify a set of core values that shows how they want individuals in the school to conduct themselves and relate to each other. A set of core values might include statements such as the following (1997, p. 24):

■ School is a place where we solve our problems peacefully.
■ School is a place where we protect and look out for one another rather than attack or hurt one another.
■ School is a place where we learn we are responsible for what we do.
■ School is a place where we learn that my way is not the only way.

Create Rules and Consequences Based on the Core Values

Rules are needed to govern classroom behavior, and those rules should be based on the school's stated values. Whereas the values state broad intentions, rules say exactly what one should and should not do. This can be seen in the following examples (1997, p. 31):

Value	*Rule*
■ School is a place where we protect and look out for one another rather than hurt or attack one another.	■ No put-downs allowed.
■ School is a place where we solve our problems peacefully.	■ Keep your hands and feet to yourselves.

Model Values with Students and Staff Members

It is essential that teachers and administrators continually model behaviors that correspond with the school values. Teachers must express their emotions nonviolently, use positive strategies to resolve conflict with students, and walk away when they receive put-downs from students. Curwin and Mendler (1997, p. 32) suggest the following as helpful to teachers. Individually or in staff meetings write on paper how you want students to express their anger toward you and how you want them to resolve classroom conflicts with you and other students. Then teach your students these techniques and use them yourself in practice.

Eliminate Interventions That Violate Core Values

Teachers everywhere tend to rely on their past experiences when responding to student misbehavior. Their responses often take the form of threats, intimidation, and using students as examples for others. Responses of these types fail to model behavior consistent with school values and tend to produce further conflict. Threats, for example, destroy student comfort in the classroom. If carried out vengefully, they produce a backlash of resentment. If made but not carried out, student behavior worsens, which calls for still more dire threats that cannot be carried out. Students in turn conclude that it is all right to threaten others, since the teacher does so. That cycle is broken by showing students the dangers of threats and teaching them alternative behaviors.

The same applies to intimidation and using students as examples. Those were mainstay tactics of a majority of teachers years ago and are still evident in many classrooms. When teachers intimidate students, students may cower (or may not), but the students in turn become more likely to treat others in the same way. It is also self-defeating to reprimand one student as an example for others. The resultant humiliation felt by the disciplined student produces a permanent effect. The primary goal of interventions is to help students learn more responsible behavior. We cannot accomplish this through hurtful tactics but instead must model positive, nonviolent behavior, use it when intervening in student behavior, and help students to use it in their interactions with others.

Specific Suggestions for Dealing with Conflict

Teachers who agree with approaches to deter violence still ask the legitimate question, "What specifically do I do when . . . ?" To answer that question, Curwin and Mendler provide many concrete suggestions, such as (1997, p. 66):

- Use privacy, eye contact, and proximity when possible. Speak privately and quietly with the students. This preserves their dignity and takes away the likelihood of their fighting back.
- Indicate to the student politely but clearly what you want. Say "please" and "thank you" (e.g., "Bill, please go to Mr. Keene's room. There's a seat there for you. Come back when you are ready to learn. I hope that doesn't take very long. Thank you, Bill.")
- Tell the student that you see a power struggle brewing that will do no one any good. Defer discussion to a later time. (e.g., "Juan, you are angry and so am I. Rather than have a dispute now, let's calm down and talk later. I'm sure we can help each other out after we cool off. Thanks a lot.")

Techniques for Dealing with Violence in the Classroom

Curwin and Mendler suggest several strategies for teachers and students to use when they encounter violence. These strategies are designed first to help everyone calm down, decide how to proceed, and take positive steps. Teachers should teach the procedures to students and model them in practice. The following are a few of the many techniques suggested (1997, pp. 94–118):

Use the six-step solution: (1) Stop and calm down. Wait a moment, take a deep breath, and relax. (2) Think—quickly explore options and foresee what will happen if you use them. (3) Decide what you want to have happen. (4) Decide on a second solution in case the first doesn't work. (5) Carry out the solution you deem best. (6) Evaluate the results—have you accomplished what you hoped? Will you use the tactic again in similar circumstances?

Solving my problems: First, name the problem, indicating specifically what somebody has said or done. Second, say what you would like to have happen. Third, say what you will do to make things happen as you would like. Fourth, make a backup plan to use in case the first doesn't work. Fifth, carry out the plan.

Learning to have patience: As we grow up we learn that our needs can't always be met when we'd like and that often we have to wait. If we don't learn to have patience, we will feel frustrated and angry because we are not getting what we want when we want it. Learning to be patient requires practice on actions such as walking away from a fight, waiting in line with a smile, and remaining calm when somebody cuts in line.

Wearing an invisible shield: Pretend you are wearing an invisible shield that deflects all bad thoughts and unkind words. It makes you immune to them. You cannot be hurt as long as you are wearing it.

Using words that work: Instead of being provoked into retaliation, you can practice saying things that will stop almost all attacks, such as (1) being polite, using words such as "please" and "thank you," (2) asking if you have done something that has upset the other person, and (3) apologizing if you have offended the person.

Planning for confrontations: Name five situations you recall in which people got into a dispute. Next to each, write down strategies you think would bring the situation calmly to a close. Practice what you would say and do should you find yourself in one of the situations.

Suggestions to Help Teachers Retrain Themselves

It is helpful for teachers to prepare themselves in advance for situations they might encounter. Curwin and Mendler suggest doing the following (1997, p. 71):

- Write down things students do or say that you find irritating.
- Determine why students do those things. What basic needs are they trying to meet? What motivates them?
- What do you presently do when students say or do irritating things?
- Are your current tactics effective in solving the problem?
- What response strategies can you think of that address the reasons for the irritating behavior while at the same time model behavior consistent with school values?
- Practice the strategies beforehand and then put them into practice at the next opportunity.

Suggestions for Working with Challenging Students

Most teachers have to work at times with students who are unusually defiant, hostile, stubborn, offensive, or unmotivated. To help those teachers be more successful, Mendler and Curwin (1999) developed an approach outlined in their book *Dignity with Discipline for Challenging Youth.* A cornerstone of the approach is helping teachers make changes *in themselves* that enable them better to meet the needs of their students. In this work, Curwin and Mendler make many practical suggestions for dealing with three major problem areas—lack of student motivation, attention problems, and gang-related behavior.

You have seen that *Discipline with Dignity* urges teachers to treat all students with dignity while emphasizing student responsibility. For working with challenging students, Curwin and Mendler add or reemphasize these suggestions:

1. *Take steps to overcome your natural resistance to working with challenging youth.* Adopt the stance that we teachers are responsible for teaching all students. Although we may not be successful with all of them, we must treat all as being worthy of our best effort. Take advantage of the fact that difficult students offer us opportunities to educate for better behavior in all aspects of life. Think of discipline as instruction for such behavior change. As a point of departure, identify the reasons for student misbehavior, do what you can to correct the causes in your class, and teach students about the causes and how to deal with them. Curwin and Mendler say students misbehave because they want to be noticed and feel connected, want to hide feelings of inadequacy, are impulsive, desire fun and stimulation, see little connection between school and life, do not empathize well with others, and need to express anger.

2. *Develop a repertoire of effective discipline strategies and be patient and persistent.* Think of discipline strategies as falling into three categories—crisis (e.g., fighting), short term (stopping misbehavior while preserving the dignity of teacher and student), and long term (working to meet the needs of students over time.) Effective crisis strategies call for specific plans of action you will take when crises arise. Short-term strategies include I-messages, PEP (privacy, eye contact, proximity), PEP notes or cards with words or phrases of appreciation or correction, privacy 3-step (privately set a limit, offer a choice, or give a consequence), and LAAD tactics (listening, acknowledging, agreeing, deferring action). Ongoing and longer-term strategies include remedying the causes of misbehavior and reframing the context in which we consider challenging students, using affirmative rather than negative labels, such as "sticks up for himself" rather than "defiant," or "has yet to find the value in lessons" rather than "lazy."

Other long-term discipline strategies include creating a caring classroom, teaching student self-control, teaching student concern for others, setting clearly defined limits on behavior, emphasizing responsibility more than obedience, teaching conflict-resolution skills that students can apply, and helping students network with others, such as classroom peers, older students, staff members, volunteers, and mentors. It is important that we always look for common ground with troublesome students and maintain the conviction that all students can change. One of the great challenges is to stay personally involved with each student without taking obnoxious, irritating, disruptive, and hurtful behavior personally. We are reminded that 70 percent of school misbehavior has its roots at home rather than at school. It is our obligation to break the cycle of hostility and aggression by not retaliating in kind.

3. *Always strive for responsible student behavior rather than mere obedience.* Do this by establishing sensible limits on behavior and allowing students choices within these limits, such as writing or drawing as a way of expressing anger. Help students learn from the consequences of their behavior and, in the process, develop a commitment to change. In all cases, place more emphasis on motivation than on discipline.

4. *Use tactics that tend to overcome student resistance.* Such tactics include personal interest, personal interaction, kindness, helpfulness, encouragement, acknowledgment of effort, and use of challenge rather than threat. Check each strategy you consider against the following:

> Does it promote dignity or humiliation?
> Does it teach responsibility or obedience?
> Does it motivate students to learn?
> Does it foster commitment?

Strengths of Curwin and Mendler's *Discipline with Dignity*

Most teachers have found ways to deal with minor behavior infractions such as talking, speaking out, chewing gum, and failing to complete homework. But all teachers dread dealing with students whose behavior is so unacceptable they not only disrupt learning but also threaten others. Such behaviors make teachers feel trapped and overwhelmed. Curwin and Mendler have provided realistic help for working with such students and for reducing behavior that is hostile, aggressive, and violent.

Initiating Curwin and Mendler's *Discipline with Dignity*

Suppose you teach a class that contains several chronically misbehaving students, and you feel the Curwin and Mendler model can help you deal with them more effectively. How do you get it in place and make it operational?

Before using the approaches Curwin and Mendler propose, you must subscribe to four principles that support their model. The first of these principles, and the most important, is that student dignity must be preserved. Students will do all in their power to protect their dignity. They don't want to appear stupid, feel incapable, or be denigrated, especially in front of their peers. When faced with a threat, students, especially the chronically misbehaved, use antisocial behavior to counter it. You must be willing to guard against threatening students' dignity, even when they threaten yours.

A second principle is that dealing with misbehavior is an important part of teaching. You are in the classroom to help your students. Those whose behavior puts them at risk of failure especially need your help, though their behavior may suggest that they want nothing to do with you. The best thing you can do for them is to find ways to encourage prosocial behavior.

A third principle is that lasting results are achieved only over time. There are no quick-fix solutions to chronic misbehavior, but by finding ways to motivate students and help them learn, you will enable many to make genuine improvement.

A fourth principle is that responsibility is more important than obedience. The ability to weigh facts and make good decisions is far more valuable in students' lives than obedience to demands. You must be willing to put students into situations in which they can make decisions about matters that concern them, be willing to allow them to fail, and then help them try again. Progressively, they will learn to behave in ways that are best for themselves and others.

Curwin and Mendler (1999, pp. 13–16) identify 12 points that provide functionality to *Discipline with Dignity.*

1. Let students know what you need.
2. Provide instruction at levels that match students' abilities.
3. Listen to what students are thinking and feeling.
4. Use humor.
5. Vary your style of presentation.
6. Offer choices.
7. Refuse to accept excuses.
8. Legitimize behavior you cannot stop.
9. Use hugs and pats when communicating with students.
10. Be responsible for yourself and allow students to be responsible for themselves.
11. Accept that you will not effectively help every student.
12. Start fresh every day.

You will have given much thought to the kind of classroom you want and how you want your students to behave. When you first meet the students, spend as much time as necessary discussing goals for the class, activities that might be helpful, and class behavior that will improve enjoyment and accomplishment for everyone. In those discussions, teacher and students should agree to class rules and consequences. It is important that students contribute to those decisions and agree to abide by them. The rules and consequences should be written out, dated, and signed by teacher and students. The document should be posted in the room and copies sent to parents and administrators.

From the outset you must seek to structure lessons to help students be active and successful. It is far better that students engage in activities they find interesting than be dragged perfunctorily through the standard curriculum. Your own energy, enjoyment of learning, and pride in teaching will affect students positively, while your willingness to help without confrontation will slowly win them over.

KEY TERMS AND CONCEPTS PRESENTED IN THIS CHAPTER

The following terms are central to the Curwin and Mendler model of discipline. Check yourself concerning their meanings:

dimensions and principles of discipline: prevention, action, resolution, no short-term solutions

instructional consequences
conventional consequences
generic consequences

logical consequences
violence
social contract

insubordination rule
behaviorally at risk
challenging youth

sense of hope
dignity
responsibility

preventing escalation

SELECTED SEVEN—SUMMARY SUGGESTIONS FROM CURWIN AND MENDLER

Richard Curwin and Allen Mendler suggest that you emphasize the following, as well as their many other suggestions:

1 Safeguard and support student dignity in all class matters. Students make every effort to preserve dignity, even if doing so requires misbehavior.

2 Do what you can to foster students' sense of hope that they will benefit from education. Students who have lost hope usually don't care how they behave.

3 Approach discipline as a very important part of teaching. It can teach students how to conduct themselves in ways that bring success in life.

4 Do not rely on short-term solutions to behavior problems. They are rarely effective.

5 Focus on student responsibility, not obedience, as the primary goal of discipline.

6 Use personal attention and good teaching to experience success with students who are considered to be chronic troublemakers.

7 In accordance with suggestions provided, prepare yourself to respond effectively to students who are hostile, disobedient, and inconsiderate.

CONCEPT CASES

■ CASE 1 *Kristina Will Not Work*

Kristina, in Mr. Jake's class, is quite docile. She never disrupts class and does little socializing with other students. But despite Mr. Jake's best efforts, Kristina rarely completes an assignment. She doesn't seem to care. She is simply there, putting forth virtually no effort. *How would Curwin and Mendler deal with Kristina?*

They would suggest the following sequence of interventions: Consider that Kristina's behavior might be due to severe feelings of incapability. She may be protecting herself by not trying. Relate to Kristina as an individual. Chat with her informally about her life and interests. Find topics that interest Kristina and build some class lessons around them. Assign Kristina individual work that helps her become more competent in her areas of special interest. Have a private conversation with Kristina. Ask for her thoughts about how you could make school more interesting for her. Show her you are interested and willing to help. As Kristina begins to work

and participate, continue private chats that help her see herself as successful.

■ CASE 2 *Sara Cannot Stop Talking*

Sara is a pleasant girl who participates in class activities and does most, though not all, of her assigned work. She cannot seem to refrain from talking to classmates, however. Her teacher, Mr. Gonzales, has to speak to her repeatedly during lessons, to the point that he often becomes exasperated and loses his temper. *What suggestions would Curwin and Mendler give Mr. Gonzales to help with Sara's misbehavior?*

■ CASE 3 *Joshua Clowns and Intimidates*

Larger and louder than his classmates, Joshua always wants to be the center of attention, which he accomplishes through a combination of clowning and intimidation. He makes wise remarks, talks back (smilingly) to the teacher, utters a variety of sound-effect noises such as automobile crashes and gunshots, and makes limitless sarcastic comments and put-downs of his classmates. Other students will not stand up to him, apparently fearing his verbal and physical aggression. His teacher, Miss Pearl, has come to her wit's end. *What do you find in Curwin and Mendler's work that might help Miss Pearl deal with Joshua?*

■ **CASE 4** *Tom Is Hostile and Defiant*
Tom has appeared to be in his usual foul mood ever since arriving in class. On his way to sharpen his pencil, he bumps into Frank, who complains. Tom tells him loudly to shut up. Miss Baines, the teacher, says, "Tom, go back to your seat." Tom wheels around and says heatedly, "I'll go when I'm damned good and ready!" *How would Curwin and Mendler have Miss Baines deal with Tom?*

QUESTIONS AND ACTIVITIES

1. In your journal, enter ideas from *Discipline with Dignity* that apply to the five principles of building a personal system of discipline.

2. In small groups, conduct practice situations in which classmates act as students who make hurtful comments to you, the teacher. Begin with the examples given here and explore new ones you have seen or think might occur. Take turns being the teacher and responding to the comments in some of the ways Curwin and Mendler suggest.

   Example 1

   Teacher: Jonathan, I'd like to see that work finished before the period ends today.

   Jonathan: [Sourly] Fine. Why don't you take it and finish it yourself if that's what you want?

   Teacher:

   Example 2

   Teacher: Desirée, that's the second time you've broken our rule about profanity. I'd like to speak with you after class.

   Desirée: No thanks. I've seen enough of your scrawny tail for one day.

   Teacher:

   Example 3

   Teacher: Marshall, I'd like for you to get back to work, please.

   Marshall: [Says nothing but nonchalantly makes a derogatory face at the teacher. Other students see it and snicker.]

   Teacher:

   Compose additional occurrences. Practice deescalating the confrontations without becoming defensive, fighting back, or withdrawing your request.

3. One of the suggestions given for motivating reluctant students was "Make your class activities events that students look forward to. Make them wonder what might happen next." For a selected grade level, brainstorm ways of complying with this suggestion.

4. Many suggestions were made for anticipating and dealing with violent, aggressive, or hostile behavior. What would you do to prepare yourself for situations involving such behavior?

YOU ARE THE TEACHER

Continuation High School Photography Lab
You teach photography lab, an elective class, in a continuation high school attended by students who have been unsuccessful for behavioral reasons in regular high school settings. Many of the students want to attend this particular school, as it is located in what they consider their turf. Some of the students are chemically dependent and/or come from dysfunctional homes. The photography lab class enrolls 15 students, all of whom are on individual study contracts.

Typical Occurrences
As students begin work, you busy yourself with a number of different tasks such as setting out needed materials,

giving advice on procedures, handing out quizzes for students who have completed contracts, examining photographs, and so forth. You see Tony sitting and staring into space. You ask him if he needs help. He shrugs and looks away. You ask him if he has brought his materials to work on. He shakes his head. You tell Tony he can start on a new part of his contract. He doesn't answer. You ask what's the matter. When Tony doesn't respond, Mike mutters, "He's blasted, man." At that moment, you hear heated words coming from the darkroom. You enter and find two students squaring off, trying to stare each other down. You ask what the problem is but get no reply. You tell the boys to leave the darkroom and go back to their seats. Neither makes the first move. As tension grows, another student intervenes and says, "Come on, you can settle it later. Be cool." You call the office and inform the counselor of the incident. The boys involved hear you do so and gaze at you insolently. The class settles back to work, and for the remainder of the period you circulate among them, providing assistance, stifling horseplay, urging that they move ahead in their contracts, and reminding everyone that they only have a limited amount of time in which to get their work done. From time to time you glance at Tony, who does no work during the period. You ask Tony again if something is bothering him. He shakes his head. You then ask him if he wants to transfer out of the class, since it is elective. Tony says, "No, man, I like it here." "That's fine," you say, "but this is not dream time. You do your work, or else we will find you another class. You understand?" "Sure, I understand." You turn away, but from the corner of your eye you are sure you see Tony's middle finger aimed in your direction.

Conceptualizing a Strategy

If you followed the suggestions of Richard Curwin and Allen Mendler, what would you conclude or do with regard to the following?

1. Preventing the problem from occurring in the first place.
2. Putting a clear end to the misbehavior now.
3. Involving other or all students in addressing the situation.
4. Maintaining student dignity and good personal relations.
5. Using follow-up procedures that would prevent the recurrence of the misbehavior.
6. Using the situation to help the students develop a sense of greater responsibility and self-control.

REFERENCES

Curwin, R. 1992. *Rediscovering hope: Our greatest teaching strategy.* Bloomington, IN: National Educational Service.

Curwin, R., and Mendler, A. 1988. *Discipline with dignity.* Alexandria, VA: Association for Supervision and Curriculum Development. Revised editions 1992, 1999, 2001. Upper Saddle River, NJ: Merrill.

Curwin, R., and Mendler, A. 1997. *As tough as necessary. Countering violence, aggression, and hostility in our schools.* Alexandria, VA: Association for Supervision and Curriculum Development.

Mendler, A., and Curwin, R. 1999. *Discipline with dignity for challenging youth.* Bloomington, IN: National Educational Service.

CHAPTER 9

Barbara Coloroso's
Inner Discipline

OVERVIEW OF COLOROSO'S MODEL

Focus

- Treating students with respect.
- Giving students the power and responsibility to make decisions.
- Providing guidance and support to help students manage their own discipline.
- Helping students accept ownership for problems and resolve them accordingly.
- Helping all students participate in putting an end to bullying.

Logic

- Teachers can help students develop inner discipline.
- Students learn decision making by making decisions and learning from the results.
- Consequences should not be punitive but should invite positive student responses.
- Students develop inner discipline by accepting ownership of misbehavior and dealing with it constructively.

Contributions

- Depicted classrooms as places to learn problem solving and develop inner discipline.
- Clarified the differential effects of consequences, rewards, bribes, and punishment.
- Explained how students can accept ownership of personal misbehavior and resolve it.
- Explained how students and teachers, working together, can break the cycle of bullying.

Coloroso's Suggestions

- Truly believe students are worth every effort you can make on their behalf.
- Treat students as you, yourself, like to be treated.
- Make an unconditional commitment to help your students develop needed behavior skills.
- Give students opportunity to solve their problems. Ask them how they plan to do so.
- Use reasonable consequences for behavior, rather than bribes, rewards, or threats.

147

About Barbara Coloroso

Barbara Coloroso

Barbara Coloroso, a former Franciscan nun, is now a parent, teacher, workshop leader, author, and affiliate instructor at the University of Northern Colorado. She contends that schools have a major duty to develop responsibility in students and that the climate for a responsibility-oriented school is based on trust cultivated by teachers and administrators. Her ideas are set forth in her books *Kids Are Worth It!: Giving Your Child the Gift of Inner Discipline* (1994, 2002), *Parenting with Wit and Wisdom in Times of Chaos and Confusion* (1999), and *The Bully, the Bullied, and the Bystander: How Parents and Teachers Can Break the Cycle of Violence* (2003). She has also made numerous contributions to educational publications on topics such as strategies for working with troubled students, creative media for students with special needs and talents, and assertive confrontations and negotiations. Her "Kids Are Worth It!" series includes videos, audiotapes, and workbooks to assist educators in developing a discipline system that creates trust, respect, and success in school. The materials are available from Kids Are Worth It!, P.O. Box 621108, Littleton, CO 80162. Coloroso can be contacted through her website at www.kidsareworthit.com.

Coloroso's Contributions to Discipline

Coloroso has identified three different categories of student misbehavior, which she calls mistakes, mischief, and mayhem, and has explained what teachers should do when they encounter each category. She describes how to use discipline rather than punishment in a manner that enables students to take charge of their lives. She contends that good discipline shows students what they have done wrong, has them assume ownership of the problem that is created, and gives them ways to solve the problem, all the while leaving their dignity intact. She stresses that children develop inner discipline by learning how to think, not just what to think. She shows how to ensure that students experience natural or reasonable consequences for their behavioral choices, and she provides the RSVP test, described later, for use when deciding on consequences. More recently, Coloroso has set forth suggestions for dealing positively with bullying, which has become a major concern in schools everywhere.

Coloroso's Central Focus

Coloroso puts major emphasis on helping students make their own decisions and then shows them how to take responsibility for their choices. She believes that in order to have good discipline, teachers must do three things: (1) Treat students with respect and dignity, (2) give them a sense of positive power over their own lives, and (3) give them opportunities to make decisions, take responsibility for their actions, and learn from their successes and mistakes. She believes that students, given adult help, have the ability to develop inner discipline and manage problems they encounter. She says that under these conditions students can grow to like themselves, think for themselves, and believe there is no problem so great it can't be solved.

Coloroso's Principal Teachings

- *Students are worth all the effort teachers can expend on them.*
  They are worth it not just when they are bright, good looking, or well behaved but always.

- *School should be neither adult dominated nor student controlled.*
  Rather, it should be a place where joint efforts are made to create a sense of community in which everyone can relate, grow, and create.

- *Teachers should never treat students in ways they, the teachers, would not want to be treated.*
  Children have dignity and innate worth, and they deserve to be treated accordingly.

- *If a discipline tactic works and leaves student and teacher dignity intact, use it.*
  Self-worth and dignity are to be maintained; anything that damages them is to be avoided.

- *Proper discipline does four things that punishment cannot do:*
  (1) shows students what they have done wrong, (2) gives them ownership of the problems involved, (3) provides them strategies for solving the problems, and (4) leaves their dignity intact.

- *In order to develop inner discipline, children must learn how to think, not just what to think.* To this end, teachers must give students responsibility and allow them to make mistakes.

- *Students have the right to be in school, but they also have the responsibility to respect the rights of those around them.*
  Rights and responsibility go hand in hand.

- *Disputes and problems are best resolved through win-win procedures.*
  Rather than rescuing students or lecturing them, teachers can give students opportunities to solve their problems in ways that everyone finds acceptable.

- *Consequences, natural and reasonable, should be clearly associated with rules.*
  Those consequences are allowed or invoked when rules are violated.

- *Natural consequences are events that happen naturally in the real world.*
  You kick a chair and the consequence is that you hurt your toe. Teachers should allow students to experience natural consequences so long as the consequences are not physically dangerous, immoral, or unhealthy.

- *Reasonable consequences are events imposed by the teacher that are related to a violation of rules.*
  If you damage material on loan from a museum, you might write a letter of apology to the museum indicating how you will repair or otherwise fix the damage and avoid a similar accident in the future.

● *Misbehavior falls into three categories: mistakes, mischief, and mayhem.*

Mistakes are simple errors that provide opportunity for learning better choices. Mischief, although not necessarily serious, is intentional misbehavior. It provides opportunity to help students find ways to fix what was done and learn how to avoid doing it again while retaining their dignity. Mayhem, which is willfully serious misbehavior, calls for application of the Three R's.

● *The Three R's provide guidance in helping students take responsibility and accept consequences.*

The first R, restitution, means to somehow repair whatever damage was done. The second R, resolution, involves identifying and correcting whatever caused the misbehavior so it won't happen again. The third R, reconciliation, entails healing relationships with people who were hurt by the misbehavior.

● *The RSVP test is used to check on consequences the teacher imposes.*

It reminds teachers that consequences must be reasonable, simple, valuable, and practical.

● *Students who experience consistent, logical, realistic consequences learn that they themselves have positive control over their lives.*

On the other hand, students who are constantly bribed, rewarded, and punished become dependent on others for approval, work only to please the teacher, and figure out how to avoid getting caught when they misbehave.

● *When reasonable consequences are invoked, students frequently try to get teachers to change their minds, but teachers must not give in.*

Students may cry, beg, argue angrily and aggressively, and sulk. They should not get their way by doing so.

● *Bullying, which devastates the morale of great numbers of students, can be brought to an end.*

Teachers and students can work together to stifle bullying. They must do so if a climate of support is to be maintained to help students profit from school.

Analysis of Coloroso's *Inner Discipline*

Coloroso's views on discipline are consistent with recent trends that assign students a more active role in taking responsibility for their behavior. She believes educators should work with students to help them develop **inner discipline,** which she defines as the ability to behave creatively, constructively, cooperatively, and responsibly without being directed by someone else.

Coloroso firmly contends that teachers must believe that their students have innate value, that those students are worth all effort expended in their behalf, and that the students can learn to be responsible for their own behavior, make their own decisions, and resolve their own problems. Students do not easily develop these qualities naturally. Most require help to do so. The best way for teachers to help is to allow students to make decisions and grow from the results of those decisions, whatever they may be. Teachers have the responsibility to make sure that student decisions do not lead to situations that are physically dangerous, morally threatening, or unhealthy. Otherwise, the role of teachers is to bring students to situations that require decisions and, without making judgments, let them proceed through the process.

What students then do will sometimes make teachers and students uncomfortable. The discomfort disappears when students resolve the problem constructively. This experience builds the power to deal with problem situations and keeps students' self-esteem intact because it gives responsibility and power to them. Teachers must trust students with this responsibility and power.

Three Types of Schools, Teachers, and Families

Coloroso describes three basic types of schools, teachers, and families that have very different effects on students. She calls the types *brickwalls, jellyfish, and backbones.*

Brickwall schools, teachers, and families are strict and rigid. They exert control on the young through power and coercion. They demand that others follow rules and they use punishment, humiliation, threat, and bribes to make them do so.

Jellyfish schools, teachers, and families are wishy-washy with little recognizable structure, consistency, or guidelines. Adults are lax in discipline, set few limits, and more or less let the young have their way, but when sufficiently provoked they turn to lecturing, put-downs, threats, and bribes. Some jellyfish teachers have little faith in students and believe that if anything is to get done they must do it themselves.

Backbone schools, teachers, and families provide support and structure necessary for the young to reason through problems and behave responsibly. Students get opportunities to make decisions and correct mistakes they make with full support from the teacher. Because the teacher neither tells them what to do nor does the work for them, they learn how to think and act on their own.

Tenets of *Inner Discipline*

Coloroso bases her work on two fundamental tenets. The first is that students are worth all the time, energy, and effort it takes to help them become resourceful, responsible, resilient, compassionate human beings. The second tenet reflects the golden rule and is worded this way: "I will not treat a student in a way I myself would not want to be treated." Discipline based on this proposition places limits on power and control while making the preservation of dignity and self-worth paramount.

Discipline, Not Punishment

In order to deal successfully with today's discipline problems, teachers must abandon punishment and rely on what Coloroso calls "discipline." She describes **punishment** as treatment that is psychologically hurtful to students and likely to provoke anger, resentment, and additional conflict. She calls it adult-oriented imposed power. Students typically respond to punishment with the **three F's**—fear, fighting back, or fleeing. They become afraid to make a mistake. Students rarely know for sure that a given act will bring punishment. They see it as depending on who the student is, which teacher catches the student, and how the teacher feels at the time.

Discipline, on the other hand, is a process that helps students see what they have done wrong and gives them ownership of the problem. It provides options and opportunities to solve problems and in so doing leaves students' dignity intact. It uses reasonable, simple, valuable, and practical (**RSVP**) consequences to help students see that they are responsible for and in control of themselves. Those consequences either occur naturally or are provided by the teacher but are always related to decisions students have made. By making clear the connections between behavior and consequences, teachers help students better understand whether their behavior has been responsible or irresponsible. Discomfort that arises from irresponsible behavior only goes away after teacher and students work together to resolve the problem constructively.

Three Types of Misbehavior

Coloroso illustrates the foregoing points in relation to three types of student misbehavior—mistakes, mischief, and mayhem—that are usually handled with either punishment or discipline. As noted earlier, **mistakes** are simply errors in behavior, made without intent to break rules. They provide opportunity to learn how to behave more acceptably. **Mischief** goes beyond mistakes. It is intentional misbehavior, though not necessarily serious, and presents an opportunity for teaching students that all actions have consequences that are sometimes pleasant and sometimes not. It also provides opportunity for showing students ways to solve their problem with dignity.

Mayhem, a more serious type of intentional misbehavior, is harmful to people and property. When it occurs, teachers should apply the **Three R's of reconciliatory justice—restitution,** which means repairing or otherwise fixing whatever damage has been done; **resolution,** which involves identifying and correcting whatever caused the misbehavior so it won't occur again, and **reconciliation,** which is the process of establishing healing relationships with people who were hurt by the misbehavior.

When students misbehave, teachers can respond with either discipline or punishment. The distinction between the two is vitally important because it affects how students learn to solve problems and deal with trauma. Discipline helps children grow up to be responsible, resourceful, resilient, compassionate humans, who feel empowered to act with integrity and a strong sense of self. Punishment, on the other hand, causes children to become adept at making excuses, blaming, and denying while feeling powerless, manipulated, and not in control (Coloroso, 1999, p. 223).

Coloroso explains why these different effects occur. She says punishment removes vital opportunities to learn integrity, wisdom, compassion, and mercy, all of which contribute to inner discipline. Discipline, in contrast, helps children learn how to handle problems positively they will encounter throughout life. It does so by providing four things (1999, p. 227):

1. It helps make students fully aware of what they have done.
2. It gives students as much ownership of the problem as they are able to handle.

3. It provides options to help students solve the problem.
4. It leaves student dignity intact.

Let's see how these ideas apply to real situations:

Anna in kindergarten. Anna is very enthusiastic about the coloring lesson, so enthusiastic that she colors beyond the paper and onto her desk with the permanent marker she is using. Anna never intended to damage her desk. It was an accident, but the marks remain. Her teacher, Mrs. Alvarez, hopes to get the marks off the desk and also prevent the accident from happening again. She believes in giving Anna partial responsibility for resolving the problem, so she asks Anna to use a special cleaner to remove as much as possible. Mrs. Alvarez also realizes that such accidents could be prevented if she would cover the desks with paper and make sure Anna and the others use washable pen or chalk for their art projects.

Fifth-grader Aaron. Aaron has shown little interest in the lessons Mr. Flynn is presenting about the Civil War. Aaron is very interested in rockets and so while Mr. Flynn tells about battles that happened far away and long ago, Aaron uses the clip from his marker to scratch a rocket on his desk. At recess Mr. Flynn notices the damage. Mr. Flynn, though distressed, knows that Aaron needs discipline, not punishment. He talks with Aaron and points out that the desk requires refinishing. He mentions various possibilities including contacting a professional refinisher, asking Aaron's father to come help, or allowing Aaron to do the job under Mr. Flynn's guidance. Aaron opts for doing it himself. He makes arrangements to remain after school. Mr. Flynn gets materials from the school custodian and shows Aaron how to remove the finish from the affected area and then apply a matching finish. Mr. Flynn's strategy of invoking reasonable consequences allows Aaron to take ownership of the problem, show responsibility for his actions, and maintain his personal dignity.

Alexis in high school. Alexis is a starting player on the high school basketball team, but because she received a detention from her chemistry teacher for several tardies, Coach Stein informs her she will have to sit out the next game. Even though this is school policy, Alexis thinks the chemistry teacher harbors a grudge against her and is upset that Coach Stein doesn't back her up. While angry, Alexis writes some unacceptable comments on the locker room wall. When Coach Stein finds the damage, she knows other girls have seen it and she feels hurt, disappointed, and angry. Her first reaction is to call Alexis in and suspend her for another game, but after considering the situation further she realizes punishment of that sort would be unproductive and might not help Alexis make better choices in the future. Coach Stein decides to encourage Alexis to accept ownership of the problem and the attendant mayhem she has created. Coach Stein realizes this can happen only in an atmosphere of compassion, kindness, gentleness, and patience. Somehow Alexis must repair the damage she did to the locker room, make a plan to ensure it won't happen again, and also mend fences with her coach, teammates, and the chemistry teacher. Coach Stein makes plans to meet with Alexis and help her acknowledge what she has done wrong, help her assume ownership of the problem, and help her identify options for dealing with the problem. Coach Stein knows all this must be done in a way that preserves Alexis's dignity.

Effective Classroom Discipline Leads to Inner Discipline

The ultimate purpose of discipline, illustrated in the Anna, Aaron, and Alexis cases, is to enable students to make intelligent decisions, accept the consequences of their decisions, and use the consequences to help them make better decisions in the future. Recognizing the relationship between decisions and their consequences teaches students that they have control over their lives, which is a requisite for the development of inner discipline.

Coloroso assigns teachers a key role in bringing about inner discipline. She believes teachers can best help by bringing students face-to-face with their problems and exposing them to tactics for resolution. She says that before teachers can see themselves in this role rather than the role to which they are traditionally accustomed, they must ask themselves two questions and answer them honestly: "What is my goal in teaching?" and "What is my teaching philosophy?" The first has to do with what teachers hope to achieve with learners, and the second with how they think they should accomplish the task. Coloroso says that because teachers act in accordance with their beliefs, it is important for them to clarify those beliefs: "Do I want to empower students to take care of themselves, or do I want to make them wait for teachers and other adults to tell them what to do and think?" Teachers who feel they must control students turn to bribes, rewards, threats, and punishment to restrict and coerce behavior. Teachers who want to empower students to make decisions and resolve their own problems give students opportunities to think, act, and take responsibility.

When given this opportunity, students will not always make the best choices. For that reason they must be provided a safe and nurturing environment in which to learn and deal with consequences. Teachers should allow and respect student decisions, even when those decisions are clearly in error, and must let students experience the consequences of their decisions. Even when consequences are unpleasant, students learn from them and at the same time learn that they have control over their lives through the decisions they make. When teachers understand this process, they see that it is counterproductive to nag, warn, and constantly remind students of what they ought to be doing.

Teaching Decision Making

Coloroso says that the best way to teach students how to make good decisions is to bring them to situations that call for decisions, ask them to make the decision (while the teacher provides guidance without judgment), and let them experience the results of their decision. This may seem inefficient, but it produces rapid growth in ability to solve one's own problems. Mistakes and poor choices become the students' responsibility. If they experience discomfort, they have the power to correct the situation in the future.

Coloroso believes that teachers should never rescue students by solving thorny problems for them. Doing so sends the message that students don't have power in their own lives and that some other person must take care of them. When students make mistakes, as they will do, teachers must not lecture them: "If you had studied more, you wouldn't have failed the test." Students already know this. What they now need is opportunity to correct the situation they have created. Coloroso suggests saying the following to them: "You have a problem. What is your plan for dealing with it?"

When students are given ownership of problems and situations, they know it is up to them to make matters better. There is no one else to blame. Teachers are there to offer advice and support but not to provide solutions. This may entail only a subtle difference in reaction. Rather than telling a student, "You can't go to the library during choice time until you finish your math assignment" (punishment), a teacher should say, "You can go to the library during choice time when you finish your math assignment" (discipline). This simple response difference better allows students to take responsibility for their mistakes rather than rationalizing them away.

The Three Cons

When students violate class rules, they should know that consequences will come into play. But even when the consequences are expected and reasonable, students will try to get out of them. Coloroso describes three ploys you can expect students to use in hopes of escaping consequences. She calls them the **three cons** and describes them as follows:

Con 1: Students beg, bribe, weep, and wail, trying to get teachers to let them by ("Oh, please, oh, please"). Some teachers give in and admonish students, saying "All right this once, but you better never do that again." Coloroso says that when teachers do this, the message they are really sending is: "I don't believe in you or trust in you. . . . I'll have to take care of you." This attitude works against students developing a sense of inner discipline. If Con 1 fails, students often follow with the second.

Con 2: Students respond with anger and aggression: "I hate this stupid class." Because Con 2 affects teachers' emotions, they tend either to become passive or lash back. Passivity invites aggression, and lashing back tends to produce counterattack. Teachers must do neither. They must remain calm and say, "I'm sorry you do, but this is the consequence we have agreed to."

Con 3: Students sulk. Sulking is the most powerful of the three cons: Students' actions say, "I'm not gonna do what you say. You can't make me." It is true that teachers cannot force students to do anything they choose not to do. But it only makes matters worse to say something like "That's right! Go ahead and pout!" Students are virtually certain to follow that suggestion. The best course is calmly to invoke the consequence in a matter-of-fact way.

Coloroso says teachers lose positive power in students' lives when they give in to pleas or bribes, become angry at students in response to students' anger, and reinforce sulking. To retain their positive power, teachers should encourage students to own both the problem and the solution.

Problem Solving

Problem solving is one of the most important skills students can learn. They will learn better and more quickly if they know that it is all right to make mistakes. They must also learn to distinguish between reality and problem, with *reality* being an accurate appraisal of what has occurred in a situation and *problem* being the discomfort caused by the reality. Coloroso says that in learning to solve problems, "We first accept (the) realities; (then) we solve the problems that come from them" (1994, p. 31). Coloroso contends that as students make the distinction between reality and problem they begin to see that there is no problem too great to be solved. But when faced with a problem, students need a way of attacking it. The approach they use should be formed in a plan, not laid out as an excuse. Coloroso suggests a problem-solving strategy that consists of six steps:

1. *Identify and define the problem.* Accurate identification of the problem is necessary if students are to resolve it effectively. Josh asks for the book he lent Melissa. He needs it for a report due on Friday. Melissa can't find the book but remembers she left it on the kitchen table near the books her mother was donating to the library. Both Josh and Melissa experience a problem—discomfort for Josh regarding the assigned report and pressure on Melissa for not returning the book. Let us look at the problem from Melissa's perspective. How is it to be resolved?

2. *List possible solutions.* Melissa's first thoughts about dealing with the problem are to say she left the book on Josh's desk or else avoid Josh. After she thinks about it a bit, she identifies three more options: See if she can find the book at the library, buy a new book for Josh, or borrow Randy's book for Josh to use.

3. *Evaluate the options.* Melissa considers the options and finds one that might work for her. Lying, the option she first identified, isn't satisfactory. Though the thought crossed her mind, Melissa decides she is unwilling to lower herself to that level. The second cannot work either: Josh is her neighbor and they usually do homework together after school. The third is a possibility: The book may have been returned to the library and can be found there. The fourth is an option but not a desirable one: Melissa borrowed the book in the first place because she didn't want to pay what a new book cost. The fifth would be only a temporary solution and, besides, Randy needs his book for himself.

Melissa's teacher has taught her to ask herself four questions about each of the options she has identified. They are:

- Is it unkind?
- Is it hurtful?
- Is it unfair?
- Is it dishonest?

Melissa recognizes that the first option would be dishonest, the second hurtful, and the fifth unfair to both Randy and Josh. She is in the process of learning that negative qualities only lead to further trouble. That leaves her two possible options: check the library again or buy a replacement book.

4. *Select the option that seems most promising.* Melissa decides she must go to the public library and see if the book can be found. If the book is located, she will explain the circumstances and get the book back.

5. *Make a plan and carry it out.* Admitting to and owning a problem, making a plan, and following through are difficult things to do for adults as well as children. It means that ex-

cuses are not acceptable, and it means one must accept responsibility for mistakes and consequences. If the plan does not work, then a new option must be tried. If Melissa cannot find the book at the library, she will have to borrow money from her parents to replace the book. That will mean taking on extra chores to repay them, but it is a responsibility she knows she must accept.

6. *In retrospect, reevaluate the problem and the solution.* Most people skip this step, but it is important for learning. Three questions should be asked:

> What caused the problem in the first place?
> How can a similar problem be avoided in the future?
> Was the problem solution satisfactory?

In this instance the problem was probably caused accidentally. However, if Melissa is often careless in misplacing things she needs, a change in her behavior is called for. She might improve by designating a special place in which to put borrowed items. In this process of solving the problem, Melissa's self-esteem has remained intact and her sense of ability to solve problems has been reinforced. No one told her what to do. She maintained positive control over her own decisions.

Natural Consequences

When students are allowed to solve their own problems, their decisions will lead to consequences they may or may not anticipate. Coloroso believes in allowing consequences to occur without adult intervention, provided the consequences are not harmful. For example, if Jacob walks to the gym without his coat, he will get cold. Being cold is a natural consequence to dressing improperly for weather and temperature. If Fazilat borrows crayons but returns them broken, her table mates will stop lending her their crayons.

But when consequences are harmful to students, the teacher should intervene to prevent them. If Jose and Zachary are fighting on the playground, it is no time for the teacher to stand aside so the boys can work out the situation between them. The teacher must intervene and the boys will have to experience reasonable consequences that have been established for fighting. The teacher must also intervene when students make decisions that are unlawful or unethical. When a student steals from another or spreads lies or engages in sexual harassment, the resultant problem may be outside the students' power to resolve. The teacher will need to step in to stop the behavior, but use it as the basis for discussions about behavior that is right and wrong.

Reasonable Consequences and RSVP

Sometimes natural consequences do not produce discomfort and, thus, are ineffective in helping students learn. This is especially the case when students decide to break rules that have been established for the good of the class, as when they shout out during instruction. To deal with behavior such as this, teacher and students should jointly agree to a set of reasonable logical consequences that will be invoked when rules are broken. Coloroso proposes a checklist she calls RSVP to use in establishing the quality of such consequences. **RSVP** stands for reasonable, simple, valuable, and practical. Reasonable, logical consequences do not punish but instead call on students to take positive steps to improve behavior. Consequences can only do this when they make students uncomfortable enough to realize there is a problem. Then in order to solve the problem the student will be helped to see what has been done wrong, understand that ownership of the problem must be accepted, and accept that a good way must be found to resolve the situation.

Dealing with Bullying

Recently, Coloroso has begun addressing the problem of bullying, which she labels "the deadliest combination going: bullies who get what they want from their target, bullied kids who are afraid to tell, bystanders who either watch, participate, or look away, and adults who see the incidents as simply 'teasing' and a normal part of childhood" (2003, jacket). Students agree that bullying is a big problem at school and something they must deal with every day.

Coloroso asserts that bullying is not about anger or conflict but rather about contempt—"a powerful feeling of dislike toward somebody considered to be worthless, inferior or undeserving of respect" (2003, p. 20). Whether it is blatant or subtle, bullying is willful and deliberate and always includes three elements: imbalance of power, intent to harm, and threat of further aggression. Bullies intend to hurt, emotionally or physically, and they enjoy it. Prolonged bullying intimidates and sustains dominance. Children who are bullied surrender themselves as powerless. They are afraid to fight back or tell anyone about the bullying. Bystanders follow or support the bullies or do nothing to stop the action. This is how the cycle of violence persists.

There are three types of bullying. **Verbal bullying** uses words to torture and torment. Examples are name-calling, taunting, false rumors and gossip, racial slurs, and sexist language. **Physical bullying** is the most visible and outwardly aggressive form but accounts for less than one-third of the bullying incidents reported by children (2003, p. 16). Hitting, slapping, punching, pinching, arm-twisting, choking, kicking, biting, and scratching are forms of physical bullying. **Relational bullying** shuns, isolates, excludes, or ignores students. It is the most difficult to recognize and is insidious because it undermines the bullied student's sense of self. Often students who are bullied are too ashamed to tell anyone about it. However, they often reveal clues through their eyes, face, body, tone of voice, and words.

Bystanders contribute to the problem by watching or supporting the bully and taking no action. Some join in. Others are passive and afraid if they say anything they will get hurt or become targets of bullying themselves. Often they simply don't know what to do.

Coloroso (2003, pp. 179–180) lists five things educators should do to reduce bullying in school. She credits Dan Olweus (1999) of the University of Norway for the following:

1. Gather information about bullying at school directly from students.
2. Establish clear schoolwide and classroom rules about bullying.
3. Train adults in the school to respond consistently and sensitively to bullying.

4. Provide adequate adult supervision, particularly in less structured areas, such as the playground and lunchroom.
5. Improve parental awareness of and involvement in working on the problem.

Coloroso goes on to say that the energy of bullies can be redirected into positive leadership. Bullied students can be helped by bringing attention to their particular strengths and talents, while bystanders can be taught and encouraged to ". . . stand up, speak out, and act against injustice" (2003, p. 202). These actions help break the cycle of violence and widen the circles of courage and caring.

Strengths of Coloroso's *Inner Discipline*

Coloroso believes in students' ability to accept ownership of their problems, resolve those problems, and live by the consequences of their decisions. She believes this process helps students take charge of their lives.

Coloroso sees discipline as a schoolwide concern and would have schools establish an overarching positive climate that permits students and teachers to make mistakes, resolve problems, and profit from the mistakes.

Within this broad climate, students would understand that they have a rightful place in school but that they also have the responsibilities to respect the rights of others and to be actively involved in their own behavior and learning. They would learn they must take ownership of their decisions and not try to rationalize mistakes, and they would do their part to end the violence of bullying. Doing these things would allow all students to maintain their personal sense of dignity.

Coloroso provides teachers a manageable approach to effective discipline. Her beliefs are humanistic and focused on preserving dignity and sense of self-worth. Coloroso believes it is through experiences with these qualities that students develop inner discipline.

Initiating Coloroso's *Inner Discipline*

To begin using Coloroso's *Inner Discipline,* you must genuinely incorporate two tenets into your beliefs about teaching:

- All students are worth all I am capable of contributing to them.
- I will not treat a student in a way I myself would not want to be treated.

With those tenets in mind, you should formalize a plan for how you will work with the class. If you follow Coloroso's suggestions, the plan will provide for the following:

1. *Develop rules to guide the class.* Involve students in helping compose them. Restrict the rules to what you can see or hear students do. Make them specific and be sure they are

linked to meaningful consequences. Both rules and consequences should be reasonable, simple, valuable, and practical.

2. *Hold class discussions on the rules, their implications, and their consequences.* Students need to hear and understand each rule, the reasons for the rule, and the consequences for violating the rule. Students need to believe they are capable of following the rules and able to make reasonable choices. Rules and consequences must be presented in such a way that students believe choice and responsible behavior are truly available to them.

3. *If a rule is broken, the teacher should concentrate immediately on the behavior and consequences.* (Do not bend a rule because of who the student is but only when the situation makes it necessary.) Apply consequences in accordance with the following:

- Help students see what they did wrong.
- Make sure students differentiate between the reality and the problem.
- Give students ownership of the problems they have created.
- Help them find ways to solve those problems.
- Do all of this in a way that leaves their dignity, and yours, intact.
- For more serious infractions, students will need to move further to the three R's of reconciliatory justice: restitution, resolution, and reconciliation. That means they need to fix what was done wrong, figure out how to keep it from happening again, and heal relationships with the people they have harmed.

4. *Get across to students that it is OK, even beneficial, to make mistakes,* and that no problem is so great that it can't be solved.

5. *Help students understand that when they have a problem, they need a plan, not an excuse.* The teacher's role is to encourage students to solve problems in constructive ways, while experiencing the real-world consequences of their choices.

6. *Take into account the fact that discipline problems are likely to result when rules are unclear and enforcement is inconsistent.* This is often the case in common areas such as halls, playgrounds, lunchrooms, and restrooms, where different people are on duty. When setting up a discipline procedure, it is best that the entire school be involved in the same program, including faculty, staff, aides, and others. When everyone is on the same page, students know the rules and consequences wherever they might be in the school.

KEY TERMS AND CONCEPTS PRESENTED IN THIS CHAPTER

The following terms and concepts are central to Coloroso's *Inner Discipline.* Check yourself to make sure you understand them:

discipline	mischief	logical consequences
punishment	mayhem	natural consequences
ownership of problem	brickwall	RSVP
inner discipline	jellyfish	the 3 R's of reconciliatory justice: res-
mistakes	backbone	olution, restitution, reconciliation

three cons   bystanders   physical bullying
bully   three F's   relational bullying
the bullied   verbal bullying

SELECTED SEVEN—SUMMARY SUGGESTIONS FROM BARBARA COLOROSO

Barbara Coloroso suggests that you emphasize the following, as well as her many other suggestions:

1 Always treat students the way you yourself want to be treated.

2 Empower students by teaching them how to make good decisions and accept responsibility for them.

3 Remember that any discipline strategy you use must leave intact the dignity of both students and teacher.

4 Strive to use "proper discipline," which does four things: (1) shows students what they have done wrong, (2) gives them ownership of the problems created, (3) provides them ways to solve the resultant problems, and (4) leaves their dignity intact.

5 Strive for win-win solutions to problems and disputes.

6 Use the Three R's to help students take responsibility for their actions—restitution (correcting any harm that was done), resolution (identifying and correcting whatever caused the misbehavior), and reconciliation (apologizing or otherwise healing the relationship with people who were hurt).

7 Work together with your students to put an end to bullying. This is necessary if a climate of support is to be maintained to help students profit from school.

CONCEPT CASES

■ CASE 1 *Kristina Will Not Work*

Kristina, a student in Mr. Jake's class, is quite docile. She socializes little with other students and never disrupts lessons. However, despite Mr. Jake's best efforts, Kristina will not do her work. She rarely completes an assignment. She is simply there, putting forth no effort at all. *How would Coloroso deal with Kristina?*

In order to convey that she believes and trusts in Kristina's ability, Coloroso might quietly say, "Kristina, I see the work is not getting done. This is not in keeping with our class agreement. It seems this might be a problem. I wonder what we can do to resolve it. Perhaps we can think of some possible solutions and come up with a plan to help you finish your work. I'd like you to see if you can do that." Kristina then might identify some options: She might ask for extra help, work with another student, copy the answers during review, or do extra problems from another assignment to make up for the ones she misses. Guiding her through the problem-solving and decision-making process, Coloroso listens to Kristina without making judgments and helps her evaluate the options. Suppose Kristina decides to work with another student. She has taken responsibility for the

problem and selected an option to help her solve it. Later that week Coloroso may say to Kristina, "Now that you have been studying with Saundra, how is this working for you? Is this a satisfactory solution for you? I appreciate that you solved this problem and now are finishing your work." If Kristina's response indicates that this option was not successful, Coloroso can support her again through the decision-making process.

■ CASE 2 *Sara Cannot Stop Talking*

Sara is a pleasant girl who participates in class activities and does most, though not all, of her assigned work. She cannot seem to refrain from talking to classmates, however. Her teacher, Mr. Gonzales, has to speak to her repeatedly during lessons, to the point that he often becomes exasperated and loses his temper. *What suggestions would Coloroso give Mr. Gonzales for dealing with Sara?*

■ CASE 3 *Joshua Clowns and Intimidates*

Larger and louder than his classmates, Joshua always wants to be the center of attention, which he accomplishes through a combination of clowning and intimidation. He makes wise remarks, talks back (smilingly) to the teacher, utters a variety of sound-effect noises such as automobile crashes and gunshots, and makes limitless sarcastic comments and put-downs of his classmates. Other students will not stand up to him, apparently fearing his size and verbal aggression. His teacher, Miss Pearl, has come to her wit's end. *Would Joshua's behavior be likely to improve if Coloroso's techniques were used in Miss Pearl's classroom? Explain.*

■ **CASE 4** *Tom Is Hostile and Defiant*

Tom has appeared to be in his usual foul mood ever since arriving in class. On his way to sharpen his pencil, he bumps into Frank, who complains. Tom tells him loudly to shut up. Miss Baines, the teacher, says, "Tom, go back to your seat." Tom wheels around, swears loudly, and says heatedly, "I'll go when I'm damned good and ready!" *How would Coloroso deal with Tom?*

QUESTIONS AND ACTIVITIES

1. In your journal, enter ideas from Coloroso's model that apply to the five principles of developing a personal system of discipline.

2. Each of the following exemplifies or relates to an important point in the Coloroso model of discipline. Identify the point illustrated by each.
   a. When Miles joined his friends to play basketball, he wore his new sneakers rather than his play shoes. When it began to rain, his new shoes got muddy and wet, which made Miles quite unhappy.
   b. Ms. Benedict is very angry and hurt that Alejo tore pages from one of her favorite read-aloud books. However, she wants to help him find a way to fix the damage, understand what he did, and make a plan so he won't do it again. Also, she wants to help him mend fences, both with her and with his classmates.
   c. When Angeline continued to be tardy to fifth-period algebra, Mrs. Wayne asked her to identify some options and come up with a plan so she could arrive to class on time. When Angeline presented her plan to Mrs. Wayne, they agreed to implement it and evaluate the results in two weeks.
   d. Brian's father is a member of the school board and his mother is active in the Parent-Teacher Association. David's mother is on welfare and does not participate in school activities. When the two boys play recklessly with tools in the wood shop class, Brian is given a verbal warning whereas David has to watch a film on proper tool handling and safety.

3. For a grade level and/or subject you select, outline in one page what you would do if you wished to implement Coloroso's ideas in your classroom.

YOU ARE THE TEACHER

Second Grade

You teach second graders in a highly transient neighborhood. You receive an average of one new student each week, and those students typically remain in your class for fairly short lengths of time before moving elsewhere. Most are from somewhat dysfunctional homes, and their poor behavior, including aggression, boisterousness, and crying, seems to reflect many emotional problems.

A Typical Occurrence

The morning bell rings, and students who have been lined up outside by an aide enter the classroom noisily.

You are speaking with a parent who is complaining that her son is being picked on by others in the class. When finally able to give attention to the class, you see that Ricky and Raymond have crawled underneath the reading table, while a group of excited children is clustered around Shawon who has brought his new hamster to share with the class. Two girls are pulling at your sleeve, trying to give you a note and lunch money. You have to shout above the din before you can finally get everyone seated. Several minutes have passed since the bell rang. Having lost much of your composure, you finally get the reading groups started when you suddenly remember the assembly scheduled for that morning. You stand up from your reading group and exclaim, "We have an assembly this morning! Put down your books and get lined up quickly! We are almost late!" Thirty-one students make a burst for the door, pushing and arguing. Rachael, a big, strong girl, shoves Amy and shouts, "Hey, get out of the way, stupid!" Amy, meek and retiring, begins to cry. You try to comfort Amy while Rachael pushes her way to the front of the line. During the assembly, Ricky and Raymond sit together. They have brought some baseball cards and are entertaining the students seated around them. When the first part of the assembly performance is over, they boo loudly and laugh instead of applaud. Under the school principal's stern eye, you separate Ricky and Raymond, but for the rest of the performance they make silly faces and gestures to each other, causing other students to laugh. Upon returning to the classroom, certain that the principal will speak to you about your class's behavior, you try to talk with the students about the impropriety of their actions. You attempt to elicit positive comments about the assembly, but several students say it was dumb and boring. The discussion has made little progress before time for recess. You sigh and direct the students to line up, reminding them again to use their best manners. As they wait at the door, Rachael is once again shoving her way to the head of the line.

Conceptualizing a Strategy

If you followed the suggestions of Barbara Coloroso, what would you conclude or do with regard to the following?

1. Preventing the problem from occurring in the first place.
2. Putting a clear end to the misbehavior now.
3. Involving other or all students in addressing the situation.
4. Maintaining student dignity and good personal relations.
5. Using follow-up procedures that would prevent the recurrence of the misbehavior.
6. Using the situation to help the students develop a sense of greater responsibility and self-control.

REFERENCES

Coloroso, B. 1994. *Kids are worth it!: Giving your child the gift of inner discipline.* New York: Avon Books. Revised edition, 2002, New York: HarperCollins.

Coloroso, B. 1999. *Parenting with wit and wisdom in times of chaos and loss.* New York: HarperCollins.

Coloroso, B. 2003. *The bully, the bullied, and the bystander: How parents and teachers can break the cycle of violence.* New York: HarperCollins.

Olweus, D. 1999. *Olweus' core program against bullying and antisocial behavior: A teacher handbook.* Research Center for Health Promotion [HEMIL], Bergen, Norway: University of Bergen. www.uib.no/psyfa/hemil/ansatte/olweus.html.

Budd Churchward's *Honor Level System of Discipline*

OVERVIEW OF CHURCHWARD'S MODEL

Focus

- Discipline that fosters aspiration to high levels of honorable behavior.
- Assisting proper behavior impartially and following through consistently.
- Comprehensive application to multiple classrooms or the entire school.
- Removing stress from discipline for both students and teachers.

Logic

- Most students behave well in school when provided the incentive for doing so.
- A behavior management program should help students stay out of trouble.
- Behavior is managed better when the entire school uses the same program.
- Behavior management is facilitated through computerized record keeping.

Contributions

- A proactive program that relates proper behavior to the concept of honor.
- A program that can be used consistently and impartially by the entire school.
- A proven way of removing stress from discipline for both students and teachers.
- A plan that allows students easily to redeem themselves after they make mistakes.

Churchward's Suggestions

- Base your discipline program on helping students stay out of trouble.
- Use high levels of responsibility as intrinsic motivators for good behavior.
- Work with fellow teachers to establish optimally effective classroom discipline.
- Manage behavior consistently and impartially in a kind and helpful manner.

About Budd Churchward

Budd Churchward

Budd Churchward, creator of the Honor Level System of discipline, taught elementary school for 12 years and middle school for 18 years. With his background in classroom and computer technology, he has successfully helped hundreds of schools in the United States and other countries to set up schoolwide discipline programs that can be managed easily through computer software. Currently he is consulting in districts in the United States, New Zealand, and Mexico. Churchward can be contacted in the United States at 1-800-441-4199 or through his Honor Level System website. A free trial offer for computer software to help manage the program is available at www.honorlevel.com.

Churchward's Contributions to Discipline

Budd Churchward has provided a system of discipline that is attractive to teachers at all levels. He has constructed his approach around four "honor levels" of behavior, hence, the title **Honor Level System.** When referring to student levels, students are said to be "on" a specific level. The level assigned to individual students indicates their record of behavior over the previous 14 calendar days. Churchward has devised an easy means of keeping track of each student's behavior. The procedure specifies consequences for positive and negative behavior, keeps track of the last 14 calendar days, and assigns students to the various honor levels for that period of time depending on their behavior.

Churchward's system removes most of the stress students and teachers usually experience in discipline. That is because of its proactive nature and its ability to keep close track of student behavior. Students know from the outset what they must do in order to reach high honor levels, and they know what the consequences will be when they misbehave. Teachers maintain a high level of consistency and spring no surprises on students. When students choose to misbehave, teachers have no reason to scold, lecture, or otherwise struggle against the students, but only follow preestablished steps that students already fully understand. Students know that when they transgress rules, they can redeem themselves by behaving well for the next two weeks or less.

As you read Churchward's description of the Honor Level System, you will see that managing the program entails considerable effort. To alleviate that concern, Churchward makes available computer software that keeps track of student misbehavior over time and prints out certificates, letters to parents, record forms, and the like. The computer can be used to keep track of all the students in a given school. In smaller schools, a secretary enters the data. In larger high schools, an assistant principal usually enters the data in order to remain aware of student levels and progress.

Churchward's Central Focus

Churchward focuses on giving students responsibility for their behavior and teaching them how to reach the top honor levels in the program. He also indicates what teachers can do to help students conduct themselves properly over time. He relies foremost on students' internal motivation to behave properly in order to reach high honor levels, but he also wants teachers to model good behavior, teach students how to behave properly, provide encouragement and help to sustain good behavior, and use a system of rules and consequences to motivate students further. Although he advises applying the Honor Level System in the entire school, it is possible for individual teachers to use the system on their own.

Churchward's Principal Teachings

- *Students should know exactly how they are to conduct themselves in school and should receive the assistance and support they need in order to do so.*

  This typically involves establishing class rules and a system of instruction, encouragement, and positive and negative consequences to help students choose proper behavior.

- *"Honor levels" of behavior strongly encourage students to behave in a manner that brings them the greatest benefits. All students have the capability of reaching the highest honor levels and are internally motivated to do so.*

  Churchward specifies four such levels, with the two highest representing acceptable behavior and the two lowest representing unacceptable behavior.

- *Behavior management usually occurs more satisfactorily when the entire school uses the same program.*

  This provides consistency throughout and students and parents react well to it. However, individual teachers can adapt the Honor Level principles for use in their classes if the entire school does not wish to be involved.

- *Honor levels of behavior motivate students to strive for the highest levels.*

  Students naturally want to be recognized as functioning at the highest honor level. They receive extra rewards when they do so, but their major motivation is intrinsic.

- *Students are assigned to a particular honor level based on their behavior over the previous 14 calendar days.*

  This time period refers to calendar days, not school days. The time period can be shortened to seven days for primary grades or special needs students. Students who get in trouble can move back to the highest level by staying out of trouble for the number of days specified in the program.

- *Students who attain high honor levels should receive certificates, certain privileges, and other types of acknowledgment.*

  However, the main incentive for proper behavior is to be known for reaching the highest level.

- *Put students in charge of their own behavior by giving then a written warning slip when they misbehave.*

  This shows students they have the power and responsibility to change their own behavior in a positive manner.

- *Positive and negative consequences should be invoked when students comply with, or violate, class rules.*

  The consequences should be invoked consistently and fairly. They will help students become better able to select proper behavior in the future.

- *Four tactics are suggested for use when students misbehave—reminders, warnings, imposing infractions, and removal from class.*

  Reminders and first warnings don't count as infractions on students' records. If a student misbehaves after being reminded and warned, an infraction is imposed. Infractions are kept in each student's record, and the number of infractions during the previous 14 calendar days determines students' individual honor levels at any given time.

- *Certain teaching tactics are recommended for helping students choose proper behavior.*

  Examples of such tactics are getting everyone's attention before proceeding, making sure everyone knows what to do, making lessons interesting, keeping the environment positive, and using I-messages rather than you-messages when talking with students.

- *Certain discipline tactics are known to backfire and should never be used.*

  Examples of such tactics are shouting at students, saying things that embarrass or degrade them, adopting a superior attitude, and backing students into a corner.

Analysis of Churchward's *Honor Level System*

Background

The Honor Level System has been developed over a period of more than 20 years by Budd Churchward, formerly an elementary and middle school teacher in Washington State. Originally developed for a single school, it is now used by a large number of schools in Arizona, California, Idaho, Michigan, Minnesota, New Mexico, Ohio, Washington, Wisconsin, Mexico, New Zealand, and elsewhere. The program is equally useful in high schools, junior high schools, middle schools, and elementary schools.

The Honor Level System is designed to help students behave properly in school. Students reach the highest honor level if they do not misbehave during a period of 14 calendar days, meaning they commit no rules infractions during that time. Should they commit infractions, they are assigned to lower honor levels. The 14 calendar day rolling period actually consists of 10 school days or even fewer. If students drop out of the highest level because of misbehavior, they can regain it fairly quickly through proper behavior. Students are intrinsically motivated to reach the highest honor level. When they do so, they receive benefits not available to students at lower honor levels. Churchward maintains, however, that the motivation to reach the highest level is primarily intrinsic and has nothing to do with the special benefits associated with that level.

The Honor Level System maintains respect for students and is easily implemented. It blends Assertive Discipline with empathetic discipline in accordance with the needs of given groups of students. The computer software that accompanies the program not only tracks students through progressive stages of disciplinary action and notifies them of detention assignments but also prints reports for parents, teachers, and administrators. Key to the Honor Level System is keeping track of student misbehavior over the past 14 calendar days. For primary grades or special needs classes, this rolling window of time can be reduced to seven days. Although a computer program is needed to handle the data for an entire school, individual teachers can use a computer or a log book for keeping track of individual student misbehavior. Parents who wish to use the Honor Level System at home with their children can manage everything on a large wall calendar.

The program gives students responsibility for their own behavior, but teachers also do what they can to help students behave acceptably in school, including teaching students how to behave appropriately. Churchward advocates a system of rules and positive and negative consequences that are applied when students behave appropriately or inappropriately. Teachers are encouraged to establish consequences they feel most effective and appropriate for their students.

The Meaning of Honor Levels

The Churchward model specifies four honor levels that students earn through their behavior. Students are encouraged and helped to attain the highest level, which is Honor Level One. Progressively lower levels are called Honor Level Two, Honor Level Three, and Honor Level Four.

Honor Level One is for students who rarely misbehave at school. To qualify for this top level, a student must not commit any infractions (i.e., be assigned to detention or sent to time-out) over a period of the last 14 calendar days. This includes their behavior on school buses and at school events. Many students take pride in reaching Honor Level One and want to stay there. By doing so, they receive special privileges such as extra recreational periods, extended lunch time breaks, and occasional spontaneous or surprise activities such as free ice-cream certificates or coupons from local merchants good for free beverages when they attend a movie or buy a hamburger. Churchward says that 70 percent to 80 percent of students usually qualify themselves for Honor Level One at any given time.

Honor Level Two is assigned to students who have committed one or two infractions in the last 14 calendar days. Certain of the extra privileges awarded Honor Level One students may also be awarded Honor Level Two students. Churchward says that 20 percent or more of students qualify for Honor Level Two at any given time.

Honor Level Three is assigned to students who have committed infractions three or more times within the last 14 calendar days. These students do not receive any of the extra privileges allowed to students in Honor Levels One and Two. Churchward says that no more than 5 percent of students are normally in this level at any given time.

Honor Level Four is assigned to students who frequently get into trouble at school. This group rarely exceeds 5 percent of the students. These students do not qualify for any of the extra activities provided for other students. A school may, at its discretion, ask them to sit in a study hall during school assemblies and not allow them to attend dances or athletic events.

The 14 Day Window

When assigning students to honor levels, as well as to negative consequences, teachers only take into account individual students' discipline records for the last 14 days. No matter how much trouble a student may get into, there is always the opportunity to work back up to Honor Level One within the 14 day window. Problems that occurred more than 14 days in the past cease to apply. Students are notified on the day they qualify for a new honor level. Most try to move up to Level One or Level Two and stay there. Teachers provide encouragement and help.

Positive and Negative Consequences

The Honor Level System advocates using positive and negative consequences to help students behave appropriately. Schools are encouraged to establish their own systems of consequences. They should make sure students perceive the overall package as fair and equitable. Some of the positive consequences students receive for being in the top two honor levels were mentioned previously. Churchward lists the following as typical negative consequences that are used to discourage misbehavior but adds that teachers should decide on the consequences most appropriate for their students:

First misbehavior: Students receive only a reminder to help them stay on track.
Second instance of the same misbehavior: Students receive a verbal or written reprimand. If they conduct themselves properly for the rest of the period or day, they may disregard or discard the reprimand. If they repeat the misbehavior, they receive an infraction notice that is entered into the records.
Penalties for infractions: These are typical negative consequences imposed for infractions during the 14-day period:

first infraction: 15-minute noon detention
second infraction: 30-minute noon detention
third infraction: after-school detention
fourth infraction: in-school suspension
fifth infraction: Saturday school
sixth infraction: suspension from school

As you can see, students can move forward and backward through these stages of consequence. Forward movement—say, from fourth to fifth consequence—occurs as any individual student is cited again and again for infractions of school rules. Backward movement—for example, from second to first—occurs when students are able to stay out of trouble over time. These movements are determined by behavior that has occurred within the past 14 days. At times, a record of undesirable behavior can be wiped clean rather quickly. The 14 day period includes weekends and holidays, and the long winter and spring breaks move all students to Honor Level One and the lowest stage of consequence. Everyone has a fresh start at least twice during the school year. You can see that the Honor Level System does not treat all students the same but instead provides different consequences for misbehavior depending on frequency of misbehavior. This differential treatment is consistent with doing the best to help every student succeed.

Understanding Student Misbehavior

Just as students function at different levels in reading and math, so do they function at different levels, or stages, of behavior. Furthermore, they often behave differently when in different situations or with different people. We can understand their behavior better in terms of **four stages of behavior** that most students move through as they mature (derived from Kohlberg, 1984).

Author's Note: Notice that in these stages of behavior, Stage 1 is lowest, or least developed, whereas Stage 4 shows the most highly developed behavior. This order is the opposite of the honor levels, in which Honor Level One is highest and Honor Level Four lowest. Please keep these rankings in mind to avoid confusion.

Stage 1. Power Behavior: Might makes right.   Students who display power behavior, for whatever reason, often refuse to follow directions, are defiant, and require a tremendous amount of teacher attention. Most are capable of moving beyond this level when they want to, but many nevertheless display this behavior from time to time. It springs from a strong imbalance of power between young children and the adults in their lives. The differential in power levels lessens as children get older, but if they are never taught a more productive style of behavior, they may continue to challenge authority and refuse to do as teachers request.

Students in school usually follow adult rules as long as the balance of power is against them. Adept assertive teachers can keep them in line, but when the teacher's back is turned, the students go out of control. If they want something, they take it if they can, and if they can get away with it, they do what they wish. They show very little concern for the feelings of others. These traits are typical of the few students who function at Honor Level Four.

Stage 2. Self-Serving Behavior: "What's in it for me?"   Students functioning at the self-serving level of behavior are easier to handle in the classroom, although they are very self-centered. They behave appropriately for one of two reasons—either because they expect to receive a reward for doing so, such as free time, candy, or other prizes, or because they don't like the negative consequences that are applied when they misbehave. They have little self-discipline. They need constant supervision. They may behave quite well in the classroom only to show lack of control once outside the classroom. These students are usually in Honor Levels Three and Four. Churchward says that older students who still behave in this manner do best in classrooms with assertive teachers.

Stage 3. Interpersonal Behavior: "How can I please you?"   Behavior based on wanting to please others is typical of most students in the middle grades. These students will conduct themselves properly if you ask them to do so. They want to please you and others. They strongly care what other people think of them, and they want to be liked. Most of them, in order to behave properly, need only gentle reminders. Most, however, are just now learning to be self-disciplined. They are seeking to trust others and build interpersonal relationships. Teachers should let these students know that proper behavior is important not only in the classroom but elsewhere as well. When carefully nurtured, these students make rapid progress toward self-discipline. These students are almost always found on Honor Level One and Honor Level Two.

Stage 4. Self-Discipline: "I behave properly because it is the right thing to do."   Students rarely misbehave in school once they have learned to conduct themselves in accordance with what they know is right and proper. Some elementary and middle school students conduct themselves in this manner part of the time, and by the time they are in high school, many do so. They are the students teachers love to work with. They can be left alone to work on a project and will remain purposeful and well behaved. They do this because, in their minds, it is the right thing to do. These students are almost always on Honor Level One. Students who function at this level do not appreciate assertive discipline, and they are bothered that certain students cause so many disruptions in the classroom. These students enjoy and profit from cooperative learning activities.

Most students work their way up through these stages in a relatively consistent manner, beginning with power behavior and moving slowly toward self-discipline. The progression is not steady, however, or always reliable. Many older students resort to power behavior, as do adults, even though they can show self-discipline when they wish. Many attempt to please others and hope to get rewarded for it. When students regress to lower levels of behavior, Churchward advises teachers to look for reasons for the regression, which are often found in problems with family members or friends, alcohol, drugs, fatigue, or the onset of illness. Take time to talk with the student and see if you can help in some way.

Learning self-discipline is akin to learning anything else. Students don't get everything right at first. They make mistakes and you have to stick with them and help when you can. If you do so, you will see progress, although it might come slowly, and you will be making a significant difference in your students' lives.

The Importance of Proactive Discipline

Churchward has quite a lot to say about the importance of proactive behavior management. He says teachers who feel they battle through every class and end the day feeling worn down and exhausted are probably trying to react to misbehavior as it arises, without preparing for it in advance. Advance preparation is what he means by being proactive, and it involves anticipating problems, forestalling most of them, and being prepared to deal effectively with those that do arise. Teachers who work in this way are better able to create happy classrooms where students feel comfortable and safe. They establish routines for most tasks so students always know what they are expected to do. *Proactive teachers* set the tenor of the room in the first few minutes, thus getting each class period off to a smooth start. This enables them to head off many potential behavior problems.

When discipline problems occur, proactive teachers use a prearranged series of discipline steps to help offending students change their behavior for the better. In well-run classes, a simple reminder is all that is usually needed. If that isn't sufficient, the teacher follows an established plan of action that is already fully understood by the students. The best tactics involve putting offending students in charge of controlling their own behavior in a dignified manner that does not provoke resistance. (Churchward's Honor Level System is designed to do that.) This plan is put in place at the beginning of the term with careful explanation and class discussion. The steps in the plan are written out and posted in the room.

Although these steps prevent a large amount of misbehavior that would otherwise occur, they do not, of course, prevent all of it. When students fail to choose appropriate behavior, the teacher takes action as stipulated in the behavior plan for the class. Throughout the process, the teacher tries to help the student choose more appropriate behavior. Negative consequences are applied only after the student is fully aware of his or her misbehavior and has received opportunity and encouragement to behave properly. The message becomes clear that in the behavior management process it is not the teacher doing something punitive to the student, but rather that the student bringing unpleasantness on himself or herself.

Reactive teachers function differently from proactive teachers. They do little to prevent misbehavior and as a result have to deal with it frequently. These resultant interruptions interfere with student learning and waste vast amounts of time. They annoy teachers and students alike, cause them to lose their tempers, add frustration for everybody, and lead to poor morale and bad attitudes. The reactive teacher typically sends students to the office time and again. Usually this is because confrontations between teacher and student escalate unnecessarily. Often the confrontations amount to little at the beginning. The teacher may ask a student to pick up crumpled paper thrown toward the wastebasket. A few seconds later they are arguing and the teacher reacts with, "Get yourself to the office, now!" Once a teacher gets caught in the reactive mode, classroom problems seem to multiply while stress builds and patience evaporates. It is not easy to switch from a reactive mode to a proactive mode, but it can be done and is eminently worth the effort involved. Churchward says the first step can be as simple as greeting the students with a warm and friendly smile as they walk through the door.

Once teachers move into the proactive mode, they focus on the behavior they want without drawing attention to misbehavior. They might only say, "Jimmy, the rest of the class is working quietly now. You need to turn around and get going with your assignment, too." There isn't much there for Jimmy to challenge, nor does he feel threatened or rebuffed. Proactive teachers recognize potential situations before they escalate and stop them before they rise to confrontations. Churchward (2003) illustrates this point with the following scenario in which the teacher defuses an argumentative student:

> During a classroom discussion, Mary is repeatedly turning around to speak with the students around her. "Mary," her teacher directs, "I think it would be better if you come sit over here for the rest of the period." Mary's face darkens and she folds her arms across her chest. "I don't want to sit over there!" Calmly, but firmly, her teacher repeats Mary's challenge. "You don't want to sit over here. I can understand that. I know you would rather sit with your friends, but I think we can help you stay out of trouble if you move over here." Mary becomes a little more anxious. She is reluctant to get up and move in front of her peers. "Why do I have to move?" "Why do you have to move?" her teacher rephrases the question. "I have tried to give you the opportunity to make things work where you are sitting. You are leaving me with fewer and fewer choices. I would like you to come sit over here. Remember our first classroom rule, Mary. I expect you to follow directions." Mary reluctantly makes her way across the room. "This isn't fair." "I'm sorry you don't think this is fair. We can talk about this later when you're less upset. Thank you for moving now." (The important thing to notice is that the teacher listens and repeats or rephrases the student's words. It is hard to argue with someone who keeps repeating what you say.)

Display the Class Rules and Discipline Steps

Identify three to five classroom rules, write them on a chart and state them in a positive fashion, and discuss them with the students. An example of a good rule is "Follow directions the first time they are given." Do the same for the four steps in discipline (these steps are explained in the next section). Explain to students that they may be asked to identify the next step if they get into trouble. Then display the rules and discipline steps conspicuously in at least two different places in the classroom. Let students know they can always look on the wall to answer your question. Also advise students that in extreme cases you reserve the right to skip immediately to more severe consequences. This may be required for certain behaviors that you simply cannot tolerate. Be specific when you explain this point and give examples.

Suppose a middle grade class has agreed on the following rules:

1. Come to class prepared and on time.
2. Leave gum, food, and beverages in your locker.
3. Follow directions the first time and give your best effort.
4. Treat others the way you like to be treated.

Now suppose Debbie chats with Alauna instead of beginning her work. All the teacher has to do is move to Debbie and whisper, "Debbie, do you see the list on the wall? Look at number 3. Are you doing that right now?" Debbie shakes her head or says nothing, and the teacher adds, "But you can, though, can't you?" Churchward says students rarely feel threatened by such reminders. The problem is usually solved at this point and nothing more need be done.

Discipline Steps Suggested for the *Honor Level System*

If you set up a discipline policy in your classroom that attempts to meet the needs of individual students, whether they are functioning at the power stage, the self-discipline stage, or somewhere in between, here are **discipline steps** to take when students misbehave. They work for students of all ages.

Step 1. Give a Reminder. Reminders are not reprimands. They help students remember what they should be doing and can be directed to individual students or to the entire class. You don't move closer to the student when using this step. Use reminders early, before a situation gets serious enough that a simple reminder is no longer enough. Here are two examples Churchward provides:

- "There is the bell, class. You should all have your homework out on your desk, now."
- "Janice and Maria, the rest of us have all started working. You need to stop talking and start too."

Churchward comments that some teachers may complain about having to remind children over and over again, but we do so because they ARE children.

Step 2. Issue a Warning. Warnings are reprimands. They may be given orally or in writing. Oral warnings shouldn't be delivered across the classroom. Approach the student closely and speak very quietly. Let the student know what he or she is expected to do. Ask the student to identify the next step. Here are two examples Churchward provides:

- Steven is sitting sideways in his chair and keeps messing with things on Maria's desk. The teacher approaches Steven and says: "Steven, I expect you to turn around in your seat and get on with your assignment. This is your warning. What is the next step?"
- During difficult independent work, Tammy suddenly speaks out: "Boy, this stuff really sucks!" The teacher walks up to her and calmly, but firmly, says, "Tammy, I expect you to raise your hand and wait to be called on before you speak. This is your warning. Now, can you tell me the next step?"

Written warnings are usually more effective than oral warnings. The teacher approaches the student and hands him or her an Honor Level System infraction slip. The teacher has checked an item on the slip and may ask the student to fill in the information at the top. The teacher says that if no further problem occurs, the student can throw the slip away at the end of the period, but if the misbehavior continues, the slip will be collected and kept. Here is an example provided by Churchward:

Jason has been teasing Janice. The teacher fills out an infraction slip and takes it to him. He says to Jason: "Here is an infraction slip with your name on it. I have marked 'Failure to treat peers with respect' because you have been bothering Janice. I will put it here on the corner of your desk. If it is still there when the bell rings, you may throw it away. If you continue to pester her, I will pick up the slip and keep it on record."

Placing a slip on the student's desk keeps it close to the student and serves as a constant reminder. If you don't teach in a classroom with desks, give the slip to the student anyway. Even in a gym class students can tuck the slip inside an elastic band somewhere or even in the shoe.

It is important that students retain possession and control of the slip. Point out that just as they are in charge of the infraction slip, so are they in charge of their own behavior. This helps students accept ownership of their actions. When the slip is in the teacher's hands, it is much easier for students to think of the responsibility belonging to someone else. But when students retain the slip, there is no doubt in their minds they have been reprimanded and no doubt as to whether they are expected to be responsible for themselves.

Step 3. Impose an Infraction. The student has already received a warning slip but misbehaves again. The teacher approaches and reminds the student that he or she has already received a warning and has now committed an infraction. If a warning slip has already been issued, the teacher takes the slip. If there has been only an oral warning, the teacher completes an infraction slip. The student is then asked to identify the next step. To illustrate, Churchward gives this example:

Nathan has been warned about staying in his seat and working on his assignment, but he keeps wandering over to argue with Jeff about a missing baseball card. The teacher marks "Failure to follow classroom rules" on an infraction slip and asks Nathan to fill in the top. She says, "Nathan, I warned you only a few minutes earlier about following directions. Yet you refuse to go to work. You will receive a detention. Can you tell me the next step?"

Nathan has refused to follow classroom rules even after being reminded and later warned. The infraction slip will be entered into the records. Nathan will be required to serve an appropriate consequence and his honor level may change. If the slip is his first, he may only serve a short detention during noon. If the slip is one of many, he may be suspended from school. In either case, the consequence is not chosen on the spur of the moment but is established in the discipline plan. The teacher should issue a reminder and a warning before enforcing the infraction slip. Only in special, extreme cases should an infraction slip be used as the first step.

Step 4. Student Is Removed from the Class. If the student has committed an infraction but misbehaves again, a special "time-out" slip is filled out and sent with the student to the office, or a "referral form" will be completed for the office later. Example:

Linda has been acting up in class quite a bit today. She has been warned and has had an infraction slip written up. Still, she continues to disrupt the class. The teacher sends her to the office. As she leaves the room, the teacher calls the office to let them know that Linda is on the way. As soon as possible, the teacher stops by the office to fill out a referral form and check with the principal. The teacher will contact the girl's parents, as well.

If the first three steps are followed faithfully, this step is rarely needed. When things do progress this far, proceed with this step in a cool, unemotional manner. There is no need for shouting or anger. Linda may try to bargain for leniency, but you must let her know you have proceeded through the established steps and have no options left. As you send her from the room, optimistically say: "Tomorrow we will try again. I'm sure we can make this work right."

Tips on Conducting Lessons

Churchward advises users of the Honor Level System to employ certain teaching techniques described in Thomas McDaniel's article, "A Primer on Classroom Discipline: Principles Old and New" that appeared in the September 1986 issue of *Phi Delta Kappan*. McDaniel's suggestions include the following:

1. Get everyone's attention before starting a lesson. Don't attempt to teach over the chatter of students. Help students understand that it is not all right for them to talk while you are presenting a lesson. Wait a few seconds for everyone to get quiet. Then begin your lesson in a quieter than normal voice.

2. Make sure everyone knows what to do and how much time they have to complete their work.
3. Monitor students while they are at work. Circulate among them and provide help when you see they need it.
4. Be the best model you can for how you want students to speak with and behave toward each other.
5. Use nonverbal cues to help students know what to do. These include facial expression, body posture, hand signals, flipping the light switch, and so forth. Normally these tactics are more effective than telling students what to do.
6. Keep the learning environment warm, cheery, and friendly.
7. Use I-messages when expressing your needs and concerns, rather than you-messages that threaten students. *Assertive I-messages* are stated as: "I need you to . . . " or "I expect you to . . . " *Humanistic I-messages* are stated as: "I am feeling very uneasy about the clutter in the room," or "I really appreciate your help in keeping the noise level down."

Discipline Techniques That Backfire

Churchward warns teachers that many discipline techniques used by teachers backfire and do more harm than good. He credits Linda Albert (1989) with identifying a number of counterproductive tactics, examples of which are shown here. He adds, "With twenty seven years in elementary and middle school classrooms I can honestly say I have tried most of these. Linda is right. They may work a few times, but not over the long haul" (Churchward, 2003).

- raising my voice
- yelling
- insisting on having the last word
- using tense body language, such as rigid posture or clenched hands
- using degrading, insulting, humiliating, or embarrassing put-downs
- using sarcasm
- attacking the student's character
- acting superior
- insisting that I am right
- preaching
- backing the student into a corner
- pleading or bribing
- holding a grudge
- nagging
- mimicking the student
- making comparisons with siblings or other students
- commanding, demanding, dominating

Strengths of Churchward's *Honor Level System*

The Honor Level System has a number of qualities teachers and students find attractive. It specifies clearly how students are expected to behave and then provides incentives and support to help them behave accordingly. It relies largely on internal motivation—students behave acceptably because they want to be seen as deserving the highest honor level. The label *honor level* itself is very appealing, and it indicates that students can, by dint of determination, control their behavior as honorable people do. Furthermore, should they get in trouble because of misbehavior, they can quickly redeem themselves and return to a high honor level. Teachers like the fact that the program has been developed and disseminated by a classroom teacher rather than someone more or less removed from daily classroom rigors. They like the fact that the entire school can use the system and that it can be managed by means of a central computer. One of the greatest strengths is that the program has the power to limit misbehavior effectively, yet maintain a positive climate in which little strife occurs between teacher and students, even when the teacher must impose negative consequences. It is a proactive program with expectations and procedures presented up front and clearly.

Initiating Churchward's *Honor Level System*

Although it is best put in place at the beginning of a term, the Honor Level System can be implemented at any time. The teacher explains to students that the system is a way of encouraging all members of the class, including the teacher, to conduct themselves in a highly responsible manner, one they will be proud of without the usual squabbling, disrupting, making excuses, bossing, threatening, or haranguing. The approach is based on honorable behavior. The four honor levels are described along with the means by which students can reach the highest levels and keep themselves there. The teacher explains the encouragement and help that will be provided to students, including making class activities enjoyable and worthwhile. Rules of behavior are then stipulated along with positive and negative consequences. The site administrator should be fully apprised of the plan before it is introduced to students. A description of the system should be written out concisely and copies sent to students' parents and posted on the school or class website. Parents will react favorably to the clarity and fairness of the approach and will appreciate the connotation of honor and honor level associated with their child.

KEY TERMS AND CONCEPTS PRESENTED IN THIS CHAPTER

The following terms and concepts are central to your understanding of the Honor Level System and your ability to implement it. Please check yourself to make sure you understand them.

Honor Level System	14 day window	self-discipline
Honor Level One	four stages of behavior	proactive teachers
Honor Level Two	power behavior	reactive teachers
Honor Level Three	self-serving behavior	discipline steps: reminder, warning,
Honor Level Four	interpersonal behavior	infraction, removal from class

SELECTED SEVEN—SUMMARY SUGGESTIONS FROM BUDD CHURCHWARD

Budd Churchward suggests that you emphasize the following, as well as his many other suggestions:

1 Make sure students know exactly how they are to conduct themselves in school and provide the assistance and support they need in order to do so.

2 Use honor levels of student behavior to motivate students to behave in accordance with the highest level, Honor Level One, which is assigned to students who have misbehaved no more than once or twice in the past 14 calendar days.

3 Work with students to make behavior expectations clear. Help students understand the benefits of behaving properly.

4 Put students in charge of their own behavior by giving then a written warning slip when they misbehave. This helps them remember they have the power and responsibility to change their own behavior in a positive manner.

5 When students misbehave, you should intervene, as appropriate, by giving a reminder, issuing a warning, imposing an infraction, or removing the student from the class. Don't count reminders and first warnings as infractions on students' records.

6 Use teaching tactics that help students behave properly, such as getting everyone's attention before proceeding, making sure everyone knows what to do, making lessons as interesting as possible, keeping the environment warm and cheery, and using I-messages rather than you-messages when talking with students.

7 Make sure to avoid teaching tactics that usually backfire, such as shouting at students, saying things that embarrass or degrade them, adopting a superior attitude, and backing students into a corner.

CONCEPT CASES

■ CASE 1   *Kristina Will Not Work*

Kristina, a student in Mr. Jake's class, is quite docile. She socializes little with other students and never disrupts the class. However, Mr. Jake cannot get Kristina to do any work. She rarely completes an assignment. She is simply there, putting forth almost no effort at all. *How would Churchward deal with Kristina?*

Churchward would probably suggest that Mr. Jake try the following:

1. Speak with Kristina in a kindly fashion. Ask if she understands the class rule about everyone trying to do their best work. Ask if something is troubling her that she would like to talk about.

2. Pair Kristina with another student who is at a high honor level and ask that student to work together with Kristina and encourage her.

3. Try to identify the probable cause of Kristina's lack of effort, such as low self-confidence, general fearfulness, mind on troubling situations outside of school, or avoidance associated with history of repeated failure in school. Take steps to deal with the cause.

4. Work directly with Kristina in a tutorial fashion or assign a class aide or volunteer to do so. Provide

warmth and comfort. Provide positive consequences when Kristina shows any signs of progress.

5. Speak with Kristina's parent or guardian. Ask for help from home.

■ CASE 2   *Sara Cannot Stop Talking*

Sara is a pleasant girl who participates in class activities and does most, though not all, of her assigned work. She cannot seem to refrain from talking to classmates, however. Her teacher, Mr. Gonzales, has to speak to her repeatedly during lessons to the point that he often becomes exasperated and loses his temper. *What suggestions would Churchward give Mr. Gonzales for dealing with Sara?*

■ CASE 3   *Joshua Clowns and Intimidates*

Larger and louder than his classmates, Joshua always wants to be the center of attention, which he accomplishes through a combination of clowning and intimidation. He makes wise remarks, talks back (smilingly) to the teacher, utters a variety of sound-effect noises such as automobile crashes and gunshots, and makes limitless sarcastic comments and put-downs of his classmates.

Other students will not stand up to him, apparently fearing his size and verbal aggression. His teacher, Miss Pearl, has come to her wit's end. *What specifically do you find in Churchward's suggestions that would help Miss Pearl with Joshua?*

■ **CASE 4   *Tom Is Hostile and Defiant***
Tom has appeared to be in his usual foul mood ever since arriving in class. On his way to sharpen his pencil,

he bumps into Frank, who complains. Tom tells him loudly to shut up. Miss Baines, the teacher, says, "Tom, go back to your seat." Tom wheels around, swears loudly, and says heatedly, "I'll go when I'm damned good and ready!" *How effective do you believe Churchward's suggestions would be in dealing with Tom?*

QUESTIONS AND ACTIVITIES

1. In your journal, enter information from the Honor Level System that pertains to the five principles of developing a personal system of discipline.

2. Churchward's model makes use of several aspects of Canter's Assertive Discipline. What differences do you see between the two models?

3. What do you consider to be (a) the most useful aspects of the Honor Level System, (b) the most complicated aspects of the Honor Level System, and (c) the requirements of the system that would be most difficult to implement?

4. Together with one or more colleagues, draft a plan for applying the Honor Level System to a single classroom (grade level of your choice) rather than the entire school. Share your plan with others and invite suggestions.

YOU ARE THE TEACHER

High School Biology
You teach advanced placement classes in biology to students from middle- to upper-income families. Most of the students have already made plans for attending college. When the students enter the classroom, they know they are to go to their assigned seats and write out answers to the questions of the day that you have written on the board. After that, you conduct discussions on text material that you assigned students to read before coming to class. During the lecture, you call randomly on students to answer questions and require that they support their answers with reference to the assigned reading. Following the lecture, students engage in lab activity for the remainder of the period.

A Typical Occurrence
You have just begun a discussion about the process of photosynthesis. You ask Sarolyn what the word *photosynthesis* means. She pushes her long hair aside and replies, "I don't get it." This is a comment you hear frequently from Sarolyn. "What is it you don't understand?" "None of it," she says. You retort, "Be more specific! I've only asked for the definition!" Sarolyn is not intimidated. "I

mean, I don't get any of it. I don't understand why plants are green. Why aren't they blue or some other color? Why don't they grow on Mercury? The book says plants make food. How? Do they make bread? That's ridiculous. I don't understand this business about photosynthesis." You gaze at Sarolyn for a while and she back at you. You ask, "Are you finished?" Sarolyn shrugs. "I guess so." She hears some of the boys whistle under their breath; she enjoys their attention. You say to her, "Sarolyn, I hope some day you will understand that this is not a place for you to show off." "I hope so, too," Sarolyn says. "I know I should be more serious." She stares out the window. For the remainder of the discussion, which you don't handle as well as usual, you call only on students you know will give correct answers. The discussion completed, you begin to give instructions for lab activity. You notice that Nick is turning the valve of the gas jet on and off. You say to Nick, "Mr. Contreras, would you please repeat our rule about the use of lab equipment?" Nick drops his head and mumbles something about waiting for directions. Sarolyn says calmly, "Knock it off, Nick. This is serious business." She smiles at you. After a moment, you complete your directions and tell the students to begin. You walk around the room, monitoring their work. You stand behind lab partners Mei and Teresa, who are having a difficult time. You do not offer them help, believing that advanced placement students should be able to work things out for themselves. But as they blunder through the activity, you find yourself shaking your head in disbelief. Although you don't intend it, you present the impression you hope the two girls will drop the class.

Conceptualizing a Strategy

If you followed the suggestions of Budd Churchward, what would you conclude or do with regard to the following?

1. Preventing the problem from occurring in the first place.
2. Putting a clear end to the misbehavior now.
3. Involving other or all students in addressing the situation.
4. Maintaining student dignity and good personal relations.
5. Using follow-up procedures that would prevent the recurrence of the misbehavior.
6. Using the situation to help the students develop a sense of greater responsibility and self-control.

REFERENCES

Albert, L. 1989. *A teacher's guide to cooperative discipline: How to manage your classroom and promote self-esteem.* Circle Pines, MN: American Guidance Service.

Churchward, B. 2003. Discipline by design: The honor level system. www.honorlevel.com.

Kohlberg, L. 1984. *The psychology of moral development: The nature and validity of moral stages.* San Francisco: Harper & Row.

McDaniel, T. 1986. A primer on classroom discipline: Principles old and new. *Phi Delta Kappan.* 68(1), 63–67.

CHAPTER 11

Spencer Kagan, Patricia Kyle, and Sally Scott's *Win-Win Discipline*

Focus

- Teachers and students working together to co-create effective discipline solutions.
- Developing self-management, responsibility, and other autonomous life skills.
- Discipline tactics for the moment of disruption, follow-up, and long-term solutions.

Logic

- Classroom disciplines should help students develop long-term, self-managed responsibility.
- Disruptive behavior is an immature attempt to meet certain unfulfilled needs.
- Teachers can lead students to adopt more responsible, fulfilling behavior alternatives.
- Responsible behavior grows out of good curriculum, instruction, and management.

Contributions

- Classification of disruptive behaviors to facilitate prevention and effective response styles.
- Identification of student "positions" to help teachers select better discipline strategies.
- A framework for a "we" approach to long-term responsibility and effective life skills.
- Differentiated discipline structures to use with various kinds of student misbehavior.

Kagan, Kyle, and Scott's Suggestions

- Provide a positive learning environment and engaging curriculum and instruction.
- Create a "we" approach in which students and teacher work toward the same end.
- Consider student positions and needs when deciding on discipline tactics.
- Seek parental support and community alliances to foster responsible student behavior.

About Spencer Kagan, Patricia Kyle, and Sally Scott

Spencer Kagan, a clinical psychologist, educational consultant, and former professor of psychology and education at the University of California, now specializes in researching and developing discipline strategies and life skills training. He heads his own company, Kagan Publishing and Professional Development. He can be contacted through Kagan Publishing and Professional Development, P.O. Box 72008, San Clemente, CA 92674-9208; telephone 1-800-933-2667 (WEE-COOP); fax 949-369-6599; website www.KaganOnline.com; email WinWin@KaganOnline.com.

Spencer Kagan

Patricia Kyle, experienced as a classroom teacher, school counselor, school psychologist, and university professor, also researches and writes about classroom discipline. She is coordinator of the School Psychology program at the University of Idaho and can be reached by email at pkyle@rmci.net.

Sally Scott is a school administrator and teacher trainer. She has been the lead Win-Win trainer since its inception. National and international educators consider Scott's school a "must-see school." She can be contacted by email at sscott@washoe.k12.nv.us.

Patricia Kyle

Kagan, Kyle, and Scott's Contributions to Discipline

Kagan, Kyle, and Scott have shown that class disruptions present fertile opportunities to teach students how to make better behavior choices while progressively learning valuable life skills such as self-control, anger management, good judgment, impulse control, perseverance, and empathy. Toward those ends, they developed the concept of Three Pillars of Win-Win Discipline, which are (1) same-side approach by teacher, students, and parents working toward building responsible behavior, (2) collaboration by teacher and students in co-creating immediate and long-term discipline solutions, and (3) helping

Sally Scott

students make responsible choices rather than creating disruptions in the classroom. Kagan, Kyle, and Scott have described four types of disruptive behavior—**aggression, breaking rules, confrontation,** and **disengagement** (the **ABCD of disruptive behavior**). They also have proposed seven **student positions** that often prompt misbehavior. The positions, described as interactions of attitudes, cognitions, and physiology which influence the type of behavior students are likely to choose, are **seeking attention, avoiding failure, being angry, seeking control,** and **being energetic, bored,** or **uninformed.** These positions occur naturally in association with needs rooted in the human condition. Kagan, Kyle, and Scott present step-by-step **discipline structures** and suggest responses for teachers to use when students make poor behavior choices in trying to meet their needs. The structures and responses are designed for use at three different occasions: for the **moment of disruption,** for **follow-up,** and for seeking **long-term solutions.**

Kagan, Kyle, and Scott's Central Focus

The overall purpose of Win-Win Discipline is twofold: (1) to help students learn to meet their needs through responsible, nondisruptive behavior, and (2) through that process to develop valuable life skills. Kagan, Kyle, and Scott emphasize that teachers and students must be on the same side in establishing good discipline. Therefore, they treat discipline as a joint responsibility of teachers and students. They have organized effective discipline interventions to use when students disrupt. The interventions are designed to help students meet their needs through responsible choices. The intervention process involves the following: looking beyond the behavior to the student's position, applying an immediate solution to the problem, following up, and working toward long-term solutions. The interventions are tailored in accordance with the type of disruption and the student's position at the time. For example, a particular misbehavior might be a confrontation (type of disruption) while the student is being angry (student's position), or disengagement while the student is being bored. A fundamental concept in Win-Win Discipline is that disruptive behavior is always a student's attempt to meet needs that are associated with a given position. Therefore, teachers are advised to look beyond the behavior to the position the student is coming from and then validate the position and help the student find responsible ways to meet the needs of the moment. Kagan, Kyle, and Scott present a large number of effective responses that can be used at the moment of disruption, for later follow-up, and for developing long-term solutions to the problem.

Kagan, Kyle, and Scott's Principal Teachings

- *Discipline is not something you do to students.*
  It is something you help students acquire.

- *Any disruptive behavior that interrupts the learning process can become an important learning opportunity.*
  The aim of discipline is to help students learn to meet their needs in a nondisruptive manner.

- *When developing an approach to discipline, use the three pillars of Win-Win Discipline: same-side approach, collaborative solutions, and shared responsibility.*
  Teacher and students are on the same side, working toward the same goal. They share responsibility for creating discipline solutions that help students conduct themselves more responsibly now and in the future.

● *Win-Win Discipline identifies four types of disruptive behavior: aggression, breaking rules, confrontation, and disengagement (the ABCD of disruptive behavior).*

By identifying the disruptive behavior, teachers are better able to select appropriate discipline responses.

● *Disruptive students occupy one or more of seven student positions.*

These positions are seeking attention, avoiding failure, being angry, seeking control and being energetic, bored, or uninformed.

● *The teacher should validate the student's position as being natural and understandable. There is no attempt to change the position. However, the disruptive behavior is not accepted. Teachers help students see how to meet their needs through behavior that is acceptable.*

This is accomplished by maintaining the student's dignity while encouraging the student to identify behavior that would be acceptable under the circumstances.

● *Teachers should work together with students on the same side.*

Teachers should openly express genuine caring for students, validate student positions, and provide support in establishing responsible alternatives to disruptive behavior.

● *Collaborative solutions made by teacher and students are especially valuable.*

Students who participate in the learning process and help create their own discipline solutions are more likely to make responsible choices.

● *The ultimate goals of Win-Win Discipline are for students to become able to manage themselves, meet their needs through responsible choices, and develop life skills that serve them well in the future.*

Win-Win Discipline is not just a strategy for ending disruptions but also one that teaches autonomous responsibility and other skills that transfer to life situations.

● *Responsible behavior is strongly affected by curriculum, instruction, and classroom management.*

Potential discipline problems are less likely to occur when students experience engaging curriculum and instruction and effective everyday procedures and management techniques.

● *Teachers must recognize the importance of parent and community alliances and creating schoolwide programs for dealing with disruptive behavior.*

When parents, teacher, and students collaborate in creating solutions—when they all see themselves as being on the same side—students become more likely to make responsible choices.

Analysis of Kagan, Kyle, and Scott's *Win-Win Discipline*

Spencer Kagan (2002) explains that Win-Win Discipline gives teachers and students a new way to view disruptive behavior and discipline. Disruptive students are not seen as "bad kids" but rather as individuals who are struggling, ineffectively, to meet their personal needs. Moreover, disruptions are not seen merely as obstacles to teaching and learning but rather as excellent opportunities for helping students learn. The Win-Win Discipline strategies are not designed to control students but to help them make responsible decisions and develop long-term life skills.

Philosophy and Nature of *Win-Win Discipline*

Kagan, Kyle, and Scott present a parable that conveys the basic philosophy of Win-Win Discipline:

> Two women are standing on a bank of a swift river. In the strong current, flailing about, desperately struggling to stay afloat, a man is carried downstream toward them. The women both jump in, pulling the man to safety. While the brave rescuers are tending the victim, a second man, also desperate and screaming for help, is carried by the current toward them. Again the women jump into the river to the rescue. As they are pulling out this second victim, they spot a third man flailing about as he is carried downstream toward them. One woman quickly jumps in to save the latest victim. As she does, she turns to see the other woman resolutely walking upstream. "Why aren't you helping?" she cries. "I am," states the other. "I am going to see who is pushing them in!" (Kagan, 2001).

The parable suggests that teachers have a fundamental decision to make when dealing with discipline problems. They can either be reactive and respond to each discipline problem as it erupts, or they can be proactive, see the place from which the discipline problem springs, and do something about it at that point. With the first choice, they must continually treat an unending stream of symptoms. With the second choice, they cure the cause of the problem by teaching how to behave responsibly rather than disruptively.

General Operating Principles

The general operating principles of Win-Win Discipline are embodied in what Kagan, Kyle, and Scott call the **Three Pillars** of Win-Win Discipline:

1. **Same Side:** Teacher, students, and parents work together on the same side rather than at odds with each other.
2. **Collaboration:** Teachers and students co-create immediate and long-term solutions to behavior problems.
3. **Learned Responsibility:** Teachers help students learn to make responsible choices in how they conduct themselves.

Types of Disruptive Behavior—ABCD

Kagan, Kyle, and Scott state that disruptive student behavior is usually one of four types—aggression, breaking rules, confrontation, or disengagement. The type of behavior suggests the type of intervention the teacher should use.

Aggression is taking hostile actions toward others. It may occur physically, verbally, or passively. Physical aggression includes hitting, kicking, biting, pinching, pulling, and slapping. Verbal aggression includes verbal put-downs, swearing, ridiculing, and name-calling. Passive aggression involves stubbornly refusing to comply with reasonable requests.

Students may **break class rules** for a variety of reasons, as when they are angry, bored, full of energy, desirous of attention, attempting to avoid failure, wanting to control, not understanding what is expected, or not having the ability to follow the rule. Common examples of breaking-the-rules behavior include talking without permission, making weird noises, chewing gum, passing notes, being out of one's seat, and not turning in work.

Confrontations are power struggles among students or between students and the teacher to get one's way or strongly argue one's point. Examples of confrontational behavior include refusing to comply, complaining, arguing, and giving myriad reasons why things should be done differently. When students don't get their way, they often pout or make uncomplimentary remarks about the task or teacher.

Students may **disengage** from lessons for a variety of reasons. They may have something more interesting on their minds, feel incapable of performing the task, or find the task too difficult or boring. Passive disengagement includes not listening, working off task, not finishing work, acting helpless, or saying "I can't." Active disengagement includes put-downs, excessive requests for help, and comments such as "I've got better things to do" or "It would be better if. . . ."

Student Positions

We noted that Win-Win Discipline proposes that disruptive behavior springs from seven student positions: seeking attention, avoiding failure, being angry, seeking control, and being energetic, bored, or uninformed. We saw that *student position* is described as an interaction of attitudes, cognitions, and physiology which influences the type of behavior students are likely to choose. Simply put, position is a state of mind that disposes the student to behave in a certain way. When students seek to meet the needs of a given position, they sometimes disrupt the class. The disruption is called misbehavior. Teacher and students can work together to understand the positions, identify the needs associated with them, and devise ways for students to meet those needs in a nondisruptive manner.

The art of using Win-Win Discipline is to look beyond behavior and see the position from which it springs. You then communicate acceptance of the student position while refusing to accept the disruptive behavior that springs from it. Positions are identified only in order to help students make more responsible choices in meeting the need associated with the position and, ultimately, to understand the long-term benefits of doing so. In short:

- Student positions are not to be considered negative; they simply reflect the student's needs at the time he or she acts out.
- Disruptive behavior springs from unmet needs inherent in student positions.
- Effective teachers try to gain the students' perspective in order to understand and deal with what is prompting students' behavior.
- Every disruption is an opportunity for helping students learn to behave more responsibly.

Preventing Disruptive Behavior

Kagan, Kyle, and Scott place heavy emphasis on preventing disruptive behavior. Win-Win Discipline enables teachers to work with students so that needs that might otherwise prompt disruptive behavior can be identified and satisfied in nondisruptive ways (Kagan, Scott, and Kagan, 2003). The **Big Three—curriculum, instruction,** and **management—** are fundamental teaching processes that have important influences on student behavior. Students do not often disrupt when engaged in a curriculum that is interesting and adequately challenging. They like to participate in cooperative learning and in activities that involve discovery, applying information, and solving problems. Students who understand expectations and procedures, and who have choices in what they learn and how they learn it, are more likely to participate, cooperate, and do their work. They very much appreciate teacher enthusiasm and willingness to vary instruction in accordance with student needs, interests, and capabilities. Kagan, Kyle, and Scott also provide a number of specific prevention strategies for particular misbehaviors. For example, a prevention strategy for aggression is using a designated cool-down area, and a prevention strategy for seeking attention is to greet students at the classroom door.

Rules in *Win-Win Discipline*

Class rules play an important role in Win-Win Discipline, but students are helped to see from the beginning that the rules don't pit teacher requirements against student desires. Good rules result from teacher and students teaming up to co-create class agreements that meet everyone's needs.

The process begins with a discussion of disruptive versus responsible ways to meet needs associated with the seven student positions. Teacher and students jointly generate agreements concerning responsible ways to meet the needs. For example, a disruptive way to meet the need for attention is to blurt out or to refuse to do an assignment, whereas a responsible way is to raise one's hand to be called on or do exceptionally well on an assignment. After students have listed disruptive and responsible things to do and say, they are asked, "Which way do we want our class to be?" Kagan, Kyle, and Scott say that without exception students choose the responsible alternatives. The class posts the responsible alternatives in the classroom and perhaps calls the agreements "The Way We Want Our Class to Be." Because students formulate and choose responsible alternatives, they do not feel the rules are imposed on them and, hence, they do not oppose them.

Although rules (or agreements) naturally vary from class to class, here are some typical examples from Kagan, Kyle, and Scott:

Ready Rule: Come to class ready to learn.
Respect Rule: Respect the rights and property of others.
Request Rule: Ask for help when needed.
Offer Rule: Offer help to others.
Responsibility Rule: Strive to act responsibly at all times.

Dealing with Disruptive Behavior

Disruptions occur when students attempt unsuccessfully to meet needs associated with a "position" from which they are operating at a given point in time. As noted, a fundamental concept in Win-Win Discipline is that disruptive behavior is always a student's attempt to meet needs that are associated with a given position.

Once the Win-Win philosophy of same-side collaboration has been internalized, students who are disruptive usually need only a reminder. This can be done by the teacher going to the chart on which rules are posted and asking, "Are we living up to the way we want our class to be?" If more is needed, the teacher might use a structure such as *Picture It Right*, which asks students to picture how they would like the class to be and verbalize what they need to do to make it that way. Win-Win Discipline provides 20 such structures for use at the moment of disruption. The purpose of these activities is not to obtain conformity to rules but rather to help everyone internalize a process of seeking mutually satisfying solutions that take needs into account.

General Protocol for Interventions

Kagan, Kyle, and Scott's many valuable suggestions can all be implemented through a general protocol for teachers to use when disruptive behavior occurs. The following protocol was not formulated by Kagan, Kyle, and Scott but is drawn logically from their other suggestions.

When Disruptive Behavior Occurs:

1. Give a reminder by referring to a class rule written on a chart posted in the room.
2. If the disruption is persistent or serious, identify and validate the disruptive student's position. Then ask the student to suggest a responsible way of meeting the needs associated with the position. For example, the teacher might say, "It's OK to need attention. From birth on, we all need attention. What do you think a responsible person might do to gain attention?"
3. Verbally support the student's choice of responsible behavior, if it is appropriate.
4. If the disruption is repeated, use a follow-up strategy such as "responsible thinking" (what would a responsible person do?) or "replacement behavior" (what might you do instead of shouting out that would help you and the class?)
5. For a long-term solution, work together with the student to plan changes that can be formalized in a student plan for self-improvement. Maintain the improvement through frequent same-side chats.

Specific Strategies for Disruptions

Kagan, Kyle, and Scott present numerous tactics for dealing with disruptive behavior. Here are a few of them:

For Attention Seeking Most individuals want to know others care about them, and when they feel they are not being cared about, they seek attention. Students wanting attention may interrupt, show off, annoy others, work more slowly than others, ask for extra help, or simply goof off. Instead of the positive results the student is hoping for, attention-seeking behavior further annoys and disrupts. Teachers usually react to attention seeking by nagging or scolding, which causes students to stop temporarily but not for long.

Dealing with disruptions that come from attention seeking: Positive interventions teachers can use at the *moment of disruption* for attention seeking include physical proximity, hand signals, I-messages, personal attention, appreciation, and affirmation. If attention seeking is chronic, teachers can ask students to identify positive ways of getting attention. They can *follow up* by meeting with students and discussing with them their need for attention and how it might be obtained in a positive manner. Suggested strategies for *long-term solutions* include focusing on the interests of the student and building self-concept and self-validation skills.

For Avoiding Failure We all have been in situations in which we rationalize our inadequacies in order to avoid pain or public embarrassment. No one likes to fail or appear stupid. The student who says, "I don't care about the stupid math quiz, so I won't study for it," knows that it is more painful to fail in front of others than not to try at all and, therefore, will rationalize the failure as lack of caring.

Dealing with disruptions that come from avoiding failure: Win-Win teachers seek to help students find ways to work and perform without feeling upset if they aren't first or best. For the *moment of disruption,* teachers can encourage students to try, assign partners or helpers, or reorganize and present the information in smaller instructional pieces. *Follow-up and long-term strategies* ask students how responsible people might deal with fear of failure. As necessary, include peer support, showing how mistakes can lead to excellent learning, and Team Pair Solo, a structure in which students practice first as a team and then in pairs before doing activities alone.

For Being Angry Everyone experiences displeasure and at times expresses it angrily. Anger is a natural reaction to many situations that involve fear, frustration, humiliation, loss, and pain. Angry students may go to the extreme because they are unable to express themselves in acceptable ways.

Dealing with disruptions that come from being angry: Teachers don't like to deal with angry students, and when doing so may experience feelings of hurt or indignation. Their immediate reaction often is to isolate the student or retaliate in some manner. However, these reactions do nothing to help students better manage their anger. Win-Win Discipline provides several structures to help teachers handle angry disruptions, including asking students to identify responsible ways of handling anger, taking time to cool down and think, and tabling the matter. *Long-term interventions* include conflict resolution conferences, class meetings, and practice in skills of self-control.

For Control Seeking We all want to feel in charge of ourselves and be able to make our own choices. This has positive and negative ramifications. On the negative side, control-seeking students may engage in power struggles with the teacher and, when challenged, argue or justify their actions. Teachers usually do not respond well to such behavior. Their reaction is to fight back to show their dominance.

Dealing with disruptions that come from control seeking: For the *moment of disruption,* Kagan, Kyle, and Scott suggest that teachers acknowledge the student's power, use Language of Choice (a structure in which the teacher provides students with choices, "You may either . . . or . . . "), or provide options for how and when work is to be done. For *follow-up* they may need to schedule a later conference or class meeting to discuss the situation, solicit student input concerning what causes students to struggle against the teacher, and consider how the struggle can be avoided. *Long-term strategies* include involving students in the decision-making process and working with them to establish class agreements concerning challenging the teacher.

For Energetic Students   All of us have experienced moments when we have so much energy we cannot sit still or concentrate. Some students are this way a good deal of the time, moving and talking incessantly.

Dealing with disruptions that come from being energetic: If energetic behavior becomes troublesome, teachers can, at the *moment of disruption,* infuse energy breaks into the lessons, provide time for progressive relaxation, remove distracting elements and objects, and channel energy productively. *Follow-up strategies* include teaching a variety of calming strategies and providing activities for students to work off energy in a positive manner. *Long-term solutions* include managing energy levels during instruction and connecting students' interests to the instruction.

For Bored Students   Students who act bored show they are not enjoying and do not want to participate in the curriculum, instruction, or activities at a given time. Boredom is communicated through body language, lack of participation, and being off task.

Dealing with disruptions that come from being bored: To help bored students at the *moment of disruption,* teachers can restructure the learning task, involve students more actively, and infuse timely energizers. As *follow-up,* they may talk privately with the students and assign them helping roles such as gatekeeper, recorder, or coach. For *long-term solutions,* teachers can provide a rich, relevant, and developmentally appropriate curriculum that actively involves students in the learning process and emphasizes cooperative learning and attention to multiple intelligences.

For Uninformed Students   Sometimes students respond or react disruptively because they simply don't know what to do or how to behave responsibly. Disruptions stemming from being uninformed are not motivated by strong emotions but by lack of information, skill, or appropriate habit. Although these disruptions are not emotional or volatile, they are nonetheless frustrating to teachers.

Dealing with disruptions that come from being uninformed: To determine whether students know what is expected, the teacher at the *moment of disruption* should gently ask if students know what they are supposed to do. If they don't, you can reteach them at the time. If they only need support, let them work with a buddy. *Follow-up strategies* include more careful attention to giving directions, modeling, and practicing the responsible behavior. *Long-term solutions* include encouragement and focusing on the student's strengths.

Responding in the Moment of Disruption

You have seen that Win-Win Discipline attempts to apply effective responses to student misbehavior in the *moment of disruption* that address the nature of the disruption and the student's position. In the moment of disruption, teachers wish to:

- End the disruption quickly and refocus all students back to the current activity in a harmonious atmosphere.
- Communicate that the disruptive behavior is unacceptable.
- Acknowledge the student position.
- Work with the student to find solutions that are mutually satisfactory.
- Take steps to create long-term learning of responsible behavior and life skills.

If after applying a suitable structure, the teacher feels the Three Pillars of Win-Win Discipline are not properly in place—same-side, joint solutions, long-term responsible behavior—he or she can use various follow-up strategies to get the class back on course. One such strategy, called the *same-side chat*, is especially effective because it shows that the teacher truly cares about the student.

Applying Consequences

Occasionally for persistently disruptive behavior, teachers may have to use more prescriptive structures, including applying consequences such as apology, restitution, or loss of activity. These are then built into the student's **personal improvement plan.** The suggested sequence for applying consequences is as follows:

1. *Warning* given to student. If more is needed, then . . .
2. *Reflection time* for the student to think about the disruptive behavior and its improvement. If more is needed, then . . .
3. *Personal improvement plan* is formulated by the disruptive student to develop responsible ways of meeting needs. If more is needed, then. . . .
4. *Phone call to parent or guardian.* If more is needed, then . . .
5. *Principal's office* visit.

Follow-Ups and Long-Term Goals

To the extent feasible, teachers should give students opportunity to resolve the problem on their own and help them develop responsibility. Kagan (2002) depicts the relationship between student positions and specific long-term goals as follows:

Student Position	*Long-Term Needs and Goals*
Attention-Seeking	Student needs self-validation
Avoiding Failure, Embarrassment	Student needs self-confidence
Angry	Student needs self-control
Control-Seeking	Student needs self-determination
Energetic	Student needs self-direction
Bored	Student needs to self-motivate
Uninformed	Student needs to self-inform

Win-Win Discipline offers a progression of follow-up structures to help students reach these long-term goals. Here are some of those structures, progressing from less directive to more directive.

Participate in Same-Side Chat. Through discussion, teacher and students get to know each other better and come to see themselves as working on the same side toward better conditions for all.

Use Responsible Thinking. Activities are used to direct students to reflect about three considerations: (1) their own and other's needs, (2) how they treat others, and (3) how they conduct themselves. Students can be asked to consider three questions:

1. What if everyone acted that way? (How would our class be if everyone acted that way?)
2. How would I like to be treated? (Did I treat others the way I would like to be treated?)
3. What would be a Win-Win solution? (What would meet everyone's needs?)

Reestablish Expectations. Discuss and if necessary reteach expectations concerning rules, procedures, and routines. This strengthens knowledge, understanding, acceptance, application, and adherence to expectations.

Use Replacement Behavior. Guide students to generate, accept, and practice responsible behavior that they can use in place of disruptive behavior.

Establish Contracts. Write out agreements in which teacher and students clarify and formalize agreements they have reached. Contracts sometimes increase the likelihood that the students will remember, identify with, and honor the agreement.

Establish Consequences. Consequences are reserved as a last resort and used only when all other follow-up efforts failed. Consequences are conditions that teacher and students have agreed to invoke when students misbehave. Consequences should be aligned with the Three Pillars of Win-Win Discipline: (1) They begin with same-side orientation. (2) They are established through teacher–student collaboration. (3) They are instructive and aimed at learning greater personal responsibility. The consequences that result from this procedure may focus on responsible thinking, apology, or restitution. When the behavior disrupts or harms others and responsible thinking is not enough, students may need to **apologize** to those they have offended. Genuine apologies have three parts: a statement of regret or remorse, a statement of appropriate future behavior, and the request for acceptance of the apology. Students may also need to make **restitution,** which means taking care of physical damage that was done. This is a tangible way of taking responsibility and dealing with the consequences of inappropriate choices. As well, it has the potential to "heal the violator."

Promoting Life Skills

One of the major goals of Win-Win Discipline is the progressive development of what Kagan, Kyle, and Scott call "life skills" that help people live life more successfully. Examples of life skills, noted earlier, are self-control, anger management, good judgment, impulse control, perseverance, and empathy. Teachers are urged to work on these skills through the curriculum as well as when responding to students at the moment of disruption, following up, and seeking long-term solutions. Kagan, Kyle, and Scott say that by fostering these life skills, teachers can escape the ineffective "pin a note" approach that can end a disruption but leave students just as likely to disrupt again in the future. They provide illustrations such as the following:

- A student puts down another student. The recipient of the put-down, having been publicly belittled, has the impulse to retaliate to give back a put-down or even initiate a fight. To the extent the student has acquired the life skills of self-control, anger management, and/or good judgment a discipline problem is averted.
- A student is finding an assignment difficult. She is tempted to avoid a sense of failure by saying to herself and others, "This assignment is stupid." To the extent the student has acquired self-motivation, pride in her work, and perseverance, a discipline problem is averted.
- A student is placed on a team with another student he does not like. He is tempted to call out, "Yuck! Look who we are stuck with!" To the extent the student has acquired relationship skills, cooperativeness, empathy, and kindness a discipline problem is averted.

Parent and Community Alliances and Schoolwide Programs

Partnerships with parent and community assist greatly in helping students make responsible behavior choices. Parents appreciate and support teachers who handle disruptive behavior in a positive manner and guide their child toward responsible behavior. The parents' input, support, follow-through, and backup strengthen the likelihood of responsible student behavior. Ongoing teacher–parent communication is essential in this regard. The degree of cooperation depends largely on how teachers reach out to parents. Rather than give up when parents are reluctant to work with them, teachers should continue to invite them to be actively involved in the process.

Win-Win Discipline provides many helpful suggestions for teacher–parent communication and interaction. Contact with parents should be made during the first week of school. Letters sent home, class newsletters, class websites, and emails are efficient ways to connect with parents. Phone calls are effective, although they take considerable time. Parent nights and open houses offer person-to-person communication opportunities. Conferences can be used to show parents they are valued as allies and may at times encourage parents to serve as mentors and tutors. Schoolwide programs such as assemblies and incentive programs encourage whole school involvement. The broader community can become involved through field trips, guest speakers, apprenticeships, and adopting and working with day care and senior centers.

Strengths of Kagan, Kyle, and Scott's *Win-Win Discipline*

Kagan, Kyle, and Scott have given teachers a system of discipline that removes the adversarial relationship between teachers and students that is a pitfall in many systems of discipline. They place teacher, students, and parents on the same side, working toward the common goal of helping students learn responsible behavior and develop life skills. They emphasize that every disruption provides a fertile moment for teaching students to make responsible choices. They help teachers see how students can meet needs associated with particular student positions. They describe how to acknowledge the student's position and implement an appropriate discipline structure. They provide an extensive set of structures designed for application at the moment of disruption, for follow-up, and for long-term benefits.

Initiating Kagan, Kyle, and Scott's *Win-Win Discipline*

Ideally, implementation of Win-Win Discipline should begin before the first day of school with advance preparation of procedures, routines, and curriculum materials designed to meet needs associated with each of the seven positions. However, if that is not possible, Win-Win Discipline can be put in place at any time. The concept and procedures will have to be taught for a while. Maintenance thereafter is relatively easy. In keeping with Kagan, Kyle, and Scott's suggestions, here is how you can introduce Win-Win Discipline to your students.

Begin by setting the tone for a win-win climate in your classroom. Let the students know that the class will be built on the Three Pillars of Win-Win Discipline—same-side approach, collaborative solutions, and learned responsibility. You might say something like this: "This is our class, and with all of us working together we will create a place where each person feels comfortable and all of us can enjoy the process of learning. As your teacher, I have a responsibility to create an environment where this can happen, but I need your help to make it work. Each of you must know that you are an important member of this class with important responsibilities and that you can help make the class a pleasant place to be. One of your main responsibilities is to help us create a positive learning atmosphere where everybody's needs are met. To accomplish this, we all must work together. I suggest that we begin by creating an agreement about how we will treat each other in this class."

Kagan, Kyle, and Scott suggest creating class agreements as follows: Begin by constructing a chart with the headings "Disruptive Behavior" and "Responsible Behavior," and subheadings under each of "Say" and "Do." Ask the students: "Let's name some of the disruptive things people say and do when they want attention." Record their responses. Then ask the class to name some of the responsible things people say and do for attention. Again, record their responses. Continue this process for each of the seven positions.

When you have reasonable lists, ask students, "How do you feel about these lists? Would you be willing to adopt the responsible behaviors as our class agreement? Can we agree to avoid the disruptive behaviors?"

It is essential that students believe their opinions and cooperation are valued. Tell them, "You and I need to be on the same side and work together to create a classroom we all enjoy where everyone can learn. You always will be included in the decision-making process. You will be able to have your say. We will learn and practice skills that are important for being citizens in a democratic society. Choosing responsible behavior will be one of the most important things we will learn."

During the first weeks, use activities that strengthen the concept of Three Pillars. This reassures students that discipline will not be done to them but will happen with them. In collaboration with the class you might decide on preferred classroom procedures, discuss discipline structures and their purposes, develop follow-ups and logical consequences, and solicit student input on some curriculum decisions. You can do all this in a series of class meetings. You also can show students how you will help them turn disruptive behavior into good learning situations. That is where reflection, follow-up, and long-term structures come into play. Remember that during the first weeks you will need to begin establishing alliances with parents.

KEY TERMS AND CONCEPTS PRESENTED IN THIS CHAPTER

The following terms are important in Kagan, Kyle, and Scott's Win-Win Discipline:

ABCD of disruptive behavior—
aggression, breaking rules,
confrontation,
disengagement
student positions—seeking
attention, avoiding failure,
being angry, seeking control,
energetic, bored, uninformed

Three Pillars—same side,
collaborative solutions,
learned responsibility
Big Three—curriculum,
instruction, management
application of discipline structures—at moment of disruption,
follow-up, long term

discipline structures
Picture It Right
personal improvement plan

SELECTED SEVEN—SUMMARY SUGGESTIONS FROM KAGAN, KYLE, AND SCOTT

Kagan, Kyle, and Scott advise you to emphasize the following as well as their many other suggestions:

1 Base your discipline program on the Three Pillars of Win-Win Discipline: same-side approach, collaboration, and long-term responsible behavior.

2 Do what you can to prevent the occurrence of misbehavior. Students seldom misbehave if the needs associated with their positions are met. Therefore, the best way to prevent misbehavior is by structuring the class to meet the needs associated with the seven positions.

3 Involve students in making decisions about class matters including behavior and discipline. Strive to reach win-win solutions to problems so that everyone benefits.

4 Respond to student misbehavior by determining the student's position at the time of disruption. Apply recommended structures for helping students meet their needs in a nondisruptive manner at the moment of disruption, at follow-up, and for long-term solutions.

5 Remember that disruptions offer prime conditions for students to learn responsible behavior and a number of other valuable life skills.

6 When a student disrupts, intervene in the following manner: First issue a *warning*, stated positively (e.g., "Jeremy, this is quiet time. Thank you."). Second, if needed, ask the student to *reflect* on his or her behavior (e.g., "Jeremy, I can see you are angry and I can understand why. But was your behavior responsible? What would be a responsible way of meeting your needs in that situation?"). Third, if needed, work out a *personal improvement plan* for meeting needs responsibly in the future to be monitored jointly by teacher and student.

7 Always maintain focus on the ultimate goal of Win-Win Discipline, which is for students to become able to manage themselves and develop long-lasting life skills.

CONCEPT CASES

■ CASE 1 *Kristina Will Not Work*

Kristina, a student in Mr. Jake's class, is quite docile. She socializes little with other students and never disrupts lessons. However, despite Mr. Jake's best efforts, Kristina will not do her work. She rarely completes an assignment. She is simply there, putting forth no effort at all. *How would Kagan, Kyle, and Scott deal with Kristina?*

Kagan, Kyle, and Scott would advise Mr. Jake to do the following: Mr. Jake would identify Kristina's disruptive behavior and ask behavior-specific questions. He also would identify and help Kristina acknowledge her position. Mr. Jake might ask Kristina how she feels about the work, determining if it is too hard (leading to avoidance of failure) or not interesting (leading to boredom). If the work is too difficult for Kristina, and her position is avoiding, or if she doesn't know how to do the work, he

might say quietly, "I really want to help you be successful, Kristina. I see this work is not getting finished. None of us wants to tackle something we know will be too hard for us. The best thing to do if something is too hard is to break it into smaller pieces, mastering a part at a time. Another good strategy is to work on the difficult pieces with others. Two heads are smarter than one. What suggestions do you have that will help you be successful?" Together they come up with possible solutions and then, if they agree that Kristina could benefit by working with a partner on smaller pieces, Mr. Jake may ask, "Would you like to work on this section with Danielle before moving on?" Throughout the interaction, Mr. Jake is attempting to help Kristina find a nondisruptive way to meet her needs. But more importantly, Mr. Jake is helping Kristina internalize a process of validating her own needs and seeking responsible rather than disruptive ways to fulfill them. As follow-up, Mr. Jake might focus on her success by saying something such as, "Kristina, I knew you could do this if we tried making the pieces smaller." His long-term solutions will include further encouragement and individual attention to Kristina's strengths.

■ CASE 2 *Sara Cannot Stop Talking*

Sara is a pleasant girl who participates in class activities and does most, though not all, of her assigned work. She cannot seem to refrain from talking to classmates, however. Her teacher, Mr. Gonzales, has to speak to her repeatedly during lessons to the point that he often becomes exasperated and loses his temper. *What suggestions would Kagan, Kyle, and Scott give Mr. Gonzales for dealing with Sara?*

■ CASE 3 *Joshua Clowns and Intimidates*

Larger and louder than his classmates, Joshua always wants to be the center of attention, which he accomplishes through a combination of clowning and intimidation. He makes wise remarks, talks back (smilingly) to the teacher, utters a variety of sound-effect noises such as automobile crashes and gunshots, and makes limitless sarcastic comments and put-downs of his classmates. Other students will not stand up to him, apparently fearing his size and verbal aggression. His teacher, Miss Pearl, has come to her wit's end. *Would Joshua's behavior be likely to improve if Win-Win Discipline were used in Miss Pearl's classroom? Explain.*

■ CASE 4 *Tom Is Hostile and Defiant*

Tom has appeared to be in his usual foul mood ever since arriving in class. On his way to sharpen his pencil, he bumps into Frank, who complains. Tom tells him loudly to shut up. Miss Baines, the teacher, says, "Tom, go back to your seat." Tom wheels around, swears loudly, and says heatedly, "I'll go when I'm damned good and ready!" *How would Tom's behavior be handled in a win-win classroom?*

QUESTIONS AND ACTIVITIES

1. In your journal on the five principles of a personal system of behavior management, add notes from Kagan, Kyle, and Scott's model as appropriate.

2. To what extent do you feel you could put Win-Win Discipline into effect in your classroom? What portions do you believe you could implement easily? What portions do you believe might present difficulty?

3. Win-Win Discipline rests on Three Pillars—same-side approach, collaborative solutions, and learned responsibility. How would you go about communicating these key principles to students?

4. In what ways are curriculum, instruction, and management linked to preventing discipline problems? How might each help with the moment of disruption, follow-up, and long-term solutions?

YOU ARE THE TEACHER

The following scenario was previously used for applying suggestions made by William Glasser. Do you see differences between suggestions Glasser would make and those Kagan, Kyle, and Scott would make?

Middle School World History

Your third-period world history class is comprised of students whose achievement levels vary from high to well below average. You pace their work accordingly, ask them to work cooperatively, and make sure everyone understands what they are supposed to do. For the most part you enjoy the class, finding the students interesting and refreshing. Your lessons follow a consistent pattern. First, you ask the students to read in groups from the textbook. Then you call on students at random to answer selected questions about the material. If a student who is called on is unable to answer a question, the group he or she represents loses a point. If able to answer correctly, the group gains a point. For partially correct answers, the group neither receives nor loses a point. For the second part of the period, the class groups do something productive or creative connected with the material they have read, such as making posters, writing a story, doing a skit, or the like. As appropriate, these efforts are shared with members of the class.

Typical Occurrences

You call on Hillary to answer a question. Although she has been participating, she shakes her head. This has happened several times before. Not wanting to hurt Hillary's feelings, you simply say, "That costs the group a point," and you call on someone else. Unfortunately, Hillary's group gets upset at her. The other students make comments under their breath. Later, Clarisse does the same thing that Hillary has done. When you speak with her about it, she replies, "You didn't make Hillary do it." You answer, "Look, we are talking about you, not Hillary." However, you let the matter lie there and say no more. Just then Deonne comes into the class late, appearing very angry. He slams his pack down on his desk and sits without opening his textbook. Although you want to talk with Deonne, you don't know how to approach him at that time. Will is in an opposite mood. Throughout the oral reading portion of the class, he continually giggles at every mispronounced word and at every reply students give to your questions. Will sits at the front of the class and turns around to laugh, seeing if he can get anyone else to laugh with him. He makes some oooh and aaaah sounds when Hillary and Clarisse decline to respond. Although most students either ig-

nore him or give him disgusted looks, he keeps laughing. You finally ask him what is so funny. He replies, "Nothing in particular," and looks back at the class and laughs. At the end of the period, there is time for sharing three posters students have made. Will makes comments and giggles about each of them. Clarisse, who has not participated, says, "Will, how about shutting up!" As the students leave the room, you take Deonne aside. "Is something wrong, Deonne?" you ask. "No," Deonne replies. His jaws are clenched as he strides past you.

Conceptualizing a Strategy

If you followed the suggestions of Kagan, Kyle, and Scott, what would you conclude or do with regard to the following?

1. Preventing the problems from occurring in the first place.
2. Putting an immediate end to the undesirable behavior.
3. Involving other or all students in addressing the situation.
4. Maintaining student dignity and good personal relations.
5. Using follow-up procedures that would prevent the recurrence of the misbehavior.
6. Using the situation to help the students develop a sense of greater responsibility and self-control.

REFERENCES

Kagan, L., Scott, S., and Kagan, S. 2003. *Win-Win discipline course workbook.* San Clemente, CA: Kagan Publishing.

Kagan, S. 2001. Teaching for character and community. *Educational Leadership, 59*(2), 50–55.

Kagan, S. 2002. What Is Win-Win Discipline? Kagan Online Magazine. *1*(15). www.KaganOnline.com.

Linda Albert's
Cooperative Discipline

Focus

- Close cooperation between teacher and students on making class decisions.
- Helping students connect with others, contribute, and see themselves as capable.
- A class code of conduct that promotes an optimal climate for learning and teaching.
- Involving parents as partners in helping students learn and show responsibility.

Logic

- To a large extent, students choose to behave the way they do.
- Students are highly motivated by the desire to sense they belong.
- Misbehavior is best understood as attempts to reach mistaken goals.
- Teachers best influence student choices through collaboration and encouragement.

Contributions

- Extended Dreikurs's discipline concepts to the classroom in a more useful form.
- Devised the Three C strategies to help students feel they belong and can succeed.
- Described dozens of good teacher interventions for use when misbehavior occurs.
- Established teacher–student–parent cooperation as pivotal in classroom behavior.

Albert's Suggestions

- Help every student feel they belong in the class and are valued members.
- Help every student connect with others, contribute to the class, and feel capable.
- Involve students and parents in planning the class discipline system.
- Turn every misbehavior into an opportunity to help students learn better behavior.

About Linda Albert

Linda Albert

Linda Albert, author and disseminator of *Cooperative Discipline*, is an educator, counselor, syndicated columnist, university professor, and former classroom teacher who works nationally and internationally with educators and parents. She has authored regular columns in *Working Mother* and *Family* magazines and has made featured appearances on NBC's *Today Show*, CBS's *This Morning*, and CNN's *Cable News*.

Albert has produced a quantity of materials and programs for educators and parents, including *An Administrator's Guide to Cooperative Discipline* (1992), *Coping with Kids* (1993), *Cooperative Discipline* (1996a, 2003a), *A Teacher's Guide to Cooperative Discipline* (1996c, 2003c), and *Cooperative Discipline Implementation Guide: Resources for Staff Development* (2003b). She has also produced two video series, *Responsible Kids in School and at Home: The Cooperative Discipline Way* (1994), and *Cooperative Discipline Staff Development Videos* (1996b), with separate materials for elementary and secondary teachers. Albert can be contacted at www.cooperativediscipline.com.

Albert's Contributions to Discipline

Influenced by Adlerian psychology and the work of Rudolf Dreikurs, Albert became convinced that students' behavior—and misbehavior—results in large part from their attempts to meet certain needs. By attending to those needs and providing much encouragement, teachers can reduce misbehavior greatly and establish classrooms in which students participate cooperatively with the teacher and each other. Albert shows how this is accomplished and provides clear techniques and strategies for classroom use. She has contributed the concepts of the Three C's (capable, connected, contributing), the classroom code of conduct, the Six-D conflict resolution plan, and the Five A's of helping students connect with teachers and peers. She has also contributed a great number of specific suggestions on what to do and say in order to prevent and redirect misbehavior.

Albert's Central Focus

Albert's main focus is on helping teachers meet student needs, thereby prompting students to cooperate with the teacher and each other. This cooperation removes the adversarial tendencies that so often exist between teacher and student. Albert believes cooperation occurs more easily when students truly feel they belong to, and in, the class. To make sure students gain that feeling, she gives heavy attention to what she calls the Three C's—helping all students feel capable, helping them connect with others, and helping them make contributions to the class and elsewhere. Albert also shows how parental support can be obtained and used to advantage. Although she gives major emphasis to developing a classroom climate that significantly diminishes misbehavior, she acknowledges that some misbehavior will occur in even the best-managed classrooms. She explains how to intervene effectively when misbehavior occurs. Beyond that, she provides strategies that minimize classroom conflict and permit teachers to deal with it in a positive manner.

Albert's Principal Teachings

- *For the most part, students choose to behave as they do.*
  How they behave is not outside their control. Virtually all students can behave properly when they feel the need to do so.

- *Students need to feel they belong in the classroom.*
  To do so, they must perceive themselves to be important, worthwhile, and valued.

- *When students misbehave, their goal is usually either to gain attention, gain power, exact revenge, or avoid failure.*
  At times, misbehavior can also occur because of exuberance or simply not knowing the proper way to behave.

- *Teachers can only influence student behavior; they cannot directly control it.*
  By knowing which goal students are seeking, teachers can exert positive influence on behavior choices that students make.

- *Teachers in general reflect three styles of classroom management: permissive, autocratic, and democratic.*
  Of the three, the democratic style best promotes good discipline. Albert refers to these three styles as hands off, hands on, and hands joined.

- *The Three C's—capable, connect, and contribute—are essential in helping students feel a sense of belonging.*
  When students feel capable, they are willing to apply themselves academically. When they can connect to others in a positive manner and can find ways to contribute to the welfare of the class, the positive relationships promote positive behaviors. With the Three C's in place, the amount of misbehavior drops dramatically.

- *Teachers should work cooperatively with students to develop a classroom code of conduct.*
  The code of conduct stipulates the kind of behavior expected of everyone in the class.

- *Teachers should also work cooperatively with students to develop a set of consequences to be invoked when the classroom code of conduct is transgressed.*
  When students participate in developing consequences, they are more likely to consider them reasonable and abide by them.

- *When conflicts occur between teacher and students, the teacher should remain calm and relaxed.*
  Teachers should adopt a businesslike attitude and use a calm, firm tone of voice.

● *Encouragement is the most powerful teaching tool available to teachers.*

Few things motivate good class behavior as much as large amounts of encouragement from teachers.

● *Teachers should remember that in order to develop a good system of discipline, they require the cooperation of students and parents.*

Both should be valued as partners and their contributions brought meaningfully into cooperative discipline.

Analysis of Albert's *Cooperative Discipline*

Albert has found that teachers everywhere are troubled, even overwhelmed, by student misbehavior. They feel incapable of dealing effectively with special-needs students, are dismayed by the number of severe classroom disruptions, and are increasingly worried about violence. These conditions are ruining the quality of teaching for many teachers and are destroying job satisfaction.

Albert says that in order to reverse this picture teachers require a discipline approach that permits them to work cooperatively with students and parents. She believes true cooperative understanding brings two prized results: First, the classroom can be transformed into a safe, orderly, inviting place for teaching and learning. Second, students have a good chance of learning to behave responsibly as well as achieving more academically.

The Goal of Classroom Discipline

The goal of classroom discipline is the same everywhere: It is to help students learn to choose responsible behavior. That goal can be reached by developing a positive relationship among teachers, students, parents, other teachers, and administrators. This relationship makes it easy to develop intervention strategies for misbehavior, encouragement strategies for building self-esteem, and collaboration strategies that involve students as genuine partners. These three strategies combine to produce positive student behavior.

Why Students Misbehave

Albert believes that most class misbehavior occurs as students attempt unsuccessfully to meet a universal psychological need—the **need to belong.** Students want to feel secure, welcome, and valued, and to a large extent their behavior influences how well those needs are met in the classroom. Although most students behave acceptably and, thus, get their needs met, some seem unable to do so. When that happens, many direct their behavior toward **mistaken goals,** so-called because students have the mistaken idea that through misbehavior they can somehow fulfill the need to belong. Albert believes students pursue four mistaken goals—attention, power, revenge, and assumed disability. Albert calls behavior that students direct at those mistaken goals **attention seeking, power seeking, revenge seeking,** and **avoidance of failure.**

Attention-Seeking Behavior

Although many students receive the attention they crave in the classroom, many others do not, so they seek it actively and passively. Active attention seeking involves what Albert calls AGMs—attention-getting mechanisms, such as pencil tapping, showing off, calling out, and asking irrelevant questions. Passive attention seeking is evident in the behavior of students who dawdle, lag behind, and are slow to comply. They behave in these ways to get attention from the teacher.

Albert says there is a silver lining to attention seeking: It shows that the offending student desires a positive relationship with the teacher but does not know how to connect. For such students, Albert suggests providing abundant recognition when they behave properly. Sometimes, attention-seeking behavior becomes excessive. For those times, Albert provides 31 intervention techniques. Two examples are (1) standing beside the offending student and (2) using I-messages such as "I find it difficult to keep my train of thought when talking is occurring."

Power-Seeking Behavior

When students do not receive enough attention to feel they belong in the classroom, some of them resort to power-seeking behavior. Through words and actions they try to show that they cannot be controlled by the teacher and will do as they please. They may mutter replies, disregard instructions, comply insolently, or directly challenge the teacher. Active power seeking may take the form of temper tantrums, back talk, disrespect, and defiance. Passive power seeking may take the form of quiet noncompliance with directions. These students are willing to hide behind labels such as lazy, forgetful, and inattentive.

Power-seeking behavior makes teachers angry and frustrated. They worry they will lose face or lose control of the class. Albert says that power seeking has its silver lining, though, in that many students who display this behavior show good verbal skills and leadership ability, as well as assertiveness and independent thinking. Keeping the silver lining in mind, teachers can prevent much power-seeking behavior by giving students options from which to choose (e.g., You may do this work alone or with a partner), delegating responsibilities, and granting legitimate power when appropriate. Once teachers find themselves engaged in a power struggle with a student, Albert advises teachers to seek a graceful exit, as described later in the chapter section entitled "Dealing with Severe Confrontations."

Revenge-Seeking Behavior

When students suffer real or imagined hurts in the class, a few may set out to retaliate against teachers and classmates. This is likely to occur when teachers have a record of dealing forcefully with students. It also happens at times when students are angry at parents or others who are too risky to rebel against. The teacher is a convenient, relatively nonthreatening target. Revenge seeking usually takes the form of verbal attacks on the teacher (e.g., "You really stink as a teacher!"), in destruction of materials or room environment, or, most frightening of all, in direct physical attacks on teachers or other students.

Strategies that are effective in dealing with power-seeking behavior are also effective when students misbehave to gain revenge (see the sections in this chapter entitled

"Avoiding and Defusing Confrontations" and "Dealing with Severe Confrontations"). Two additional tactics are helpful for decreasing revenge-seeking behavior. The first is to work at building caring relationships with all students. This includes students whose behavior is often unacceptable. The second is to teach students to express hostility in acceptable ways, such as through talking about their problems or developing a personal anger management plan.

Avoidance-of-Failure Behavior

Many students have an intense dread of failure. A few, especially when assignments are difficult, withdraw and quit trying, preferring to appear lazy rather than stupid. Albert advises teachers not to allow students to withdraw, but instead alter assignments and provide plentiful encouragement to keep students involved. Specific suggestions include (1) using concrete learning materials that students can see, feel, and manipulate, (2) using computer-based instruction, taking advantages of the latest technology and many students' natural interest in computers, (3) teaching students to accomplish one step at a time so they enjoy small successes, and (4) teaching to the various intelligences described by Howard Gardner (1983). This last strategy encourages students to use special talents they might have in areas referred to as linguistic, mathematical, visual, kinesthetic, rhythmic, intrapersonal, and interpersonal. In addition, special help can be provided by the teacher or by remedial programs, adult volunteers, peer tutoring, or commercial learning centers. It is important that withdrawn students be constantly encouraged to try. The teacher must show belief in them and help remove their negative thoughts about their ability to succeed.

Albert's Plethora of Strategies

Albert puts great stock in strategies that serve to prevent misbehavior, but she puts equal emphasis on strategies teachers can employ at what she calls "the moment of misbehavior." She states that her intention is to give teachers so many specific strategies that they are never at a loss for what to do next when a student misbehaves. Space within this chapter does not permit presentation of the numerous strategies she describes. Readers are directed to the Appendixes of *Cooperative Discipline* (2003b), especially Appendix C, which provides a summary chart of the numerous effective interventions she advocates.

The Three C's of Cooperative Discipline

The fundamental approach to Cooperative Discipline is embodied in what Albert calls the **Three C's** of helping students see themselves as **capable, connected** with others, and **contributing** members of the class.

The First C—Capability

Albert contends that one of the most important factors in school success is what she calls students' **I-can level.** The I-can level refers to the degree to which students believe they are capable of accomplishing work given them in school. Albert advises teachers to consider the following tactics to increase students' sense of capability.

1. *Make mistakes okay.* The fear of making mistakes undermines students' sense of capability, and when they are fearful, many stop trying. To minimize this fear, Albert would have teachers talk with students about what mistakes are, help them understand that everyone makes mistakes, and show students that mistakes are a natural part of learning. Teachers can point out that the more an individual undertakes, the more mistakes he or she will make. Albert urges teachers to be careful how they correct student mistakes. Too many corrections are overwhelming, as often seen in assignments that are returned covered with red ink. Teachers should correct mistakes in small steps, focusing on only one or two mistakes at a time.

2. *Build confidence.* In order to feel capable, students must have confidence that success is possible. To raise student confidence, teachers should convey to students that learning is a process of improvement, not an end product. When students improve, teachers should acknowledge the improvement. This is done by comparing the student's work only to his or her own past efforts, not against other students or grade level expectations. It should be remembered that people can be successful in a number of ways that do not involve written work. Students may show neatness, good handwriting, persistence, and a number of other specific abilities. Teachers should provide activities that bring all such talents into play.

New tasks seem difficult to practically everyone, so there is little point in telling students a task is "easy" or saying, "Oh, anybody can do this." It is better to say, "I know this may seem difficult at first, but keep at it. Let's see how you do." When students succeed in tasks they consider difficult, their sense of capability increases.

3. *Focus on past successes.* Very few people are motivated by having their mistakes pointed out. When they know they are being successful, however, they tend to be enthusiastic. Success depends on two factors—belief in one's ability and willingness to expend effort. Albert says teachers should ask students why they think they were successful in activities or assignments. If they say it was because the task was easy, teachers can say, "It seemed easy because you had developed the skills to do it." If they say it was because they tried hard, teachers can say, "You surely did. That is one of the main reasons you were successful."

4. *Make progress tangible.* Teachers should provide tangible evidence of student progress. Grades such as "B" and "satisfactory" are ineffective because they tell little about specific accomplishments. Albert suggests more effective devices such as I-can cans, accomplishment albums and portfolios, and talks about yesterday, today, and tomorrow. She describes these devices as follows:

I-can cans are empty coffee cans, decorated and used by primary-grade students, in which students place strips of paper indicating skills they have mastered, books they have read, and so forth. As the cans fill, they show how knowledge and skills are accumulating. These cans are useful for sharing in parent–teacher conferences.

Accomplishment albums and portfolios are better for older students. Students can place in them evidence of accomplishments, such as papers written, books read, projects completed, and special skills attained. Students should not be allowed to compare their accomplishment albums against each other. The emphasis is solely on personal growth, shown by what students can do now that they couldn't do before.

Talks about yesterday, today, and tomorrow help students visualize improvements they have made. "Remember when you couldn't spell these words? Look how easy they are now. You are learning fast. By the end of the year you will be able to . . . " or "Remember three weeks ago when you couldn't even read these Spanish verbs? Now you can use all of them in present tense. By next month, you'll be able to use them in past tense as well."

5. *Recognize achievement.* Albert believes that sense of capability increases when students receive attention from others for what they've accomplished. She suggests that teachers have class members acknowledge each other's accomplishments, recognize students at awards assemblies, set up exhibits, and make presentations for parents and other classes. Other suggestions include giving self-approval for achievements and providing positive time-out in which students are sent to administrators, counselors, or librarians for a few minutes of personal attention.

The Second C—Helping Students Connect

Albert feels it is essential that all students *connect,* meaning that they establish and maintain positive relationships with peers and teachers. As students make these connections, they become more cooperative and helpful with each other and more receptive to teachers. The **Five A's**—acceptance, attention, appreciation, affirmation, and affection—are important in making connections.

Acceptance means communicating that it is all right for each student to be as he or she is, regardless of culture, abilities, disabilities, and personal style. Teachers need not pretend that whatever students do is all right but should always indicate that the student is a person of potential, worthy of care.

Attention means making oneself available to students by sharing time and energy with them. Albert suggests greeting students by name, listening to what they say, chatting with them individually, eating in the cafeteria with them occasionally, scheduling personal conferences, recognizing birthdays, making bulletin boards with students' baby pictures on them, sending cards and messages to absent students, and showing real interest in students' work and hobbies.

Appreciation involves showing students that we are proud of their accomplishments or pleased by their behavior. It is made evident when we give compliments, express gratitude, and describe how students have helped the class. Appreciation can be expressed orally, in writing, or behaviorally in how we treat others. In showing appreciation, it is important to focus on the deed, not the doer. Albert suggests making statements of appreciation that include three parts: (1) the action, (2) how we feel about it, and (3) the action's positive effect. For example, a teacher might say, "Carlos, when you complete your assignment as you did today, it makes me very pleased because we can get all our work done on time."

Affirmation refers to making positive statements about students that recognize desirable traits, such as courage, cheerfulness, dedication, enthusiasm, friendliness, helpfulness, kindness, loyalty, originality, persistence, sensitivity, and thoughtfulness. By consciously looking for such traits, teachers can find something positive to say about every student, even those with difficult behavior problems. Albert suggests phrasing affirmations as follows: "I have noticed your thoughtfulness" and "Your kindness is always evident."

Affection refers to displays of closeness and caring that people show each other. Albert points out that affection is quite different from reward when kindness is shown only when the student behaves as desired. Affection is freely given, with nothing required in return. As Albert (1996a, p. 117) puts it: "[affection] is a gift with no strings attached. It is not 'I like you when' or 'I'd like you if.' Instead, it is simply 'I like you.' " Unlike appreciation, which is directed at what the student has done, affection is always addressed to the student personally, regardless of the deed. It helps students believe their teacher likes them even when they make mistakes.

The Third C—Helping Students Contribute

Students who have no sense of being needed often see school as purposeless. They see no reason to try to make progress. Albert suggests that one of the best ways to help students feel they are needed is to make it possible for them to contribute. Some of the ways she suggests doing this are:

1. *Encourage student contributions in the class.* Ask students to state their opinions and preferences about class requirements, routines, and other matters. Students can also furnish ideas about improving the classroom environment. Sincerely indicate you need their help and appreciate it.

2. *Encourage student contributions to the school.* Albert suggests creating *Three C Committees* whose purpose is to think of ways to help all students feel more capable, connecting, and contributing. Teachers and administrators can assign school service time when students perform such tasks as dusting shelves, beautifying classrooms, and cleaning the grounds, all of which help build a sense of pride in the school.

3. *Encourage student contributions to the community.* Albert makes a number of suggestions in this regard, including:

   ■ adopting a health care center and providing services such as reading, singing, and running errands for residents of the center.
   ■ contributing to community drives such Meals on Wheels, Toys for Tots, and disaster relief funds.
   ■ promoting volunteerism in which students volunteer their services to local institutions.
   ■ encouraging random acts of kindness, such as opening doors for people and providing help with their packages.

4. *Encourage students to work to protect the environment.* One of Albert's suggestions is for the class to adopt a street or area of the community and keep it litter free.

5. *Encourage students to help other students.* Albert's suggestions include:

- establishing a **circle of friends** who make sure that everyone has a partner to talk with, to sit with during lunch, and to walk with between classes.
- doing peer tutoring, in which adept students help students who are having difficulty.
- doing peer counseling, in which students talk with other students who are experiencing certain difficulties in their lives.
- providing peer mediation when students mediate disputes between other students.
- giving peer recognition, in which students recognize efforts and contributions made by fellow students.

The Classroom Code of Conduct

Albert strongly advises teachers to work together with their classes to establish a **classroom code of conduct** that specifies how everyone, including the teacher, is to behave and interact. In accordance with the code of conduct, every person is held accountable for his or her behavior all the time.

Developing a Code of Conduct

Albert would have the code of conduct replace the sets of rules that teachers normally use. Rules, she says, cause difficulty because students interpret the word *rule* as meaning what teachers do to control students. Moreover, rules are limited in scope, whereas a classroom code of conduct covers a wider variety of behavior. The code of conduct is developed as follows:

1. *Envision the ideal.* Spend time thinking about how you would like your classroom to be, if everything were just as you wanted. What would it look and sound like? How would the students behave toward each other?

2. *Ask students for their vision of how they would like the room to be.* Usually, students want the same conditions that teachers want. It is easy to merge the two visions.

3. *Ask for parents' input.* Albert suggests involving parents by sending them a letter summarizing the ideas students have expressed and asking for comments and suggestions. This increases parental support for the code of conduct.

Albert (2003a) presents several examples of codes of conduct developed in elementary, middle, and secondary schools. They are quite similar at the various grade levels. This is one such example for the secondary level:

I am respectful.
I am responsible.
I am safe.
I am prepared.

Because "Excellence in Education" is our motto, I will:

- do nothing to prevent the teacher from teaching and anyone, myself included, from participating in educational endeavors.
- cooperate with all members of the school community.
- respect myself, others, and the environment.

Teaching the Code of Conduct

The code of conduct can be taught in three steps:

1. *Identify appropriate and inappropriate behaviors.* Begin by asking students to identify specific behaviors that are appropriate for each operating principle. For example, in discussing what one does when "treating everyone with courtesy and respect," students might suggest:

- Use a pleasant tone of voice.
- Listen when others are speaking.
- Use proper language.
- Respond politely to requests from teachers and classmates.

Behaviors that these same students might list as inappropriate might include sneering, putting others down, pushing and shoving, ridiculing others, and making ethnic jokes.

Albert says it doesn't matter if these lists become long. They are not for memorizing. Their purpose is to help students develop the judgment and understanding needed for evaluating their own behavior choices and for accepting responsibility for all their behavior all the time.

2. *Clarify appropriate and inappropriate behaviors.* It is not enough simply to list student suggestions. They must be clarified so that every student knows exactly what each suggestion means. This is accomplished through explanation, modeling, and role playing.

3. *Involve parents.* Students can write a letter to parents explaining the code of conduct and listing the appropriate and inappropriate behaviors they have identified. The teacher can add a postscript to the letter asking parents to save the letter for discussions with their children.

Enforcing the Code of Conduct

Albert advises teachers to do the following when misbehavior occurs:

1. *Check for understanding.* Ask questions to make sure students grasp that their behavior is inappropriate as relates to the code. Examples of questions are:

- What behavior are you choosing at the moment?
- Is this behavior on our *appropriate list* or *inappropriate list* of behaviors?
- Can you help me understand why you are violating our code of conduct at this moment?
- Given our code of conduct, what should I say to you right now?

These questions are asked in a businesslike manner, with no accusatory tone.

2. *Problem-solve when disagreements occur.* Students may at times disagree with the teacher about whether a behavior is appropriate or inappropriate. These disagreements should be resolved in one of three ways:

- with a student–teacher conference
- in a class meeting dealing with the behavior
- by any other mediation or conflict resolution process

3. *Post the code of conduct.* Make sure the code of conduct is displayed in the classroom. When prominently displayed, the teacher can:

- walk to the display, point to the operating principle being violated, and make eye contact with the offending student.
- write the number of the principle being violated on an adhesive note and put it on the student's desk.
- point to the operating principle and say, "Class, notice principle number three, please."
- point to the operating principle being violated and say, "Tell me in your own words, Clarissa, what this principle means."

Reinforcing the Code of Conduct

Regular repetition and review are needed in helping students become proficient in monitoring and judging their behavior. Albert makes these suggestions:

- Review the code of conduct daily or weekly.
- Model self-correction. When the teacher makes a mistake, such as yelling at the students, the violation should be admitted, with a description of how it will be done correctly the next time.
- Encourage student self-evaluation. Ask students to make lists of their own behaviors that show how they are complying with or violating the code of behavior.

Involving Students and Parents as Partners

The effectiveness of Cooperative Discipline is increased when supported by students and parents. Albert makes many suggestions for obtaining their invaluable support.

For Enlisting Students as Partners

1. *Discuss with students the fundamental concepts in Cooperative Discipline:* (1) Behavior is based on choice. Students choose to behave as they do. (2) Everyone needs to feel they belong in the class and should be helped to do so. (3) The four goals of misbehavior are attention, power, revenge, and avoidance of failure. (4) The Three C's help everyone feel capable, connected, and contributing.
2. *Involve students in formulating the classroom code of conduct.*
3. *Involve students in establishing consequences for misbehavior.*
4. *Involve students in decision making about classroom and curriculum.*

For Enlisting Parents as Partners

1. *Inform parents about Cooperative Discipline and the class code of conduct that teacher and students have been discussing. Ask for parents' comments.* This is best done through newsletters sent home to parents and may be reinforced through parent group presentations.

2. *Establish guidelines for the style of communicating with parents.* Teachers should use objective terms when referring to students and their behavior, limit the number of complaints made to parents, and anticipate student success because every parent needs to have hope for their child's improvement.

3. *Notify parents when behavior problems occur.* Begin with a positive statement about the student, then identify the problem, and end with another positive statement about the student.

4. *Structure parent–teacher conferences for success.* When it is necessary to have a conference with a parent, use the **Five A's** strategy:

   - Accept the parent without prejudice.
   - Attend carefully to what the parent says.
   - Appreciate the parent's efforts and support.
   - Affirm the child's strengths and qualities.
   - Affection for the child is made evident to the parent.

Avoiding and Defusing Confrontations

Teachers fear situations in which students defy their authority. It is important to think through and practice how you want to conduct yourself when students challenge you through power or revenge behaviors. Albert suggests practicing how to:

1. *Focus on the behavior, not on the student.* To do this, a teacher can

   - Describe the behavior that is occurring but without evaluating it. Use objective terms to tell the student exactly what he or she is doing. Do not use subjective words such as *bad, wrong,* or *stupid.*
   - Deal with the moment. This means talking only about what is happening now, not what happened yesterday or last week.
   - Be firm but friendly. Indicate that the misbehavior must stop, but at the same time show students continuing care and interest in their well-being.

2. *Take charge of negative emotions.* This refers to teachers' negative emotions. In confrontations, teachers feel angry, frustrated, or hurt, but acting in accord with those emotions is counterproductive. One should, therefore:

   - Control negative emotions. Teachers should practice responding in a calm, objective, noncombative manner. This blocks the student's intention to instigate conflict and helps everyone calm down so the problem can be resolved.
   - Later, release the negative emotions. Emotions, though controlled, will remain after the confrontation. Albert suggests that teachers release those emotions as soon as possible through physical activity such as walking, playing tennis, or doing house or yard work.

3. *Avoid escalating the situation.* This recommendation dovetails with controlling negative emotions. Certain teacher reactions make situations worse, not better. Albert provides an extensive list of behaviors teachers should avoid, such as raising their voice, insisting

on the last word, using tense body language, using sarcasm or put-downs, backing the student into a corner, holding a grudge, mimicking the student, making comparisons with siblings or other students, and commanding or demanding.

4. *Discuss the misbehavior later.* At the time of the confrontation, make a brief, direct, friendly intervention that will defuse tensions. When feelings are running strong, most matters cannot be resolved immediately. Wait an hour or until the next day when both parties have cooled down.

5. *Allow students to save face.* Students know teachers have the ultimate power in confrontations, so eventually they comply with teacher expectations. However, to save face with their peers and make it seem they are not backing down completely, they often mutter, take their time complying, or repeat the misbehavior one more time before stopping. Albert advises teachers to overlook these behaviors rather than confront the student anew. When allowed to save face, students are more willing to settle down and behave appropriately.

Dealing with More Severe Confrontations

Suppose that a very upset student is having a real tantrum, yelling and throwing things. What does the teacher do then? Albert offers a number of suggestions that she calls **graceful exits,** which allow teachers to distance themselves from the situation. These exits are made calmly, with poise and without sarcasm.

- Acknowledge the student's power. Recognize that you can't make the offending student do anything and be willing to admit it to the student. But also state your expectation: "I can't make you write this essay, but it does need to be turned in by Friday. Let me know your plan for completing the assignment."
- Move away from the student, putting distance between the two of you. Try stating both viewpoints, such as: "To *you* it seems I'm being unfair when I lower your grade for turning in an assignment after the due date. To *me* it's a logical consequence for not meeting an important deadline."
- Remove the audience. By this, Albert means deflecting onlookers' attention when a confrontation arises. This can be done by making an announcement or raising an interesting topic for discussion.
- Table the matter. When emotions are running high or when the entire class is likely to become embroiled in a confrontation, say "You may be right. Let's talk about it later," or "I am not willing to talk with you about this right now."
- Call the student's bluff and deliver a closing statement. "Let me get this straight. I asked you to _____ and you are refusing. Is this correct?" The teacher stands ready with pencil and clipboard to write down what the student says. Albert also suggests using a closing statement, which she calls a one-liner to communicate that the confrontation has ended, for example, "You've mistaken me for someone who wants to fight. I don't."

- If you feel yourself losing control, take a teacher time-out. Say something like "What's happening right now is not okay with me. I need some teacher time-out to think about it. We'll talk later."
- If you see that the student will not calm down, have the student take time-out in the classroom, principal's office, or designated room.

Implementing Consequences

When a student seriously or repeatedly violates the classroom code of conduct, particularly through power or revenge behavior, you should invoke consequences in keeping with previous agreements. Think of consequences as an excellent teaching tool for helping students learn to make better behavior choices. Although negative consequences are usually unpleasant to the student, they are never harmful physically or psychologically. Albert refers to the **Four R's of consequences**—related, reasonable, respectful, and reliably enforced. By *related*, she means that the consequence should call on students to do something related directly to their misbehavior. Betsy continues to talk disruptively; her consequence is isolation in the back of the room where she cannot talk to others. She should not be kept after class for talking, as the penalty has no logical connection with the offense. By *reasonable*, Albert means that the consequence is proportional to the misbehavior. She reminds us that consequences are used to teach students to behave properly, not to punish them. If Juan fails to turn in an assignment, the consequence should be to redo the assignment. By *respectful*, Albert means that the consequence is invoked in a friendly but firm manner, with no blaming, shaming, or preaching. By *reliably enforced*, Albert means that teachers invoke consequences and follow through in a consistent manner.

Albert describes four categories of consequences that teachers should discuss with their class:

- loss or delay of privileges, such as loss or delay of a favorite activity
- loss of freedom of interaction, such as talking with other students
- restitution, such as return, repair, or replacement of objects, doing school service, or helping students that one has offended
- relearning appropriate behavior, such as practicing correct behavior and writing about how one should behave in a given situation

Resolution of more serious misbehavior or repeated violations of the classroom code of conduct should be done in a private conference with the student. The purpose of the conference is never to cast blame but rather to work out ways for helping the student behave responsibly. Albert presents a **Six-D conflict resolution plan** to help resolve matters under dispute for use in conferences or between students in the classroom. The plan is as follows:

1. Define the problem objectively, without blaming or using emotional words.
2. Declare the need; that is, tell what makes the situation a problem.

3. Describe the feelings experienced by both sides.
4. Discuss possible solutions. Consider pros and cons of each.
5. Decide on a plan. Choose the solution with the most support from both sides. Be specific about when it will begin.
6. Determine the plan's effectiveness. A follow-up meeting is arranged after the plan has been in use for a time in order to evaluate its effectiveness.

Strengths of Albert's *Cooperative Discipline*

Cooperative Discipline powerfully helps students achieve their ultimate goal of belonging, which in turn reduces their amount of misbehavior. For use on occasions when students do misbehave, Albert has developed approximately 70 proven procedures for dealing with misbehavior, procedures that stress teaching proper behavior rather than punishing transgressors. She has provided a clear rationale for Cooperative Discipline and a detailed guide for implementing and maintaining the program. She recognizes the importance of strong support from administrators and parents and provides many suggestions for ensuring that support.

Initiating Albert's *Cooperative Discipline*

Cooperative Discipline can be put into effect at any time. Teacher and class, working together, envision an environment that would meet their needs. They identify specific behaviors that would contribute to such an environment as well as behaviors that would work against it. They clarify these behaviors through discussion, demonstration, and role playing. Teachers and students jointly decide on the consequences to be invoked for violations of the standards they have agreed to, remembering that consequences should be related to specific misbehaviors. They write out the agreement, which becomes known as the classroom code of conduct. Before it is finalized, copies of the classroom code are sent to parents for input and support. When the code of conduct is finalized, it is posted in the room. The behaviors it calls for must be taught, not taken for granted, and the code should be discussed regularly. This keeps it in the foreground for reminding students and for use when correcting misbehavior. When serious violations of the code occur, procedures of conflict resolution are applied. All the while, teachers make ongoing efforts to help students feel capable, connected with others, and contributors to the class and elsewhere.

Doing these things may require some changes that make one feel somewhat uncomfortable. Albert tells teachers to expect those feelings and urges them to stick with the changes until they become second nature. Change is more easily accomplished when teachers visualize success and give themselves encouragement with statements they repeat over and over, such as:

This may be hard, but I can do it.
With practice I can master this strategy.
I am going to be able to make my classroom better.

Role playing with trusted colleagues is also helpful in becoming comfortable with new tactics. Albert reminds teachers that success with new discipline strategies depends not so much on how quickly they are learned but on how persistently they are applied.

KEY TERMS AND CONCEPTS PRESENTED IN THIS CHAPTER

The following terms and concepts are important in Albert's Cooperative Discipline. Check yourself to make sure you understand their meanings.

Cooperative Discipline
goals of student behavior and misbehavior (genuine, mistaken, belonging, attention-seeking, power-seeking, revenge-seeking, avoidance of failure)
Three C's (capable, connected, contributing)
I-can level

accomplishment albums and portfolios
I-can cans
circle of friends
Three C Committee
Five A's of connecting (acceptance, attention, appreciation, affirmation, affection)
classroom code of conduct

self-control
graceful exits
Four R's of consequences
Six-D conflict resolution plan

SELECTED SEVEN—SUMMARY SUGGESTIONS FROM LINDA ALBERT

Linda Albert suggests that you emphasize the following, as well as her many other suggestions:

1. Do what you can to help students perceive themselves to be important, worthwhile, and valued.

2. Remember, you can only influence how your students behave. You cannot control their behavior directly.

3. Liberally use encouragement (as distinct from praise). Encouragement is the most powerful teaching tool available to teachers.

4. A sense of belonging is important to good behavior. To promote a sense of belonging in the class, help students feel capable, show them how to connect with others, and help them contribute to the class (the Three C's).

5. Work together cooperatively with your students to develop a classroom code of conduct, which stipulates the kind of behavior expected of everyone in

the class. Involve parents in this process, too, as valued partners.

6. When you must deal with misbehavior, do the following: (a) Describe the behavior that is occurring but without evaluating it. (b) Deal only with what is happening now (not what happened in the past). (c) Be firm but friendly. Being firm means indicating that the misbehavior must stop. Being friendly means showing students continuing care and interest.

7. When you must invoke consequences for misbehavior, make sure they are related to the particular offense, reasonable, respectful, and reliably enforced (the Four R's of consequences).

CONCEPT CASES

■ CASE 1 *Kristina Will Not Work*

Kristina, a student in Mr. Jake's class, is quite docile. She socializes little with other students and never disrupts lessons. However, despite Mr. Jake's best efforts, Kristina will not do her work. She rarely completes an assignment. She is simply there, putting forth no effort at all. *How would Albert deal with Kristina?*

Albert would advise Mr. Jake to do the following: Work hard at the Three C's with Kristina. Give her work she can do easily so she begins to feel more capable. Then gradually increase the difficulty, teaching one new step at a time. Help her connect through a buddy system with another student and through participation in small group work. Give her opportunities to contribute by sharing information with the class about hobbies, siblings, and the like. Perhaps she has a skill she could teach to another student. Encourage her at every opportunity. Talk with her; ask her if there is something that is preventing her from completing her work. Show that you will help her however you can.

■ CASE 2 *Sara Cannot Stop Talking*

Sara is a pleasant girl who participates in class activities and does most, though not all, of her assigned work. She cannot seem to refrain from talking to classmates, however. Her teacher, Mr. Gonzales, has to speak to her repeatedly during lessons to the point that he often becomes exasperated and loses his temper. *What suggestions would Albert give Mr. Gonzales for dealing with Sara?*

■ CASE 3 *Joshua Clowns and Intimidates*

Larger and louder than his classmates, Joshua always wants to be the center of attention, which he accomplishes through a combination of clowning and intimidation. He makes wise remarks, talks back (smilingly) to the teacher, utters a variety of sound-effect noises such as automobile crashes and gunshots, and makes limitless sarcastic comments and put-downs of his classmates. Other students will not stand up to him, apparently fearing his size and verbal aggression. His teacher, Miss Pearl, has come to her wit's end. *Would Joshua's behavior be likely to improve if Albert's techniques were used in Miss Pearl's classroom? Explain.*

■ CASE 4 *Tom Is Hostile and Defiant*

Tom has appeared to be in his usual foul mood ever since arriving in class. On his way to sharpen his pencil, he bumps into Frank, who complains. Tom tells him loudly to shut up. Miss Baines, the teacher, says, "Tom, go back to your seat." Tom wheels around, swears loudly, and says heatedly, "I'll go when I'm damned good and ready!" *How would Albert have Miss Baines deal with Tom?*

QUESTIONS AND ACTIVITIES

1. Make entries in your journal from Albert's Cooperative Discipline that are pertinent to the five principles of building a personal system of discipline.

2. Indicate and describe the student and parent support structures you would implement to make Cooperative Discipline maximally effective.

YOU ARE THE TEACHER

High School English

You teach English to high school students, all of whom have a history of poor academic performance. Most of them have normal intelligence, although a few have been diagnosed with specific learning disabilities. Several live in foster homes or with relatives other than their parents. Many are bused from a distant neighborhood.

Some of the students are known to be affiliated with gangs.

Typical Occurrences

The students enter the classroom lethargically, find their seats, and as directed, most of them begin copying an assignment from the board. Something is going on between Lisa and Maria, who shoot hateful glances at each other. Neither begins work. When the students are settled, you review the previous day's lesson and then begin instruction on how to write a business letter. You ask the class to turn to an example in their textbooks. Five of the 14 students do not have their books with them, although this is a requirement you reemphasize almost daily. Students without books are penalized points that detract from their course grade. You see that Lisa has her book and you ask her to open it to the correct page. Lisa shakes her head and puts her head down on the desk. You give her the option of time out. Lisa leaves the room and sits by herself at a table outside the door. You go on with the lesson. You ask the students to work in pairs to write a letter canceling a magazine subscription and requesting a refund. You let them pick their own partners but find after a while that several students have formed no partnerships. Lisa's absence leaves an odd number of students. Maria asks if she can work by herself. You grant her request, but Maria continually glances back at Lisa. Two other girls, Marcia and Connie, have taken out mirrors and are applying makeup instead of working on their assignment. You inform them that you intend to call on them first to share their letter with the class. After the allotted work time, ask for volunteers to read their letters. With prodding, a pair of boys is first to share. You then call on Marcia and Connie. They complain that they didn't understand how to do the assignment. You tell them they must complete the letter for homework.

They agree to do so, but you know they will not comply and you expect them to be absent the next day. Other students read their letters. Some are good, while others contain many mistakes. The students do not seem to differentiate between correct and incorrect business letter forms. You attempt to point out strengths and weaknesses in the work, but the class applauds and makes smart-aleck remarks impartially. At the end of the period, you ask the students to turn in their letters. You intend for them to refine their work the next day. You find that two papers are missing and that Juan and Marco have written on theirs numerous A+ symbols and gang-related graffiti.

Conceptualizing a Strategy

If you followed the suggestions of Linda Albert, what would you conclude or do with regard to the following?

1. Preventing the problems from occurring in the first place.
2. Putting a clear end to the misbehavior now.
3. Involving other or all students in addressing the situation.
4. Maintaining student dignity and good personal relations.
5. Using follow-up procedures that would prevent the recurrence of the misbehavior.
6. Using the situation to help students develop a sense of greater responsibility and self-control.

REFERENCES

Albert, L. 1992. *An administrator's guide to cooperative discipline: Strategies for schoolwide implementation.* Circle Pines, MN: American Guidance Service.

Albert, L. 1993. *Coping with kids.* Circle Pines, MN: American Guidance Service.

Albert, L. 1994. *Responsible kids in school and at home.* [Series of 6 videos]. Circle Pines, MN: American Guidance Service.

Albert, L. 1996a, 2003a. *Cooperative discipline.* Circle Pines, MN: American Guidance Service.

Albert, L. 1996b. *Cooperative discipline staff development. Videos and materials for elementary and secondary level.* Circle Pines, MN: American Guidance Service.

Albert, L. 1996c, 2003c. *A teacher's guide to cooperative discipline.* Circle Pines, MN: American Guidance Service.

Albert, L. 2003b. *Cooperative discipline implementation guide: Resources for staff development.* Circle Pines, MN: American Guidance Service.

Gardner, H. 1983. *Frames of mind: The theory of multiple intelligences.* New York: Harper & Row.

CHAPTER 13

C. M. Charles's
Synergetic Discipline

Focus

- Teaching in a way that increases energy, responsibility, and desirable behavior.
- Preventing misbehavior by addressing its causes.
- Involving students cooperatively in making decisions about the class.
- Intervening positively and respectfully when misbehavior occurs.

Logic

- Moderately high levels of class energy promote learning and ensure good behavior.
- Learning and behavior are greatly affected by student needs.
- Misbehavior is best addressed by dealing with its causes.
- Students become more cooperative when involved in making decisions about the class.

Charles's Contributions

- A way of teaching that produces energy and satisfaction for all concerned.
- An approach to discipline that addresses the causes of misbehavior.
- A comfortable, dignified, effective way of helping students learn and conduct themselves responsibly.

Charles's Suggestions

- Ensure that your approach to teaching is compatible with student needs.
- Involve students cooperatively in making decisions about behavior and the class.
- Organize your discipline plan to address known causes of misbehavior. Discuss the causes and ways of resolving them with your students.
- Energize your class through selected activities, good communication, and charisma.

About C. M. Charles

C. M. Charles, born in 1931, began his teaching career in New Mexico in 1953. In 1961, he earned a Ph.D. in curriculum and educational psychology at the University of New Mexico and thereafter was on the faculties of education at Teachers College Columbia University and San Diego State University, where he is now professor emeritus. Charles directed innovative programs in teacher education and five times received outstanding professor and distinguished teaching awards. He also served on several occasions as advisor in teacher education and curriculum to the governments of Peru and Brazil. Charles has authored a number of books that have attracted wide audiences in the United States and abroad, with translations into several foreign languages. Those having to do most directly with school discipline are *Teachers' Petit Piaget* (1974); *The Synergetic Classroom: Joyful Teaching and Gentle Discipline* (2000); and *Essential Elements of Effective Discipline* (2002). Charles can be contacted through his website: www.teacherweb.com/ca/sdsu/charles.

C. M. Charles

Charles's Contributions to Discipline

Charles describes a way of teaching and working with students that produces quality learning and good student behavior, while removing the stress usually associated with misbehavior. He calls his approach *Synergetic Teaching* and its behavior management component *Synergetic Discipline*. The approach involves developing same-side cooperation between teacher and students, focusing on student needs, energizing the class, and eliminating or limiting the usual causes of misbehavior. These steps lead to quality instruction and responsible student behavior.

Charles's Central Focus

Charles focuses on energizing the class to increase motivation, while removing the usual causes of misbehavior. Teachers do not make demands on students, do not struggle against them, and do not use coercive measures to force them to behave. Instead, they obtain the willing cooperation of students by meeting their needs in a helpful manner and treating them with respect. Charles also stresses establishing a sense of community in the classroom and emphasizing ethical behavior.

Charles's Principal Teachings

● *Discipline at its best occurs as a natural, functional, ongoing part of teaching.*
It is not something separate from teaching to be used when students misbehave.

● *Students have seven predominant needs that motivate their behavior in school.*

Those needs are for security, hope, acceptance, dignity, power, enjoyment, and competence.

● *We now know how to ensure quality teaching, good learning, and responsible behavior in the classroom.*

These results occur when teachers help students meet their needs in a helpful, considerate manner.

● *Misbehavior is caused by a number of specific factors that teachers can address.*

Most misbehavior can be prevented by eliminating those causal factors or taking steps to reduce their effects.

● *Students naturally resist when teachers try to force them to work or conduct themselves in certain ways.*

Teachers who are most effective do not try to use force but instead encourage desirable behavior through cooperation between teacher and students to make the class enjoyable and productive.

● *A number of specific teacher qualities attract students and make them inclined to cooperate with teachers.*

Chief among the teacher qualities that appeal to students are trust, charisma, personal attention, and helpfulness.

● *In the most successful classes, students and teachers often experience synergy, a condition characterized by heightened enthusiasm and sense of purpose.*

Synergy increases enjoyment and productivity for everyone. When it is present, very little misbehavior occurs.

● *It is possible to establish classroom conditions that lead reliably to synergy.*

This is done by making the class interesting, providing activities that students enjoy and find meaningful, and using cooperative methods that lead to significant outcomes for the group.

● *When you first have contact with students, begin working out agreements with them concerning instruction, learning activities, and personal behavior.*

From that point forward they should always help students abide by the agreements and accept responsibility for their actions and for the well-being of the class.

● *When misbehavior occurs, which it sometimes does even in a trusting, supportive atmosphere, teachers should deal with it in a helpful, nonconfrontational manner.*

Teachers should never argue with students, put them down, or back them into a corner. Instead, they should show continual willingness to try to correct whatever is troubling the students and help resolve problems and conflicts equitably.

● *To deal with misbehavior, the teacher should look for the cause and attempt to correct it.*

Ask misbehaving students, "Is there a problem I can help you with?" or "Can you help me understand why this is happening? I'd like to help fix the problem." Show you are interested in helping, not punishing. Don't fight against students. Your challenge is to win them over, not show that you can dominate.

Analysis of Charles's *Synergetic Discipline*

Synergy and *Synergetic Discipline*

Synergy, a condition that sometimes occurs during social interaction between two or more people, is characterized by heightened energy. It often leads to creativity, productivity, satisfaction, and enjoyment. It occurs when the individuals involved interact in ways that increase each other's psychic energy. In school, this effect is most noticeable when students get caught up in group spirit and sense of purpose. Many teachers note that during episodes of synergy, discipline problems are almost nonexistent.

Synergetic Discipline is an integral part of **Synergetic Teaching.** It calls on students and teacher to work cooperatively to establish agreements concerning personal behavior in class. Teacher and students do all they can to eliminate or reduce the causes of misbehavior, work through problems in a positive manner, and energize the class through stimulating activities and mutual support and encouragement.

The following is a basic procedure that can effectively establish Synergetic Discipline in your classroom:

1. Invite your students sincerely to work with you in creating and maintaining an interesting, inviting program for learning, one that is free from fear and based on personal dignity and consideration for others.
2. Cooperatively establish a set of agreements about how the class is to function and class members are to conduct themselves.
3. Discuss and demonstrate conditions that elevate class spirit and energy. Ask the class continually to help identify topics and activities they find appealing.
4. Discuss the factors that are known to lead to misbehavior in the classroom. Ask students to work with you to eliminate or reduce those factors.

Dealing with the Causes of Misbehavior

The best way to deal with misbehavior is through attention to its causes. Thirteen types of student misbehavior are *inattention, apathy, needless talk, moving about the room without permission, annoying others, disruption, lying, stealing, cheating, sexual harassment, aggression and fighting, malicious mischief,* and *defiance of authority.* In the paragraphs that follow, 25 **causes of misbehavior** are reviewed. Classroom misbehavior declines as those causes are eliminated or reduced. The causes are grouped in accordance with where they seem to reside.

Causes That Reside in Individual Students

Nine causes of misbehavior reside within individual students: unmet needs, thwarted desires, expediency, urge to transgress, temptation, inappropriate habits, poor behavior choices, avoidance, and egocentric personality.

1. *Unmet needs.* Students continually try to meet classroom needs related to *security, belonging, hope, dignity, power, enjoyment,* and *competence.* When any of these needs is not being satisfied, students become unsettled or distracted and more inclined to misbehave.

Resolution By observing students and talking with them, you can help them meet most of their needs in an acceptable manner.

2. *Thwarted desires.* When students fail to get something they want badly, they may complain, become destructive, sulk, pout, or act out.

Resolution Tell students you can see they are troubled or distracted. Ask if there is anything you can do to help. Be sympathetic, but don't dwell on the problem. Try to get them interested in something else.

3. *Expediency.* Students always look for ways to make their lives easier and more enjoyable. They take shortcuts, conveniently forget what they are supposed to do, look for ways to get out of work, and intentionally break rules.

Resolution Expedient behavior is seldom a problem in classes that are interesting and enjoyable but appears often in those that are dull and boring. Hold discussions about expediency and its troublesome effects. Ask students why they sometimes take the easy way, such as reading book summaries or reviews rather than the assigned book, rushing through a writing assignment, or copying others' ideas. If they are comfortable enough to answer honestly, they will probably say they do so because they don't like the work, don't see the point in it, or don't want to spend time on it. Ask them what *would* encourage them to give their best effort. Listen to their suggestions and make use of them if you can.

4. *Urge to transgress.* All of us feel the urge to transgress rules and regulations and we often do so, knowing there is a chance we will get caught or even harm ourselves or others. Students succumb to this urge frequently, especially when class activities are not appealing, and cheat, take shortcuts, tell lies, break class rules, and annoy others.

Resolution Discuss this urge, its effects, and how it can be controlled sensibly. Discuss the reasons for rules, including how they reduce potential harm, equalize opportunity, and help us live together harmoniously. If students are old enough, ask if they understand what ethics, ethical conduct, and personal character mean. Ask why ethical people are generally admired.

5. *Temptation.* Students regularly encounter objects, situations, behaviors, and people they find powerfully attractive. Examples include music and lyrics, desirable objects, ways of speaking, styles of clothing, ways of conducting oneself, and cheating on tests and assignments. Although pursuit of these temptations can sometimes result in mild or severe misbehavior, students nevertheless find them so attractive they will succumb to them even though forbidden to do so.

Resolution Conduct discussions with your students in which together you analyze temptation and help students understand why certain objects, styles, and opportunities are so seductive. Help students foresee the undesirable consequences of following disapproved styles and manners. Help them clarify the lines that separate the approved from the disapproved and reinforce their resolve to resist factors that are likely to harm them.

6. *Inappropriate habits.* Inappropriate habits are ingrained ways of behaving that violate established standards and expectations. Jason uses profanity at school. Maria is discourte-

ous, inconsiderate, and calls others names. Larry always looks for a way to get out of doing his work. Some of these habits are learned in school, but most come from the home or community.

Resolution   Bring inappropriate habits to students' attention without pointing a finger at anyone. Discuss their harmful effects and, if necessary, teach students acceptable alternatives to habits such as name-calling, teasing, verbal put-downs, cheating, lying, and disregard for others.

7. *Poor behavior choices.*   The behaviors students use in attempting to meet their needs are sometimes acceptable, sometimes not. Levels of acceptability may not be clear to students, who seldom put much thought into how they can meet their needs appropriately. Alicia, in trying for attention, annoys others so much they avoid her. Alan, trying to meet his need for power, refuses to do what the teacher requests, thereby distressing the class. Alicia and Alan are trying to meet legitimate needs but do not consider how their behavior choices are harming themselves or the class.

Resolution   To help students such as Alicia and Alan, ask the class: What are some of the things you have seen students do to (e.g., get attention, be acknowledged, get better grades than they deserve, get out of work, become members of groups)? Does their behavior usually get them what they want? What could those students do that would probably bring better results?

8. *Avoidance.*   No one likes to face failure, intimidation, ridicule, or other unpleasant situations and treatment. One way to escape them is to avoid situations in which they might occur, but in school we can't always do that. Consider Norona, who refuses to participate in a group assignment. Her refusal seems to show disdain for the teacher, but her real reason for refusing is that she is intimidated by the prowess of her peers and doesn't want them to think she is inept.

Resolution   To help students such as Norona behave advantageously in circumstances they dislike by showing them how to face unpleasant situations and work through them. Rather than singling out Norona, ask the following in a group discussion: Are there things you try to avoid in school, such as people, events, or activities you find frightening or embarrassing? Which of those things could best be dealt with through avoidance (e.g., a clique that is maligning other students)? Which of those things cannot be dealt with through avoidance (e.g., giving an oral report in front of the class)? What is the worst thing that can happen in class if we make a mistake? Can mistakes help us learn? What could a person do to reduce fear of mistakes or unpleasant situations? (Perhaps practice in pairs, then small groups, then large groups.)

9. *Egocentric personality.*   Students with egocentric personalities focus primarily on themselves, believe they are superior to others, and think they do no wrong. Most classes contain one or more such students.

Resolution   To help these students behave more appropriately, ask questions such as the following in class discussions: Are the needs and interests of all students important, or do only certain students deserve attention? Is one person often entirely right and everyone else entirely wrong? Is everyone entitled to an equal opportunity in the class? How should you and I react to a person who always wants to dominate, be first, be right, and quarrel with those who don't agree? (Make sure the proffered suggestions are positive in nature, not negative.)

Causes That Reside in Class Peers and Groups

Two significant causes of misbehavior reside in class peers and groups—*provocation* and *group behavior*. Here are suggestions for dealing with them.

10. *Provocation.* A great amount of school misbehavior results from students' provoking each other or being provoked by annoyance, insult, or boredom. Heather is trying to study but Art's incessant chatter frustrates her to the bursting point. Marty calls Jerry a name and Jerry responds hotly. Randall is trying to pay attention but finally disengages from the lesson because he neither understands nor sees any point to it.

Resolution Provocation often produces strong emotions that reduce self-control and increase combativeness. Discuss this phenomenon with your class. Ask: Can you name some things people say or do that upset you so much you want to retaliate? How do you feel when this happens? If you retaliate, is it likely to improve the situation or make it worse? What might you do that would resolve the incident peacefully? Is provoking others consistent with the class character we are trying to build?

11. *Group behavior.* Students often succumb to peer pressure or get caught up in group emotion, and as a result they may misbehave in ways they would not consider if by themselves. It is difficult for students to disregard peer pressure, easy to get swept up in group energy and emotion, and easy to justify one's misbehavior as "only what others were doing." Because Kerry and Lee want to look cool to their peers, Kerry defaces school property, and Lee bullies a weaker member of the class, even though those acts are not what Kerry and Lee would do if by themselves.

Resolution Discuss this phenomenon with your class in ways such as the following:

- Tell the class about some event in which a friend of yours, let's say Sarah, behaved badly just because others were doing so. Indicate that Sarah is now very embarrassed about her behavior and wishes no one knew about it.
- Ask your students if they know any stories like Sarah's they can share, without mentioning names the class might recognize. (Tell them they must not mention family matters or members—doing so is a sure way to get parents upset at you.) If they share stories, guide the class in analyzing one or two of them. If they don't contribute a story, have a fictional one ready for their consideration. After hearing or recounting the story, ask questions such as:

    Is the behavior something the person will be proud of later?

    Why do you suppose the person behaved that way? (e.g., for fun, comradeship, testing limits, being seen as clever or "cool")

    What do you think the long-term results will be for the person? (e.g., an unpleasant story to remember, regret, guilt, getting caught, being found out, worry, disappointing one's family, possible punishment, living with knowing you did the wrong thing)

How do you think the possible benefits compare with the probable harmful effects?

Once you do something you are ashamed of, is there any way to make amends?

How can you stay away from, or keep out of, group activities that are unlawful, unethical, or against the rules?

Causes That Reside in Instructional Environments

Four causes of misbehavior reside in instructional environments and all can be easily corrected. They are physical discomfort, tedium, meaninglessness, and lack of stimulation.

12. *Physical discomfort.* Students become restless or frustrated when made uncomfortable by inappropriate temperature, poor lighting, or unsuitable seating or workspaces.

Resolution Attend to comfort factors in advance and ask students about them. Make corrections as necessary.

13. *Tedium.* Students begin to fidget after a time when an instructional activity requires continued close attention, especially if the topic is not appealing.

Resolution Break the work into shorter segments or add something that increases the interest level.

14. *Meaninglessness.* Students grow restless when required to work at topics they do not comprehend or for which they see no purpose.

Resolution Make sure the topic is meaningful to students—that they understand it and see its relevance and importance in their lives.

15. *Lack of stimulation.* The topic and learning environment provide little that is attractive or otherwise stimulating. Students take no interest in the lesson.

Resolution Select topics and activities in which students have natural interest. When that is not possible, introduce elements students are known to enjoy, such as novelty, mystery, movement, competition, group work, and role playing.

Causes That Reside in Teachers and Other School Personnel

Presently we will see how teachers sometimes misbehave. Other school personnel occasionally misbehave as well, including administrators, librarians, clerical staff, health personnel, cafeteria personnel, custodial personnel, and family members working in the school. Here are ten factors that can cause misbehavior by school personnel, with suggestions for attending to them.

16. *Poor habits.* Educators sometimes unknowingly acquire ineffective or counterproductive ways of dealing with students. They may become set in those ways.

Resolution Watch closely to see how students react to you. Do they seem friendly? Afraid? Attracted to you? Eager to cooperate? Eager to please? If they are reticent, fearful, uncooperative, or unfriendly, analyze your interactions with them and try to determine if your behavior is contributing to the problem.

17. *Unfamiliarity with better techniques.* Some educators have not had occasion to learn some of the newer, more effective ways of teaching and relating with today's students.

Resolution Ask students about things school people do that they really like. Hold discussions with fellow educators about effective teaching techniques and ways of working with students. See if the school can place professional books and journals in the teachers' lounge. Ask other teachers about Internet sites that provide helpful information. There are many such sites.

18. *Presenting poor models of behavior.* At times all of us are inconsistent, irresponsible, and short on self-control, and we sometimes treat students with discourtesy or disregard. We can't expect to be perfect, but we must realize that when we treat students poorly— which is to say in ways we would not want to be treated—we not only damage relationships but also encourage students to imitate our poor behavior.

Resolution Always be the best model you can for your students, who watch you very closely and often pattern their behavior after yours (especially when you misbehave). If you do anything inappropriate, call attention to it, explain why it was wrong, and apologize if necessary.

19. *Showing little interest in or appreciation for students.* We sometimes fail to show interest in students or appreciation for them as individuals, despite knowing they want our attention and want us to be interested in their lives. If we disregard them repeatedly, students become wary of us or may disruptively seek our attention.

Resolution Give each student as much personal attention as possible. Greet them personally, exchange a friendly word, show you are aware of their difficulties, try to help them feel at ease, and acknowledge their progress.

20. *Succumbing to personal frustration.* Some educators are beaten down from continually having to deal with student misbehavior or inconsiderate parents. This leaves them stressed and makes it difficult for them to work with students in a kind, helpful manner.

Resolution Educators who experience intense frustration are often trying unsuccessfully to force students to comply with their expectations. Force does not work well. Replace it with encouragement and enticement. Frustration will diminish as students become cooperative, willing to learn, and considerate.

21. *Succumbing to provocation.* Students sometimes do and say things intentionally to get under your skin, hoping to see you become upset and befuddled and perhaps lose self-control.

Resolution Do not allow students to provoke you. When they try to do so, disregard their comments and actions and proceed as if nothing has happened. If you feel it necessary to respond, say, "Something is causing violations of our agreement about being considerate of others. Can you help me understand? Perhaps we can fix the problem."

22. *Providing ineffective guidance and feedback.* Without proper guidance and feedback, students do not understand what is expected of them, how much progress they have made, or how they can improve.

Resolution Make sure students understand clearly what they are supposed to do and how they should do it. Check to determine they know what is expected. During assigned activities, and again after they are completed, tell students what they have done well or poorly and indicate how they can improve. Ask them to give their opinions about the activity and their efforts.

23. *Using ineffective personal communication.* Some educators are not adept at communicating with students on a personal level. This can be easily corrected. Students want you to know their names and exchange pleasantries with them. They sometimes want to know your views on various matters and want to tell you their views. This provides them a measure of personal validation.

Resolution Speak regularly with students in a friendly way. Avoid comments that hurt feelings or dampen enthusiasm. Say things that increase optimism and bolster confidence. Build students up when you can, but do so honestly. You can find genuinely positive things to say to, and about, each of your students.

24. *Failure to plan proactively.* Many educators do not plan ahead sufficiently to foresee potential problems. Then, when unexpected events occur, they have difficulty saying or doing what would be best under the circumstances.

Resolution Think carefully about problems that might arise in class or possible student reactions to topics, lessons, your requests, or unexpected events. By anticipating potential difficulties, you can avoid most problems and can prepare yourself to deal with whatever might eventuate. Think through what you will do when people are injured or become suddenly ill, grow defiant, or get into fights. Decide what you will do and say if an unauthorized visitor approaches you, if a parent berates you, if the class moans when you give an assignment, and so forth. Determine how you can respond decisively to such eventualities yet maintain positive relationships.

25. *Using coercion, threat, and punishment.* Students don't like to be forced to do anything and they don't like to be threatened. If you treat them abrasively, they keep a watchful eye on you, fearful of being scolded, embarrassed, or demeaned, and they will almost certainly develop negative attitudes toward you and school.

Resolution Give up coercion, threat, and punishment (meaning intimidation, belittlement, and humiliation). Replace them with considerate helpfulness, personal attention, and good communication.

Recognizing and Correcting Teacher Misbehavior

It would be remiss not to acknowledge frankly that we teachers do misbehave at times. Despite our dedication and concern for students, we sometimes do or say things that provoke antagonism, inhibit student progress, and leave the class dispirited. Five types of **teacher misbehavior** are *inducing fearfulness, denigrating students, being demanding and abrasive, presenting poor models of behavior,* and *not making classes interesting and worthwhile.* We misbehave in these ways because we are fearful of losing control of our classes or simply do not know how to use positive tactics that work well. The next several pages show how to eliminate these types of teacher misbehavior.

Establishing a Set of Agreements Concerning Class and Behavior

On the first day of class begin formalizing a set of agreements with your students about how the class is to function concerning teaching, learning, and behavior. Approximately seven short sessions are needed to reach those agreements. For young children, the sessions will require about 10 minutes each, whereas for older students the sessions will require no more than 15 or 20 minutes each.

For all sessions, students should be seated in a close circle. Explain that these class meetings, used for student input and discussion, will occur regularly and that the circular seating arrangement allows eye contact and encourages discussion.

In *Session 1*, begin to establish rapport with your students. Smile. Look into their faces. Tell them you are pleased to see them and are looking forward to working with them. Tell them you want to discuss with them some ideas for making the class enjoyable and useful, but first you want to begin getting acquainted with them. Call their names and ask if you have pronounced them correctly. Tell students just a bit about yourself, including your special interests and why you became a teacher. Then tell the students you'd like to learn more about them. Using the class roster, call on individual students. As appropriate to their age, ask about siblings, pets, hobbies, and special interests. Call on as many as time allows and end the session by saying you hope to know all of them better as quickly as you can.

In *Session 2*, draw the students out concerning how they'd like the class to function. Tell them the overriding class purpose is always to learn and to have an enjoyable time doing so. Ask the following and make notes on a chart as indicated:

- Ask them what are some of the things they like best about school. List their comments on the left side. They will probably include playing, being with friends, sports, art, and music. Some may mention plays, concerts, and athletics.
- Ask what they like, specifically, about each of the things you've written on the chart. Make notes on the right side of the chart.
- Ask if they think any of the things they've mentioned might be possible in this class. Circle things they indicate.

Thank them for their contributions and tell them you want the class to be as they'd like it, insofar as possible. Assure them you will consider their suggestions carefully and make use of as many as possible.

In *Session 3*, give feedback concerning the suggestions students made in Session 2. Beforehand, redo the chart and indicate the suggestions you think you can incorporate into the class. Ask students if they have further thoughts or suggestions. Turn to a fresh page on the chart and elicit comments about the kind of teacher they prefer.

- Ask if they have had a teacher they really enjoyed or respected. Ask them not to mention names but to indicate what that teacher did that made such a good impression. They will say things such as nice, interesting, helpful, fair, and sense of humor. They may also mention favorite activities and special teacher talents. Note the preferred traits on the left side of the chart.
- Review the traits with the class. Ask for examples or further details, such as what they mean by "helpful" or "really fun." Make these notes on the right side of the chart.
- Tell students that all teachers are different but you want to be the kind of teacher they prefer to the extent you are able. Tell them you want to study their comments and will give them feedback at the next session. Thank them for their helpfulness.

In *Session 4*, show students a clean copy of the traits they have identified in teachers they like. Ask if they have additional comments. Tell them you will do your best to be the kind of teacher they appreciate. If you can't do so in every respect, tell them so, and why. Next, draw students out about how they feel they should behave in the class.

- Ask students to think of a classmate who has behaved in ways they admired or appreciated. Without giving names, have them tell what the student was like or what he or she did. List the descriptions on the left side of a clean page.
- When several behaviors have been listed, go back and ask students *why* they appreciated those behaviors. Make notes accordingly.
- Now ask students how they like for other members of a class to treat them. Make notes on a clean page. Go back and once more ask *why*.
- Next, ask what kind of behavior they most appreciate from other students when they are working together on assignments. Ask why.
- Finally, ask students if they think it would be possible to have the kinds of behavior in this classroom that are listed on the chart. Thank them for their input and tell them you'll review their suggestions at the next session.

In *Session 5*, give students feedback on behaviors they have indicated they like and appreciate. Ask if they have further comments.

- Now ask what they *dislike* fellow students doing in class. Make notes as usual.
- When that is done, ask if they have ideas about how to keep those unwanted behaviors from occurring.
- Ask students if they feel they have control over how they, themselves, behave in the class. Follow with "What makes you decide whether to behave properly or improperly?" Ask them if they feel they could almost always behave properly, for their own sake and for the good of the class.

- Say: Suppose despite everything we do, someone decides to misbehave (to break a class agreement). What should we do then? Students will typically suggest punishment or loss of privileges. If they do, say: "I would want the person to understand that the behavior is hurtful to the class. I wouldn't be interested in punishing the person. When there is a problem, we need to fix it. Now put yourself in the place of a student who has misbehaved. How would you like for me to treat you?

Thank the students for their input and tell them you will provide feedback later.

In *Session 6*, ask students to respond to a summary you have made of their suggestions so far. Show them a chart you have prepared that lists (1) things students like best in school, (2) traits they like in teachers, (3) behaviors they appreciate in classmates, (4) behaviors they dislike in classmates, and (5) a plan you have made for helping students want to behave properly in the classroom. Review the first four items and ask if you have understood correctly. Then move into your plan, which indicates:

- Why you think misbehavior won't often occur if the class is interesting, the teacher is helpful, and students treat each other considerately.
- How students can resolve most of their disputes in a friendly manner.
- How you will talk with students who misbehave to try to correct whatever is causing their misbehavior.

Ask the class to comment on the plan and make suggestions. Thank them and indicate you hope the group can formalize some agreements to live by in class.

In *Session 7*, work toward a set of class agreements. Bring back the chart used in the previous session. Put it to the side, in view. Using a blank chart, tell the students you hope they can finalize statements about the following:

- Class activities that are valuable and enjoyable.
- The teacher's way of teaching and treating students.
- The students' ways of treating each other and the teacher.
- How students will work at assigned tasks.

When satisfactory statements have been made, ask the class if they feel they can abide by the agreements. Tell them you will do your best to adhere to them and help students do so as well. Later, prepare a chart of the agreements and post it prominently in the room.

Establishing Conditions That Elevate Class Spirit and Energy

Synergetic Teaching requires putting in place certain conditions that maintain interest and enhance personal relations. We all try to involve ourselves with people, places, objects, situations, and activities we like, while avoiding those we dislike. The following paragraphs summarize what students almost always like and respond well to in class. They also indicate what students dislike and resist. This information is distilled from contributions made by Steve Biddulph (1997), Cynthia Mee (1997), William Glasser (1998), Jean Piaget (2001), Harry Wong (2001), and a number of experienced educators. In these discussions, the word *likes* is used as a noun, meaning conditions that students enjoy, prefer, or seek out.

Emphasize Likes Related to Needs

Students like, seek out, or try to achieve the following, which are associated with basic needs:

> Security, the feeling of safety without worry
> Sense of hope, the feeling that school is worthwhile and success is possible
> Personal dignity, feeling respected and worthwhile
> Belonging, feeling a part of things, being valued, having a place in the class
> Sense of power, with some control of and input into events in the class
> Enjoyment, of activities that are pleasurable or rewarding
> Competence, capable of doing what others can do and what is expected

Conversely, students strongly dislike any conditions that prevent these needs being met. You will find it a real struggle to try to force students to engage in topics or activities they dislike. To the extent possible, reduce or eliminate topics and activities that students clearly do not like or that affect them adversely.

Emphasize Likes Related to Class Life and Activities

Students strongly like and seek:

> Teachers who are friendly, enjoyable, and interesting
> Attentive support and help from the teacher
> Camaraderie—enjoyable associations with classmates
> Interesting topics to learn about that are intriguing and worthwhile
> Enjoyable instructional activities
> Opportunity for, and likelihood of, success and accomplishment
> Having attention drawn tactfully to personal accomplishments

Conversely, students usually dislike the following, which they often encounter in school. By guarding against them, you can cut down greatly on misbehavior. (However, some students do not object to these activities or conditions.)

> Sitting still for long periods
> Keeping quiet for long periods
> Working by oneself
> Memorizing facts for tests
> Completing lengthy writing assignments
> Doing repetitive busy work
> Completing long reading assignments

Engaging in individual competition when there is little or no chance of winning
Having little or no choice in activities, assignments, or assessment

Work to Develop Ethics and Trust

Ethics refers to doing the right thing given the circumstances. Ethical teacher behavior is essential for building trust in the class. Students see teachers as ethical if they are unwaveringly kind, considerate, helpful, fair, honest, and show faith in students. It is also essential to build a sense of **trust** in the classroom. To trust people means we believe we can count on them, that they will come through for us if they possibly can, and that they will support and not harm us. Trust is essential to the synergetic classroom.

Increase Your Personal Charisma

Charisma is a quality people have that attracts others. Students greatly enjoy charismatic teachers and flock to them, eager to follow their lead. Most people think charisma is static, that each of us has a certain fixed amount of it. In fact, charisma is not fixed and can certainly be increased. It comprises talent, experience, knowledge, and understanding of others and is dependent on how these qualities are displayed through smiles, body language, gestures, friendliness, enthusiasm, and sensitivity.

Improve the Quality of Communication

Except for trust, no element of synergy is more important than communication. The type of communication that contributes most to synergy is verbal give-and-take between teacher and students. It involves listening sensitively, showing genuine interest, and speaking encouragingly rather than arguing, moralizing, or giving unsolicited advice.

Make Use of Coopetition

Coopetition, pronounced "co-opetition," refers to members of groups cooperating together in order to compete against other groups. Coopetition is not given a great deal of attention in teaching, but it contributes powerfully to synergy. Probably the greatest example of synergy in education involves athletic teams competing against each other, often bringing the entire school to a fever pitch. Coopetition can be incorporated into almost all areas of the curriculum. Students usually respond to it more enthusiastically than to any other activity.

Resolve Problems and Conflicts Productively

A **problem** is a nonconflict situation that affects the class seriously enough to require attention, whereas a **conflict** is a strong disagreement between students or between teacher and student.

How to Address Problems Suppose students in a high school geometry class are troubled by a heavy load of homework. Or suppose a middle school teacher is greatly embarrassed when the principal visits and finds the room very untidy. When such a situation hinders teaching or learning, or if it causes feelings to run high, it should be addressed immediately. In times past, the teacher would tell the class how to deal with the problem. In Synergetic Teaching, the teacher, having sensed the problem and its nature, might say, "Class, something is going on that I think we need to talk about. Let's move our chairs into a circle." The problem is then clarified, possible solutions are sought, and a solution is selected and tried.

How to Address Conflicts Conflicts are interpersonal situations characterized by strong disagreements, which may or may not include misbehavior. If the individuals involved do not know how to find a peaceful solution, they tend to fight each other verbally, or sometimes physically, thus posing threats to personal dignity that is strongly defended. Examples of conflict situations include disputes over who won a contest, who is entitled to play with a toy, whether work was turned in on time, and whether work has met the standards expected. Conflict is best resolved through a win-win approach in which agreements are reached that allow both sides to get most of what they want. To make such agreements possible, do the following:

- Make sure each person has a chance to express himself or herself.
- Try to make sure all observations and suggestions are presented in a friendly manner.
- Encourage both sides to be open and honest but tactful.
- Encourage each person to try to see things from the other's point of view.
- Keep attention focused on areas of agreement between the disputants.
- Help disputants formulate solutions as if they are joint agreements.
- Don't allow arguing back and forth, defending oneself, or debating.

Intervening When Students Misbehave

Although Synergetic Discipline emphasizes prevention of misbehavior, it can also deal quite effectively with misbehavior that does occur. A typical sequence of intervention steps is shown here. The sequence can be modified in accordance with the age of the students and severity of the misbehavior.

Step One. Subtly remind students of expected behavior. Do this with physical proximity, eye signals, or facial expressions. If these reminders don't work, point to the chart of class agreements and say, "Class, let's please remember our agreement about. . . ."

Step Two. If it seems advisable, identify what is causing the misbehavior. This cause may be apparent, as when students seem to find the lesson boring and, therefore, disengage from it, or it may be obscure, as when Jason and Nathan continue an emotional dispute that originated outside the classroom. Even if you think you know the cause, check with students to make sure. Ask, "Is this too boring for you?" or "Boys, is there a problem I can help you with?" or "Something is causing us to violate our class agreement about being considerate of others. What do you suppose it is?" When the cause is identified, ask students, "How can we deal with this cause in a responsible manner?"

Step Three. If it seems advisable, correct or limit the cause to the extent possible. You may or may not be able to change what is causing students to misbehave. You can usually remove the cause easily if it resides in activities, classroom, or teacher behavior. You can lessen its effects when it involves student needs simply by trying to provide what students crave. It is more difficult to limit causes that have to do with egocentric personalities. You can say, "Jason, something is causing you to call out and disrupt the lesson. That makes it difficult for me to teach and for other students to learn, and violates our class agreement. Can you help me understand what is causing you to do that?"

Step Four. If the misbehavior involves, or leads to, a confrontational dispute, help those involved identify the cause of the disagreement and work together to find a solution.

If the confrontation is between students, as when Jason and Nathan are speaking angrily to each other, consider the following:

1. Ask, "Boys, this is disturbing the class. Can you work the problem out between your-selves, or do you need my help?" (If they say they can work it out between them-selves, ask them if they can keep their dispute from affecting the class. Ask them if they would mind telling you later what they have decided.)

2. If the conflict is such that they can't resolve it themselves, get together with the boys at a suitable time. In a nonthreatening manner:

   ■ Ask each boy to tell you calmly what is troubling him. (Explain that you need to hear each clearly, so please no interrupting or arguing while each is talking.)
   ■ Ask Jason what he would like for Nathan to do differently. Nathan listens carefully.
   ■ Ask Nathan what he would like for Jason to do differently. Jason listens carefully.
   ■ Ask each of the boys if he feels he could do part, or most, of what the other wants.
   ■ If they agree on a possible solution, thank them and leave it at that. If they cannot reach a solution, ask them if they'd mind the class discussing the matter in order to learn more about resolving disputes considerately.
   ■ If they agree, bring up the matter at the next class meeting. If they decline permis-sion, say, "Boys, it is not good for any of us in the class when bad feelings exist. How can we resolve this matter so both of you feel all right? What ideas do you have?" If they reach a settlement, thank them. If they can't, say, "I'm disappointed we can't settle this matter so both of you feel all right. But since we can't, I need to ask you to control yourselves, for the sake of the class." It is unlikely that the con-flict negotiations will ever reach this point; the boys will agree to a solution earlier in the process.

If the conflict is between you and a student, consider the following: When you are help-ing a misbehaving student, your efforts will seldom lead to conflict provided you treat the student with consideration. But if conflict should occur, you need to deal with it in a way that brings resolution while preserving positive feelings. Suppose Melissa has once again failed to do her homework. You ask her kindly if there is a problem that is preventing her complying with the class agreement. For some reason your question strikes a nerve and Melissa retorts, "There wouldn't be a problem if you didn't assign this stupid stuff!" What do you do?

   ■ Say, "Melissa, can you help me understand why you think the homework is stupid? I'd like your opinion because I want it to be helpful to your progress. What can you suggest that would help make it better?" Melissa may apologize, say nothing, come back with another snide remark, or give you an explanation for her feelings. If she says nothing or remains uncooperative, consider saying:

■ "Now is not a good time for us to discuss the matter. Perhaps we can do so later, just the two of us. Could you meet with me for a minute or two at (name a time and place)?" When you meet, tell her you are willing to listen if she has something she needs to talk about. If she declines, assure her you are interested in her views and are always ready to help.

If Melissa apologizes or explains her feelings or talks about some other problem in her life that is probably her real cause of concern, consider saying: "Thank you, Melissa, for informing me. If I can make good changes in the homework or otherwise help with your situation, I'd like to do so. Do you have suggestions?"

Strengths of Charles's *Synergetic Discipline*

Synergetic Discipline provides a structure for increasing student interest and involvement in class activities, which in turn significantly reduces misbehavior, increases student achievement, and produces satisfaction for all concerned. It focuses on identifying and attending to causes of misbehavior. It puts teacher and students on the same side, working collaboratively to maintain a quality program. It increases student responsibility and ethical behavior and it results in a strong sense of satisfaction. It is easy to implement and maintain, and students respond to it positively. Parents like it, too, because it helps and encourages their children in a respectful manner. Synergetic Discipline not only prevents misbehavior but also provides an effective means of addressing misbehavior when it occurs. It does this without offending students and without producing the turmoil and stress that are often associated with discipline.

Initiating Charles's *Synergetic Discipline*

Synergetic Discipline is used only to encourage students helpfully, never to try to coerce them. It acknowledges students' feelings, supports their interests, shows them respect, and provides help for success. It does this in a dignified manner. You saw how to introduce Synergetic Discipline earlier in the chapter, in the section entitled "Establishing a Set of Agreements Concerning Class and Behavior."

KEY TERMS AND CONCEPTS PRESENTED IN THIS CHAPTER

The following terms and concepts are central to your understanding of Synergetic Discipline. Check yourself to make sure you understand them

| basic student needs | belonging | dignity |
| security | hope | power |

enjoyment	Synergetic Teaching	causes of misbehavior
competence	ethics	charisma
student likes and dislikes	trust	coopetition
synergy	problem	class agreements
Synergetic Discipline	conflict	teacher misbehavior

SELECTED SEVEN—SUMMARY SUGGESTIONS FROM C. M. CHARLES

C. M. Charles suggests that you emphasize the following, as well as his many other suggestions:

1 In discipline, your challenge is to help students conduct themselves considerately and responsibly, not to show you can dominate them.

2 Much student misbehavior results from thwarted needs. Make sure your educational program is consistent with student needs for security, hope, acceptance, dignity, power, enjoyment, and competence.

3 Use qualities and techniques that attract students and make them inclined to cooperate with you, such as trust, charisma, personal attention, and helpfulness.

4 Guard against teacher misbehavior such as inducing fearfulness, denigrating students, being demanding and abrasive, presenting poor models of behavior, and failing to make classes interesting and worthwhile.

5 Establish conditions that lead reliably to synergy (when it would be helpful), such as studying interesting topics, providing activities that students enjoy, and using cooperative methods that lead to significant outcomes for the group.

6 When you have first contact with your students, begin working on agreements with them concerning instruction, learning activities, and personal behavior. From that point forward, always help students and encourage them to abide by the agreements and accept responsibility.

7 When misbehavior occurs, deal with it in a helpful, nonconfrontive manner. Never argue with students, put them down, or back them into a corner. Instead, show continual willingness to correct whatever is troubling the students and resolve problems and conflicts equitably. Show you are interested in helping, not punishing.

CONCEPT CASES

■ CASE 1 *Kristina Will Not Work*

Kristina, a student in Mr. Jake's class, is quite docile. She socializes little with other students and never disrupts lessons. However, despite Mr. Jake's best efforts, Kristina will not do her work. She rarely completes an assignment. She is simply there, putting forth no effort at all. *How would Charles deal with Kristina?*

Charles would advise Mr. Jake to do the following: First, Mr. Jake should quickly appraise Kristina's efforts and general demeanor to see if he can determine why Kristina is not working. Then in a quiet, friendly tone, he might say, "Kristina, I see this work is not getting done. Our class agreement is that we will always try to do our best. Is there something about the assignment that bothers you?" If she indicates a difficulty, such as the work is too hard or she doesn't understand it, Mr. Jake could reply, "What do you think might help?" or "Is there something I could do to help you get started?" Probably Kristina will begin working. If she does not, Mr. Jake could say, "Kristina, I think this work is important and I want to help you get it done. Would you like to try . . . ?" Mr. Jake lists two options, such as working with another student to complete the assignment or doing an alternative assignment that he names. In the unlikely possibility this still doesn't get Kristina started, Mr. Jake might say, "Kristina, I want to do everything possible to help you enjoy the class and learn successfully. I know I can't make you learn if you don't want to. Frankly, I'm not sure what to suggest now. Can you think of anything?" If she cannot, ask if she would allow the class to discuss the situation in their next class meeting as a way to learn better how to help each student learn.

■ CASE 2 *Sara Cannot Stop Talking*
Sara is a pleasant girl who participates in class activities and does most, though not all, of her assigned work. She cannot seem to refrain from talking to classmates, however. Her teacher, Mr. Gonzales, has to speak to her repeatedly during lessons, to the point that he often becomes exasperated and loses his temper. *What suggestions would Charles give Mr. Gonzales for dealing with Sara?*

■ CASE 3 *Joshua Clowns and Intimidates*
Larger and louder than his classmates, Joshua always wants to be the center of attention, which he accomplishes through a combination of clowning and intimi-

dation. He makes wise remarks, talks back (smilingly) to the teacher, utters a variety of sound-effect noises such as automobile crashes and gunshots, and makes limitless sarcastic comments and put-downs of his classmates. Other students will not stand up to him, apparently fearing his size and verbal aggression. His teacher, Miss Pearl, has come to her wit's end. *Would Joshua's behavior be likely to improve if Synergetic Discipline were used in Miss Pearl's classroom? Explain.*

■ CASE 4 *Tom Is Hostile and Defiant*
Tom has appeared to be in his usual foul mood ever since arriving in class. On his way to sharpen his pencil, he bumps into Frank, who complains. Tom tells him loudly to shut up. Miss Baines, the teacher, says, "Tom, go back to your seat." Tom wheels around, swears loudly, and says heatedly, "I'll go when I'm damned good and ready!" *How would Tom's behavior be handled in a synergetic classroom?*

QUESTIONS AND ACTIVITIES

1. In your journal, add information from this chapter that helps elaborate the five principles for building a personal system of discipline.

2. To what extent do you feel you could put Synergetic Teaching and Discipline into effect in your classroom? What portions do you believe you could implement easily? What portions do you believe might be difficult?

3. Synergetic Discipline neither punishes students for misbehavior nor does it apply penalties or other measures to try to force student compliance. Do you think

students will take advantage of Synergetic Discipline's softer nature, that they will disregard the teacher because they have no fear of the consequences? Is there anything in Synergetic Discipline that would prevent them from doing so?

4. If you introduce Synergetic Discipline as Charles suggests, a few days might pass before students have reached complete agreement on class behavior and preferences. Can you think of four or five strategies you might use to keep students from misbehaving while the program is taking effect?

YOU ARE THE TEACHER

This scenario was used previously for applying Budd Churchward's Honor System tactics. Note the differences in Churchward's and Charles's approaches.

High School Biology
You teach advanced placement classes in biology to students from middle- to upper-income families. Most of the students have already made plans for attending college. When the students enter the classroom, they know

they are to go to their assigned seats and write out answers to the questions of the day that you have written on the board. After that, you conduct discussions on text material that you assigned students to read before coming to class. During the lecture, you call randomly on students to answer questions and require that they support their answers with reference to the assigned reading. Following the lecture, students engage in lab activity for the remainder of the period.

A Typical Occurrence

You have just begun a discussion about the process of photosynthesis. You ask Sarolyn what the word *photosynthesis* means. She pushes her long hair aside and replies, "I don't get it." This is a comment you hear frequently from Sarolyn. "What is it you don't understand?" "None of it," she says. You retort, "Be more specific! I've only asked for the definition!" Sarolyn is not intimidated. "I mean, I don't get any of it. I don't understand why plants are green. Why aren't they blue or some other color? Why don't they grow on Mercury? The book says plants make food. How? Do they make bread? That's ridiculous. I don't understand this business about photosynthesis." You gaze at Sarolyn for a while, and she back at you. You ask, "Are you finished?" Sarolyn shrugs. "I guess so." She hears some of the boys whistle under their breath; she enjoys their attention. You say to her, "Sarolyn, I hope some day you will understand that this is not a place for you to show off." "I hope so, too," Sarolyn says. "I know I should be more serious." She stares out the window. For the remainder of the discussion, which you don't handle as well as usual, you call only on students you know will give correct answers. The discussion completed, you begin to give instructions for lab activity. You notice that Nick is turning the valve of the gas jet on and off. You say to Nick, "Mr. Contreras, would you please repeat our rule about the use of lab equipment?" Nick drops his head and mumbles something about waiting for directions. Sarolyn says calmly, "Knock it off, Nick. This is serious business." She smiles at you. After a moment, you complete your directions and tell the students to begin. You walk around the room, monitoring their work. You stand behind lab partners Mei and Teresa, who are having a difficult time. You do not offer them help, believing that advanced placement students should be able to work things out for themselves. But as they blunder through the activity, you find yourself shaking your head in disbelief. Although you don't intend it, you present the impression you hope the two girls will drop the class.

Conceptualizing a Strategy

If you followed the suggestions of C. M. Charles, what would you conclude or do with regard to the following?

1. Preventing the problems from occurring in the first place.
2. Putting a clear end to the misbehavior now.
3. Involving other or all students in addressing the situation.
4. Maintaining student dignity and good personal relations.
5. Using follow-up procedures that would prevent the recurrence of the misbehavior.
6. Using the situation to help the students develop a sense of greater responsibility and self-control.

REFERENCES

Biddulph, S. 1997. *Raising boys.* Sydney, Australia: Finch Publishing.

Charles, C. 1974. *Teaches' petit Piaget.* Belmont, CA: Fearon.

Charles, C. 2000. *The synergetic classroom.* Boston: Allyn and Bacon.

Charles, C. 2002. *Essential elements of effective discipline.* Boston: Allyn and Bacon.

Glasser, W. 1998a. *The quality school: Managing students without coercion.* New York: HarperCollins.

Glasser, W. 1998b. *The quality school teacher.* New York: HarperCollins.

Mee, C. 1997. *2,000 voices: Young adolescents' perceptions and curriculum implications.* Columbus, OH: National Middle School Association.

Piaget, J. 2001. *The psychology of intelligence.* London: Routledge & Kegan Paul.

Wong, H. 2001. Summary of major concepts covered by Harry K. Wong. www.glavac.com/harrywong.htm.

CHAPTER 14

Alfie Kohn's
Beyond Discipline

Focus

- Teaching that promotes thinking, decision making, and consideration for others.
- Developing a sense of community in the classroom with shared responsibility.
- Involving students in resolving classroom problems, thus removing aversive control.

Logic

- Coercive discipline has no place in enlightened teaching: It harms rather than helps.
- Students develop self-control and responsibility when trusted and allowed initiative.
- Effective teachers use collaborative problem solving instead of coercive control.

Contributions

- Urged "constructivist teaching" as the best approach to education.
- Showed how coercive discipline limits the development of caring human beings.
- Popularized the concept of classroom as community with equal participation by all.
- Provided guidance to help teachers transform their classrooms into communities.

Kohn's Suggestions

- Involve students seriously in discussing curriculum, procedures, and class problems.
- Organize the curriculum to attend to student interests and promote in-depth thinking.
- Always ask the question: How can my students help decide on this matter?
- Use participative classroom management to resolve problems that occur in the class.

About Alfie Kohn

Formerly a teacher, Alfie Kohn is now a full-time writer and lecturer. He has several influential books to his credit, including *The Brighter Side of Human Nature: Altruism and Empathy in Everyday Life* (1990); *No Contest: The Case Against Competition* (1986, 1992); *Punished by Rewards: The Trouble with Gold Stars, Incentive Plans, A's, Praise, and Other Bribes* (1993, 1999); *Beyond Discipline: From Compliance to Community* (1996, 2001); and *The Schools Our Children Deserve: Moving Beyond Traditional Classrooms and "Tougher Standards"* (1999). He has also published numerous journal articles related to motivation, grading, discipline, and developing caring people. Recognized as one of the most original thinkers in education, Kohn has appeared on over 200 radio and television programs, including *Oprah* and *The Today Show,* and his work has received mention in scores of national newspapers and magazines. He speaks frequently at major conferences and conducts workshops across the nation. He can be reached at his website www.alfiekohn.org.

Kohn's Central Focus

Kohn's critical analyses of schooling and teaching have focused mainly on helping teachers develop caring, supportive classrooms in which students pursue in depth topics of interest to them and participate fully in solving class problems, including problems of behavior. He has roundly criticized teaching and approaches to discipline that do things *to* students rather than *involving* students as partners in the process. Particularly scathing have been his attacks on discipline schemes that involve reward and punishment. He says that nothing valuable comes from reward and punishment—that the process is actually counterproductive, not only because it produces side effects such as mistrust, avoidance, and working for rewards only, but also because it causes students to mistrust their own judgment and thwarts their becoming caring and self-reliant. He advises teachers to forget the popular systems of discipline and work instead toward developing a **sense of community** in their classes, where students feel safe and are continually brought into making judgments, expressing their opinions, and working cooperatively toward solutions that affect themselves and the class.

Kohn's Contributions to Discipline

Kohn has made two significant contributions to discourse on classroom discipline. The first is his proposition that instruction should be based on **constructivist theory,** which holds that students cannot receive knowledge directly from teachers but must construct it from experience. A corollary of this view is that for instruction to be effective students must be involved deeply in topics they consider important, and when they do so there is little need for discipline controls of any sort. The second contribution is his rationale and prescription for developing a sense of community in the classroom, which he judges essential for developing caring, responsible students. This sense of community would more effectively bring about purposeful activity and concern for others, which is what teachers normally hope to achieve through discipline techniques.

Kohn's Principal Teachings

- *Educators must abandon teaching that "does things to" students and replace it with teaching that takes students seriously, involves them in decisions, and helps them explore in depth topics they consider important.*

  Students quickly forget most of what they learn in traditional teaching because the learning is superficial and of little importance from the students' point of view.

- *Educators must look beyond the techniques of discipline and ask the question: What are we attempting to accomplish with discipline?*

  Doing this, he says, will make evident that most teachers are thinking in terms of making students compliant and quiet, conditions that do not develop the kinds of people we'd like students ultimately to become.

- *Virtually all popular discipline programs are based on threat, reward, and punishment, which are used to gain student compliance.*

  Essentially, discipline programs differ only in how kindly and respectfully the teacher speaks to students while using threat, reward, and punishment.

- *When students are rewarded (or punished) into compliance, they usually feel no commitment to what they are doing.*

  They have no real understanding of why they are doing the act and are not becoming people who *want* to act this way in the future.

- *Teacher-made rules are of no practical value in the classroom.*

  This is because students learn how best to behave not from being told but from having the opportunity to behave responsibly.

- *Some teachers—and most authorities in discipline—have an unrealistically negative view of students' basic motives.*

  They consider students to be predisposed to disobedience and troublemaking. They seem also to ignore that the curriculum powerfully influences student interest and involvement.

- *Student growth toward kindness, happiness, and self-fulfillment occurs as they work closely with fellow students.*

  This includes students' disagreeing and arguing with each other, which can have positive benefits.

● *When concerns arise, the teacher should always ask students, "What do you think we can do to solve this problem?"*

This question is pivotal in helping students develop a sense of capability and responsibility.

● *Class meetings offer the best forum for addressing questions that affect the class. Education must be reformed so that classrooms take on the nature of communities.*

A classroom community is a place where students are cared about and care about others, are valued and respected, and think in terms of *we* instead of *I*.

● *Teachers who wish to move beyond discipline must do three things:*

Provide an engaging curriculum based on student interests, develop a sense of community, and draw students into meaningful decision making.

Analysis of Kohn's *Beyond Discipline*

Discipline *per se* makes no sense except in relation to what the teacher is attempting to accomplish in the classroom. If the teacher is primarily concerned with keeping order and maintaining quiet, there are a number of effective discipline systems to use. If, on the other hand, the teacher is primarily concerned with developing self-directed, responsible, caring students who explore in depth topics they consider interesting and relevant, then an entirely different approach is required. Before we can properly understand what discipline means to Kohn, we need to examine his views concerning education and teaching.

The Trouble with Today's Teaching

Kohn thinks *traditional teaching* is falling well short of the expectations we hold for it. When he says traditional teaching, he means the type that is seen in classrooms everywhere in which the teacher selects the curriculum, does the planning, delivers the lessons through lecture, demonstration, guided discussion, reading assignments, worksheets, and homework, and tests students to assess their progress. Emphasis in that kind of instruction is placed on helping students reach certain specific objectives—information and skills that students can demonstrate behaviorally. Little attention is given to exploring ideas, seeking new solutions, looking for meaning or connections, or attempting to gain deeper understanding of the phenomena involved. Students remain relatively passive during traditional instruction. They listen, read assignments, answer questions when called on, and complete worksheets. There is little give-and-take. Instruction and learning are deemed "successful" to the extent that students show on tests that they have reached most of the stated objectives.

What is wrong with this kind of teaching? After all, it has been the predominant method of teaching for many years. Kohn (1999, p. 28) says that it counterproductively puts emphasis on *how well* students are doing rather than *on what* they are doing. Instruction concerned with *how well* tends to focus on outcomes that are shallow, relatively insignificant, and of little interest or relevance to learners. Students come to think of correct answers and good grades as the major goals of learning. They rarely experience the satisfaction of exploring in depth a topic of interest and exchanging their views and insights with others. Kohn says an impressive and growing body of research shows that the traditional approach produces several undesirable outcomes, such as:

- undermining student interest in learning
- making failure seem overwhelming
- not leading students to challenge themselves
- reducing the quality of learning (that is, learning that has little depth or relevance)
- causing students to think of how smart they are instead of how hard they are trying

He goes on to say that students taught in this way develop a poor attitude toward learning. They think of learning as getting the work done rather than something they could be excited about exploring. Once they have done the "stuff," they quickly forget much of it as they move on to learn more new stuff. They strive to get the right answer, and when they do not, or if they don't make top scores on the test, they experience a sense of failure that is out of place in genuine learning in which making mistakes is the rule rather than the exception. They never have reason to challenge themselves intellectually. Their learning is superficial and their desire to learn for its own sake is nonexistent. The overall result is that although students seem to be learning well, they are actually doing poorly because they are not thinking widely and exploring ideas thoughtfully.

How Instruction Should Be Done

Kohn argues for instruction that is very different from traditional teaching. He says, first, that students should be taken seriously. By that he means teachers must honor them as individuals and seek to determine what they need and enjoy. Good teachers, he says, use a constructivist approach, knowing that students must construct knowledge and skills out of the experiences provided in school. These teachers look for where students' interests lie, continually trying to imagine how things look from the child's point of view and figuring out what lies behind the child's questions and mistakes. Such teachers know knowledge cannot be absorbed from the teacher. They, therefore, lead students to explore topics, grapple with them, and make sense of them. They provide challenges and emphasize that making mistakes is an important part of learning. Kohn has much to say about the role of mistakes in learning. He gives an example (1999, pp. 138–139) in which the teacher asks the class how many legs an insect has. A boy answers, "Twelve or fifteen or more." The teacher is tempted to say "No . . . " but instead decides to try to get a feeling for what the boy is thinking. She asks if he can give an example, and he replies, "a caterpillar." This unexpected answer opens up a good discussion about adult insects, larvae, and the possibility of mutations.

How do teachers help students move into deeper levels of thinking? Kohn says the best way is by asking them for examples or asking the question, "How do we know that?" This helps students maintain a critical mind, a healthy skepticism, a need for evidence, a willingness to hear different points of view, and a desire to see how things are connected.

It encourages them to appraise the importance of what they are learning and to explore how it can be useful in their lives.

From his constructivist position, Kohn argues for a curriculum that allows students to be purposefully active most of the time rather than passive. He says the way to bring that about is to " . . . start *not* with facts to be learned or disciplines to be mastered, but with questions to be answered" (1999, p. 145). He says these questions should not lead students to correct answers but make students pause, wonder, and reflect. Kohn gives examples of what he means in questions such as, "How could you improve the human hand?" and "Why were the founding fathers so afraid of democracy?" (1999, p. 146).

Kohn urges educators to remember three key facts about teaching: (1) Students learn most avidly and have their best ideas when they get to choose which questions they want to explore; (2) all of us tend to be happiest and most effective when we have some say about what we are doing; and (3) when student choice and control over learning is not allowed, achievement drops. Given these facts and the difference they make in learning, it is astonishing that present-day instruction tends systematically to ignore them. It is unnerving to most teachers, at least at first, to try to organize instruction in accordance with Kohn's suggestions. Kohn, however, says it is breathtaking to be involved in learning when students have a say in the curriculum and can decide what they will do, when, where, with whom, and toward what end. Kohn points out that this approach must be adjusted to the maturity levels of students, but he maintains it is a rule of thumb that "the more students' questions and decisions drive the lesson, the more likely (it is) that real learning will occur" (1999, p. 151). The best teachers, he insists, are those who ask themselves, "Is this a decision I must make on my own, or can I involve students in it?"

To summarize, Kohn's description of good teaching includes the following:

- Teachers taking students seriously by treating them as individuals with needs to be met, including the opportunity to delve deeply into topics of interest.
- Strong student involvement in making decisions about what is to be learned and how progress will be demonstrated.
- Curriculum and instruction organized in large part around questions students want to explore.
- Questions explored in depth, rather than superficially, and opinion, evidence, relevance, and interconnectedness examined critically.
- Students encouraged to work actively, purposefully, and often cooperatively, with give-and-take.
- Teachers assisting students by helping to obtain needed resources, listening, urging and encouraging, exploring mistakes and showing students how to use mistakes productively, and helping them make sense of what they are learning.
- Progress demonstrated not in test results but in productivity, insight, and ability to explain and analyze critically.

Where Discipline Fits in Kohn's Views on Teaching

It is time, Kohn says (2001, p. 54), to decide just what it is we hope to accomplish with discipline. We should take a serious look beyond the *methods* of discipline and give careful consideration to the *goals* of discipline. This statement gives pause. Most people have taken for granted that the goal of discipline is to control student behavior (or enable students to control their own behavior in accordance with adult expectations) so that teaching and learning may proceed as intended. But Kohn persists in putting the question: "Just what is it we are trying to do here?"

This question presents an issue, he says, that people who write about and do research in discipline never address. They expound on "effective discipline," but effective in regard to what? The obvious answer is that discipline is considered to be effective when it causes students to behave as teachers wish them to. Therein lies the rub, in Kohn's view. All approaches to discipline, when analyzed, reveal a set of assumptions about students, learning, and the role of the teacher. Because these assumptions are seldom made explicit, even in the writings of the most respected authorities, they directly suggest that (1) students are by nature predisposed to disrupt the learning program and deal misery to teachers, (2) learning occurs best in an atmosphere of structure, quiet, and order, and (3) the teacher's role in discipline is to make students obedient, compliant, and above all quiet.

Kohn contends that all three assumptions are ill-founded and he, therefore, finds fault with virtually all the popular approaches to classroom discipline. He points, for example, to the work of Jacob Kounin (see Chapter 2), one of the first writers to attempt a scientific analysis of classroom behavior related to discipline. Preeminent among several teacher traits that Kounin found helpful in discipline is one called "withitness." Teachers display this trait when they are attentive to what all students are doing in the classroom at all times and make sure the students are aware of it. Such teachers are more effective than their "withoutit" colleagues, to use Kohn's words. But to what does the word *effective* refer? Kohn points out that Kounin used it to mean getting student conformity and obedience. In other words, it means that students keep busy at their assigned work and don't do anything the teacher considers inappropriate. Kohn (2001) says:

> Now, if a good classroom is one where students simply do what they're told, we shouldn't be surprised that a teacher is more likely to have such a classroom when students are aware that she can quickly spot noncompliance. (p. 55)

Kohn levels some of his sharpest criticisms against the Canters' Assertive Discipline but is also troubled by contentions in many of the "newer" approaches to discipline. He alludes to what he calls the rhetoric that accompanies these supposedly more humane discipline systems, saying:

> . . . I have reluctantly concluded . . . that the New Disciplines are just as much about getting compliance as is the more traditional approach. The overriding goal is to get students to do what they are supposed to be doing . . . (and) to learn what's acceptable to the teacher and what's not. (p. 59)

The Trouble with Compliance

Thus, Kohn is deeply troubled by the notion that schooling is usually structured to force, or at least entice, **compliant behavior** from students. Most teachers are delighted when students comply with their expectations, so what is wrong with compliance? Kohn describes how he often begins workshops with teachers by asking the question: "What are your long-terms goals for the students you work with? What would you like them to be—to be like—long after they've left you?" (2001, p. 60). Teachers say they want their students to be caring, happy, responsible, curious, and creative, a conclusion that

> . . . is unsettling because it exposes a yawning chasm between what we want and what we are doing, between how we would like students to turn out and how our classrooms and schools actually work. We want children to continue reading and thinking after school has ended, yet we focus their attention on grades, which have been shown to reduce interest in learning. We want them to be critical thinkers, yet we feed them predigested facts and discrete skills—partly because of pressure from various constituencies to pump up standardized test scores. We act as though our goal is short-term retention of right answers rather than genuine understanding. (Kohn, 2001, p. 61)

Many teachers rely heavily on class rules and rewarding students who behave or respond as teachers want. But Kohn points out that even when students are rewarded into compliance, they usually feel no commitment to what they are doing, no genuine understanding of the act or why they are doing it, and no sense that they are becoming people who *want* to act this way in the future. Moreover, classroom rules are self-defeating because they cause students to look for ways of subverting the rules and cast teachers as police officers who feel obliged to take action when students break the rules. Kohn (2001) concludes that the entire process of behavior management works against what we hope to achieve:

> The more we "manage" students' behavior and try to make them do what we say, the more difficult it is for them to become morally sophisticated people who think for themselves and care about others. (p. 62)

Kohn says that if compliance is *not* what teachers are looking for in the long run, then we are faced with a basic conflict between our ultimate goals for learners and the methods we are using to achieve those goals. One or the other, Kohn asserts, has got to give.

What Is Needed in Classroom Management

If we give up reward and punishment as means of ensuring desired behavior, indeed if we move away from compliance entirely as the goal of discipline, then what are we left with? Most people ask, "Aren't there times when we simply need students to do what we tell them?" Kohn begins his reply to that question by suggesting that teachers think carefully about how often "students need to do what the teacher tells them." He notes that the number of such occasions varies widely from one teacher to another, which suggests that the need for student compliance is seated in the teacher's personality and background. Teachers ought to examine their preferences and bring them to the conscious level: If one teacher needs students to be more compliant than another, is that teacher then entitled to use a coercive discipline program to meet his or her particular needs?

When reflecting on this point, many teachers are inclined to ask whether this means that anything goes, whether students don't have to comply with expectations that they participate and learn, and whether they can ignore assignments, shout obscenities, and create havoc.

This concern, Kohn explains, misses the point. The question isn't whether it's all right for students to act in those ways, but rather, are they likely to do so if their teacher does not demand control and compliance, but instead emphasizes a curriculum that appeals to students. Teachers do not have to choose between chaos on the one hand and being a strong boss on the other. There is another, and better, option available to teachers, which is to work with students in creating a democratic community where the teacher is not much concerned with personal status and only rarely with demanding compliance.

Kohn contends that students in such classrooms are likely to comply with teacher expectations when it is truly necessary for them to do so, and he acknowledges that there are such times, as when personal abuse or safety or legal matters are concerned. Even then, students are more apt to comply willingly when bonds of trust have been built between teacher and students. Teachers who make a habit of trusting students find that students come to trust and respect them in return.

The Value of Conflict

Student growth toward kindness, happiness, and self-fulfillment depends more on working closely with fellow students, including disagreeing and arguing with them, than with following rules and learning discrete bits of information. Kohn says that it is more important for students to wrestle with dilemmas, clash with others' ideas, and take others' needs into account than to follow sets of rules. The sound of children arguing (at least in many circumstances) should be music to teachers' ears. True, conflict can become destructive, in which case it must be stopped and the problem ironed out. But disagreement presents golden opportunities for learning and, therefore, should not be suppressed. Even hurtful conflict needs to be resolved rather than pushed aside. Kohn notes that teachers should be wary of various versions of conflict resolution that do not examine the deeper issues involved, including people's motives and the possibility that something valuable may be gained from dealing with the conflict. Kohn expresses suspicion about classrooms that operate too smoothly and cleanly. To him, they suggest that conflict may have been conveniently suppressed by the teacher.

Teachers question the practicality of stopping planned lessons in favor of lessons about resolving conflict. Certainly, many situations do not permit an extended discussion at the time they occur. When that is the case, the teacher may wish to ask for a conversation about the matter later on. The enlightened point of view, hard though it may be to accept at first, is that teachers should expect and welcome students' arguments about the rules. Students become thinkers when they try to make sense of things in their own minds. Students who cannot voice their opinions find ways of expressing them in ways far less productive than rational argument. Kohn says that discipline writers are wrong in suggesting that teachers should do everything possible to keep classroom misbehavior from occurring. Kohn (2001) suggests instead that

. . . the real quantum leap in thinking is not from after-the-fact to prevention, where problems are concerned. It involves getting to the point that we ask, "What exactly is construed as a problem here—and why?" It means shifting from eliciting conformity and ending conflict to helping students become active participants in their own social and ethical development. (p. 77)

Regarding Structure and Limits

Most teachers feel it is necessary to place structure and limits on student behavior if the class is to function efficiently. Is their belief justified? Kohn presents criteria for determining how defensible a structure or limit is in terms of how much it resembles plain teacher control. Here are some of his criteria:

- *Purpose.* A restriction is legitimate to the extent its objective is to protect students from harm as opposed to imposing order for its own sake.
- *Restrictiveness.* The less restrictive a structure or limit is the better. Kohn says that it is harder, for example, to justify a demand for silence than for quiet voices.
- *Flexibility.* Although some structure is helpful, one must always be ready to modify the structure in accordance with student needs.
- *Developmental appropriateness.* Kohn uses the example that although we need to make sure that young children are dressed for winter weather, it is better to let older students decide on such matters for themselves.
- *Presentation style.* The way in which restrictions are presented makes a big difference in how students accept them. Kohn cites a study that found no negative effects when guidelines for using art supplies were presented respectfully to students. But when the identical rules were presented to another group in a tone that ordered them to comply, the students showed less interest and did less creative work.
- *Student involvement.* Most importantly, it is student input that makes structure acceptable. When concerns arise, the teacher can ask students, "What do you think we can do to solve this problem?"

Class Meetings

Kohn agrees with many other authorities that class meetings offer the best forum for addressing questions that affect the class. He makes the following points about class meetings:

- *Sharing.* Class meetings are a place to talk about interesting events. Students decide whether or not they want to speak up.
- *Deciding.* Class meetings are ideal places for deciding on matters that affect the class, such as furniture arrangement and procedures for working on projects.
- *Planning.* Class meetings are places where planning should be done for field trips, raising money, inviting chaperones, and so forth. Teachers should always be asking themselves, "Wait a minute: How can I bring the students in on this?"
- *Reflecting.* Class meetings are good places to think about progress, what has been learned, what might have worked better, and what changes might help the class.

Holding good class meetings is not as easy as it sounds. Sometimes participants can't agree on a solution. Some don't participate. Some behave in an unkindly manner to someone's idea or don't pay attention. Sometimes one or two students dominate the meeting. Kohn reminds us that these are not problems for the teacher to solve alone. They are to be brought up for consideration and dealt with by the group.

Many teachers say they like the idea of class meetings but can't find time in their schedules to include them. Kohn gives a simple response to that concern: Make the time. Class meetings are too important to leave by the wayside. They bring social and ethical benefits, foster intellectual development, motivate students to become more effective learners, and greatly cut down on the need to deal with discipline problems. Kohn tells of a secondary math teacher who regularly devotes time to class meetings even though the class is limited to a total of 45 minutes per day. In their meetings the students reflect on how the class is going, exchange ideas on their independent projects, decide when the next test should be scheduled, and decide when it would be appropriate to work in small groups.

Making Decisions

The process of making decisions produces many benefits for students, such as helping them become more self-reliant, causing them to think issues through, and encouraging them to buy-in to the school program. This is not a matter to be reserved for older students alone. As Kohn says, it is experience with decisions that helps children become capable of handling them.

But students long accustomed to being told what to do may need time to get used to deciding on things for themselves. Kohn cautions that students may respond to increased freedom in several different ways—ways that can be discouraging to educators who aren't prepared for reactions such as:

- *Acting out.* As students adjust to greater freedom, teachers may see a lot more behavior of every kind, including negative behavior. This is not especially pleasant, Kohn says, but he urges teachers to keep thinking, "Bring the kids in on it." In class meetings ask them if they can figure out what's going on and what to do about it.
- *Testing the teacher.* Students may test teachers in several ways in order to see whether the teacher means what he or she says about wanting students to express themselves. They may be trying to see whether the teacher really means it when saying, "This is *our* classroom!"
- *Outright resistance.* Students may simply refuse to do what the teacher asks. That is a good time to discuss with them questions such as, "What is the teacher's job? And what about yours? Are you old enough to participate in such decisions? Do you learn better in a classroom where someone is always telling you what to do?"
- *Silence.* Some students will not participate in class discussions, even when asked for their opinion. The teacher should reflect on why this is happening. It might be that the student has nothing to say for the moment, doesn't feel safe with the teacher or classmates, is chronically shy, or has trouble handling new responsibility.
- *Parroting.* Some students will make glib remarks in discussions, hoping to say what the teacher wants to hear. When that occurs, the teacher might want to invite deeper

reflection rather than taking that response at face value. In so doing, the teacher should be careful not to criticize the individual student.

School and Classrooms as Communities

Kohn writes at length about the importance of transforming schools and classrooms into **communities.** By *community* Kohn (2001) means

> a place in which students feel cared about and are encouraged to care about each other. They experience a sense of being valued and respected; the children matter to one another and to the teacher. They have come to think in the plural: they feel connected to each other; they are part of an "us." And, as a result of all this, they feel safe in their classes, not only physically but emotionally. (pp. 101–102)

Kohn suggests various strategies that will help teachers and schools move toward a greater sense of community. Among them are the following:

Building Relationships between Teachers and Students

Students come to behave more respectfully when important adults in their lives behave respectfully toward *them*. They are more likely to care about others if they know *they* are cared about. If their emotional needs are met, they show a tendency to help meet other people's needs rather than remaining preoccupied with themselves.

Enhancing Connections among Students

Connections among students are established and enhanced through activities that involve interdependence. Familiar activities for enhancing connections include cooperative learning, getting-to-know-you activities such as interviewing fellow students and introducing them to the class, and finding a partner to check opinions with on whatever is being discussed at the moment. Kohn also suggests using activities that promote **perspective taking,** in which students try to see situations from another person's point of view.

Undertaking Classwide and Schoolwide Activities

To develop a sense of community, students need plenty of opportunity for the whole class to collaborate on group endeavors. This might involve producing a class mural, producing a class newsletter or magazine, staging a verse choir performance, or doing some community service activity as a class. Kohn contends that the overall best activity for involving the entire group is a class meeting, as discussed earlier. Such meetings at the beginning of the year can be particularly helpful in establishing a sense of community. Kohn suggests posing questions at these first meetings, such as: "What makes school awful sometimes? Try to remember an experience during a previous year when you hated school, when you felt bad about yourself, or about everyone else, and you couldn't wait for it to be over. What exactly was going on when you were feeling that way? How was the class set up?"

Kohn says that not enough teachers encourage this sort of reflection, particularly in elementary schools where an aggressively sunny outlook pervades. Students' feelings of anger or self-doubt do not vanish just because their expression is forbidden.

Using Academic Instruction

The quest for community is not separate from academic learning. Class meetings can be devoted to talking about how the next unit in history might be approached or what the students thought was best and worst about the math test. Academic study pursued in co-operative groups enables students to make connections while learning from each other. Units in language arts and literature can be organized to promote reflection on helpfulness, fairness, and compassion.

Strengths of Kohn's *Beyond Discipline*

Kohn brings into public debate intriguing ideas about how education can be done to produce people who lead full lives and contribute to society. He is very critical of traditional education for being shallow and unattractive to learners. But he doesn't stop with criticism—he sets forth compelling alternatives that he believes will make education the dynamic force it should be. His suggestions have to do mostly with curriculum and teaching and little to do directly with discipline. This is understandable because he advocates building curriculum around topics students find interesting and relevant, while eschewing topics that have no appeal or relevance to real life. When students are afforded the opportunity to delve into such topics, and when their progress is not driven by getting answers right on tests, they will eagerly explore learning in depth, enjoy give-and-take with other students, and seek out connections that help them make sense of things. When thus engaged in learning, students have little reason to misbehave. Should personal problems arise, they are sorted out by those involved or, if necessary, addressed by the class as a whole. Yet, Kohn does make suggestions to strengthen relationships among members of the class, as seen in the next section on implementing his ideas.

Implementing Kohn's *Beyond Discipline*

Teachers who wish to move beyond discipline must do three things: provide an engaging curriculum, develop a caring community, and provide students latitude in making choices. When this is accomplished, Kohn says, the result can be properly called a **democracy**. In this kind of classroom, the teacher's point of departure when problems occur is to ask: *How can I work with students to solve this problem? How can I turn this into a chance to help them learn?*

Kohn offers 10 suggestions that he believes will be helpful to teachers who wish to move beyond discipline but find that their efforts do not produce the desired results:

1. Work on establishing a trusting, caring relationship with your students. It's hard to work with a student to solve a problem unless the two of you already have a relationship on which to build.

2. Work diligently toward acquiring for yourself, and developing in your students, skills of listening carefully, remaining calm, generating suggestions, and imagining someone else's point of view.

3. When an unpleasant situation occurs, your first effort should be to diagnose what has happened and why. If you have a trusting relationship with students, you can gently ask them to speculate about why they hurt someone else's feelings, or why they keep coming to class late.

4. To figure out what is really going on, be willing to look beyond the concrete situation. Do not immediately identify the student as the sole source of the problem while letting yourself off the hook. You should ask yourself, or the student or the class, what is really going on here. Can you do anything to help? Try sitting down in a friendly way and see if a plan can be made that will resolve the problem.

5. Maximize student involvement in making decisions and resolving problems. Individual students should be asked, "What do you think we can do to solve this problem?" Involving students is far more likely to lead to a meaningful, lasting solution than having the teacher decide unilaterally what must be done.

6. Work with students on coming up with authentic solutions to problems. This requires an open-ended exploration of possibilities and reflection on motive.

7. When students do something cruel, our first priority is to help them understand that what they did is wrong, and why it is wrong, to discourage its happening again. Then an examination should be made of ways to make restitution or reparation, such as trying to restore, replace, repair, clean up, or apologize. Making amends is important and should be viewed as an essential part of the process, but more importantly, students must construct meaning for themselves around concepts of fairness and responsibility, just as they would around concepts in mathematics and literature.

8. When new plans or strategies are put into effect, be sure to review them later to see how they have worked.

9. Remain flexible and use judgment concerning when you need to talk with a student about a problem. Sometimes it is better to delay the talk for a while so the student will feel more inclined to discuss the problem.

10. On the rare occasions when you must use control, do so in a way that minimizes its punitive impact. Sometimes, despite your every effort, you will have to control misbehavior. A student may be disrupting the class, despite repeated requests not to do so. In that case you may have to isolate the student or send him or her from the room. But even then your tone should be warm and regretful and you should express confidence that the two of you will eventually solve the problem together.

KEY TERMS AND CONCEPTS PRESENTED IN THIS CHAPTER

The following terms are used with special meaning in Kohn's model of discipline. Check yourself to make sure you understand them.

compliant behavior
constructivist theory
democracy

goals of discipline versus methods
   of discipline
perspective taking

sense of community
traditional teaching

SELECTED SEVEN—SUMMARY SUGGESTIONS FROM ALFIE KOHN

Alfie Kohn suggests that you emphasize the following, as well as his many other suggestions:

1 Take students seriously and organize your class so it takes on the nature of a community, where students take part in making decisions, cooperate, explore topics in depth, support each other, and think in terms of "we" rather than "I."

2 Make regular and frequent use of classroom meetings as forums for discussion and group decision making.

3 Students come to behave more respectfully when important adults in their lives behave respectfully toward *them*. They are more likely to care about others if they know *they* are cared about.

4 You can largely remove misbehavior as a problem if you provide an engaging curriculum based on stu-

dent interests, develop a sense of community, and draw students into meaningful decision making.

5 Allow students to work closely with each other and help them show kindness and find happiness and fulfillment.

6 When class concerns arise, ask students, "What do you think we can do to solve this problem?"

7 You cannot transfer your knowledge to students. The best you can do is lead students to explore topics, grapple with them, and make sense of them. Provide challenges and emphasize that making mistakes is an important part of learning.

CONCEPT CASES

■ CASE 1 *Kristina Will Not Work*

Kristina, a student in Mr. Jake's class, is quite docile. She socializes little with other students and never disrupts lessons. However, despite Mr. Jake's best efforts, Kristina will not do her work. She rarely completes an assignment. She is simply there, putting forth no effort at all. *How would Kohn deal with Kristina?*

From the first day Kristina was in his class, Kohn would have begun establishing a trusting, caring relationship with her and all other students. He would try to put himself in her place and imagine her situation, hoping thereby to understand her reluctance to participate. He would examine the class situation and himself to see if the problem lay there. He would chat with Kristina and gently sound her out. He would ask why she didn't feel like participating, if she could suggest a solution, and if there was a way he might help her. He would see if the two of them could devise a plan to resolve the problem. He would ask her opinions and involve her fully. After deciding on a possible solution, he would remain flexible, talk with her, and be ready to alter the plan if the need were indicated.

■ CASE 2 *Sara Cannot Stop Talking*

Sara is a pleasant girl who participates in class activities and does most, though not all, of her assigned work. She cannot seem to refrain from talking to classmates, however. Her teacher, Mr. Gonzales, has to speak to her re-

peatedly during lessons to the point that he often becomes exasperated and loses his temper. *What suggestions would Kohn give Mr. Gonzales for dealing with Sara?*

■ CASE 3 *Joshua Clowns and Intimidates*

Larger and louder than his classmates, Joshua always wants to be the center of attention, which he accomplishes through a combination of clowning and intimidation. He makes wise remarks, talks back (smilingly) to the teacher, utters a variety of sound-effect noises such as automobile crashes and gunshots, and makes limitless sarcastic comments and put-downs of his classmates. Other students will not stand up to him, apparently fearing his size and verbal aggression. His teacher, Miss Pearl, has come to her wit's end. *Would Joshua's behavior be likely to improve if Kohn's techniques were used in Miss Pearl's classroom? Explain.*

■ CASE 4 *Tom Is Hostile and Defiant*

Tom has appeared to be in his usual foul mood ever since arriving in class. On his way to sharpen his pencil, he bumps into Frank, who complains. Tom tells him loudly to shut up. Miss Baines, the teacher, says, "Tom, go back to your seat." Tom wheels around, swears loudly, and says heatedly, "I'll go when I'm damned good and ready!" *How would Kohn deal with Tom?*

QUESTIONS AND ACTIVITIES

1. In your journal, make notes from Kohn's *Beyond Discipline* that apply to the five principles of constructing a personal system of discipline.

2. Compare Kohn's views on discipline with those of Canter (Chapter 3). Which do you feel more accurately depicts classroom realities and makes the better suggestions for helping students?

3. In pairs or small groups, discuss (a) what you think of Kohn's views, (b) the extent to which you feel his views are grounded in the realities of classrooms and students, (c) whether you yourself would consider implementing his suggestions and why, and (d) the changes, if any, you would have to make in your views of discipline before you could enthusiastically endorse his suggestions.

YOU ARE THE TEACHER

Sheltered English Kindergarten

You teach a sheltered English kindergarten class comprised of 18 students, only three of whom speak English at home. The ethnic/racial makeup of the class is a mixture of Vietnamese, Laotian, Chinese, Samoan, Iranian, Latino, Filipino, African American, and Caucasian. The emphasis of the class is rapid English language development. For the most part, the students work in small groups, each of which is directed by a teacher, aide, or parent volunteer. The groups rotate every half hour so as to have a variety of experiences.

A Typical Occurrence

Shortly before school begins, a new girl, Mei, is brought into the class. She speaks very little English and is crying. She tries to run out of the classroom but is stopped by the aide. When you ring your bell, the students know they are to sit on the rug, but those already at the play area do not want to do so. You call them three or four times, but you finally have to get up and physically bring two of them to the rug. As the opening activities proceed, you repeatedly ask students to sit up. (They have begun rolling around on the floor.) Kinney is pestering the girl next to him. Twice you ask him to stop. Finally, you send him to sit in a chair outside the group. He has to sit there until the opening activities are finished. Then he can rejoin his group for the first rotation at the art table. As soon as the groups get under way, you hear a ruckus at the art table, which is under the guidance of Mrs. García, a parent volunteer. You see that Kinney has scooped up finger paint and is making motions as if to paint one of the girls, who runs away squealing. Mrs. García tells him to put the paint down. Kinney, who speaks English, replies, "Shut up, you big fat rat!" You leave your group and go to Kinney. You tell him,

"You need time out in Mrs. Sayres's room (a first grade next door to your kindergarten)." Kinney, his hand covered with blue paint, drops to the floor and refuses to move. He calls you foul names. You leave him there, go to the phone, and call the office for assistance. Kinney gets up, wipes his hand first on a desk and then on himself, and runs out the door. He stops beside the entrance to Mrs. Sayres's room, and when you follow he goes inside and sits at a designated table without further resistance. You return to your group. They sit quietly and attentively but do not speak. You are using a Big Book on an easel, trying to get the students to repeat the words you pronounce but with little success. When it is time for the next rotation, you go quickly to Mrs. Sayres's room and bring Kinney back to the class. He rejoins his group. As you begin work with your new group, you see Rey and Duy at the measuring table pouring birdseed on each other's heads. Meanwhile, the new girl, Mei, continues sobbing audibly.

Conceptualizing a Strategy

If you followed the suggestions of Alfie Kohn, what would you conclude or do with regard to the following?

1. Preventing the problem from occurring in the first place.
2. Putting a clear end to the misbehavior now.
3. Involving other or all students in addressing the situation.
4. Maintaining student dignity and good personal relations.
5. Using follow-up procedures that would prevent the recurrence of the misbehavior.
6. Using the situation to help the students develop a sense of greater responsibility and self-control.

REFERENCES

Kohn, A. 1986, 1992. *No contest: The case against competition.* Boston: Houghton Mifflin.

Kohn, A. 1990. *The brighter side of human nature: Altruism and empathy in everyday life.* New York: Basic.

Kohn, A. 1993, 1999. *Punished by rewards: The trouble with gold stars, incentive plans, A's, praise, and other bribes.* Boston: Houghton Mifflin.

Kohn, A. 1999. *The schools our children deserve: Moving beyond traditional classrooms and "tougher standards."* Boston: Houghton Mifflin.

Kohn, A. 2001. *Beyond discipline: From compliance to community.* Upper Saddle River, NJ: Merrill/Prentice Hall. 1996 edition published Alexandria, VA: Association for Supervision and Curriculum Development.

CHAPTER 15

Working Effectively with All Students

CHAPTER PREVIEW

This chapter presents information for working more effectively with students who are members of various ethnic, economic, cultural, and linguistic groups. In the United States, almost 40 percent of the public school population is comprised of students designated as minority or culturally or economically diverse. This chapter reviews some of the characteristics of students in those groups and indicates how they can be educated more effectively. It also gives attention to working more productively with students identified as behaviorally at risk of failure, ADHD (Attention Deficit Hyperactivity Disorder), prone to ATOD abuse (alcohol, tobacco, and other drugs), and those prone to bullying and hate crimes. Please keep in mind that although important differences exist among these groups, for the most part, students have the same set of needs and are much more alike than they are different.

Working with Economically Disadvantaged Students

Economically disadvantaged is synonymous with living **in poverty.** A family and its members are said to be in poverty if they have to spend more than one-third of their disposable income for food adequate to meet the family's nutritional needs. By this definition, just over 10 percent of American families live in poverty (U.S. Census Bureau, 2001).

Economically disadvantaged students tend to have life views that are different from those of the dominant society. Ruby Payne (2001), investigating the effects of economic disadvantage in education, has identified a number of views and behaviors of students in poverty that impinge on their education. She says that each economic class has its own set of **hidden rules** that helps it survive. Schools and teachers reflect and use middle-class hidden rules, which include future time orientation, planning ahead, strong work ethic, competition, individuality, verbal learning, and willingness to take risks. However, students who are economically disadvantaged have a set of hidden rules that differs from those of the middle class. The result is misunderstanding and conflict. Payne advises teachers to learn some of the hidden rules of poverty in order to understand and communicate better with students, such as:

- *Speech and language*—Students in poverty often use a casual, informal style of speech, whereas school emphasizes a more formal style of speech. Teachers should point out the difference, help students use the appropriate language for various situations, and help them understand that a formal style is helpful in school and the workplace.
- *Money*—is to be used, to be spent. The school suggests it is to be managed, saved, and made to grow.
- *Personality*—highly valued and appreciated for entertainment. The school places higher value on achievement than on personality.
- *Major thought about food*—is there enough? Middle-class concern is if you liked it.
- *Clothing*—is an expression of personality.
- *Time*—the present is most important. School emphasizes looking to the future.
- *Language*—casual, about survival. School language is more formal, about negotiation.
- *Family structure*—is in many cases matriarchal, whereas Anglo American society is usually patriarchal.
- *Broader view*—tends to be local for students of poverty, while national for the dominant society.
- *Driving forces in life*—survival, relationships, entertainment. School emphasizes driving forces of work and achievement.
- *Background noise*—high, with television almost always on, and participatory conversation, with more than one person talking at a time. Schools value quiet, with speakers taking turns.
- *School discipline*—seen as punishment rather than help for improvement. Students may laugh when disciplined as a way of saving face.
- *Teachers*—likeable ones are to be pleased. Others are not worth the trouble.
- *Conflict*—settled verbally and physically rather than with calm reason.

Working with Recently Arrived Immigrant Students

Immigrant students have needs not only for academic learning but also (and sometimes more importantly) for socialization and language development. Student success is increased when parents, family, and community are involved, along with health and counseling services. Suggestions for working productively with newly arrived immigrant students have been put forth by several writers (see Lucas, Henze, and Donato, 1990; Walsh, 1991; National Coalition of Advocates for Students, 1994; Benard, 1997; "Qualities of Effective Programs . . . ," 1998; Krovetz, 1999; Chavkin and Gonzalez, 2000). Here is a summary of their advice:

- Have a repertoire of instructional approaches that upholds high expectations of students, while affirming the acceptance of differences among students.
- Be knowledgeable about issues of acculturation and second language acquisition and teach with materials that reflect a diversity of cultures, experiences, and perspectives.
- Learn as much as possible about students' families. Teachers can serve students better when they know the educational backgrounds of their families. This information is valuable in developing academic support in the home.

- Show appreciation for and enjoyment of ethnic language and culture.
- Hold high expectations of students and frequently recognize their achievement publicly.
- Become familiar with English as a Second Language (ESL) and sheltered English instruction. Learn a bit of the students' native language.
- Find ways to give much personal attention to each student.
- Use a flexible approach that involves, when appropriate, peer tutoring, language experience, process writing, reciprocal teaching, whole language, mentoring by sympathetic adults, home–school liaisons, and links with community agencies.
- Establish supportive relationships with students and their parents, emphasizing encouragement from school personnel and other adults.
- Work to increase student self-esteem, motivation, and willingness to accept responsibility.
- Emphasize prosocial skills and academic success.
- Rely on personal relationships with students to motivate them.

Working with African American Students

African American students comprise approximately 16.5 percent of the public school population. Many are bright and talented, whereas others have become alienated from formal education. Male students, especially, often drop behind academically at around the third or fourth grade (Kunjufu, 1984) and continue to fall farther behind and many drop out of school. During their teenage years, they tend to engage in adolescent risk taking that can lead to delinquency, early fathering, drug use, and violence (Ascher, 1991).

Schools have been making a concerted effort to redress this situation. Attempts include decreasing the suspension and expulsion rates for African American students, increasing their representation in programs for the gifted and talented, and improving the recruitment and training of teachers and counselors in predominantly black schools (Gibbs, 1988; Reed, 1988). More recently, investigators have been focusing on linguistic and cultural factors. They make the following suggestions (see Diller, 1999; Foster, 1999; McCollough, 2000; Ladson-Billings, 2000; Bempechat, 2001; Schwartz, 2001):

- Express cultural understanding and acceptance.
- Show solidarity with students and eagerness to help.
- Emphasize the knowledge, skills, and values needed for school success and a healthy cultural identity.
- Link curriculum content to students' out-of-school experiences.
- Become knowledgeable about African American social styles.
- Take into account the knowledge, culture, values, and abilities of African American students.
- Cease to speak disparagingly of African American traditions.
- Attempt to mentor students, especially the troublesome, rather than avoid them.
- Create a more hospitable environment by communicating the expectation that all students can succeed, providing the opportunity for them to do so, and evaluating them on the basis of their strengths, not their weaknesses.

- Develop class behavior codes that are culturally sensitive and stress responsibility and respect.
- Use a discipline system that emphasizes modeling good behavior rather than punishment and gives students a voice in deciding how it will function.
- Keep family members informed about their child's school performance and behavior, good and bad, and ask them to work with you for the child's benefit.

Working with American Indian/Alaska Native Students

Susan Faircloth and John Tippeconnic reported in 2000 that there were approximately 500,000 American Indian and Alaska Native (AI/AN) students attending K–12 schools in the United States, just over 1 percent of the total school population. These students come from more than 500 tribal groups that have their own government and social systems and speak an estimated 200 different languages.

Overall the students from these various tribal groups are not enjoying much success in school. Their achievement level is below that of other groups, and they have the highest dropout rate of all racial/ethnic groups in the United States (U.S. National Center for Education Statistics, 2001). The reasons for AI/AN students' relative lack of success in school are not known (St. Germaine, 1995), although speculation centers on impoverished home and community experiences, a curriculum that is unconnected to students' lives, and the fact that success in school is interpreted as selling out older traditions in favor of "white man's ways."

There is reason to believe that AI/AN students have learning styles that differ somewhat from those of students in the dominant culture (Cornett, 1983; Swisher, 1991). Many have very strong capabilities for learning visually, perceptively, and spatially, as opposed to the verbal processes emphasized in school. They may tend to use mental images in thought processes rather than word associations. They may learn better by seeing, from the outset, the entire picture of what is to be learned, rather than learning bits of information that slowly build up to the full picture. They show an affinity for manipulatives and hands-on activities and seem to work and learn better in cooperative groups than individually. They seem to show the ability to learn from experience without constant supervision and feedback. They best demonstrate their learning in contexts similar to those from which they have learned.

Anglo teachers usually consider AI/AN students to be quiet and not very talkative in the classroom. Although these students may be hesitant to participate in large and small group recitations, they are said to be more talkative than other students when working in student-led group projects (Philips, 1983). Philips explained that AI/AN students tend to acquire competence through a process of observation, careful listening, supervised participation, and individualized self-correction or testing.

Other studies point out that AI/AN students become uncomfortable when asked, in school, to behave in ways not valued in the communities where they live. For example, most AI/AN students are more cooperative and less competitive than Anglo students, a trait that probably contributes to lower school achievement. AI/AN behavior stresses group achievement rather than individual achievement, which is frowned on. For that reason, very able students often hide their academic competence to avoid appearing superior. Individuals simply do not try to advance above others or display self-importance (Brown, 1980).

A number of suggestions have been made to help teachers work more effectively with students from AI/AN groups (Cox and Ramirez, 1981; Cornett, 1983; Cajete, 1986; Swisher, 1991; Butterfield, 1994). Although no set of expectations can apply fully to all students, the following suggestions should be helpful:

- Get to know the norms and values of the community from which students come.
- Learn all you can about students' background knowledge and experiences.
- Fit new learning into the contexts of home, community, and school.
- Note students' preferred ways of learning and the ways student behaviors change from situation to situation. Discuss these matters with students and take their learning styles into account.
- Provide activities that are more cooperative and less competitive. However, encourage independent learning, too.
- Provide feedback that is immediate, helpful, and private.
- Allow students to use direct personal experience as much as possible in learning.
- Emphasize art and creative writing about personal experiences.
- While providing familiar, comfortable, successful experiences, gradually introduce new ways of learning.
- Evaluate student progress in terms of goal attainment, student behavior, and involvement.
- Employ a flexible time framework for activities rather than always staying on a rigid schedule.
- Remember that most AI/AN students do not like to be in the spotlight.

Working with Asian American Students

Jianhua Feng (1994) points out that the term *Asian American* covers a variety of national, cultural, and religious groups, more than 29 of which differ in language, religion, and customs. Among them are four major groups, identified as East Asian, Southeast Asian, South Asian, and Pacific Islanders. Although these distinct groups often get lumped together as "Asian," they differ considerably from each other. Some students have only recently arrived and, therefore, experience difficulty with language and customs, whereas others are native born, speak English fluently, and are highly acculturated.

Asian Americans are generally viewed as successful, law-abiding, conforming, and high achieving. Their school behavior is much in keeping with those perceptions, and only occasionally do they present behavior problems for teachers. They tend to be strongly group and family oriented, which for newly arrived students may hamper their adaptation to the independence, competition, and individualism emphasized in Western education.

Students from many East and Southeast Asian cultures are imbued with Confucian ideals, which include learning, respect for elders, responsibility for relatives, deferred gratification, and self-discipline. They tend to view failure as a lack of individual will. They tend to be conforming and willing to place family welfare over individual wishes. They are usually self-effacing, willing to wait patiently (Feng, 1994), and seem to learn best in well-structured, quiet environments (Baruth and Manning, 1992). They tend to dislike having attention drawn to them as individuals. Many have been socialized to listen carefully, think before they speak, use soft voices, and show modesty in personal dress and grooming.

In conversations and other verbal communication, Asians seldom speak their minds as plainly as do Westerners. They often display verbal hesitancy and ambiguity to avoid giving offense, and they do not make spontaneous or critical remarks (Kim, 1985). Their body language is noticeably different from that of Westerners, too, characterized by head nodding and lack of eye contact (Matsuda, 1989). The Japanese and Vietnamese are noted for being unwilling to use the word "no" even when they actually disagree with you (Coker, 1988; Wierzbicka, 1991). Seldom are Asian students, their family members, or their teachers aware of the cultural differences that affect communication. This leads to one side or the other being misunderstood or ignored.

A sense of time unfamiliar to teachers in Western schools can also cause difficulties. Many Asian cultures operate on what is called "polychronic time" as distinct from the "monochronic time" familiar to Western people (Storti, 1999). Polychronic time allows different social interactions to happen at the same time, whereas monochronic time is linear—you do one thing at a time, in a fixed sequence. This difference in time orientation sometimes causes misunderstandings because Asians may not be prompt or ready to get down to business as quickly as Westerners would like.

Li-Rong Cheng (1998) points out that Asian students with school experience elsewhere are accustomed to learning through listening, observing, reading, and imitating; responding to teachers' questions based on lectures and textbooks; and taking tests that require only the recall of factual information. They may be left feeling ambivalent and confused by classroom activities that involve group work, discussions, and creative activities, at which times the following behaviors may be observed:

- *Delay or hesitation.* Students may be unsure of an answer, unfamiliar with the discourse style, or simply disengaged and lost.
- *Failure to stick with the topic.* This may be due to insufficient knowledge, unfamiliarity with how to gain the floor, or fear and avoidance of interactions.
- *Inappropriate nonverbal expressions.* Students will often avoid eye contact with adults (a sign of respect), frown (in concentration, as opposed to displeasure), or giggle (from embarrassment or lack of understanding, not in response to something perceived as humorous).
- *Short responses.* Students may not be proficient enough to reply in long, cohesive utterances, or they may be too shy to respond.
- *Overly soft voice.* This is typical for children in some Asian cultures.
- *Unwillingness to take risks.* Students may fear being embarrassed or ridiculed.
- *Lack of participation.* In some Asian classrooms volunteering information is considered overly bold.

- *Embarrassment over receiving praise.* Students' native culture may value humility and self-criticism.
- *Atypical greetings.* Students may appear impolite or unfriendly because they look down, out of respect or fear, when the teacher approaches instead of offering a greeting.

Matsuda (1989), Baruth and Manning (1992), Trueba and Cheng (1993), Huang (1993), Feng (1994), and Cheng (1996, 1998) make a number of suggestions to help teachers work more effectively with Asian students, including:

- Learn about the values, traditions, and customs of the cultures from which your students come.
- Carefully observe and understand students' sense of communication and time, and adjust your interactions accordingly.
- Learn at least a few words of the students' native languages. Ask students to teach them to you.
- Help students understand that, while at school, they may offer their opinions and challenge the views of others.
- Explain to family members that parental involvement in their child's education is a tradition in the Western world.
- Be patient during verbal exchanges. Consider periods of silence opportunities for reflection on what has been said. Be attentive to nonverbal cues.
- When you can do so, use individual rather than group meetings and oral communication rather than written memos.
- Encourage students to join student clubs to increase their exposure to language, socialization, and different types of discourse.
- Facilitate students' transition into mainstream culture through activities and discussions of culturally unique experiences and celebrations, such as birthday parties and Thanksgiving.
- Role play, practice colloquialisms, and act out skits that involve typical verbal exchanges.
- Read to students to increase their vocabulary, and expose them to various narrative styles used in letters, stories, articles, biographies, and poetry.

Working with Hispanic American Students

Hispanic American students, often called Latinos, are members of various ethnic groups whose native or ancestral language is Spanish. These students now comprise approximately 17 percent of public school enrollment, up from 6 percent in 1972 and expected to reach 25 percent by the year 2025 (Latinos in School: Some Facts and Findings, 2001). Large numbers of these students have blended into the dominant society, speak English perfectly, and assume leadership roles. However, as a group, Hispanic students are the second most likely, after AI/AN students, to drop out of school. Their high school completion rate in 1999 was 63 percent, as compared with 81 percent for African Americans and 90 percent for Anglo Americans. The dropout rate among Hispanic immigrants is double that of U.S.-born Hispanic students—44 percent compared to 21 percent. The reason for this high dropout rate is not clear but is usually associated with attendance at overcrowded, inadequately staffed, and underresourced schools that fail to meet students' educational and social needs, while at the same time serving as breeding grounds for antisocial activities. Many of these students live in economically distressed areas and do not believe that remaining in school will materially improve their present or future lives.

Wendy Schwartz (2000) and Anne Lockwood and Walter Secada (2000) have presented several suggestions for improving the quality of classroom experiences for Hispanic American youth, including:

- Make the classroom a safe and inviting place to learn.
- Personalize instruction and give students the opportunity to assume positions of leadership and responsibility. Encourage these students into prosocial roles and protect them from intimidation.
- Provide help in reducing student anger and building trust as a means of countering attitudes produced by negative experiences with schools and adults.
- Treat Hispanic students' language and culture as desirable resources.
- Convey high expectations, present options, and provide resources needed for an effective education.
- Emphasize the prevention of problems and respond effectively to early warning signs that a student is beginning to disengage from school.
- Teach content so it interests and challenges Hispanic students.
- Respect and show interest in students' language, culture, and ethnicity.

The school as a whole can contribute to this effort by doing the following:

- Identify for each Hispanic student an adult in the school who is committed to nurturing a sense of self-worth and supporting the student's efforts to succeed. Such mentors can help students withstand the peer, economic, and societal pressures that lead to dropping out.
- Find ways to provide smaller classes or a lower student–teacher ratio to increase personal attention to each student.
- Seek out and replicate programs being used effectively in other schools. Continually try to improve them.
- Engage family members and the community in the education of their children.
- Look for ways to improve communication with Hispanic families.
- Recruit Hispanic family members into a partnership to envision a future for their children and a reasonable plan for realizing it.

Working with Students Who Are Behaviorally at Risk of Failure

Behaviorally at risk refers to students whose behavior severely inhibits learning and puts them in danger of failing in school. Richard Curwin and Allen Mendler (1992) have taken a special interest in these students, whom teachers usually consider lazy, turned off, angry, hostile, irresponsible, disruptive, withdrawn, having attitude problems, or out of control. Curwin and Mendler point out that these students have received, but do not respond to, most of the punishments and/or consequences offered by the school. They have low self-concepts in relation to school and little or no hope they will be successful there. They associate with and are reinforced by students similar to themselves. Many do not care how they behave in the classroom. It does not worry them if they fail, bother the teacher, or disrupt the class.

However, most of these students can become reasonably successful in school, provided they regain a sense of hope. Richard Curwin (1992) says we can often restore hope simply by treating these students with respect, while making instruction more interesting and worthwhile. In addition, these students must experience pleasure and success often and regularly if they are to persevere. We can help them significantly by working with them as follows:

- Always treat them with dignity. Respect them as individuals, show concern for their needs, and understand their viewpoints.
- Don't allow discipline to interfere with student motivation. Any discipline technique that reduces motivation to learn is self-defeating.
- Emphasize responsibility rather than obedience. Obedience means "do as you are told." Responsibility means "make the best decision possible."

We don't often think of using programs of accelerated learning to help students who are at risk. However, such programs offer promise, as indicated in the following provisions of the Accelerated School Program used for students at risk (Levin, 2002):

- Enhance academic growth through challenging and stimulating activities instead of slowing down student learning with remediation.
- Treat "at-risk" students as gifted and talented students by identifying and building on their strengths instead of lowering expectations for these children.
- Incorporate the entire staff into governance and decision making for creating powerful learning experiences for *all* children, instead of using state- and district-mandated "canned" curriculum packages as solutions to learning challenges for the children.

Working with Students Who Have Attention Deficit and Hyperactivity Disorder (ADHD)

Attention Deficit and Hyperactivity Disorder (**ADHD**) is a behavior syndrome involving poor attention span, weak impulse control, and hyperactivity, three traits that generally inhibit learning and lead to misbehavior. ADHD can begin in infancy and extend into adulthood, with negative effects on the individual's life at home, in school, and in the community. It is now estimated that ADHD afflicts 3 to 5 percent of the school-age population. Its exact cause is not known. Males are more likely than females to have the condition. Among afflicted students, males typically have ADD with hyperactivity, whereas females typically have it without hyperactivity (Amen, 2001).

Dianna McFarland, Rosemarie Kolstad, and L. D. Biggs (1995), Dawn Hogan (1997), and the Attention Deficit Disorders Association, Southern Region (2002) provide a number of suggestions to help teachers work more effectively with ADHD students:

- Maintain cordial relationships with students. Engage in personal, friendly conversation, show you value their opinions, include them in the decision-making process when possible, and provide activities in which they can excel.
- Provide a calm, structured, positive learning environment. Keep the classroom uncluttered and well organized to minimize distractions.
- Seat students near you.
- Establish clear standards of behavior, with realistic, predictable consequences for infractions. Model positive behavior. Help students develop an awareness of their behavior and discuss incidents and possible solutions together.
- Assign work that is within the student's capabilities. The material may need to be broken into tasks that can be accomplished in short amounts of time.
- When ADHD students become upset, use time-out to allow them to think quietly about the problem and resolve it on their own.
- Avoid fatigue, stress, and pressure, which can easily overwhelm students' self-control and lead to inappropriate behavior. Provide opportunities for rest and relaxation. Let overactive students run errands, sharpen pencils, water plants, and stand up when called on in class.
- Develop consistent daily routines and prepare students for any change in the procedure to avoid disorientation.
- Make sure homework can be completed easily and gets done. Communicate closely with parents and encourage their involvement in students' homework.
- Provide frequent reinforcement in the form of nods, smiles, pats on the back, and words of praise. If stronger reinforcement is needed, consider point systems or tangible items. Encourage self-talk, where students talk about how good behavior is self-gratifying.
- Make instructions clear and concise. Give only one direction at a time. Make eye contact before giving instructions. Ask students to repeat instructions you have given.
- Coach students on how to make friends and relate to others.
- Avoid power struggles. Give directions one to three times as needed. Speak clearly and slowly, use a gentle touch, and make eye contact using an encouraging expression.
- Be accepting of these students' limitations. You cannot change them through repeated criticism. Much of their misbehavior is not intentional and cannot be completely eliminated. You get better results through tolerance and respect.

Working with Students Who Abuse Drugs and Alcohol

Teachers, schools, and communities are very concerned about students' use of drugs and alcohol. Just over 50 percent of high school students report they use alcohol at least once a month (Bosworth, 1997). The use of illicit drugs is almost as prevalent, with about 40 percent of high school seniors admitting they have used an illicit drug at least once, and 24 percent reporting they use drugs at least once a month. Students are generally becoming less convinced that drugs and alcohol are bad for them.

For three decades, significant public and private resources have been expended in attempting to discourage youth from using alcohol, tobacco, and other drugs (abbreviated **ATOD**). Emphasis has been placed on scare tactics, providing information on ATOD and their effects, self-esteem building, values clarification, large assembly presentations, and didactic presentation of material (Tobler and Stratton, 1997). None of those efforts has proved reliably effective. Other approaches, however, have shown some potential for success. The following seem most likely to help (Bosworth 1997):

- *Normative education.* Help students realize that use of ATOD is not the norm for teenagers. Students generally overestimate the proportion of their peers actively involved in ATOD, making it easier to be pressured by the myth that "everybody is doing it." Surveys and opinion polls can be used to help students understand actual use rates.
- *Social skills.* Help students increase their ease in handling social situations. Decision making, communication skills, and assertiveness skills are particularly important during early adolescence, when puberty prompts changes in the social dynamics among young people as well as with the adults in their lives.
- *Social influences.* Use advertising, role models, and peer attitudes to help students realize the external pressure for using ATOD. Help them learn how to resist such pressures.
- *Perceived harm.* Help students understand the risks and short- and long-term consequences of using ATOD. The message must come from credible sources and be reinforced in multiple settings.
- *Protective factors.* Emphasize close association with peers who provide positive support. Encourage students to focus on positive aspects of life such as helping, caring, setting goals, and meeting challenges successfully.
- *Refusal skills.* Stress ways of effectively refusing involvement with ATOD while maintaining friendships. Recent research indicates refusal skills are helpful in supporting teens who do not want to use drugs. They appear to be more effective when used in conjunction with other activities such as social influences and normative education.
- *Interactive learning.* Lecture presentations do not seem to produce the desired results. More promising are role plays, simulations, Socratic questioning, brainstorming, small group activities, cooperative learning, class discussions, and engaging students in self-examination and learning. Refusal skills need to be practiced in the classroom through role plays in the context of realistic settings where ATOD might be offered. Videos and multimedia software that are set in real-world environments can be used to provide models of appropriate behavior and stimulate discussion.
- *Adult modeling.* Teachers and other adults at school should set high expectations, open up supportive communication with students, and show they care and want to help. They can also use prevention messages from literature, movies, songs, or current events that portray substance use/abuse.

Working with Students Prone to Violence, Bullying, and Hate Crimes

A few years ago, the United States government formulated a set of educational goals the country was to reach by the year 2000. The seventh of those goals was that "All schools in America will be free of drugs and violence and the unauthorized presence of firearms and alcohol, and will offer a disciplined environment that is conducive to learning." To help reach that goal, Congress passed the Safe and Drug-Free Schools and Communities Act of 1994, which supported programs of drug and violence prevention.

Sorry to say, we didn't reach the goal, nor even come close to it. In 1998, a survey by the U.S. National Center for Education Statistics (NCES) showed that out of a sample of 1,234 schools, 37 percent reported that students had, at school, committed from one to five crimes. About 20 percent of the schools reported six crimes or more. Ten percent reported at lease one serious violent crime—murder, rape, sexual battery, assault with a weapon, or robbery. Sixty-five percent of school-associated violent deaths were students, 11 percent were teachers or other staff members, and 23 percent were community members who were killed on school property.

Efforts to Deal with Violence

Among schools' efforts to deal with violence, four approaches stand out, with varying degrees of effectiveness. They are:

- Zero-tolerance policies, used where there is high incidence of violence, alcohol, drugs, firearms, and other weapons
- Increased school security, although only about 2 percent of schools use stringent security measures, such as full-time guards and daily metal detection checks. Others use part-time guards, protective fencing, and alarms, whereas 3 percent do not use security measures at all.
- Formal violence prevention programs, used in 78 percent of schools surveyed.
- Programs in character development, problem resolution, and anger control. These programs attempt to develop stronger individual character and better personal relations. They vary considerably and their results are inconclusive. The Center for Disease Control and Prevention (1999) has suggested using (1) curricula that emphasize the development of problem-solving skills, anger management, and other social skills, (2) adult mentoring for young people, and (3) full involvement of the community in developing a sense of ownership of the problem of violence and its solutions.

Bullying and Hate Crimes

Bullying and hate crimes have devastating effects on student morale. **Bullying** is defined as committing intentional, repeated hurtful acts against others. It is a daily occurrence in most schools. It may consist of physical aggression, sexual aggression, name-calling, threatening, taunting, intimidating, or shunning. Not only does it harm its intended victims, but it also has a negative effect on school climate and opportunity for all students to learn.

Four kinds of bullying are common: *Physical bullying* includes punching, poking, strangling, hair pulling, beating, biting, kicking, and excessive tickling. *Verbal bullying* includes hurtful name-calling, teasing, and gossip. *Emotional bullying* includes rejecting, terrorizing, extorting, defaming, humiliating, blackmailing, rating/ranking of personal characteristics such as race, disability, ethnicity, or perceived sexual orientation, manipulating friendships, isolating, ostracizing, and peer pressure. *Sexual bullying* includes many of the actions just listed as well as exhibitionism, voyeurism, sexual propositioning, sexual harassment, abuse involving physical contact, and sexual assault.

Large numbers of students report they have been victims of bullying at school. Among middle school students, one in four is bullied on a regular basis, whereas one in five admits to bullying others. About one in seven says he or she experienced severe reactions to the abuse.

Acts of bullying usually occur away from the eyes of teachers or other responsible adults. As perpetrators go undetected, a climate of fear develops that affects victims adversely. Grades may suffer because attention is deflected away from learning. Fear may lead to absenteeism, truancy, or dropping out. If the problem persists, victims occasionally feel compelled to take drastic measures, such as fighting back, carrying weapons, and occasionally attempting suicide.

Bystanders and peers of victims can suffer harmful effects as well. They may be afraid to associate with the victim for fear of lowering their own status or of retribution from the bully. They may not report bullying incidents because they do not want to be called a "snitch," a "tattler," or an "informer." Some experience feelings of guilt or helplessness for not standing up to the bully on behalf of their classmate. They may feel unsafe, with loss of control and inability to take action.

Hate crimes are similar to bullying but are related to a dislike for other races, ethnic groups, or religions. They typically involve intimidation, harassment, bigoted slurs or epithets, force or threat of force, or vandalism.

The incidence and effects of bullying and hate crimes are usually grossly underreported. Educators, family members, and children concerned with violence prevention must be concerned with hate crimes and their linkage to other violent behaviors. Excellent suggestions on limiting bullying and hate crimes are seen in *Preventing Bullying: A Manual for Schools and Communities.* (U.S. Department of Education, 1998) and in Barbara Coloroso's 2003 book, *The Bully, the Bullied, and the Bystander: How Parents and Teachers Can Break the Cycle of Violence.* Here are a few of the many suggestions provided in those two resources:

- Schedule regular classroom meetings during which students and teachers engage in discussion, role playing, and other activities to reduce bullying, hate crimes, and other forms of school violence.
- Immediately intervene in all bullying incidents.

- Involve parents or guardians of bullies and victims of bullying and hate crimes. Receive and listen receptively to family members who report bullying. Establish procedures whereby such reports are investigated and resolved expeditiously.
- Form "friendship groups" or other supports for students who are victims of bullying or hate crimes.
- Popularize antibullying efforts within the community.
- Closely supervise students on the grounds and in classrooms, hallways, rest rooms, cafeterias, and other areas where bullying occurs.
- Conduct assemblies and teacher/staff in-service training to raise awareness of bullying and hate crimes, communicating zero tolerance for such behavior.
- Post and publicize clear behavior standards, including rules against bullying, for all students. Consistently and fairly enforce such standards.
- Establish a confidential reporting system that allows children to report victimization. Keep records of the incidents.
- Ensure that your school has in force all legally required policies and grievance procedures for sexual discrimination. Make these known to family members and students.
- Provide students with opportunities to talk about bullying and hate crimes and enlist their support in defining bullying as unacceptable behavior.
- Involve students in establishing classroom rules against bullying. Such rules may include a commitment from the teacher not to ignore incidents of bullying.
- Develop an action plan to ensure that students know what to do when they observe a bully/victim episode.
- Confront bullies in private rather than in front of their peers, which might enhance their status and lead to further aggression.
- Don't try to mediate a bullying situation. The difference in power between victims and bullies may cause victims to feel further victimized by the process or believe that they are somehow at fault.

Getting Parents on Your Side

Insofar as you can, try to get parents interested and involved in your program. Their participation increases support from home and results in better student behavior at school. Richard Riles, former U.S. Secretary of Education, states (Lounsbury, 2000):

> Thirty years of research show that when family and community members are directly involved in education, children achieve better grades and higher test scores, have much higher reading comprehension, graduate at higher rates, are more likely to enroll in higher education, and are better behaved.

For many years, teachers have been advised to write out their discipline plans and send copies to parents for their commentary and approval. Copies are signed by parents and returned to the teacher. This keeps parents informed about discipline standards and procedures and gives them an opportunity for some input. At present, teachers are more frequently creating home and web pages for their classes and are using them to communicate their programs to families at home. Typically, these pages contain announcements, homework assignments, discipline procedures, and other news and information of interest to parents. Setting up a web page is not difficult. If you don't know how to do it, a media person at your school or fellow teacher will show you, or you can learn through any number of manuals on the topic. Your school district may have its own server dedicated to this purpose, and most servers for electronic mail include provisions for establishing a website in their service package. You can find these by using keywords such as "free space" or "free Web hosting." Sites available to you usually have enough space for you to use multiple pages, if you wish. The home page need not be elaborate in appearance. Parents want information, not frills.

Message contents for discipline should include the following, stated briefly in your own words:

1. What your program is intended to do for students.
2. How students should conduct themselves to profit most from the program.
3. Class rules or agreements concerning work and behavior.
4. How you will help students abide by class agreements.
5. How you will intervene positively when students break rules or agreements.

KEY TERMS AND CONCEPTS PRESENTED IN THIS CHAPTER

The following terms and concepts are important in understanding this chapter. Check yourself to make sure you understand them.

economic disadvantage	behaviorally at risk of failure	bullying
in poverty	ATOD	hate crimes
hidden rules	ADHD	

QUESTIONS AND ACTIVITIES

1. Enter into your journal information from this chapter that applies to the five principles for developing your personal system of discipline.

2. Identify the three most important differences teachers are likely to encounter between a typical mainstream American student and
   - a typical Hispanic American student
   - a typical Chinese American student
   - a typical American Indian student
   - a typical African American student
   - a typical student living in poverty
   - a typical student afflicted with ADHD
   - a typical student at risk of failure due to misbehavior
   - a typical student who bullies or is bullied

3. What fallacies do you see in considering any individual students as "typical" for a group? What errors in judgment might result from doing so? Given the likelihood of errors in judgment, is there any value in comparing the "typical" behavior of various groups? If so, what is the value?

4. What do you see as advantages and disadvantages of trying to maintain closer relationships with students' parents?

REFERENCES

Amen, D. 2001. *Healing ADD: The breakthrough program that allows you to see and heal the six types of Attention Deficit Disorder.* New York: G. P. Putnam's Sons.

Ascher, C. 1991. School programs for African American males. ERIC Digest. New York: ERIC Clearinghouse on Urban Education.

Attention Deficit Disorders Association, Southern Region, ADD/ADHD. 2002. www.adda-sr.org/BehaviorManagementIndex.htm.

Baruth, L., and Manning, M. 1992. *Multicultural education of children and adolescents.* Boston: Allyn and Bacon.

Bempechat, J. 2001. Fostering high achievement in African American children: Home, school, and public policy influences. http://eric-web.tc.columbia.edu/monographs/ti16_index.html.

Benard, B. 1997. Drawing forth resilience in all our youth. *Reclaiming Children and Youth, 6*(1): 29–32.

Bosworth, K. 1997. Drug abuse prevention: School-based strategies that work. ERIC Digest. Washington, DC: ERIC Clearinghouse on Teaching and Teacher Education.

Brown, A. 1980. Cherokee culture and school achievement. *American Indian Culture and Research Journal, 4,* 55–74.

Butterfield, R. 1994. Blueprints for Indian education: Improving mainstream schooling. ERIC Digest. Charleston, WV: ERIC Clearinghouse on Rural Education and Small Schools.

Cajete, G. 1986. Science: A Native American perspective (A Culturally Based Science Education Curriculum). Ph.D. dissertation, International College/William Lyon University, San Diego, CA.

Center for Disease Control and Prevention. 1999. Facts about violence among youth and violence in schools. U.S. Government. Media Relations Division.

Chavkin, N., and Gonzalez, J. 2000. Mexican immigrant youth and resiliency: Research and promising programs. Urbana, IL: ERIC.

Cheng, L. 1996. Enhancing communication: Toward optimal language learning for limited English proficient students. *Language, Speech and Hearing Services in Schools, 28*(2), 347–354.

Cheng, L. 1998. Enhancing the communication skills of newly-arrived Asian American students. ERIC/CUE Digest No. 136. New York: ERIC Clearinghouse on Urban Education.

Coker, D. 1988. The Asian students in the classroom. *Education and Society, 1*(3), 19–20.

Coloroso, B. 2003. *The bully, the bullied, and the bystander: How parents and teachers can break the cycle of violence.* New York: HarperCollins.

Cornett, C. 1983. What you should know about teaching and learning styles (Fastback No. 191). Bloomington, IN: Phi Delta Kappa Foundation.

Cox, B., and Ramirez, M. 1981. Cognitive styles: Implications for multiethnic education. In J. Banks (Ed.), *Education in the 80s: Multiethnic Education* (pp. 61–71). Washington, DC: National Education Association.

Curwin, R. 1992. *Rediscovering hope: Our greatest teaching strategy.* Bloomington, IN: National Educational Service.

Curwin, R., and Mendler, A. 2001. *Discipline with dignity.* Upper Saddle River, NJ: Merrill.

Diller, D. 1999. Opening the dialogue: Using culture as a tool in teaching young African American children. *Reading Teacher, 52*(8), 820–858.

Faircloth, S., and Tippeconnic, J. 2000. Issues in the education of American Indian and Alaska Native students with disabilities. ERIC Digest. Charleston, WV: ERIC Clearinghouse on Rural Education and Small Schools.

Feng, J. 1994. Asian-American children: What teachers should know. ERIC Digest. Urbana, IL: ERIC.

Foster, M. 1999. Teaching and learning in the contexts of African American English and culture. *Education and Urban Society, 31*(2), 177ff.

Gibbs, J. (Ed.). 1988. *Young, black, and male in America: An endangered species.* Dover: Auburn Publishing Company.

Hogan, D. 1997. ADHD: A travel guide to success. *Childhood Education, 73*(3), 158–160.

Huang, G. 1993. Beyond culture: Communicating with Asian American children and families. ERIC/CUE Digest Number 94. New York: ERIC.

Kim, B. 1985. (Ed.). *Literacy and languages. The Second Yearbook of Literacy and Languages in Asia, International Reading Association Special Interest Group.* Selection of Speeches and Papers from the International Conference on Literacy and Languages (Seoul, South Korea, August 12–14, 1985).

Kunjufu, J.1984. *Developing positive self-images and discipline in black children.* Chicago: African American Images.

Krovetz, M. 1999. *Fostering resiliency: Expecting all students to use their minds and hearts well.* Thousand Oaks, CA: Corwin Press.

Ladson-Billings, G. 2000. Fighting for our lives: Preparing teachers to teach African American students. *Journal of Teacher Education, 51*(3), 206–214.

Latinos in school: Some facts and findings. 2001. ERIC Digest Number 162.

Levin, H. 2002. The Accelerated Schools Program. www.acceleratedschools.org.

Lockwood, A., and Secada, W. 2000. Transforming education for Hispanic youth: Exemplary practices, programs, and schools. ERIC Digest. www.ncbe.gwu.edu/ncbepubs/resource/hispanicyouth/hdp.htm.

Lounsbury, J. 2000. Understanding and appreciating the wonder years. Month of the young adolescent. National Middle School website at www.nmsa.org/moya/moyajhl.htm.

Lucas, T., Henze, R., and Donato, R. 1990. Promoting the success of Latino language minority students. An exploratory study of six high schools. *Harvard Educational Review, 60,* 315–340.

Matsuda, M. 1989. Working with Asian family members: Some communication strategies. *Topics in Language Disorders, 9*(3), 45–53.

McCollough, Shawn. 2000. Teaching African American students. *Clearing House, 74*(1), 5–6.

McFarland, D., Kolstad, R., and Briggs, L. 1995. Educating Attention Deficit Hyperactivity Disorder Children. *Education, 115* (4), 597–603.

National Coalition of Advocates for Students. 1994. Delivering on the promise: Positive practices for immigrant students. Boston: Author.

Payne, R. 2001. *A framework for understanding poverty.* Highlands, TX: aha! Process, Inc.

Philips, S. 1983. *The invisible culture.* New York: Longman.

Qualities of effective programs for immigrant adolescents with limited schooling. 1998. ERIC Digest. Washington, DC: ERIC.

Reed, R.1988. Education and achievement of young black males. In J. W. Gibbs (Ed.), *Young, black, and male in America: An endangered species.* Dover: Auburn Publishing Company.

Schwartz, W. 2000. New trends in language education for Hispanic students. ERIC/CUE Digest Number 155. New York: ERIC.

Schwartz, W. 2001. School practices for equitable discipline of African American students. ERIC Digest. New York: ERIC Clearinghouse on Urban Education.

St. Germaine, R. 1995. Drop-out rates among American Indian and Alaska Natives students: Beyond cultural discontinuity. ERIC Digest. Charleston, WV: ERIC Clearinghouse on Rural Education and Small Schools.

Storti, C. 1999. *Figuring foreigners out: A practical guide.* Yarmouth, ME: Intercultural Press.

Swisher, K. 1991. American Indian/Alaskan Native learning styles: Research and practice. ERIC Digest.

Tobler, N., and Stratton, H. 1997. Effectiveness of school-based drug prevention programs: A meta-analysis of the research. (Cited in Bosworth, K. 1997. Drug abuse prevention: School-based strategies that work. ERIC Digest. Washington, DC: ERIC Clearinghouse on Teaching and Teacher Education.)

Trueba, H., and Cheng, L. 1993. *Myth or reality: Adaptive strategies of Asian Americans in California.* Bristol, PA: Falmer Press.

U.S. Census Bureau, Poverty 2001. www. census.gov/hhes.

U.S. Department of Education. 1998. *Preventing bullying: A manual for schools and communities.* www.cde.ca.gov sp-branch/ssp/bullymanual.htm.

U.S. National Center for Education Statistics. 1998. Violence and discipline problems in U.S. public schools: 1996–97. U.S. Government. NCES publication 98-030.

U.S. National Center for Education Statistics. 2001. http://nces.ed.gov.

Walsh, C. 1991. Literacy and school success: Considerations for programming and instruction. In C. Walsh and H. Prashker (Eds.), *Literacy development for bilingual students.* Boston: New England Multifunctional Resource Center for Language and Culture Education.

Wierzbicka, A. 1991. Japanese key words and core cultural values. *Language in Society, 20*(3), 333–385.

CHAPTER 16

Formalizing Your Personal System of Discipline

CHAPTER PREVIEW

This chapter helps you put the finishing touches on a personal discipline system, one that meets the needs of your students and your own needs as well. From the beginning of this book, you have been encouraged to explore various philosophical, theoretical, and practical views on discipline, with an eye ultimately to organizing a discipline approach that you believe will be most effective for you.

The Five Principles and Your Personal System of Discipline

To begin this final activity, take a few minutes to review the five principles for building a personal system of discipline and then proceed to clarifying your thoughts concerning your personal views on the philosophy, theory, and practice of discipline. Summarized, the five principles are:

Principle 1. Present and conduct yourself in a professional manner.
Principle 2. Clarify how you want your students to behave, now and in the future.
Principle 3. Establish classroom conditions that help students become the kind of people you hope they will be.
Principle 4. Do all you can to help students conduct themselves acceptably.
Principle 5. Intervene in a helpful manner when misbehavior occurs.

In addition to the five principles, it is important that you clarify your answers to the following questions (for now, just read through the questions; we will come back to them presently):

1. What is classroom misbehavior and why does it require attention?
2. What is the purpose of discipline? What sorts of results do you hope for?
3. What do you consider to be essential components of a good discipline system?

4. How do those components relate to or influence each other?
5. What makes you believe those components will produce the results you desire?
6. What can teachers do to limit the occurrence of misbehavior?
7. How can teachers react most effectively when students misbehave?
8. How can teachers help students to actually want to behave more responsibly?

The first two questions have to do with your **philosophy of discipline**—what you believe discipline to be, how important you think it is, and what you believe it will help you accomplish.

Questions 3, 4, and 5 have to do with your **theory of discipline.** A theory is a tentative explanation of a large-scale phenomenon. It typically includes the components that seem to play important roles in the phenomenon under consideration and suggests how those components interact with each other.

Questions 6, 7, and 8 have to do with your views concerning the **practice of discipline,** that is, how discipline should be implemented in the classroom. Practice should be guided by philosophy and theory, but most teachers overlook those basic considerations and move ahead to what they will do and say when students misbehave. However, if they would clarify their philosophy and theory of discipline, they could more effectively compose a system attuned to student needs and what they hope to achieve in the class.

Clarifying Your Philosophy of Discipline

Edward Savage, a high school math teacher who recently retired, was asked about the views he had on discipline when he first began teaching in 1961, and in particular if at that time he had thought through a philosophy or theory of discipline. He shook his head and said, "No, I don't think I ever thought much about a philosophy or theory of discipline. If you are asking how I approached discipline, well . . . my methods changed over the years, but I knew when students were behaving improperly and so did they, and I stopped them from doing it. I don't think I was tyrannical. They knew how they were supposed to act in class. Everybody had students who liked to see what they could get away with. When my students were out of line I asked them to stop, and they usually did. Sometimes if they kept at it I gave them detention or made them do extra work. I had confrontations with students occasionally, which left me feeling pretty bad afterward." Prompted again about philosophy and theory of discipline, Mr. Savage said, "No, I really am not sure what that means. What do you mean by that?"

Mr. Savage gave a candid description of his views on discipline during his career. Those same views are held by many teachers today. Mr. Savage was considered to be a good disciplinarian, but he relied mainly on strength of personality. He got by with that because his students were more compliant than students are today.

Your philosophy about any matter—life, education, politics, teaching, what have you—summarizes what you believe to be true, good, and correct about that matter, and conversely, what is false, bad, and incorrect about it. Philosophy gives direction to how you think and what you do. Humans (including Mr. Savage) philosophize every day. For example, we are all keenly interested in human nature and behavior, but few of us can explain what we actually believe about them, that is, what they are like, what is good and bad about them, whether or not they can be changed, and if so, for what purpose, to what extent, and under what conditions. Let's consider the questions that were listed earlier:

What is classroom misbehavior and why does it require attention? In Chapter 1, classroom misbehavior was defined as any behavior that, through *intent or thoughtlessness*, interferes with teaching or learning, threatens or intimidates others, or oversteps society's standards of moral, ethical, or legal behavior. Such behavior requires attention because it disrupts learning in class. If you truly want to do the best you can for all your students, you must help them learn to choose responsible behavior that serves them well and does not impinge on the rights of other students. To make this possible, help your students formulate clear agreements about how they will work and conduct themselves. Help them understand why violations of those agreements are detrimental to the class, why intervention is required when agreements are transgressed, and how mistakes can be turned into valuable learning experiences.

What is the purpose of discipline? What sorts of results does one hope for? The purpose of discipline is to help students learn more easily, relate better with others, and become more self-directed and responsible. Students do not respond well to forceful discipline, but they appreciate discipline that is helpful.

Clarifying Your Theory of Discipline

We noted that theory helps us understand larger events and processes when there is not enough factual information to provide certainty. Theories of education, teaching, and discipline are useful in helping us work more effectively with the young. All educators, students, parents, and other adults have beliefs about discipline they seldom articulate. When classroom discipline is mentioned, most people envision a beleaguered teacher trying to lay down the law to unruly students. If asked to explain the nature of discipline, what it's for and how it works, most would say only that it involves misbehavior and the steps taken to correct it. But teachers require a more encompassing view of discipline. They need to know its purpose, the elements that comprise it, and how it is managed positively, so that behavior improves while motivation and dignity remain intact.

What seem to be the essential components of an effective system of discipline? The answer to this question depends on your philosophy of discipline. To illustrate this point, observe the contrasts in three different philosophical views and the theories that emerge from them. Remember, these are only three of a number of different possibilities, and none mentions self-control, self-direction, responsibility, or learning from mistakes, which most teachers would like to emphasize.

Philosophy 1. Discipline is for making students behave. If you believe, as did Mr. Savage, that the overriding purpose of discipline is to make students behave themselves in class, you have only two main elements to be concerned about—misbehavior and enforcement. Teachers who adhere to this philosophy, and many still do, often tell their students exactly what kinds of misbehavior they will not tolerate. Others do no more than react to whatever displeases them at the moment, assuming that their students "know better." When students misbehave, these teachers make students so uncomfortable they stop misbehaving. Their favorite tactics include scowling, scolding, lecturing, moralizing, and punishing.

Philosophy 2. Discipline is for helping students get along together and sense they belong. If your philosophy holds that the goal of discipline is to help students get along with each other and that students misbehave mainly when they cannot satisfy their desire to belong in the group, class, or school, your theory of discipline will include four main elements: (1) what "getting along well" and "sense of belonging" mean, and how they affect each other, (2) the types of misbehavior students engage in when they have no sense of belonging, (3) what can be done to provide the sense of belonging students crave, and (4) tactics that direct misbehavior back to acceptability when it goes awry.

Philosophy 3. Discipline is for identifying and correcting causes of misbehavior. If your philosophy holds that misbehavior has many identifiable causes, that students misbehave when a range of needs goes unmet, and that student behavior improves when those causes of misbehavior are limited or removed, your theory of discipline will contain a number of elements. First, there is a list of student needs that discipline should help meet. Second, there are the agreements, formulated jointly by teacher and students, that indicate behavior that best serves individuals and the group. Third, there is a list of factors that often cause students to violate class agreements. Fourth, there are the preventive procedures done in advance to remove or limit the causes of misbehavior. Fifth, there are steps taken to build trust between teacher and students. And, sixth, there are the dignified interventions the teacher uses to remove causes of misbehavior and redirect students who have transgressed agreements.

How do the components in your theory relate to or influence each other? The elements in discipline interact in ways we call *cause–effect* and *means–end.* **Cause–effect** occurs in two significant ways, illustrated in these examples: (1) Jon is in class. He becomes bored (cause) and to relieve his boredom begins to talk to his neighbor (effect). Here, a factor (boredom) has caused Jon to misbehave. (2) Jon misbehaves by talking to his neighbor. Mrs. Abel moves closer to him (cause) and Jon stops talking (effect).

Means–end is illustrated as follows: We want Jon to behave properly (the end result) so in advance we take actions (means) that will encourage him to do so. In other words, we remove or reduce the potential causes of misbehavior. Means–end is central to *preventive discipline,* a prominent feature of many discipline systems.

Although prevention is extremely important and useful, all teachers, novice and experienced, are keenly interested in how to stop Jon's misbehavior once it occurs. They invariably want to know what to do when Jon is disrespectful, doesn't do his homework, bothers others, or sits and does nothing. They ask the question as though there were a single reliable answer, but as we have seen, there can be a number of effective answers as well as lots of ineffective ones.

Suppose Jon gets up and wanders around the room bothering others when he is supposed to be working. What do we really want for Jon, both for now and for the long term?

- Stop wandering around and bothering others, period.
- Stop misbehaving but maintain a good attitude.
- Learn how to behave more appropriately.
- Show more self-control, self-direction, and responsibility.
- Show consideration for the well-being of the class.

When we decide what we want for Jon, what do we do then? Ideally, in keeping with agreements reached in the class, Jon would never get up and wander around in the first place. But given the fact that he has done so, what should we do? Consider the following possibilities:

- We can work on the cause of Jon's misbehavior. To do this, we must first determine why Jon is misbehaving (breaking class agreements). Possibilities might include boredom, frustration, desire for attention, poor habits, or self-centeredness. Once we have identified the cause, we can remove or limit it. The various models of discipline analyzed earlier suggest tactics for preventing boredom and fatigue, teaching in charismatic ways, managing lessons to hold student attention, and holding students accountable for learning. These tactics deal with some of the known causes of misbehavior.
- We can provide direct help to Jon. We might talk with him and see if he is experiencing a problem we might assist with. If he identifies a problem, we need to show willingness to deal with it if possible. If he says there is no problem, we might want to ask for his cooperation so the lesson can continue without further disruption. We might also consider arranging for him to work with another student or altering the lesson by shortening it or changing activities.
- We should make sure the intervention has a positive effect on Jon. A good intervention should stop the misbehavior and help Jon behave properly in the future with a positive attitude. We can usually accomplish this by speaking to him in a kindly manner and showing respect without giving personal offense.

What makes you believe the components in your theory of discipline will produce the results you desire? Four sources can validate the effectiveness of the components in your theory of discipline. *First,* there is a body of research you can rely on that deals with behavior shaping, communication, lesson management, and other topics important in discipline. That information has been presented in earlier chapters. *Second,* there is the persuasive logic of authorities who have devoted much of their careers to improving class discipline. This too is provided in the models. *Third,* there is an abundance of teacher experience that helps us understand what works well with students and what does not. You may have some of this experience yourself, or you may glean it from other teachers. *Fourth,* you can rely on your own logical thought based on what you know about human nature and how you, yourself, react to guidance and intervention. Simply recognizing how students are likely to behave and knowing how you would like to be treated in those circumstances provides excellent guidance. You almost never go wrong when you treat others as you would like them to treat you.

Clarifying Your Practice of Discipline

Here we move to a consideration of how your system of discipline works in the classroom. This should be derived logically from your philosophy and theory of discipline. Let's consider the remaining questions posed at the beginning of the chapter.

What will you do to prevent or limit the occurrence of misbehavior? This question takes us back to preventive discipline. Any misbehavior you prevent saves you many minutes of instructional time and helps maintain interpersonal relations and positive attitudes toward school and learning. The preventive aspect of discipline entails removing, in advance, the known causes of misbehavior or limiting their effects to the extent possible. An extensive list of causes was presented in Chapter 13, along with suggestions for dealing with them. All in all, we can prevent most misbehavior by attending to the following:

Treatment of Students

- Show students that each and every one is a valued member of the class.
- Give personal attention to each individual student as often as possible.
- Never threaten students or back them into a corner.

Trust and Responsibility

- Develop bonds of trust with students through helpfulness and fair treatment.
- Give students responsibility for making decisions and show them it is all right to make mistakes.
- Use mistakes as excellent opportunities for learning.

Communication

- Learn students' names quickly and chat with each of them as often as feasible.
- Always speak respectfully; don't preach to students, speak derisively, or use sarcasm.
- Use I-messages rather than you-messages when discussing problem situations.

Instruction

- Make instructional activities as interesting and worthwhile as possible.
- Give constant attention to students' needs for security, hope, enjoyment, and competence.
- Always ask yourself how you can be of most help to your students right now.

Teacher Personality

- Present yourself as enthusiastic, energetic, and eager.
- Tactfully share information about your life, aspirations, and interests.
- Always be a model of kindness, consideration, and good manners.

Class Agreements

- Involve your students in making class agreements about instruction and behavior.
- Encourage students to accept the agreements as the code that guides the class.
- Think of misbehavior not just as violations of the code but as opportunities to learn.

How can you react most effectively when students misbehave? Despite your diligent efforts to prevent misbehavior, students will still misbehave, sometimes for reasons outside your control and sometimes as willful transgressions of class agreements. This brings us again to the question all teachers ask: "What do I do when . . . ?" There is no single correct answer to that question, of course. Let's examine some good possibilities for various occasions, such as when students first become restive, when they transgress class rules, and when they behave immorally or viciously.

When you see students becoming restive. Even the most accomplished teachers expect at some point to see their students begin to fidget, doodle, look out the window, smile or make gestures at each other, whisper, and otherwise indicate they are disengaging from the lesson. You can cut down considerably on this sort of behavior by making your instructional activities especially interesting. It is sometimes difficult to do this, and in truth some important topics are so boring that your best ingenuity is required.

Let us suppose you have shown an awareness of what students are doing in all parts of the room at all times. Your students realize this and will often glance at you to see if you are noticing their behavior. Your eye contact is often enough to get them going again. If that isn't sufficient, you might move to the student involved and ask a question about the work in progress. (All the while you are beginning to ask yourself if the lesson is interesting enough to hold student attention much longer.) You may need to make a comment such as, "Class, I'll really appreciate it if you can stick with the lesson for five more minutes." If they like and trust you, they will probably comply with your request. If they don't comply, you might ask, "Class, I see that the lesson is not holding your attention. What seems to be the trouble?" Based on their comments, you might make modifications that resolve the problem.

When students thoughtlessly break class agreements. Most of the time when students transgress class agreements they do so unintentionally or without malice by talking, calling out, moving about, goofing off, or not completing work. What do you do? Here are some suggestions offered by authorities:

- Use body language such as eye contact, physical proximity, and attention.
- Remind the students of the class agreements they have helped formulate.
- Stop the class and say, "This lesson doesn't seem to be holding your attention. What might I do to help?"
- Stop the class and say, "We seem to have a problem here. What do you think we can do to resolve it?"
- In no case should you call offending students to task publicly.
- Conduct class meetings to discuss ongoing incidents and explore solutions. Here you must be careful not to single out individual students. You want their cooperation, not their enmity.

All of these tactics are effective. It is for you to decide which makes most sense to you personally and which you can use on a daily basis. Just remember it is self-defeating to scold or deride the offending students. You and they will both be better off if you can help them abide by class rules willingly.

When students misbehave seriously. The vast majority of student misbehavior is benign. Although it interferes with learning, wastes time, and annoys the teacher and perhaps other students, it can be dealt with fairly easily. Occasionally, however, students behave in ways considered immoral, outrageous, or violent. These behaviors range from lying and cheating to stealing, sexual immorality, bullying, cruelty, aggression, and violence. Although these behaviors are relatively rare, they affect everyone strongly. You should carefully think through how you will react to them. Before any matters of this type occur, hold a class meeting. Tell the class there are certain kinds of behaviors so serious they are bound to cause problems if they occur. Mention the kinds of behaviors you are concerned about. Indicate that although you don't expect the behaviors to occur in the class, you feel it is important to bring them out in the open. That way, students will be mindful of them and perhaps can help determine how to react to them.

Should a serious transgression occur, conceal your distress and maintain your composure. If possible, say either privately to the individual or to the entire class if all are affected, "This is a serious problem. I'd like us to resolve it together. Let's try. But if we can't, I'll need to ask for help from the vice principal."

Meanwhile, begin working immediately toward positive solutions with the students involved. Show your willingness to help them choose behavior that serves them and the class productively. Later, bring the topic up for discussion in class meetings, provided it is not a private matter.

You can usually handle lying, cheating, stealing, and sexual innuendo or harassment without having to call for expert assistance. Sexual innuendo and harassment should be squelched immediately. Without singling out the individuals involved, point out what is occurring and why it is forbidden in the classroom. If the behavior continues, speak with the culpable individual privately and explain once more why those acts are not permitted in the class or school. Remind yourself that your goal is not to punish but to help. Ask the individual to meet with you privately and, without casting blame, explain your concern frankly. Some students will admit what they've done; others will deny it. Don't try to make students admit wrongdoing. Don't threaten them or use logic in trying to persuade them, and never insist they apologize, as that can work against the relationship you hope to preserve. When you talk with an offending student, admit you might be wrong, then explain your perception of the situation. Ask students if they understand why, when they behave in those ways, others lose trust in them and don't want to associate with them. Ask them if they can identify more responsible ways of behaving. Assure offending students that you want to help them learn and be the best persons they can. Show them kind personal attention. Go out of your way to be helpful. This is as much as you can realistically do. If that does not resolve the problem, you should inform the school counselor or administrator and let that person take over from there.

For behavior that is threatening, dangerous, or wantonly cruel—such as severe bullying, intimidation, fighting, or possession of weapons or dangerous substances—be ready to call for help immediately. You are not expected to deal with those conditions. Some authorities suggest including a "severe clause" in class agreements, which makes clear to students that dangerous or threatening behavior will result in immediate notification of the school administrator and removal from the classroom. From that point, the matter moves out of your hands into those of persons with special training. To make sure what you are expected to do in those circumstances, discuss the matter with your school administrator.

How can teachers help students actually want to behave more responsibly? The dream of all teachers is to work with students who behave responsibly because they feel it is the proper thing to do. Many years ago Rudolf Dreikurs made "social interest" a prime ingredient in his scheme of classroom discipline. He sought to help students see that they prospered individually when the class prospered as a whole. He pointed out that the best way for students to help themselves was to help the class function well. Social interest can be developed through making joint decisions, assuming personal responsibility, developing a sense of community, and producing class synergy, as described in the following paragraphs.

Making joint decisions. Students like to have a sense of power in the classroom. When power is not available to them, some try to seize it by rebelling. Wise teachers give students power by involving them in helping make decisions that affect the class. This gives students a feeling of being in control, and when they help make decisions they become more likely to comply with them. When they see that what benefits the class also benefits them personally, they become predisposed to work toward the betterment of the class.

Assuming responsibility. Students desire freedom and power but often do not understand that responsibility is tied to them. Teachers are being advised to give students more responsibility, so they put them in charge of keeping the room tidy, managing the media or science equipment, helping take care of plants and pets, and so forth. This is one kind of responsibility, certainly, and it does contribute to a sense of concern about the class. There is, however, another kind of responsibility that of necessity is tied to freedom and power. This is responsibility in accepting the results of one's actions and learning from them. When students are allowed to make decisions about what goes on in the class, they must be helped to understand that they must deal with the results of their decisions. If the class decides to forgo preparation for an upcoming test and students do poorly, they must accept that they are to blame, not the teacher. They need to see, too, that they can learn from the situation so that they do better in the future. Mr. Abrams always stands ready to help the class overcome difficulties. He allows them to make decisions, but when they do poor work he does not excuse them. This same principle applies when students decide to work in groups but find that some students are not doing their part. They must assume responsibility for working things out. Mr. Abrams will help them find ways to do so, but the working-through process is up to them. In this manner students begin to realize that they have a collective responsibility to make things run smoothly for the class. Given the opportunity, most students would rather be involved in this process than have the teacher make all decisions for them.

Developing a sense of community. Joint decision making and responsibility help build a sense of community in the class. Alfie Kohn places prime emphasis on working toward establishing this sense of community, which he describes as a place where students feel valued and connected to each other and think in terms of "we" instead of "I." Kohn believes sense of community grows when teachers consistently show they care about students and behave respectfully toward them. He says that when students' personal needs are met, they show increased tendency to help meet their classmates' needs rather than remaining preoccupied with their own.

Developing synergy. Teachers have long recognized the value of group spirit, where students reach high levels of energy and involvement. It is usually seen in connection with athletic contests and to a slightly lesser degree in school plays, concerts, and other productions. It can also occur in the classroom. Most teachers have experienced it and know that it provides a time of happy learning, joyful teaching, and few or no discipline problems. However, teachers have not understood clearly what causes it or how they can make it occur.

C. M. Charles calls the phenomenon "class synergy" and says it occurs when members of a class begin, through interest or excitement, to feed psychic energy to each other. When the energy level becomes high enough, students work together eagerly with little thought for themselves as individuals. They communicate, cooperate, share resources, and find pleasure in the process. Learning occurs rapidly. Goodwill predominates and misbehavior disappears.

Charles says the elements of synergy can be put in place by teachers and that with practice they can cause synergy to occur when desired. He lists elements of synergy such as trust, teacher charisma, communication, interest, class agreements, coopetition, human relations, and problem resolution. Although synergy can occur without all the elements being in place, it cannot be made to occur reliably when certain of them are absent, especially trust, communication, charisma, and interest.

Two Sample Approaches to Discipline

Here are two approaches to discipline constructed and used by experienced teachers. You will see that they differ. The first places emphasis on rules and consequences that are applied when students misbehave. The second places emphasis on student–teacher cooperation and preventing misbehavior. You might wish to use either of them as a guide to planning your discipline system, modify either to make it more appropriate for your situation, or turn to yet another approach that suits you better.

Sample 1. An Approach That Emphasizes Rules and Consequences

Many teachers use discipline plans that feature rules and consequences. Teachers who use such plans believe the teacher should be firmly yet sensitively in control and see that everyone behaves as they should in the classroom. They feel their approach cuts down on disruptions and allows students to learn in an environment free from worry. Discipline plans of this type usually contain the following:

- *Rules.* A set of rules that indicates what students are allowed and not allowed to do in class. Students may help compose the rules.
- *Consequences.* Consequences (results that follow behavior) are attached to the rules and made plain to students. Positive consequences are pleasant experiences that students enjoy when they follow the rules. Negative consequences are unpleasant experiences that students experience when they break the rules.
- *Procedure.* A series of steps is established for applying the consequences. When students behave properly, they receive something they like, such as compliments, bonus points, privileges, or a favorite activity. When they behave unacceptably, they receive negative consequences—conditions they don't like—that may grow progressively unpleasant if students continue to repeat the misbehavior. Parents are kept fully informed about the rules, consequences, and procedures of enforcement.

This approach has served hundreds of thousands of teachers for many years and continues to be widely popular. To see how a present-day teacher uses the rules-consequences-procedure protocol, adjusted to her needs, examine the following program developed by third-grade teacher Deborah Sund.

Deborah Sund's Third-Grade Discipline Program

Deborah Sund, who had been teaching for two years when she devised this program, was seeking a discipline approach that provided structure for herself and her students while at the same time meeting students' needs. She felt structure was important for helping everyone know exactly what was expected. Notice in the plan that Ms. Sund clarifies her students' needs, her own needs, and her special dislikes, then builds her discipline system so all are taken into account.

My Students' Needs
- To learn interesting and useful information, especially that which promotes skills in reading, math, and language.
- A learning environment that is attractive, stimulating, free from threat, and conducive to productive work.
- A teacher who is helpful, attentive, and kind.
- The opportunity to interact and work cooperatively with other students.
- To be accepted and feel part of the group.
- To learn how to relate to others humanely and helpfully.
- To have the opportunity to excel.

My Own Needs
- Orderly classroom appearance; good room arrangement; materials neatly stored; interesting, well-thought-out displays.
- Structure and routines: a set schedule that is flexible and allows for improvisation when needed.
- Attention and participation: students pay attention to directions and speakers and participate willingly in all instructional activities.
- Situationally appropriate behaviors: quiet attention during instruction, considerate interaction during group activities.
- Enthusiasm from me and my students.
- Warmth as reflected in mutual regard among all members of the class.
- Positive, relaxed classroom environment reflecting self-control, mutual helpfulness, and assumption of responsibility.

My Dislikes
- Inattention to speaker, teacher, other adult, or class member.
- Excessive noise: loud voices, inappropriate talking and laughing.
- Distractions: toys, unnecessary movement, poking, teasing, and so on.
- Abuse of property: misusing, wasting, or destroying instructional materials.
- Unkind and rude conduct: ridicule, sarcasm, bad manners, and physical abuse.

Class Rules I ask students on the first day of school to tell me how they would like to be treated by others in the room. I also ask them what they especially dislike. We discuss their contributions at length, making sure through examples that we have a clear understanding of their wishes. By the next day, I have written out some statements that summarize what they have said. I ask them if these ideas seem good ones to live by in the room. They invariably say yes and we call the statements our class rules. We spend some time practicing how we will behave and speak in accordance with the rules. In the days that follow, I demonstrate to students the prompts, cues, hints, and other assistance I will give to help them abide by the behaviors we have agreed on.

The following are class rules that typically emerge from discussions with my students:

1. Be considerate of others at all times. (Speak kindly. Be helpful. Don't bother others.)
2. Do our best work. (Get as much done as possible. Do work neatly, to be proud of it. Don't waste time.)
3. Use quiet voices in the classroom. (Use regular speaking voices during class discussions. Speak quietly during cooperative work. Whisper at other times.)
4. Use signals to request permission or receive help. (I explain the signal systems for assistance, movement, restroom pass.)

Positive Consequences I emphasize that I will always try to show I am pleased when students follow the rules we have agreed to. I tell them:

- Mostly I will give them smiles, winks, nods, and pats when they are behaving well.
- Sometimes I will say out loud how pleased I am with the way they are working or behaving toward each other.
- Once in a while, when the whole class has behaved especially well, I will give them a special privilege (go early to recess, do one of their favorite activities, see a video.)
- From time to time I will send a complimentary note to their parents or call their parents and comment on how well they are doing.

Negative Consequences When discussing the class rules, I ask students what they think should happen when someone breaks a rule. They usually suggest punishment. I tell them that because I want them always to be as happy as possible, I don't want to punish them. I say that instead of punishment, I will do the following:

- Give them "pirate eyes" or a stern glance with disappointed or puzzled expression.
- Remind them of what rule is being broken: "I hear noise." "Some people are not listening."
- Tell them exactly what they are doing wrong: "Gordon, you did not use the signal. Please use the signal."
- Separate them from the group until they can control themselves.
- Contact their parents to see how they can help.

To Prevent Misbehavior I discuss with my students a number of things I will do to help them feel more like behaving properly, such as:

- Show respect for each student as entitled to the best education I can provide.
- Look for the positive and enjoyable qualities in each student.
- Take time to know each student better on a personal level.
- Each day assess students' feelings and discuss them if necessary.
- Talk with students in ways that imply their own competence, such as, "Okay, you know what to do next."
- Involve them in establishing rules and assuming responsibility for proper behavior.
- Keep a good room environment to prevent their feeling strained, tired, or inconvenienced (proper lighting, temperature, traffic patterns, attractiveness).
- Emphasize, model, and hold practice sessions on good manners, courtesy, and responsibility.
- Provide a varied, active curriculum with opportunities for physical movement, singing, interaction, and times of quiet.
- Communicate with parents in the following ways:
  1. Send letters outlining expectations and the discipline system.
  2. Make short, positive phone calls to parents.
  3. Send home with children notes concerning good work and behavior.
- End each day on a positive note, with a fond good-bye and hope for a happy and productive tomorrow.

Intervening When Students Misbehave When students begin to misbehave, I do the following:

- Move close to the student.
- Show interest in the student's work.
- Modify the lesson or activity if it seems to be causing difficulty.
- Invoke the negative consequences that we have agreed to.

Sample 2. An Approach That Emphasizes Prevention and Student–Teacher Cooperation

The following approach emphasizes preventing misbehavior through meeting student needs and building personal relationships. The rationale for this approach is, first, that it is difficult to confront misbehavior head-on without producing undesirable side effects, such as student resentment, desire to retaliate, and reluctance to cooperate, and, second, that working with students in this manner helps teachers find greater satisfaction and enjoyment in teaching. When needs are met rather than thwarted, students become more inclined to cooperate and less interested in outsmarting or disdaining their teachers. Moreover, when causes of misbehavior are addressed rather than the dignity of the student, positive feelings are kept intact. Plans of this sort emphasize the following:

- Attending continually to students' needs for security, hope, acceptance, dignity, power, enjoyment, and competence.
- Communicating effectively and regularly with students and their parents.

- Making sure to give all students attention, encouragement, and support.
- Making class activities consistently enjoyable and worthwhile.
- Ensuring that all students accept responsibility and experience success.
- Establishing agreements about how everyone will interact and behave.
- Discussing and practicing manners, courtesy, and responsibility.
- Involving all students meaningfully in the operation of the class.
- Dealing with misbehavior by attending to its causes.

Teachers who adopt this discipline strategy feel it allows them to relate with students in a way that builds positive relationships and produces relatively little stress. Gail Charles uses a discipline plan that incorporates many of these qualities.

Gail Charles's Discipline Plan—Eighth-Grade English

The following narration is in Gail Charles's words:

> I have been teaching for almost 25 years. For many years, my students misbehaved much more than I thought they should, and I tried to control their misbehavior with scowls, reprimands, lectures, threats, and detentions. My students grudgingly behaved themselves well enough to learn most of what I intended, but I'm sure they felt under siege. I know I did, and the effort it required left me continually frustrated and exhausted.
>
> Seven or eight years ago I began to understand that I am more effective and enjoy my work more when I organize the curriculum to accommodate, even embrace, the needs of my adolescent students and then work cooperatively with them. While I still provide a strong and challenging curriculum, I have switched from a coercive to a collaborative way of teaching. I now try to guide, encourage, and support students' efforts rather than endlessly push and prod. The result has been fewer power struggles, more success, and happier students and teacher.
>
> **Winning My Students Over**   My students want to feel part of the group. They want to feel accepted and valued by each other and especially by me. They want to feel safe, so I forbid all ridicule and sarcasm. I've never ridiculed a student, but sorry to say, I have spoken sarcastically many times when struggling against students who defied my rules. I no longer use sarcasm or allow students to belittle each other in any way.
>
> I give my students a voice in class matters and listen to them sincerely. I allow them to make decisions about where they sit and with whom they wish to work. I do this as part of trying to make learning enjoyable. They like to work with each other, participate, talk, and cooperate.
>
> **Meeting My Needs**   We discuss the importance of making classwork enjoyable, and I tell my students that the class needs to be enjoyable for me, too. I tell them up front what I need in order to feel good about the class—that I want the tone to be positive, with everyone showing patience, tolerance, good manners, and mutual respect. I tell them that I want them to be enthusiastic and do the best work they can. I say I need

their attention and that I want them to help care for materials and keep the room clean. I promise to treat them with respect, and they usually want to reciprocate.

Rules and Student Input My new approach to discipline has required me to make changes in my curriculum and ways of establishing rules. I have learned to request and make use of student input concerning expectations, operating procedures, and codes of conduct. Formerly, I greeted new students with a printed set of rules and consequences, but they always saw them as impositions rather than cooperative agreements they wanted to support. Now when I meet a new class, I discuss their needs and mine and focus on how we can meet those needs and make our class productive. I give students power to make many decisions and show that I respect what they say.

Together we write a plan for how we will work and behave in the class. Because I want them to make thoughtful suggestions, I ask them, for their first homework assignment, to think back on previous years in school and write brief responses to the following:

1. When have you felt most successful in school?
2. What did the teacher do to help you feel successful?
3. What kinds of class activities have you found most helpful and enjoyable?
4. What suggestions do you have for creating a classroom in which all can work, learn, and do their best?

The next day I organize students into small groups to share and discuss what they have written. Volunteers present each group's responses, which I list on the overhead projector. Occasionally I may add a suggestion of my own. We then streamline, combine, reword, and sometimes negotiate until we reach a set of agreements we think best. Before the next class, I type up the agreements and ask each student and his or her parent to sign, indicating their support. I do this for each of my five classes. The agreements turn out to be quite similar from class to class.

Prevention In classes of 35 students, distractions abound. It is up to me to keep students successfully engaged in activities they enjoy and find rewarding. I have had considerable success using reading and writing activities in which students choose books to read and respond to them in writing. I present mini-lessons that address common needs I see in the class. Students evaluate their own work and make it the best possible for inclusion in their Showcase Portfolios, which are displayed for parents, teachers, administrators, and others at a Writers' Tea. In addition, students complete at least one project per quarter. They have choices on what they will pursue in their projects and how they will show what they have learned. Always there is a high emphasis on quality.

During these efforts, I try to interact personally with every student. It is not easy to forge relationships with 160+ students, but I try to do so in order to show I "see" and like them. At the beginning of the year I write a letter to my students introducing myself and telling a bit about my family, hobbies, interests, and goals. I ask them to do the same so I can know them better. I keep a birthday calendar to remember student birthdays. I try to comment on new hairstyles, new outfits, or how great a now brace-free set of teeth looks. I chaperone field trips and dances, supervise the computer writing lab after school, and make myself available for conversation before and after school. These little things mean a lot to students.

For their part, many students like to involve themselves in the workings of the classroom. I assign them tasks such as classroom librarian, bulletin board designer, plant caretaker, and class secretary. Their involvement makes them feel important and useful.

More than anything else, I have found that if I want respect from my students, I must show them respect. I want them to enjoy writing, so I write along with them. I want them involved in learning, so I get involved with them. I want them to show good manners, humor, and kindness, so I exemplify those qualities the best I can in my behavior and dealings with them. I make mistakes in these efforts and lots of them, but the more sincerely I try, the more forgiving my students become.

Interventions   With the collaborative plan in place, I have few discipline problems and little difficulty dealing with those that occur. Most often, a simple reminder is all that is needed to get students back on track. For the occasional student who repeatedly misbehaves despite our agreements, I ask the counselor to set up a meeting with the students' parents and, sometimes, with other teachers. We discuss the problem and how it can be resolved. Only two or three times has a student behaved in a dangerous manner or prevented my teaching. When that happens, I call the vice principal for assistance.

Finalizing Your Personal System of Discipline

Given the structure and information needed for a personal system of discipline, we move ahead to formalizing your personal approach, which can be done easily in a series of five steps.

Step 1. Specify How You Will Present and Conduct Yourself at School

Indicate how you will abide by professional standards, ethical standards, and legal considerations.

Step 2. Specify the Goals and Aspirations You Have for Your Students

Explain how would like your students to conduct themselves, now and in the future. Compare your views with the following reminders.

- Show positive attitude.
- Behave considerately toward others.
- Take initiative.

- Show self-direction.
- Make a strong effort to learn.
- Assume personal responsibility for behavior.

Step 3. Describe the Classroom Conditions You Want to Maintain

Specify the physical and psychosocial conditions you intend to maintain in your classroom. You might wish to consider the following list of reminders.

- Good environment for learning
- Sense of community
- Positive attention
- Good communication
- Consideration for others
- Trust
- Interesting activities
- Student knowledge of expectations
- Continual helpfulness
- Preservation of dignity
- Minimizing causes of misbehavior
- Teacher charisma
- Student involvement in planning the program

Step 4. Specify How You Will Work Individually or Cooperatively with Students to Help Ensure Appropriate Behavior

You might wish to refer to the following list of reminders.

- Help students meet their needs in a responsible manner.
- Involve students in helping formalize the class program, including discipline.
- Establish class agreements concerning behavior, interactions, and instruction.
- Identify and minimize factors that lead to misbehavior.
- Show each student personal attention as often as possible.
- Develop trust with and among class members.
- Seek frequently to energize the class.
- Select instructional topics and activities students enjoy and find rewarding.
- Use congruent communication and I-messages.
- Encourage student initiative and responsibility.
- Seek parental support for the class program.
- Teach students to use win-win methods for resolving problems and conflicts.
- For misbehavior, use established interventions that preserve personal dignity.
- When students misbehave, help them assume responsibility for correction and restitution.

Step 5. Indicate How You Will Intervene When Misbehavior Occurs or Appears Imminent

You might wish to consider the following reminders.

- Show interest in the students' work and ask cheerful questions, make favorable comments, or provide hints.
- Catch students' eyes, send private signals, or move closer to students.
- Provide a light challenge: "Can you get five more problems done before we stop?"
- Ask students if they are having difficulty. Ask what you might to do help.
- If the work is boring or too difficult, restructure it or change the activity.
- For more serious infractions, follow procedures that have been clearly established in advanced, with student involvement and approval. (Indicate what those procedures might involve.)
- Teach students how to use win-win conflict resolution. If they have disputes, ask them to try to resolve their conflict.
- Talk with offending students calmly and respectfully. Don't lecture, threaten, impugn their dignity, or back them into a corner. Always try to help the student and the class.
- Remain pleasant and composed. Don't argue with students. Remind them they have helped make the agreements and have indicated they will abide by them.
- Conduct the interventions in a consistent manner. Don't give in to student wheedling or begging. Remind them that everything will be all right so long as they follow class agreements and they can now make a fresh start.

KEY TERMS AND CONCEPTS PRESENTED IN THIS CHAPTER

The following terms and concepts are important for understanding this chapter. Check yourself to make sure you understand them:

philosophy of discipline	practice of discipline	means–end
theory of discipline	cause–effect	

The following are terms featured in the models of discipline and supporting chapters in this book. When appropriate, authorities who originated and/or helped popularize the term are indicated.

ABCD of disruptive behavior (Kagan, Kyle, and Scott): Aggression, breaking rules, confrontations, disengagement.

Acceptable choice (Nelsen, Lott, and Glenn): A behavior option the teacher considers worthwhile, made available to students.

Accomplishment albums and portfolios (Albert): Albums and portfolios in which students place samples of their best work to document progress.

Accountability (Kounin): Holding each student responsible for active involvement in what is being taught.

Accountability mentality (Nelsen, Lott, and Glenn): Students' predisposition to accept responsibility for their actions. Contrasts with victim mentality in which blame is placed on other factors or people.

Active listening (Gordon): Listener showing obvious attention by providing responses to what speaker is saying.

ADHD: Attention Deficit and Hyperactivity Disorder.

Aggression (Kagan and others): A type of misbehavior that directs hostility or unwanted attention toward others.

Application of discipline structures (Kagan, Kyle, and Scott): Times when teachers apply discipline tactics—at moment of disruption, follow-up, and long term.

Appraising reality (Redl and Wattenberg): Helping students become aware of a discipline situation, especially as concerns reward and punishment.

Appreciative praise (Ginott): Praise that expresses gratitude or admiration for effort, rather than accomplishment.

Appropriate choices (Nelsen, Lott, and Glenn): Acceptable behavior options that teachers make available to students.

Assertive response style (Canter and Canter): Responding to student behavior in a helpful manner while insisting that class rules be followed.

Assertive teachers (Canter and Canter): Teachers who clearly, confidently, and consistently reiterate class expectations and attempt to build trust with students.

ATOD: Alcohol, tobacco, and other drugs.

At risk, behaviorally: Students who are likely to fail in school because of unacceptable behavior.

Attention (various): A basic need of most individuals.

Attention-getting mechanisms (Albert): Tactics such as pencil tapping, showing off, calling out, and asking irrelevant questions, used to get attention from teacher and peers.

Autocratic teachers (Dreikurs): Teachers who command, demand cooperation, dominate, and criticize.

Aversive discipline (Dreikurs): Controlling behavior through use of threats and harsh consequences.

Avoidance of failure behavior (Albert): Nonproductive efforts students make to avoid being considered stupid or incapable.

Backbone teachers and schools (Coloroso): Teachers and schools that have in place clear expectations and standards of conduct.

Backup system (Jones): The planned action teachers take when students misbehave seriously and refuse to comply with positive teacher requests—typically means being sent to the principal's office.

Barriers to relationships (Nelsen, Lott, and Glenn): Teacher behaviors that are disrespectful and discouraging to students.

Basic needs: Psychological and physical requirements that, when not satisfied over time, interfere with normal functioning.

Basic student needs (Charles): Student needs for security, belonging, hope, dignity, power, enjoyment, and competence.

Behavior: The sum total of what individuals do, think, and feel.

Behavior as choice (Glasser and others): The contention that students choose their behavior at any given time.

Behavior journal (Canter and Canter): A log book in which students write accounts of their misbehavior, why they broke a rule, and what a better behavior choice would have been.

Behavior management: Attempts to get students to behave in particular ways.

Behavior modification (Skinner's followers): The use of Skinnerian principles of reinforcement to control or shape behavior.

Behavior shaping (Skinner): The process of gradually modifying behavior through reinforcement.

Behaviorally at risk (Curwin and Mendler): Students whose behavior prevents their learning and puts them in serious danger of failing in school.

Bell work (Jones): Work students do to begin a class period, such as reading, writing in journals, or completing warm-up activities, which do not require instruction from the teacher.

Belonging (Dreikurs; Glasser; Albert): A basic human need for legitimate membership in groups that are significant to the individual.

Big Three of discipline (Kagan, Kyle, and Scott): Curriculum, instruction, and management.

Body carriage (Jones): Posture and movement that indicate to students whether the teacher is well, ill, in charge, tired, disinterested, or intimidated.

Body language (Jones): Nonverbal communication transmitted through posture, eye contact, gestures, and facial expressions.

Boss teachers (Glasser): Teachers who set the tasks, direct the learning activities, ask for little student input, and grade student work.

Breaking rules (Kagan, Kyle, and Scott): One of four basic types of classroom misbehavior identified in the Win-Win system of discipline.

Brickwalls (Coloroso): Schools and teachers that rigidly use power and coercion to control students.

Builders of relationships (Nelsen, Lott, and Glenn): Teacher behaviors that show respect and encouragement to students.

Bullied: The person being bullied.

Bullying: Students systematically inflicting physical or emotional harm on other students.

Bystanders (Coloroso): Those present observing bullying.

Causes of misbehavior (Charles): Factors known to foster misbehavior, such as boredom and threat to personal dignity. Charles identifies 22 such factors.

Challenging youth (Curwin and Mendler): Students who are difficult to manage in school because of absence of motivation or high levels of anger, hostility, aggression, stubbornness, or offensiveness.

Charisma (Charles): Personal allure that invites attention and cooperation.

Choice Theory (Glasser): Theory that we all choose how to behave at any time, we cannot control anyone's behavior but our own, and all behavior is purposeful in meeting basic needs.

Choices, good (Glasser): Student behavior choices that benefit the student and the class.

Choices, poor (Glasser): Student behavior choices that are detrimental to the student and the class.

Circle of friends (Albert): Organized relationships that help all students feel they belong and are interconnected with others.

Class agreements (Charles; Albert; others): Agreements or codes composed jointly by teacher and students that indicate how behavior, instruction, and other matters are to occur.

Agreements jointly formulated by teacher and students that regulate behavior, routines, expectations, and the like.

Class rules: Written statements about acceptable and unacceptable behavior in the classroom.

Classroom meetings (Glasser and others): Meetings held in the classroom for communication and addressing and solving problems.

Classroom meetings: eight building blocks for (Nelsen, Lott, and Glenn): A list of suggestions for organizing and conducting classroom meetings more effectively.

Classroom structure (Jones): Classroom organization, including room arrangement, class rules, class routines, chores, and the like.

Climate: The feeling or tone that prevails in the classroom.

Code of conduct (Albert): Specification of how everyone in the class is supposed to behave and interact, including the teacher. Considered preferable to lists of rules.

Collaborative rule setting (Gordon): A procedure in which teachers and students work together to establish rules for making the classroom safe, efficient, and harmonious.

Communication roadblocks (Gordon): Various things teachers do, such as moralizing and preaching, that tend to shut down communication with students.

Community (Kohn): Classrooms and schools where students feel cared about and care about each other, are valued and respected, are involved in decision making, and have a sense of "we" rather than "I."

Compliant behavior: Calm student acquiescence to teacher expectations, held as a main purpose of discipline by many teachers.

Conferring dignity (Ginott; Curwin and Mendler): Respecting students by putting aside their past history, treating them considerately, and being concerned only with the present situation.

Conflict (Charles): A problem situation, such as a dispute, that involves a strong clash of wills.

Confrontation (Kagan, Kyle, and Scott): One of four types of classroom misbehavior identified by Kagan, Kyle, and Scott.

Congruent communication (Ginott): A style of communication in which teachers acknowledge and accept students' feelings about situations and themselves.

Consequences: Penalties or rewards to be applied when rules are violated or complied with.

(Curwin and Mendler): Conditions invoked for misbehavior, such as reminders, warnings, and isolation from the group.

(Canter and Canter): Penalties invoked by teachers when students interfere with others' right to learn, together with positive rewards given when students comply with expectations.

(Glasser): Students' agreement that when they break rules, they will try, with the teacher's help, to correct the underlying problem.

Also see *Instructional consequences.*

Consequences, generic (Curwin and Mendler): Common reminders, warnings, choosing, and planning that teachers invoke when they see students misbehave.

Constant reinforcement (Skinner): Providing a reinforcing stimulus every time the student behaves appropriately.

Constructivist theory: A theory of school learning that holds that students cannot receive knowledge directly from teachers but must construct it from experience.

Controlling the conversation (Marshall): Asking questions as a means of causing others to reflect on concerns you consider important.

Conventional consequences: Consequences ordinarily provided in the classroom, such as disapproval and reprimand.

Cooperative Discipline (Albert): A type of discipline in which teacher and students collaborate in making decisions.

Coopetition (Charles): Cooperation by members of a group engaged in competition against other groups.

Correcting by directing (Ginott): Teachers correcting student misbehavior simply by telling students respectfully what they should be doing rather than dwelling on what they are doing wrong.

Corrective actions: Steps taken by the teacher to stop student misbehavior.

Democratic classrooms (Dreikurs): Classrooms in which teachers give students responsibility and involve them in making decisions.

Democratic teachers (Dreikurs): Teachers who show friendly guidance and encourage students to take on responsibility, cooperate, and participate in making decisions.

Diagnostic thinking (Redl and Wattenberg): A process of analyzing misbehavior, by forming a first hunch, gathering facts, exploring hidden factors, and taking action, while remaining flexible.

Dignity (Ginott; Curwin and Mendler): Respect for oneself and others.

Dimensions of discipline (Charles): Prevention, support, correction.

(Curwin and Mendler): prevention, action, resolution.

Directions (Canter and Canter): Statements that apply only to a given activity, in contrast to *rules* that are always in effect.

Disciplinary problem (Charles): A situation involving transgression of class rules or agreements.

Discipline: What teachers do to help students conduct themselves appropriately in class. Also used to refer to the quality of student conduct in class.

(Jones): Teacher efforts to engage students in learning in the most positive, unobtrusive fashion possible.

(Coloroso): What teachers do to help students become aware of their behavior, accept responsibility for it, and make amends.

Discipline, principles of (Curwin and Mendler): The duty to deal with misbehavior, the ineffectiveness of short-term solutions, the need to treat students with dignity, the maintenance of student motivation, and the importance of responsibility rather than obedience.

Discipline, preventive (Charles and others): Steps teachers take in advance to prevent or reduce the occurrence of misbehavior.

Discipline, supportive (Charles and others): Tactics teachers use to help students remain on-task when they show first signs of incipient misbehavior.

Discipline hierarchy (Canter and Canter): Levels of consequences and the order in which they will be imposed within the period or day.

Discipline structures (Kagan, Kyle, and Scott): Discipline tactics used to deal with various types of disruptive behavior.

Disengagement: Withdrawing from an activity. Not paying attention.

Displaying inadequacy (Dreikurs): Student withdrawal and failure to try.

Diversity, student: Refers to the numerous differences in ethnic, racial, linguistic, and economic characteristics of school students.

Economic disadvantage: Traits and conditions of students living in poverty that interfere with expected educational progress.

Economic diversity: The variation in economic conditions among school students.

Eight building blocks for classroom meetings (Nelsen, Lott, and Glenn): Eight suggestions for establishing and maintaining good classroom meetings.

Encouragement (Dreikurs): Showing belief in students and stimulating them to try, as distinct from praising students for their accomplishments.

Ethics in the classroom (Charles): A principle of behavior management that stresses ethical behavior as part of developing trust in the classroom.

Ethnic diversity: The variation is ethnic origins among students in school.

Evaluative praise (Ginott): Praise that expresses judgment about students' character or quality of work.

Considered to be detrimental by Ginott and various other authorities.

External motivation: Synonymous with extrinsic motivation—that which comes from outside the individual.

Extinction (Skinner): The gradual removal of a given behavior, accomplished by withholding reinforcement.

Five A's of connecting with others (Albert): Acceptance, attention, appreciation, affirmation, and affection.

Five key principles in a personal system of discipline (Charles): Developing your professionalism, clarifying your goals for students, establishing optimal classroom conditions, helping students accept responsibility for their behavior, and intervening helpfully when misbehavior occurs.

Four classical virtues (Marshall): Prudence, temperance, justice, and fortitude.

Four personal skills needed in self-discipline (Nelsen, Lott, and Glenn): Intrapersonal, interpersonal, strategic, and judgmental.

Four R's of good consequences (Albert): Consequences should be related to the misbehavior, reasonable, respectful, and reliably enforced.

Four-step problem-solving process (Nelsen, Lott, and Glenn): A problem-solving strategy for students to use in resolving their disputes: (1) Ignore the situation, (2) talk it over respectfully with the other student, (3) agree with the other student on a solution, and (4) if no solution is found, put the matter on the class meeting agenda.

Fourteen-day window (Churchward): A rolling window of the past 14 calendar days used in keeping track of student behavior.

Freedom (Glasser): A basic student need that is met when students are allowed to make responsible choices concerning what they will study, how they will do so, and how they will demonstrate their accomplishments.

Fun (Glasser): A basic student need for pleasure that is met when students are permitted to pursue activities they find intriguing and interact with others.

General rules (Jones): General rules of behavior that apply at all times, as distinct from specific rules related to certain activities.

Generic consequences: The usual consequences teachers provide such as approval or disapproval following student behavior.

Genuine discipline: That which leads to student self-control and responsibility.

Genuine goal of class behavior (Dreikurs; Albert): Belonging, a fundamental desire to acquire sense of place and value in a group.

Genuine incentives (Jones): Incentives that truly motivate students to work or behave appropriately, as contrasted with vague incentives such as "become a better person."

Getting attention (Dreikurs): A mistaken goal of student behavior, involving disruption and showing off, to gain attention from the teacher and other students.

Goals of discipline versus methods of discipline (Kohn): Focusing on what we hope to accomplish through discipline rather than on the procedure itself.

Goals of student behavior (Dreikurs, Albert, Nelsen): Belonging, attention, power, avoidance of failure.

(Glasser): Survival, belonging, power, freedom, fun.

(Charles): Security, belonging, hope, dignity, power, enjoyment, competence.

Graceful exits (Albert): Steps teachers can take to distance themselves gracefully from confrontations with students who are very upset.

Grandma's rule (Jones): "First eat your vegetables, then you can have your dessert," or "Finish your work first, then you can do something you especially enjoy."

Group alerting (Kounin): Getting students' attention and quickly letting them know what they are supposed to do.

Group behavior (Redl and Wattenberg): Different from the ways individuals typically behave—more conforming combined with more risk taking.

Group concern (Jones): A condition in which every student has a stake in the behavior that permits the group to earn preferred activity time.

Group dynamics (Redl and Wattenberg): Psychological forces that occur within groups and influence the behavior of group members.

Guided choices (Marshall and others): Allowing students to select from a small group of acceptable behaviors.

Hate crimes: Crimes committed against people because of their race, culture, or fundamental beliefs.

Helping skills (Gordon): A cluster of skills teachers can employ when the student owns a problem to be dealt with.

Helpless handraising (Jones): A condition in which a student sits with hand raised, not working unless the teacher is hovering nearby.

Hidden asset, the teacher's (Ginott): Sincerely asking students, "How can I help you?"

Hidden rules: Unsuspected values and guidelines that direct the behavior of various ethnic and socioeconomic groups.

Hierarchy of social behavioral levels (Marshall): Anarchy, bossing, conformity, and democracy.

Honor levels (Churchward): Four levels of behavior, identified for individual students by the number of transgressions they have committed during the previous 14 calendar days.

Honor Level System (Churchward): A system of discipline that motivates students to behave in an honorable manner.

Hope, sense of (Curwin and Mendler): Anticipation of success and well-being, which inspires us, enables us to live meaningfully, and provides courage and incentive to overcome barriers.

Hostile response style (Canter and Canter): Bossing, putting down, and ordering students about.

Hostile teachers (Canter and Canter): Teachers who are openly disrespectful to students.

I-can cans (Albert): Receptacles in which primary-grade students place records of personal accomplishment.

I-messages (Ginott; Gordon): Teachers expressing their personal feelings and reactions to situations, such as "I have trouble teaching when there is so much noise in the room."

Inadequacy (Dreikurs): A mistaken goal of behavior in which the individual feigns inadequacy or inability to perform a task.

Incentive (Jones): Something outside of the individual that entices the individual to act.

Incentive, genuine (Jones): Incentive that motivates all members of the class rather than just a few.

Infraction (Churchward): One of the steps in dealing with misbehavior in the Honor Level System.

Inner discipline (Coloroso): The ability to control one's own behavior and make responsible decisions.

In poverty: Any member of a family that has to spend more than one-third of its disposable income for food adequate to meet the family's nutritional needs.

Instructional consequences (Curwin and Mendler): Consequences that teach students how to behave properly rather than punish.

Insubordination rule (Curwin and Mendler): If a student does not accept the consequence after breaking a class rule, then he or she will not be allowed to participate with the class until the consequence is accepted.

INTASC: The Interstate New Teacher Assessment and Support Consortium that has described competencies needed by teachers.

Interior loop (Jones): A classroom seating arrangement with wide aisles that allows teachers to move easily among students at work.

Intermittent reinforcement (Skinner): Reinforcement provided occasionally, not on a fixed schedule.

Internal motivation: Synonymous with intrinsic motivation—coming from within the individual.

Interpersonal behavior skills (Nelsen, Lott, and Glenn): Dialogue, sharing, listening, empathizing, cooperating, negotiating, and resolving conflicts—skills needed for working cooperatively with others.

Inviting cooperation (Ginott): Encouraging and enticing students into activities and giving them choices, rather than demanding their participation.

I-statements: Statements that begin with "I" and tell how the speaker feels. The same as I-messages.

Jellyfish teachers and schools (Coloroso): Teachers and schools that are wishy-washy, with unclear expectations or standards of conduct.

Judgmental skills (Nelsen, Lott, and Glenn): The ability to evaluate situations and make good choices.

Labeling is disabling (Ginott): Ginott's warning about the bad effects that occur when teachers label students verbally.

Laconic language (Ginott): Brevity of teacher's comments about misbehavior, such as "This is work time."

Lead teachers (Glasser): Teachers who explore with students what the students wish to learn and how they prefer to learn, provide necessary help, and encourage students to do quality work.

Legal concerns: Aspects of legality concerning discipline and other procedures in working with students.

Linguistic diversity: Variations among students in terms of native language.

Logical consequences (Dreikurs): Conditions invoked by the teacher that are logically related to behavior students choose, such as making amends for what was done wrong.

(Coloroso): Positive behavior to be taken by students in response to breaking rules; the behavior is to be responsible and related to the broken rule.

Massive time wasting (Jones): A condition Jones found to prevail in many classrooms in which discipline was not done efficiently.

Mayhem (Coloroso): Intentional misbehavior that calls for reconciliatory justice.

Misbehavior: Behavior that is considered inappropriate for the setting or situation in which it occurs.

(Gordon): An adult concept in which a student's behavior causes a consequence that is unpleasant to the teacher.

(Charles): Any behavior that, through intent or thoughtlessness, interferes with teaching or learning, threatens or intimidates others, or oversteps society's standards of moral, ethical, or legal behavior.

(Kagan, Kyle, and Scott): Students meeting legitimate needs in a disruptive manner.

Misbehavior, teacher (Charles): Anything teachers do in the classroom that adversely affects learning or human relations, or that is unprofessional in any way.

Misbehavior, types of (Coloroso): Mayhem, mischief, mistakes.

(Charles): Inattention, apathy, needless talk, moving about the room, annoying others, disruption, lying, stealing, cheating, sexual harassment, **aggression and fighting, malicious mischief, defiance of authority.**

Mischief (Coloroso): Intentional misbehavior—presents an opportunity for teaching students that all actions have consequences, sometimes pleasant and sometimes not.

Mistaken goals (Dreikurs; Albert): Attention, power, revenge, and avoidance of failure that students turn to in the mistaken belief they will bring positive recognition.

Mistakes (Coloroso): Errors in behavior, made without intent to break rules.

Modifying the environment (Gordon): A way of dealing with student misbehavior that involves changing the room or eliminating distractions.

Momentum (Kounin): Refers to teachers getting activities started promptly, keeping them moving ahead, and bringing them to efficient closure or transition.

Natural consequences (Dreikurs, Coloroso): Consequences that occur naturally (i.e., are not imposed by the teacher) when students misbehave.

Needs of students (Dreikurs, Albert): Belonging.

(Glasser): Survival, belonging, power, fun, and freedom.

(Charles): Survival, belonging, hope, dignity, power, enjoyment, competence.

(Canter and Canter, concerning helping students learn): Extra attention, extra motivation, firmer limits.

Negative consequences: Something unpleasant that occurs, or is made to occur, to students when they misbehave.

Negative reinforcement (Skinner): Removing aversive stimuli, thereby strengthening desired behavior.

No-lose method of conflict resolution (Gordon): An approach that finds a mutually acceptable solution to a disagreement, so that neither party is made to feel a loser.

Nonassertive response style (Canter and Canter): Teacher responses that let students get by with misbehavior in the classroom.

Nonassertive teachers (Canter and Canter): Teachers who take a passive, hands-off approach in dealing with students.

Noncoercive behavior management (Glasser and others): Discipline in which teachers invite and encourage proper behavior rather than using demands or threats.

Noncongruent communication (Ginott): Teacher communication that is not harmonious with students' feelings about situations and themselves.

Noncontrolling influence (Gordon): Same as noncoercive behavior management.

Nondisciplinary problem (Charles): A difficulty affecting the class, such as noise from outside, that does not involve violations of class rules or agreements.

Nonverbal communication (Jones): Communicating with students via body language.

Obedience (Curwin and Mendler): Unquestioning compliance. Not the goal of discipline: Responsibility is the true goal.

Omission training (Jones): An incentive plan for an individual student who, by cutting down on undesired behavior, can earn preferred activity time for the entire class.

Operant conditioning (Skinner): The process of shaping behavior through reinforcement.

Operant behavior (Skinner): Any behavior that an organism produces voluntarily.

Overlapping (Kounin): Refers to teachers attending to two or more issues in the classroom at the same time.

Ownership of behavior problem (Coloroso): Students taking responsibility for their actions so they can work out appropriate solutions.

Participative classroom management (Gordon and others): An operating procedure in which teachers share power and decision making with their students.

Permissive teachers (Dreikurs): Teachers who put few if any limits on student behavior and do not invoke consequences for disruptive behavior.

Personal accountability (Coloroso; Nelsen, Lott, and Glenn): Assuming personal responsibility for one's own behavior.

Personal improvement plan (Kagan, Kyle, and Scott): A plan devised in cooperation with a student to help curtail the student's disruptive behavior.

Personal power to influence (Nelsen, Lott, and Glenn): One of the three self-perceptions—believing one has the power to influence events and other people.

Personal system of behavior management (Charles): The contention that each teacher, in order to be authentic and effective, should develop a personal style of working with students.

Perspective taking (Kohn): Doing one's best to see and understand a situation from another person's point of view.

Philosophy of discipline: The beliefs one has about the nature, purpose, and value of discipline.

Physical proximity (Redl and Wattenberg and others): The teacher's moving close to a student who is misbehaving.

Picture It Right (Kagan, Kyle, and Scott): A tactic in which students are asked to picture how they would like the class to be and verbalize what they need to do to make it that way.

Poor choices (Glasser and others): Students' behavioral choices that are inappropriate and detrimental to the individual or the class.

Positive consequence: Something pleasant that occurs, or is made to occur, to students who behave in accordance with class rules.

Positive outlook (Marshall): Maintaining an air of optimism and inclination to focus on the best.

Positive recognition (Canter and Canter): Giving sincere personal attention to students who behave in keeping with class expectations.

Positive reinforcement (Skinner): Supplying reinforcing stimuli as a means of strengthening a particular behavior.

Positive repetition (Canter and Canter): Correcting a misbehaving student by commenting on what another student is doing properly—used in primary grades.

Positive support (Canter and Canter): Providing willing, optimistic help to students.

Poverty, in: Any member of a family that has to spend more than one-third of its disposable income for food adequate to meet the family's nutritional needs.

Power (Glasser): A basic student need for control, satisfied when students are given significant duties in the class and are allowed to participate in decisions about class matters.

Power-seeking behavior (Dreikurs; Albert): Behaviors such as temper tantrums, back talk, disrespect, and defiance that students use to try to show they have power over the teacher.

Practice of discipline (Charles): How discipline is put into effect and conducted in the classrooms—follows from one's philosophy and theory of discipline.

Praise: Laudatory comments, which teachers often use to encourage responsible behavior.

(Dreikurs; Ginott): Approval given to students for accomplishment: It is ineffective; encouragement should be used instead.

Praxis: A series of tests published by Educational Testing Service for assessing the competency levels of teachers.

Preferred activity time (Jones): Time allocated for students to engage in activities of their preference; used as an incentive to encourage responsible behavior.

Preventing escalation of conflicts (Curwin and Mendler): Employing tactics such as allowing a cool-off period or rescheduling the work for a more appropriate time.

Preventive discipline (Charles): The aspect of discipline that removes factors likely to promote misbehavior.

Prevention of misbehavior: Same as preventive discipline.

Proactive teacher behavior (Canter and Canter; Churchward): Preplanned reactions to student misbehavior that, when practiced, can help teachers remain calm and effective in tense situations.

Problem (Gordon): A situation that causes discomfort for someone.

(Charles): A difficulty that does not involve a clash of wills.

Problem resolution process (Coloroso): A process that resolves problems through three phases—*resolution* of the immediate problem, *restitution* to the person who has been damaged, and *reconciliation* between offender and offended.

Proper breathing (Jones): Breathing technique, slow and deep, that helps teachers remain calm when facing student misbehavior.

Providing help efficiently (Jones): A technique in which the teacher quickly provides enough help to get a student working again, then moves away. To be accomplished in 20 seconds or less.

Proximity: Moving close to a student who is misbehaving.

Proximity praise (Canter and Canter): Giving praise to a properly behaving student who is seated near a misbehaving student.

Punishment (Dreikurs): Action taken by the teacher to get back at misbehaving students and show them who is boss.

(Gordon): Aversive treatment of students; has overall negative effects.

(Redl and Wattenberg): Planned, unpleasant consequences, not physical, the purpose of which is to change behavior in positive directions.

(Skinner): Supplying aversive stimuli, a process that may or may not result in behavior change.

(Coloroso): Psychologically harmful consequences applied by teachers to students; likely to provoke resentment and retaliation.

Quality curriculum (Glasser): A program of study that emphasizes excellence in learnings that students consider useful.

Quality education (Glasser): Education in which students acquire knowledge and skills that the students themselves see as valuable.

Quality learning (Glasser): Learning in which students attain high competency in knowledge and skills they judge to be important in their lives.

Quality schoolwork (Glasser): Learning activities centered around knowledge and skills that students find important and engaging.

Quality teaching (Glasser): Instruction in which teachers help students become proficient in knowledge and skills the students consider important.

Racial diversity: Variations in racial origins among students.

Raise Responsibility (Marshall): A key element in improving student self-control and self-direction.

Reactive posture: A tendency to react to events rather than plan ahead, foresee events, and decide in advance what to do about them.

Reactive teacher behavior (Canter and Canter; Churchward): Reactions to student behavior that are not thought through in advance. Frequently inappropriate and counterproductive.

Reasonable consequences (Coloroso): Consequences arranged by teacher and students that make sense and are appropriate to the violation of a given rule.

Reconciliation (Coloroso): A human relations skill in which individuals who have been in dispute take steps to resolve and smooth over their differences.

Reflective questions (Marshall): Questions posed to students to help them make better behavioral choices and assume responsibility.

Reinforce: See *Reinforcement.*

Reinforcement (Skinner): Supplying (or, in some cases, removing) stimuli in such a manner that the organism becomes more likely to repeat a given act.

Reinforcer: See *Reinforcing stimuli.*

Reinforcing stimuli (Skinner): Stimuli received by an organism immediately following a behavior that increases the likelihood that the behavior will be repeated.

Related-respectful-reasonable (Nelsen, Lott, and Glenn): The Three R's that describe the nature of good consequences.

Reminder: A step in the process of applying consequences for misbehavior, usually the first step.

Removal from the class: A step in the process of applying consequences for misbehavior, usually a final step.

Resolution (Coloroso): Ironing out the problem, one of the follow-up steps in dealing with misbehavior.

Resolution dimension (Curwin and Mendler): An aspect of discipline that focuses on helping chronically misbehaving students learn to make and abide by decisions that serve their needs.

Responsibility (Glasser; Marshall): In discipline, students taking charge of their behavior by becoming self-directing, accepting the consequences of their actions, and learning from the process.

Responsibility versus rules (Marshall): Responsibility encourages students to behave in ways they know are proper, whereas rules expect students to behave in accordance with teacher stipulations.

Responsible choices (Gordon; Marshall): Behavioral choices based on ethical values.

Restitution (Coloroso): Repairing or replacing damage done in disruptive behavior—one of the steps in resolving the problem.

Revenge (Dreikurs; Albert): A mistaken goal toward which students sometimes turn when thwarted in their desire to find acceptance in the group.

Rewards: Payoffs used to control student behavior. (Gordon, Glasser, and many others consider them ineffective or even detrimental in the long run.)

Roadblocks to communication (Gordon): Things teachers say, such as preaching, advising, and analyzing, that inadvertently shut off student willingness to talk.

RSVP of consequences (Coloroso): Consequences should be reasonable, simple, valuable, and practical.

Rules: Statements that specify how students are to behave.

Rules, general (Jones): Classroom rules that define the teacher's broad guidelines, standards, and expectations for work and behavior, as distinct from the specific behaviors expected of students.

Sane messages (Ginott): Teacher messages that address situations rather than students' character.

Satiation (Kounin): Getting all one can tolerate of a given activity, resulting in frustration, boredom, or listlessness.

Say, See, Do Teaching (Jones): A teaching method that uses repeated short cycles of teacher input followed by student output.

Seeking power (Dreikurs; Albert): Student behavior that attempts to gain control over teachers through arguing, lying, throwing temper tantrums, and refusing to follow directions.

Seeking revenge (Dreikurs; Albert): Student behavior intended to hurt the teacher or other students.

Self-control: See *Self-discipline.*

Self-diagnostic referral (Marshall): A self-diagnosis done by a disruptive student and submitted as a plan for improvement—includes description of what was done wrong and the steps that will be taken to improve.

Self-discipline (Dreikurs; Albert; others): Self-control, which grows out of freedom to make decisions and having to live by the consequences.

Self-evaluation (Glasser): Students appraising the quality of their own work; a key step leading to improvement and quality work.

Self-serving behavior (Churchward): Stage Two of four stages of behavioral development that students pass through—this is the "what's in it for me" stage.

Sense of community (Kohn): Classes where students feel safe and are continually brought into making judgments, expressing their opinions, and working cooperatively toward solutions that affect themselves and the class.

Sense of hope (Curwin and Mendler): The belief that things will get better in the future, or that present tasks will be worthwhile. Many students have lost a sense of hope concerning the value of education.

Separating student from the behavior (Marshall and others): Clearly separating in one's comments the character of the student from the nature of the misbehavior.

Setting limits: Clarifying with the class exactly what is expected of them.

Severe clause (Canter and Canter; Curwin and Mendler): Invoking the most severe penalty in the discipline hierarchy when extreme behaviors such as fighting occur: usually means being sent to the principal.

Shaping behavior (Skinner): The process of using reinforcement to produce desired behavior in students.

Short-term solutions (Curwin and Mendler): Steps to stop misbehavior, such as scolding, lecturing, or detention, that are not likely to have lasting positive effect.

Significant seven (Nelsen, Lott, and Glenn): Three self-perceptions (personal capability, significance in primary relationships, and personal power) and four essential skills that contribute significantly to success in life (intrapersonal skill—understand and control self; interpersonal skill—communicate, cooperate, and work with others; strategic skill—flexible, adaptable, and responsible; and judgmental skill—ability to evaluate situations).

SIR (Glasser): An acronym standing for the process of self-evaluation, improvement, and repetition, used until quality is achieved.

Situational assistance (Redl and Wattenberg): Providing help to students who, because of the difficulty of the task, are on the verge of misbehaving.

Six-D conflict resolution plan (Albert): A six-step tool for helping resolve matters under dispute.

Smoothness (Kounin): Teachers' avoidance of abrupt changes that interfere with students' activities or thought processes.

Social contract (Curwin and Mendler): The agreement concerning rules and consequences that teacher and students have decided should govern behavior in the classroom.

Social contract test (Curwin and Mendler): A test to prevent students from using the excuse that they didn't understand the rules. This test deals with class rules and consequences.

Social interest (Dreikurs): The concept that one's personal well-being is dependent on the well-being of the group; thus, one acts in ways that benefit the group.

Specific rules (Jones): Classroom rules that detail specifically what students are to do and how they are to do it.

Strategic skills (Nelsen, Lott, and Glenn): Responding to the limits and consequences of everyday life with responsibility, adaptability, flexibility, and integrity.

Structures (Kagan, Kyle, and Scott): Discipline approaches used for specific combinations of disruptions and needs.

Student dislikes (Charles): Activities, situations, topics, people, and the like that students do not enjoy or for some other reason dislike. They should be avoided.

Student likes (Charles): Activities, situations, topics, people, and the like that students typically enjoy. They should be emphasized in the educational program.

Student needs (Glasser): Survival, belonging, power, fun, and freedom, upon which curriculum and teaching should be based.

(Charles): Survival, belonging, hope, dignity, power, enjoyment, competence.

Student positions (Kagan, Kyle, and Scott): A conglomerate of factors that lead to students conducting themselves in the following ways: seeking attention, being angry, avoiding failure, being bored, seeking control, or being energetic or uninformed.

Student responsibility (Glasser and others): The contention that students have the obligation to consider their behavior choices, how they affect themselves and others, and deal with the consequences.

Student rights (Canter and Canter): The right to be treated with respect and have teachers who do all they can to help provide success.

Student roles (Redl and Wattenberg): Roles students assume in the classroom, such as instigator, clown, leader, and scapegoat.

Success, genuine: Student success based on true accomplishment.

Successive approximations (Skinner): Behavior that, through reinforcement, moves progressively closer to the desired goal.

Supporting self-control (Redl and Wattenberg): Doing things that help students maintain self-control when they are on the verge of misbehaving.

Supportive discipline (Charles): The facet of discipline in which teachers use reminders and encouragement to keep students behaving properly.

Survival (Glasser; Charles): A basic need that motivates student behavior and sometimes misbehavior.

Synergetic Discipline (Charles): Discipline based on synergetic teaching, which removes most causes of misbehavior and energizes the class. Also the method of correcting misbehavior by dealing with whatever is causing the misbehavior.

Synergetic Teaching (Charles): Teaching in a manner that energizes the class. Done by putting in place combinations of elements known to produce heightened classroom energy.

Synergy (Charles): A heightened state of energy that can occur when two or more entities feed energy to each other.

Teacher misbehavior (Charles): Anything teachers do in the classroom that adversely affects learning or human relations, or that is unprofessional in any way.

Teacher rights (Canter and Canter): Opportunity to teach in a professional manner with the backing of administrators and support of parents.

Teacher roles (Redl and Wattenberg): Various roles students expect teachers to play, such as surrogate parent, arbitrator, disciplinarian, and moral authority.

Teacher self-discipline (Ginott): Teacher self-control, which is of paramount importance in helping students conduct themselves appropriately.

Teachers at their best (Ginott): Teachers when using congruent communication that addresses situations rather than students' character, invites student cooperation, and accepts students as they are.

Teachers at their worst (Ginott): Teachers when they name-call, label students, ask rhetorical "why" questions, give long moralistic lectures, and make caustic remarks to their students.

Teachers' hidden asset (Ginott): Eagerness to help any given student at any given moment.

Teaching proper behavior (Canter and Canter and others): Actually teaching students how to conduct themselves properly in various situations.

Teaching the discipline plan (Canter and Canter; Marshall; and others): Teaching students the ins and outs of the discipline plan being used.

Theory of discipline: An overall explanation of the elements that comprise discipline and how they work together, influence each other, and produce certain outcomes.

Theory X and Theory Y (Marshall): Theories of managing people. Theory X holds that people must be directed and controlled, whereas Theory Y holds that people should be encouraged and given responsibility.

Three cons, student response to consequences (Coloroso): Imploring, complaining, sulking.

Three C's (Albert): Albert's prescription for ensuring student sense of belonging in the class: feel capable, connect with others, and contribute to the class.

Three C Committee (Albert): A school committee whose purpose is to think of ways to help all students feel more capable, connected, and contributing.

Three F's (Coloroso): The three ways students typically respond to threat—fear, fighting back, or fleeing.

Three perceptions that promote self-control (Nelsen, Lott, and Glenn): Perceptions of personal capability, significance in primary relationships, and personal power to influence one's own life.

Three Pillars of Win-Win Discipline (Kagan, Kyle, and Scott): Teacher and students on the same side, sharing responsibility, and emphasizing behavior that meets students' needs in a nondisruptive manner.

Three R's of Reconciliatory Justice (Coloroso): Restitution, resolution, and reconciliation.

Three R's of solutions (Nelsen, Lott, and Glenn): Solutions for correcting misbehavior that are related to what was done wrong, respectful of the persons involved, and reasonable.

True discipline: Defined by most authorities as inner discipline; self-discipline; self-control.

Trust (Charles and others): Students' confidence that the teacher is working in their best interest and will not harm them. Desirable in teaching and necessary for synergy.

Types of classroom misbehavior

(Coloroso): Three types of student misbehavior are mistakes (unintentional), mischief (intentional light misbehavior), and mayhem (more serious misbehavior).

(Kagan, Kyle, and Scott): Four types of student misbehavior are aggression, breaking rules, confrontation, and disengagement.

(Dreikurs; Albert): Four types of student misbehavior are attention seeking, power seeking, revenge seeking, and feigned helplessness.

(Charles): Thirteen types of student misbehavior are inattention, apathy, needless talk, moving about the room without permission, annoying others, disrupting, lying, stealing, cheating, sexual harassment, aggression and fighting, malicious mischief, and defiance of authority.

Unequal treatment (Curwin and Mendler): The best discipline does not treat all students equally. It treats them differently in accordance with their individual needs.

Unobtrusive tactic (Marshall): A discipline tactic directed at a particular students that is unnoticed by most of the class members, such as facial expression, eye contact, hand signal, or physical proximity.

Useful work (Glasser): Schoolwork that deals with skills and information that students deem valuable in their lives.

Value judgments (Glasser): In Glasser's earlier work, the contention that when students misbehave, they should be required to make judgments about their actions. Now refers to Glasser's insistence that students appraise the quality of their own work.

Verbal recognition (Canter and Canter): Vocal recognition of students who are following class agreements, such as remaining on task, behaving responsibly, and so forth.

Victim mentality (Nelsen, Lott, and Glenn): A predisposition to blame others for one's own shortcomings. Contrasts with accountability mentality.

Violence (Curwin and Mendler): Verbal abuse, physical threat or action against a person, or damage done maliciously to the property of another person.

VIP (Jones): Visual instruction plan, a graphic posted in the classroom that reminds students what to do next and how to do it, so they won't have to ask the teacher.

Visual instruction plan (VIP) (Jones): Picture prompts that guide students through the process of the task or performance at hand.

Warning: Often the first step teachers take when applying consequences for misbehavior.

Why questions (Ginott): Counterproductive questions that teachers put to students, asking them to explain or justify their behavior. For example, "Why did you . . . ?"

Win-Win solutions (Kagan, Kyle, and Scott): Solutions to disruptions or disputes that produce positive results for students and teachers alike.

Win-lose conflict resolution (Gordon): Conflict resolution in which one person emerges as "winner"
and the other as "loser." This method is to be
avoided in favor of "no-lose" or "win-win" conflict
resolution.

Withitness (Kounin): The teacher's knowing what is
going on in all parts of the classroom at all times.

Work the crowd (Jones): Moving about the class while
teaching and interacting with students frequently
on an individual basis.

You-messages (Ginott; Gordon): Teacher messages
that attack students' character, such as "You are acting like barbarians." These messages carry heavy
blame and put-downs.

BIBLIOGRAPHY

Albert, L. 1989. *A teacher's guide to cooperative discipline: How to manage your classroom and promote self-esteem.* Circle Pines, MN: American Guidance Service.

Albert, L. 1992. *An administrator's guide to cooperative discipline: Strategies for schoolwide implementation.* Circle Pines, MN: American Guidance Service.

Albert, L. 1993. *Coping with kids.* Circle Pines, MN: American Guidance Services.

Albert, L. 1994. *Responsible kids in school and at home.* [Series of 6 videos]. Circle Pines, MN: American Guidance Service.

Albert, L. 1996a, 2003a. *Cooperative discipline.* Circle Pines, MN: American Guidance Service.

Albert, L. 1996b. Cooperative discipline staff development. Videos and materials for elementary and secondary level. Circle Pines, MN: American Guidance Service.

Albert, L. 1996c, 2003c. *A teacher's guide to cooperative discipline.* Circle Pines, MN: American Guidance Service.

Albert, L. 2003b. *Cooperative discipline implementation guide: Resources for staff development.* Circle Pines, MN: American Guidance Service.

Amen, D. 2001. *Healing ADD: The breakthrough program that allows you to see and heal the six types of Attention Deficit Disorder.* New York: G. P. Putnam's Sons.

Ascher, C. 1991. School programs for African American males. ERIC Digest. New York: ERIC Clearinghouse on Urban Education.

Attention Deficit Disorders Association, Southern Region, ADD/ADHD. 2002. www.adda-sr.org/BehaviorManagementIndex.htm.

Baruth, L., and Manning, M. 1992. *Multicultural education of children and adolescents.* Boston: Allyn and Bacon.

Bempechat, J. 2001. Fostering high achievement in African American children: Home school, and public policy influences. http://eric-web.tc.columbia.edu/monographs/ti16_index.html.

Benard, B. 1997. Drawing forth resilience in all our youth. *Reclaiming children and families.* ERIC/CUE Digest Number 94. New York: ERIC.

Biddulph, S. 1997. *Raising boys.* Sydney, Australia: Finch Publishing.

Bosworth, K. 1997. Drug abuse prevention: School-based strategies that work. ERIC Digest. Washington, DC: ERIC Clearinghouse on Teaching and Teacher Education.

Brown, A. 1980. Cherokee culture and school achievement. *American Indian Culture and Research Journal, 4,* 55–74.

Butterfield, R. 1994. Blueprints for Indian education: Improving mainstream schooling. ERIC Digest. Charleston, WV: ERIC Clearinghouse on Rural Education and Small Schools.

Cajete, G. 1986. Science: A Native American perspective (a culturally based science education curriculum). Ph.D. dissertation, International College/William Lyon University, San Diego, CA.

Canter, L. 1978. Be an assertive teacher. *Instructor, 88*(1), 60.

Canter, L. 1988. Let the educator beware: A response to Curwin and Mendler. *Educational Leadership, 46*(2), 71–73.

Canter, L. 1996. First, the rapport—then, the rules. *Learning, 24*(5), 12, 14.

Canter, L., and Canter, M. 1976, 1992, 2002. *Assertive Discipline: A take-charge approach for today's educator.* Seal Beach, CA: Lee Canter & Associates. The second and third editions of the book, published in 1992 and 2002, are entitled *Assertive Discipline: Positive behavior management for today's classroom.*

Canter, L., and Canter, M. 1993. *Succeeding with difficult students: New strategies for reaching your most challenging students.* Santa Monica, CA: Lee Canter & Associates.

Center for Disease Control and Prevention. 1999. Facts about violence among youth and violence in schools. U.S. Government. Media Relations Division.

Charles, C. 1974. *Teaches' petit Piaget.* Belmont, CA: Fearon.

Charles, C. 2000. *The synergetic classroom.* Boston: Allyn and Bacon.

Charles, C. 2002. *Essential elements of effective discipline.* Boston: Allyn and Bacon.

Chavkin, N., and Gonzalez, J. 2000. Mexican immigrant youth and resiliency: Research and promising programs. Urbana, IL: ERIC.

Cheng, L. 1996. Enhancing communication: Toward optimal language learning for American students. *Journal of Teacher Education, 51*(3), 206–214.

Cheng, L. 1998. *Enhancing the communication skills of newly-arrived Asian Americans.* Chicago: African American Images.

Churchward, B. 2003. Discipline by design: The honor level system. www.honorlevel.com.

Coker, D. 1988. The Asian students in the classroom. *Education and Society, 1*(3), 19–20.

Coloroso, B. 1990. *Discipline: Creating a positive school climate.* Booklet; video; audio. Littleton, CO: Kids are worth it!

Coloroso, B. 1990. *Winning at teaching . . . without beating your kids.* Booklet; video; audio. Littleton, CO: Kids are worth it!

Coloroso, B. 1994. *Kids are worth it!: Giving your child the gift of inner discipline.* New York: Avon Books. Revised edition, 2002, New York: HarperCollins.

Coloroso, B. 1999. *Parenting with wit and wisdom in times of chaos and loss.* New York: HarperCollins.

Coloroso, B. 2003. *The bully, the bullied, and the bystander: How parents and teachers can break the cycle of violence.* New York: HarperCollins.

Cornett, C. 1983. What you should know about teaching and learning styles (Fastback No. 191). Bloomington, IN: Phi Delta Kappa Foundation.

Cox, B., and Ramirez, M. 1981. Cognitive styles: Implications for multiethnic education. In J. Banks (Ed.), *Education in the 80s: Multiethnic education* (pp. 61–71). Washington, DC: National Education Association.

Curtiss, K. 2003. Welcome. www.kathycurtiss.com.

Curwin, R. 1992. *Rediscovering hope: Our greatest teaching strategy.* Bloomington, IN: National Educational Service.

Curwin, R., and Mendler, A. 1988. *Discipline with dignity.* Alexandria, VA: Association for Supervision and Curriculum Development.

Curwin, R., and Mendler, A. 1997. *As tough as necessary. Countering violence, aggression, and hostility in our schools.* Alexandria, VA: Association for Supervision and Curriculum Development.

Danielson, C. 1996. *Enhancing professional practice: A framework for teaching.* Alexandria, VA: ASCD.

Diamond, M., and Hopson, J. 1998. *Magic trees of the mind: How to nurture your child's intelligence, creativity, and healthy emotions from birth through adolescence.* New York: Dutton.

Diller, D. 1999. *Opening the dialogue: Using culture as a tool in teaching young.* Dover: Auburn Publishing Company.

Dr. Discipline. (2004, ongoing) National Education Association. www.nea.org/neatoday/9809/discipline/messages/17.html.

Dreikurs, R., and Cassel, P. 1995. *Discipline without tears.* New York: Penguin-NAL. Originally published in 1972.

Drye, J. 2000. Tort liability 101: When are teachers liable? Atlanta, GA: Educator Resources. www.Educator-Resources.com.

Faircloth, S., and Tippeconnic, J. 2000. Issues in the education of American Indian and Alaska Native students with disabilities. ERIC Digest. Charleston, WV: ERIC Clearinghouse on Rural Education and Small Schools.

Feng, J. 1994. Asian-American children: What teachers should know. ERIC Digest. 2001 edition: Upper Saddle River, NJ: Merrill.

Foster, M. 1999. Teaching and learning in the contexts of African American English and culture. *Education and Urban Society, 31*(2), 177ff.

Gardner, H. 1983. *Frames of mind: The theory of multiple intelligences.* New York: Harper and Row.

Gibbs, J. (Ed.). 1988. *Young, black, and male in America: An endangered species.* Dover: Auburn Publishing Company.

Ginott, H. 1971. *Teacher and child.* New York: Macmillan.

Ginott, H. 1972. I am angry! I am appalled! I am furious! *Today's Education, 61,* 23–24.

Ginott, H. 1973. Driving children sane. *Today's Education, 62,* 20–25.

Glasser, W. 1965. *Reality therapy: A new approach to psychiatry.* New York: Harper and Row.

Glasser, W. 1969. *Schools without failure.* New York: Harper and Row.

Glasser, W. 1977. 10 steps to good discipline. *Today's Education, 66,* 60–63.

Glasser, W. 1978. Disorders in our schools: Causes and remedies. *Phi Delta Kappan, 59,* 331–333.

Glasser, W. 1986. *Control theory in the classroom.* New York: HarperCollins.

Glasser, W. 1992. The quality school curriculum. *Phi Delta Kappan, 73*(9), 690–694.

Glasser, W. 1998a. *The quality school: Managing students without coercion.* New York: HarperCollins.

Glasser, W. 1998b. *The quality school teacher.* New York: HarperCollins.

Glasser, W., and Dotson, K. 1998. *Choice theory in the classroom.* New York: HarperCollins.

Glenn, H., and Nelsen, J. 2001. *Raising self-reliant children in a self-indulgent world: Seven building blocks for developing capable young people.* Roseville, CA: Prima.

Glenn, H., Nelsen, J., Duffy, R., Escobar, L., Ortolano, K., and Owen-Sohocki, D. 2001. *Positive discipline: A teacher's A–Z guide.* Rocklin, CA: Prima.

Goorian, B., and Brown, K. 2002. Trends and issues: School law. ERIC Clearinghouse on Educational Management. http://eric.uoregon.edu/trends_issues/law/index.html.

Gordon, T. 1970. *Parent Effectiveness Training: A tested new way to raise responsible children.* New York: New American Library.

Gordon, T. 1974, 1987. *T.E.T.: Teacher Effectiveness Training.* New York: David McKay.

Gordon, T. 1989. *Discipline that works: Promoting self-discipline in children.* New York: Random House.

Hogan, D. 1997. ADHD: A travel guide to success. *Childhood Education,* 73(3), 158–160.

Huang, G. 1993. Beyond culture: Communicating with Asian American children and families. ERIC/CUE Digest Number 94. New York: ERIC.

Interstate New Teacher Assessment and Support Consortium. 2003. Model standards for beginning teacher licensing, assessment and development: A resource for state dialogue. www.ccsso.org/content/pdfs/corestrd.pdf.

Jones, F. 1979. The gentle art of classroom discipline. *National Elementary Principal,* 58, 26–32.

Jones, F. 1987a. *Positive classroom discipline.* New York: McGraw-Hill.

Jones, F. 1987b. *Positive classroom instruction.* New York: McGraw-Hill.

Jones, F. 1996a. Did not! Did, too! *Learning,* 24(6), 24–26.

Jones, F. 2001. *Fred Jones's tools for teachers.* Santa Cruz, CA: Fredric H. Jones & Associates.

Jones, F. 2003. Tools for teachers. www.fredjones.com.

Jones, J. 1993. *Instructor's guide: Positive classroom discipline—a video course of study.* Santa Cruz, CA: Fredric H. Jones & Associates.

Jones, J. 1996a. *Instructor's guide: Positive classroom discipline—a video course of study.* Santa Cruz, CA: Fredric H. Jones & Associates.

Jones, J. 1996b. *Instructor's guide: Positive classroom instruction—a video course of study.* Santa Cruz, CA: Fredric H. Jones & Associates.

Jones, J. 2002. *The video toolbox.* Santa Cruz, CA: Fredric H. Jones & Associates.

Kagan, L., Scott, S., and Kagan, S. 2003. *Win-Win Discipline course workbook.* San Clemente, CA: Kagan Publishing.

Kagan, S. 2001. Teaching for character and community. *Educational Leadership,* 59(2), 50–55.

Kagan, S. 2002. What is Win-Win Discipline? Kagan Online Magazine, 1(15). www.KaganOnline.com

Kagan, S., Kyle, P., and Scott, P. 2004. *Win-win discipline.* San Clemente, CA: Kagan Publishing.

Kim, B. 1985. (Ed.). *Literacy and languages. The Second Yearbook of Literacy and Languages in Asia, International Reading Association Special Interest Group.* Selection of Speeches and Papers from the International Conference on Literacy and Languages (Seoul, South Korea, August 12–14, 1985).

Kohn, A. 1986, 1992. *No contest: The case against competition.* Boston: Houghton Mifflin.

Kohn, A. 1990. *The brighter side of human nature: Altruism and empathy in everyday life.* New York: Basic.

Kohn, A. 1993, 1999. *Punished by rewards: The trouble with gold stars, incentive plans, A's, praise, and other bribes.* Boston: Houghton Mifflin.

Kohn, A. 1996. *Beyond discipline: From compliance to community.* Alexandria, VA: Association for Supervision and Curriculum Development.

Kohn, A. 1999. *The schools our children deserve: Moving beyond traditional classrooms and "tougher standards."* Boston: Houghton Mifflin.

Kounin, J. 1971. *Discipline and group management in classrooms.* New York: Holt, Rinehart & Winston. Reissued in 1977.

Krovetz, M. 1999. *Fostering resiliency: Expecting all students to use their minds and hearts well.* Thousand Oaks, CA: Corwin Press.

Kunjufu, J. 1984. *Developing positive self-images and discipline in black children.* Chicago: African American Images.

Ladson-Billings, G. 2000. Fighting for our lives: Preparing teachers to teach African Languages in Asia, *International Reading Association Special Interest Group.* Selection of Speeches and Papers from the International Conference on Literacy and Languages (Seoul, South Korea, August 12–14, 1985).

Latinos in school: Some facts and findings. 2001. ERIC Digest Number 162.

Levin, H. 2002. The Accelerated Schools Program. www.acceleratedschools.org.

Lockwood, A., and Secada, W. 2000. Transforming education for Hispanic youth: Limited English proficient students. *Language, Speech and Hearing Services in Schools, 28*(2), 347–354.

Lounsbury, J. 2000. Understanding and appreciating the wonder years. Month of the young adolescent. www.nmsa.org/moya/moyajhl.htm.

Lucas, T., Henze, R., and Donato, R. 1990. Promoting the success of Latino language minority students. An exploratory study of six high schools. *Harvard Educational Review, 60*, 315–340.

Marshall, M. (Monthly since August 2001). Promoting Responsibility: The Monthly Newsletter. www.MarvinMarshall.com.

Marshall, M. 1998. *Fostering social responsibility.* Bloomington, IN: Phi Delta Kappa Educational Foundation.

Marshall, M. 2001. *Discipline without stress, punishments, or rewards: How teachers and parents promote responsibility & learning.* Los Alamitos, CA: Piper Press.

Maslow, A. 1954. *Motivation and personality.* New York: Harper.

Matsuda, M. 1989. Working with Asian family members: Some communication strategies. *Topics in Language Disorders, 9*(3), 45–53.

McCollough, Shawn. 2000. Teaching African American students. *Clearing House, 74*(1), 5–6.

McDaniel, T. 1986. A primer on classroom discipline: Principles old and new. *Phi Delta Kappan, 68*(1), 63–67.

McFarland, D., Kolstad, R., and Briggs, L. 1995. Educating Attention Deficit Hyperactivity Disorder children. *Education, 115*(4), 597–603.

McGregor, D. 1960. *The human side of enterprise.* New York: McGraw-Hill.

Mee, C. 1997. *2,000 voices: Young adolescents' perceptions and curriculum implications.* Columbus, OH: National Middle School Association.

Mendler, A., and Curwin, R. 1999. *Discipline with dignity for challenging youth.* Bloomington, IN: National Educational Service.

National Coalition of Advocates for Students.1994. Delivering on the promise: Positive practices for immigrant students. Boston: Author.

National Education Association. 1975. Code of Ethics of the Education Profession. www.nea.org/aboutnea/code.html.

Native students: Beyond cultural discontinuity. ERIC Digest. Charleston, WV: ERIC Clearinghouse on Rural Education and Small Schools.

Nelsen, J. 1987. *Positive discipline.* New York: Ballantine. Revised edition 1996.

Nelsen, J., and Lott, L. 2000. *Positive discipline for teenagers: Empowering your teens and yourself through kind and firm parenting.* Roseville, CA: Prima.

Nelsen, J., Lott, L., and Glenn, H. 1993. *Positive discipline in the classroom.* Rocklin, CA: Prima. Revised editions 1997, 2000.

Olweus, D. 1999. *Olweus' core program against bullying and antisocial behavior: A teacher handbook.* Research Center for Health Promotion [HEMIL], Bergen, Norway: University of Bergen. www.uib.no/psyfa/hemil/ansatte/olweus.html.

Payne, R. 2001. *A framework for understanding poverty.* Highlands, TX: aha! Process.

Philips, S. 1983. *The invisible culture.* New York: Longman.

Piaget, J. 2001. *The psychology of intelligence.* London: Routledge & Kegan Paul.

Qualities of effective programs for immigrant adolescents with limited schooling. 1998. ERIC Digest. Washington, DC: ERIC.

Redl, F., and Wattenberg. W. 1951. *Mental hygiene in teaching.* Rev. ed. 1959. New York: Harcourt, Brace, and World.

Reed, R. 1988. Education and achievement of young black males. In J. W. Gibbs (Ed.), *Young, black, and male in America: An endangered species.* Dover: Auburn.

Schwartz, F. 1981. Supporting or subverting learning: Peer group patterns in four tracked schools. *Anthropology and Education Quarterly, 12*(2), 99–120.

Schwartz, W. 2000. New trends in language education for Hispanic students. ERIC/CUE Digest Number 155. New York: ERIC.

Skinner, B. 1953. *Science and human behavior* New York: Macmillan.

Skinner, B. 1954. The science of learning and the art of teaching. *Harvard Educational Review, 24*, 86–97.

Skinner, B. 1971. *Beyond freedom and dignity.* New York: Knopf.

St. Germaine, R. 1995. Drop-out rates among American Indian and Alaska Natives students: Beyond cultural discontinuity. ERIC Digest. Charleston, WV: ERIC Clearinghouse on Rural Education and Small Schools.

Storti, C. 1999. *Figuring foreigners out: A practical guide.* Yarmouth, ME: Intercultural Press.

Swisher, K. 1991. American Indian/Alaskan Native learning styles: Research and practice. ERIC Digest.

Tobler, N., and Stratton, H., 1997. Effectiveness of school-based drug prevention programs: A meta-analysis of the research. (Cited in Bosworth, K. 1997. Drug abuse prevention: School-based strategies that work. ERIC Digest. Washington DC: ERIC Clearinghouse on Teaching and Teacher Education).

Trueba, H., and Cheng, L. 1993. *Myth or reality: Adaptive strategies of Asian American in California.* Bristol, PA: Falmer Press.

U.S. Census Bureau, Poverty 2001. www.census.gov/hhes.

U.S. Department of Education. 1998. *Preventing bullying: A manual for schools and communities.* www.cde.ca.govspbranch/ssp/bullymanual.htm.

U.S. National Center for Education Statistics. 1998. Violence and discipline problems in U.S. public schools: 1996–97. U.S. Government. NCES publication 98-030.

U.S. National Center for Education Statistics. 2001. http://nces.ed.gov.

Utah State Department of Education. 2003. www.ed.utah.edu/TandL/NCATE/correlationINTASC-PRAXIS.pdf.

Walsh, C. 1991. Literacy and school success: Considerations for programming and instruction. In C. Walsh and H. Prashker (Eds.), *Literacy development for bilingual students.* Boston: New England Multifunctional Resource Center for Language and Culture Education.

Wierzbicka, A. 1991. Japanese key words and core cultural values. *Language in Society, 20*(3), 333–385.

Wong, H. 2001. Summary of major concepts covered by Harry K. Wong. www.glavac.com/harrywong.htm.

INDEX